KV-637-678

THE ACADEMY OF INTERNATIONAL BUSINESS

Published in association with the UK & Ireland Chapter of the Academy of International Business

Titles already published in the series:

INTERNATIONAL BUSINESS AND EUROPE IN TRANSITION (Volume 1)
Edited by Fred Burton, Mo Yamin and Stephen Young

INTERNATIONALISATION STRATEGIES (Volume 2)
Edited by George Chryssochoidis, Carla Millar and Jeremy Clegg

THE STRATEGY AND ORGANIZATION OF INTERNATIONAL BUSINESS
(Volume 3)
Edited by Peter Buckley, Fred Burton and Hafiz Mirza

INTERNATIONALIZATION: PROCESS, CONTEXT AND MARKETS (Volume 4)
Edited by Graham Hooley, Ray Loveridge and David Wilson

INTERNATIONAL BUSINESS ORGANIZATION (Volume 5)
Edited by Fred Burton, Malcolm Chapman and Adam Cross

INTERNATIONAL BUSINESS: EMERGING ISSUES AND EMERGING MARKETS
(Volume 6)
Edited by Carla C.J.M. Millar, Robert M. Grant and Chong Ju Choi

INTERNATIONAL BUSINESS: EUROPEAN DIMENSIONS (Volume 7)
Edited by Michael D. Hughes and James H. Taggart

MULTINATIONALS IN A NEW ERA: INTERNATIONAL STRATEGY AND
MANAGEMENT (Volume 8)
Edited by James H. Taggart, Maureen Berry and Michael McDermott

INTERNATIONAL BUSINESS (Volume 9)
Edited by Frank McDonald, Heinz Tüselmann and Colin Wheeler

INTERNATIONALIZATION: FIRM STRATEGIES AND MANAGEMENT (Volume 10)
Edited by Colin Wheeler, Frank McDonald and Irene Greaves

THE PROCESS OF INTERNATIONALIZATION (Volume 11)
Edited by Frank McDonald, Michael Mayer and Trevor Buck

INTERNATIONAL BUSINESS IN AN ENLARGING EUROPE (Volume 12)
Edited by Trevor Morrow, Sharon Loane, Jim Bell and Colin Wheeler

MANAGERIAL ISSUES IN INTERNATIONAL BUSINESS (Volume 13)
Edited by Felicia M. Fai and Eleanor J. Morgan

ANXIETIES AND MANAGEMENT RESPONSES IN INTERNATIONAL BUSINESS
(Volume 14)
Edited by Rudolf R. Sinkovics and Mo Yamin

Also by Gregory Jackson

CORPORATE GOVERNANCE IN JAPAN: Institutional Change and Organizational Diversity *(co-editor with H. Miyajima and M. Aoki)*

Also by Roger Strange

THE WTO AND DEVELOPING COUNTRIES *(co-edited with H. Katrak)*

SMALL-SCALE ENTERPRISES IN DEVELOPING AND TRANSITIONAL ECONOMIES *(co-edited with H. Katrak)*

THE EUROPEAN UNION AND ASEAN: TRADE AND INVESTMENT ISSUES *(co-edited with J. Slater and C. Molteni)*

TRADE AND INVESTMENT IN CHINA: the European Experience *(co-edited with J. Slater and L. Wang)*

BUSINESS RELATIONSHIPS WITH EAST ASIA: the European Experience *(co-edited with J. Slater)*

MANAGEMENT IN CHINA: the Experience of Foreign Businesses

JAPANESE MANUFACTURING INVESTMENT IN EUROPE: its Impact on the UK Economy

Corporate Governance and International Business

Strategy, Performance and Institutional Change

Edited by

Roger Strange

and

Gregory Jackson

First published 2008 by
PALGRAVE MACMILLAN
Houndmills, Basingstoke, Hampshire RG21 6XS and
175 Fifth Avenue, New York, N.Y. 10010
Companies and representatives throughout the world

PALGRAVE MACMILLAN is the global academic imprint of the
Palgrave Macmillan division of St. Martin's Press, LLC and of
Palgrave Macmillan Ltd. Macmillan® is a registered trademark in
the United States, United Kingdom and other countries.
Palgrave is a registered trademark in the European
Union and other countries.

ISBN-13: 978–0–230–20339–6   hardback
ISBN-10: 0–230–20339–6   hardback

This book is printed on paper suitable for recycling and made
from fully managed and sustained forest sources. Logging,
pulping and manufacturing processes are expected to conform
to the environmental regulations of the country of origin.

A catalogue record for this book is available from the British Library.

Library of Congress Cataloging-in-Publication Data

Corporate governance and international business : strategy,
    performance and institutional change / edited by Roger Strange and
    Gregory Jackson.
        p. cm. — (Academy of international business series)
    Includes bibliographical references and index.
    ISBN 0–230–20339–6 (alk. paper)
    1. Corporate governance.   2. International trade.   I. Strange,
    Roger. II. Jackson, Gregory, 1971–
    HD2741.C77492 2008
    658.4'2—dc22

                                                           2008000203

10   9   8   7   6   5   4   3   2   1
17   16   15   14   13   12   11   10   09   08

Printed and bound in Great Britain by
CPI Antony Rowe, Chippenham and Eastbourne

For Emma and Tom
Henri, Ella and Franzine

Contents

List of Tables

List of Figures

Notes on the Contributors

Mark G. Albon was born and educated in Bloemfontein South Africa. He gained an undergraduate degree in Political Science, Industrial Sociology and History from the University of Natal (Durban) in 1988. He served as a South African diplomat in Israel, Switzerland and the Netherlands from 1989 to 2003. In 2003 he joined the global pulp and paper manufacturer Sappi as Corporate Communications Manager. He moved to the global IT solutions company, Dimension Data, in 2007 as the Global Internal Communications Manager. In 2006 he completed a Masters in Business Leadership (MBL) with Unisa School of Business Leadership.

Tord Andersson, Colin Haslam, Edward Lee and Nick Tsitsianis work with a group of academics in the Centre for Research in Finance and Accounting (CRiFA) which is based in the Business School at the University of Hertfordshire. CRiFA provides a focus for the development of critical and informative research in the area of finance and accounting. Current research on the US S&P 500 and European 170 is being employed to review corporate performance and construct financialized accounts. The financial interests of managers and investors are aligned and this, coupled with fair value reporting for shareholders, is forcing a reorientation of cash distribution towards equity stakeholders and modifying corporate governance as managers struggle to hold the financial line. As part of a more general programme of research CRiFA was involved in the production of a report on the Alternative Investment Market (AIM) in 2007 which revealed that bigger IPO bets are being placed on firms where there is also increased value at risk.

Petra Bouvain is a Lecturer in Marketing at the University of Canberra. She is the Australian convenor of ProfNet, a global network of academics interested in Internet-related research. As part of this network she has undertaken comparative research in the car industry, banking and investor relations. She has undertaken consultancies for both private and public sector clients. Currently she is enrolled in the PhD programme at the Australian National University, working on corporate social responsibility. She holds a Diplôme Ingénieur and a Wirtschaftsingenieur from the University of Applied Sciences Niederrhein and a Bachelor of Adult Education from the CCAE.

Trevor Buck is a Professor in International Business at Loughborough University, with current research interests in executive pay in different institutional environments (United Kingdom, Germany, China). His work on China extends beyond executive pay to include an investigation into the stability or otherwise of national cultural attributes and research on returnee entrepreneurs. This work has attracted grants from the ESRC, British Council and Leverhulme Trust.

Jian Chen is currently a Senior Lecturer in Finance in the Business School at the University of Greenwich. He is an active researcher on the issues of corporate governance, corporate finance and their applications in the Chinese economy. He received his PhD in Finance from King's College London. He was the President of the Chinese Economic Association in the UK (2003–2004).

Stephen Chen is an Associate Professor of Management at Macquarie University. Previously he has held academic appointments at Henley Management College, the Open Business School (UK), City University Business School, Manchester Business School, the Anderson School of Management at UCLA and the Australian National University. He has also held R&D, IT, management and consultancy posts in industry. He holds an MBA from Cranfield Management School and a PhD in Business Policy from Imperial College, London. His current research interests include the impact of globalization and non-economic factors on business strategies, corporate social responsibility and business ethics.

Amon Chizema is Lecturer in International Business and Strategy at Loughborough University. His research interests include corporate governance, the dynamics of institutions, and economic development. He has published in *International Business Review* and has presented his work at major conferences such as the Academy of Management and Academy of International Business. He received his PhD in International Management from Loughborough University.

Ruth Clarke is an Associate Professor in the H. Wayne Huizenga School of Business and Entrepreneurship at Nova Southeastern University and Chair for International Business. She holds a PhD in Strategic Management from the University of Massachusetts, Amherst. Her current focus of research is on emerging markets in general, with a focus on international new ventures; uncertainty and risk in the international environment; social capital and international entrepreneurship; export channel integration; ethics and corporate governance.

Enrico Cotta Ramusino is Full Professor of Corporate Finance and Strategic Management at the University of Pavia. He has authored five books and several articles on strategic management and corporate finance.

John H. Dunning is Emeritus Professor of International Business at the University of Reading in the United Kingdom and at Rutgers University in the United States. He earned his doctorate in Economics from the University of Southampton in 1957, and since then has received five honorary doctorates. He is an ex-President of both the Academy of International Business, and the International Trade and Finance Association. His research interests include the theory and international political economy of international business activity. He has written or edited 48 books and 250 articles in professional journals.

Natalya Dyomina is a mathematician by training and a researcher at REB-Consulting in Moscow, a leading consultancy specializing in business surveys in Russia. She has published in the *Journal of International Business Studies* and the *Journal of Development Studies*.

Saul Estrin is Professor of Managerial Economics and Strategy, and (since 2006) Head of the Department of Management at the London School of Economics, and previously Professor of Economics at the London Business School, where he also served as Adecco Professor of Business and Society, Director of the Centre for New and Emerging Markets, and Deputy Dean (Faculty and Research). His publications include *Privatisation in Central and Eastern Europe* (Longman, 1994), *Foreign Direct Investment in Central and Eastern Europe* (Cassell, 1997), *Investment Strategies in Emerging Markets* (Edward Elgar, 2004), and numerous papers in scholarly journals (including the *Quarterly Journal of Economics, Journal of Development Economics, Journal of Public Economics* and *European Economic Review*). His main areas of research include labour and industrial economics, transition economics and economic development, privatization and foreign direct investment. He has been a Visiting Professor at Stanford University, Michigan Business School, Cornell University, and the European University Institute, and is a Fellow of the Centre for Economic Policy Research (CEPR), the Institute for the Study of Labor (IZA) and the William Davidson Institute.

Simon Harris, formerly strategic planner in the textile industry and investment manager and adviser in businesses worldwide, now lectures in International Strategic Management at the University of Edinburgh. He works with companies concerning their strategic development and their international growth, doing so with managers and chief executives in Scotland, the Netherlands, France, Germany, Sweden, China, Italy and Finland. His research focuses on the different ways that CEOs internationally develop strategies for their firms, and develop their operations in other countries. This has been helped by a major EU research grant, by the 2003 Gunnar Hedlund award for doctoral research, by collaboration with other scholars, and by the support of managements of some large European multinational firms.

Charles Harvey is Professor of Business History and Management and Dean of Faculty at Strathclyde Business School. He holds a PhD in International Business from the University of Bristol. His interests span the fields of strategy, organization studies and comparative business from a long-run perspective. He is the author of eight books, five edited books and numerous journal articles, including contributions to the *Journal of Management Studies*, *Human Relations*, *Organization Studies*, the *Economic History Review*, the *Business History Review* and *Business History*. He has twice won the Wadsworth Prize for excellence in business history.

Bruce Hearn is currently completing his ESRC-funded doctorate in the Department of Management at King's College London. He has a BSc from the University of Edinburgh, a Postgraduate Certificate in Finance and an MSc in International Business, both from Birkbeck College, University of London. He has worked as an analyst at several financial institutions in the City of London, including BNP Paribas and Gulf (Saudi) International Bank. His research focuses on the extent and benefits of integration amongst the equity markets of Africa, and he has several publications in this field. His research has further benefited from extensive travel in Africa, including visits to the majority of equity markets that feature in his research.

Richard Hyman is Professor of Industrial Relations at the London School of Economics and Political Science (LSE), and is the founding editor of the *European Journal of Industrial Relations*. He has written extensively on the themes of industrial relations, collective bargaining, trade unionism, industrial conflict and labour market policy, and is author of a dozen books (including *Strikes and Industrial Relations: a Marxist Introduction*) as well as numerous journal articles and book chapters. He co-edited the 17-country text *Changing Industrial Relations in Europe*. His comparative study *Understanding European Trade Unionism: Between Market, Class and Society* (Sage, 2001) is widely cited by scholars working in this field.

Gregory Jackson is Reader in Strategy and Comparative Management at King's College London. He graduated from the University of Wisconsin–Madison, received his PhD in Sociology from Columbia University and was formerly a Research Fellow at the Max-Planck-Institute for the Study of Societies in Cologne, Germany (1996–2002). He was also a Fellow at the Research Institute of Economy, Trade and Industry (RIETI) (2002–2004).

Rostislav Kapelyushnikov is Chief Researcher at the Institute of World Economy and International Relations of the Russian Academy of Sciences. He is Deputy Chief Editor of the quarterly bulletin *The Russian Economic Barometer*, and Deputy Director of the Centre for Labour Market Studies at the

State University – Higher School of Economics, Moscow. His research interests are focused on labour economics, economics of transition, institutional
economics and corporate governance. He has authored several books including *Russian Unemployment: Dynamics, Composition, and Specificity* (2003) and
numerous papers in Russian and Western academic journals.

Andrei Kuznetsov is Professor at Lancashire Business School, University of
Central Lancashire. His research focuses on corporate governance, cross-
cultural management, knowledge transfer and corporate social responsibility.
He is on the editorial board of the *Journal of East–West Trade*. He has written
and edited several books on post-communist transition, including *Russian
Corporation: the Strategies of Survival and Development* (2001). He has pub-
lished in journals such as *Europe-Asia Studies* and the *Journal for East European
Management Studies*.

Christel Lane is Professor of Economic Sociology in the Faculty of Social
and Political Sciences, Cambridge University. She has been a Fellow at St
John's College since 1990. Her recent and current research has been in two
inter-linked areas. First, she has been concerned with an understanding of
the different varieties of capitalism in Europe and how increasing economic
globalization has interacted with and changed national institutions and business organizations. Second, her project on 'The globalizing behaviour of UK
firms in comparative context' investigates how companies organize their
value chains – what functions/activities are kept in-house and which are
externalized in processes of outsourcing and in-licensing. It establishes the
organizational structures adopted to this end, the locational decisions made
and the rationale for patterns adopted. The study is comparative of three
industries (textiles and clothing, pharmaceuticals and book publishing) and
four countries. It has entailed fieldwork in the UK, US, Germany, Japan, as
well as in China, Turkey and Romania. Her publications include *The Rites of
Rulers: Ritual in Industrial Society* (Cambridge University Press, 1981), *Management and Labour in Europe, Industry and Society in Europe* and, edited with
R. Bachmann, *Trust Within and Between Organizations* as well as numerous
book chapters and refereed articles in a wide range of journals.

Mairi Maclean is Professor of International Business at Bristol Business
School. She holds an MA and PhD from the University of St Andrews, and an
MBA from the University of Bath. Her interests include corporate governance,
business elites, business history, business transformation and transition. Her
recent books include *Business Elites and Corporate Governance in France and
the UK*, written with Charles Harvey and Jon Press, and funded by the Leverhulme Trust and Reed Charity; and *Economic Management and French Business
from de Gaulle to Chirac*. She is the author of four books, editor of three, and

has published numerous articles in journals such as *Human Relations, Business History* and *West European Politics*.

Viola Makin is a Full Professor (Strategy and Governance) with seventeen years' experience as an academic member of the Strategy and International Business division of the University of South Africa's Graduate School of Business Leadership. She has also been on the Faculty of University of Maryland University College for the past three years. Professor Makin has a DBA from the University of Pretoria. She is a board member for Alexkor, and has prior business experience in patents, the diplomatic service and television production.

Hideaki Miyajima is Professor at the School of Commerce and Vice Director of the Institute of Finance at Waseda University. He is also a faculty fellow of the Research Institute of Economy, Trade and Industry (RIETI), a special research fellow of the Policy Research Institute (Ministry of Finance), and adjunct professor of Chung-Ang University (Seoul). He was a Research Associate at the Institute of Social Sciences, Tokyo University before moving to Waseda University. He studied as a graduate student at Tokyo University and received his PhD in Commerce from Waseda University.

Jenifer Piesse is Professor of International Business at King's College London and Visiting Professor at University of Stellenbosch, Republic of South Africa. She has a BA in Economics and Statistics from Columbia University, an MSc in International Accounting and Finance from the London School of Economics, and a PhD in Economics from Birkbeck College, University of London. Her research is concerned with developing and emerging country financial systems and their impact on economic growth.

Mari Sako is Professor of Management Studies at the Said Business School, University of Oxford. After reading PPE (Philosophy, Politics and Economics) at the University of Oxford, she studied for her MSc in Economics at the LSE, MA in Economics at the Johns Hopkins University, and PhD in Economics at the University of London. She has also taught at the London School of Economics, and has been a visiting scholar at Kyoto University, Tokyo University, RIETI (Research Institute of Economy, Trade and Industry in Tokyo), and the Ecole Polytechnique, Paris. She has published numerous books and articles on international business strategy, comparative business systems, and human resources. She has been, since 1993, a principal researcher of the MIT International Motor Vehicle Program (IMVP), which funded her research on outsourcing, modularity, and supplier parks in the global auto industry. Since 2003, she has been a Fellow of the ESRC-EPSRC Advanced Institute of Management Research (AIM), and has studied the implications of out-sourcing/offshoring of business services on corporate strategy and national competitiveness.

Roger Strange is Senior Lecturer in Economics at King's College London. His current research focuses on three main areas: (a) the effects of corporate governance factors on foreign direct investment decisions and upon firm per-formance; (b) the determinants of MNE subsidiary location, and the effects of location on competitiveness; and (c) the reasons for, and the implications of, the growing trend towards manufacturing outsourcing and the 'external-ization' of production. He is the author of five books, seven edited books, and numerous journal articles including papers in the *Journal of International Business Studies, International Business Review, Transnational Corporations* and *Management International Review*.

Zhonghua Wu is a PhD candidate at the Business School, National Univer-sity of Singapore. Her main interests include boards of directors, executive compensation and political control in emerging economies.

Antonella Zucchella is Full Professor of Innovation Management and Mar-keting at the University of Pavia, and Lecturer in International Marketing at Strasbourg University Robert Schuman. She has authored several articles in international journals, Italian monographs and a book on *International Entrepreneurship and Sourcing*.

Glossary of Acronyms

ACP	African, Caribbean and Pacific
ADF	Augmented Dickey-Fuller (test)
ADR	American depository receipt
AMC	asset management company
AMF	Autorité des Marchés Financiers (France)
APT	arbitrage pricing theory
ARDL	autoregressive distributed lag (model)
BVAR	bivariate autoregressive (model)
CAPM	capital asset pricing model
CCP	Chinese Communist Party
CEE	Central and Eastern Europe
CEO	chief executive officer
CIA	comparative institutional analysis
CIS	Commonwealth of Independent States
CMA	Common Monetary Area
CME	coordinated market economy
CMF	Conseil des Marchés Financiers (France)
COB	Commission des Opérations de Bourse (France)
COE	collective-owned enterprise
COO	chief operating officer
COSSE	Committee of SADC Stock Exchanges
CSD	Central Securities Depository (Kenya)
CSI	corporate social irresponsibility
CSR	corporate social responsibility
CSRC	China Securities Regulatory Commission
DAX	Deutsche Aktien Xchange (Germany)
EBO	employee buy-out
EBRD	European Bank for Reconstruction and Development
EC	European Commission
EPRD	European Programme for Reconstruction and Development
EPS	earnings per share
ESO	executive stock option
EU	European Union
FASB	Financial Accounting Standards Board
FDI	foreign direct investment
FPI	foreign portfolio investment
FSC	foreign sales corporations
FTSE	Financial Times Stock Exchange (index)
GAAP	Generally Accepted Accounting Principles

GCC	global commodity chain
GDP	gross domestic product
GDR	general depository receipts
GNP	gross national product
GPN	global production network
GVC	global value chain
HGB	Handelsgesetzbuch (German commercial code)
HK	Hong Kong
IAS	International Accounting Standards
IASB	International Accounting Standards Board
IB	international business
IBS	international business strategy
IFRS	International Financial Reporting Standards
IMF	International Monetary Fund
IPC	intellectual property crime
IPO	initial public offering
IPR	intellectual property rights
ISI	import substitution industrialization
ISIN	International Security Identification Number (system)
IV	instrumental variable
JIBS	*Journal of International Business Studies*
JSE	Johannesburg Securities Exchange
LME	liberal market economy
LP	legal person (share)
M&A	mergers and acquisitions
MBO	management buy-out
MEBO	management and employee buy-out
METI	Ministry of Economy, Trade and Industry (Japan)
MNC	multinational corporation
MNE	multinational enterprise
MV	market value
NASDAQ	National Association of Securities Dealers Automated Quotations (market)
NEPAD	New Partnership for Africa's Development
NIE	new institutional economics
NIS	new institutional sociology
NPV	net present value
NRE	nouvelles régulations économiques (France)
NYSE	New York Stock Exchange
OECD	Organization for Economic Cooperation and Development
OIE	old institutional economics
OLS	ordinary least squares
OTC	over-the-counter
PBR	price-book ratio

PCAOB	Public Company Accounting Oversight Board
PCB	printed circuit board
PDG	Président Directeur Général
PPP	purchasing power parity
PRC	People's Republic of China
QFII	qualified foreign institutional investor
REB	Russian Economic Barometer
ROA	return on assets
ROCE	return on capital employed
ROE	return on equity
S&P	Standard & Poor's
SADC	Southern African Development Community
SEC	Securities and Exchange Commission (United States)
SETS	Shares Electronically Traded System (London Stock Exchange)
SFAS	Statement of Financial Accounting Standards
SHSE	Shanghai Stock Exchange
SZSE	Shenzhen Stock Exchange
SOE	state-owned enterprise
SOX	Sarbanes-Oxley Act (United States)
SSA	sub-Saharan Africa
TAR	threshold autoregressive (model)
TFP	total factor productivity
TOB	takeover bids
UK	United Kingdom
UNCTAD	United Nations Conference on Trade and Development
UNRISD	United Nations Research Institute for Social Development
US	United States (of America)
VAR	vector autoregressive (model)
VC	venture capital
VECM	vector error correction (model)
WTO	World Trade Organization

1

Why Does Corporate Governance Matter for International Business?

Gregory Jackson and Roger Strange

Introduction

Corporate governance relates to the structure of rights and responsibilities among the parties with a stake in the firm (Aoki, 2001). Effective corporate governance employs mechanisms to ensure executives respect the rights and interests of company stakeholders, as well as making those stakeholders accountable for acting responsibly with regard to the protection, generation and distribution of wealth invested in the firm (Aguilera et al., 2008). Effectiveness may relate to different dimensions of corporate governance, ranging from monitoring and control over managerial discretion to promoting entrepreneurial leadership and innovation. On this basis, a large and diverse set of research now looks at corporate governance based on agency theory in economics, organizational and institutional literatures in sociology, or law and economics approaches – to name just a few.

Much of the empirical literature on corporate governance has attempted to understand corporate governance in terms of agency theory and explored links between different corporate governance practices and firm performance. This literature argues that by reducing principal-agent conflicts between shareholders and managers, firms will operate more efficiently and perform better. The empirical findings related to this hypothesis remain varied, and depend highly on the historical, sectoral and national contexts being studied. Corporate governance has also been studied from other theoretical perspectives that stress its relation to business strategy and the evolution of firms. Strategic management scholars have emphasized how corporate governance may influence access to critical firm resources and the formation of firm-specific capabilities (O'Sullivan, 2000). One set of arguments from resource dependency theory suggests that firms will respond to demands made by external actors or organizations upon whose resources they are heavily dependent, but also that organizations may seek to buffer against or minimize that external dependence (Pfeffer and Salancik, 1978). For example, the degree and nature of external finance is likely to influence the demands placed on corporate governance for transparency or board independence. Likewise, the resource-based view of the firm stresses the internal capabilities of the firm, such as skills, knowledge and information (Barney, 1991; Mahoney and Pandian, 1992). Corporate governance may play an important role in firm-internal coordination and the motivation of critical employees, depending on the nature of skills and knowledge that are critical for the firm's competitive advantage. For example, the essential or non-essential nature of human assets of managers and workers impacts the effectiveness of different modes of corporate governance (Aoki and Jackson, 2008).[1] These arguments highlight how the effectiveness of corporate governance is mediated by various strategic resources, which are critical within the context of firms' organizational, market, sectoral or institutional environments (Aguilera et al., 2008). Since the nature and salience of these resources varies rather than being universal, an important agenda now links corporate governance to organizational strategy (Whitley, 1999), organizational life-cycle (Filatotchev and Wright, 2005) and the involvement of different stakeholders (Connolly et al., 1980).

Comparative institutional theory has examined how corporate governance impacts both agency costs and strategic management across different institutional environments (Aoki, 2001). A large literature now documents the diversity of national systems of corporate governance, described variously in terms of insider versus outsider, bank versus market, or shareholder versus stakeholder-oriented systems. This institutional perspective stresses how corporate governance is related to the legitimacy of managerial control over corporations (Davis, 2005), and hence part of a wider set of political dynamics (Roe, 2003). However, different sets of institutions are widely argued to have different sets of strengths and weaknesses in promoting accountability, as well as distributional consequences for different stakeholders (Aguilera and Jackson, 2003; Gourevitch and Shinn, 2005). Despite the importance of institutional diversity, internationalization has led to rapid changes in corporate governance around the world, leading to a debate over the diffusion of new regulatory forms such as codes (Aguilera and Cuervo-Cazurra, 2004), various forms of convergence in the function and form of corporate governance (Gilson, 2000) and the change of institutions through the adaptation or hybridization across different national patterns (Ahmadjian and Robbins, 2005).

Corporate governance has, until recently, not been a major topic for IB scholars. IB research focuses on the strategies of multinational enterprises (MNEs) for global expansion in diverse regions and countries. The emphasis here is on the corporate and business level strategies themselves, rather than the processes of strategic decision-making and hence corporate governance. However, we suggest that corporate governance and international business can be usefully linked in at least three ways. First, the corporate governance institutions in a particular country influence its attractiveness for international investment and may shape the form of that investment, such as FDI or portfolio investment. At a macro-level, the flow of international economic activity is strongly influenced by the legal rules, informal institutions and governance-related business practices across countries. Second, the power, influence and expertise of different stakeholders within corporate governance have a strong influence on strategic decision-making, in general, and internationalization strategies, in particular. The institutions of corporate governance in a particular home country may influence its ability to relocate operations, or the pattern of competitive advantage of the firm. Host country corporate governance institutions likewise pose a barrier to some types of business practices, such as due to differences in the protection of investors or the participation of employees in strategic decisions. Third, internationalization and the activities of MNEs impact corporate governance, by exposing firms to diverse sets of institutions and stakeholder pressures. Internationalization may bring pressures from foreign investors for greater shareholder value or changes in regulation towards international standards. This book pursues these three themes in greater depth, drawing upon a number of different disciplinary approaches and methodological styles.

Corporate governance, strategy and performance

Part I of the book contains seven chapters linking corporate governance with issues of strategy and performance in an international context. Much of the recent interest in corporate governance among IB scholars relates to the particular context of transition and emerging economies. In these countries, corporate governance institutions are often institutionally or culturally distant to those in the home countries of MNEs. Moreover, this diversity often relates to vastly different levels of investor protection, which exacerbate problems of agency and create very different incentives for MNE strategy. Chapter 2 presents an overview of the economics literature on the impact of privatization on company performance. The next three chapters address the influence of corporate governance systems at a macro-level, focusing on the composition of equity foreign investment inflows (Chapter 3), the international integration of equity markets (Chapter 4), and upon the interaction with national cultural values in the formulation of firm strategy (Chapter 5). The latter three chapters provide more micro-analysis, and consider how the introduction of new equity capital may impact on firms' internationalization strategies (Chapter 6), how ownership concentration affects firm performance (Chapter 7) and the practice of tunnelling by controlling shareholders (Chapter 8).

In Chapter 2, Saul Estrin first outlines the rationale for the privatization of state-owned enterprises (SOEs) in transition economies. He contrasts the different objectives of SOEs and private firms, but also emphasizes that a system of private ownership places more effective internal and external constraints upon discretionary managerial behaviour and thus encourages better resource allocation and efficiency. He goes on to stress that the scale of the privatization required in the transition economies of Central and Eastern Europe (CEE) and the Commonwealth of Independent States (CIS) was substantial, and that the stock of domestic private savings in these countries was insufficient to purchase the assets being offered. As a result, many countries used management buy-outs (MBOs) or employee buy-outs (EBOs) as their method of privatization, others used 'mass privatization' schemes to issue share vouchers to the general population, but only a few encouraged the sale of assets to foreigners. But, as Estrin notes, mass privatization may lead to dispersed ownership, or to concentrated ownership in the hands of insiders, and thus may not provide appropriate incentives for effective corporate governance. Finally, Estrin undertakes a meta-analysis of previous studies on the impact of ownership structure on company performance. He reports *inter alia* that private ownership tends to have a positive effect on performance, and that the effect is larger with foreign investors than with domestic investors. Furthermore, new foreign firms appear to be more efficient than new domestic firms, and the latter are no less efficient than firms privatized to domestic owners.

As noted above, foreign equity capital is sought as a supplement to the funds available for domestic investment in many emerging and transition economies. In principle, foreign equity capital may be introduced through foreign direct investment (FDI), foreign portfolio investment (FPI), or through indigenous firms issuing shares on overseas stock exchanges. Yet the typical emerging economy is characterized by weaker legal protection for investors, or other institutional problems related to insecure property rights or high levels of corruption. In these contexts, many perceived 'best practices' for corporate governance may receive relatively little support through formal institutions. In Chapter 3, Roger Strange and Jian Chen argue that the information asymmetries and agency problems resulting from the weak legal protection of investors mean that potential foreign investors will favour FDI, notwithstanding the illiquid and indivisible nature of the investment, rather than purchasing shares – either those traded domestically or overseas – in an indigenous company. They proceed to examine the development of the corporate governance system in China since the early 1990s, during which time many of the large state-owned enterprises (SOEs) were incorporated whilst many of the smaller SOEs were effectively privatized. Listings on the domestic or overseas stock exchanges were at the discretion of the Chinese authorities and did not attract substantial foreign investment. But Strange and Chen argue that the situation has changed dramatically since the turn of the century as a result of the deteriorating government fiscal situation and the prospect of increasing competition following WTO accession in 2001. They catalogue a range of initiatives introduced by the Chinese authorities, and show how these have been accompanied by a dramatic change in the composition of foreign investment inflows. They interpret this change in the composition of the foreign investment inflows as strong evidence of a secular improvement in the corporate governance regime in China.

In 2001, the African Union (AU)[2] adopted a strategic framework called the New Partnership for Africa's Development (NEPAD) to promote sustainable growth and development in the continent, and to halt the perceived marginalization of Africa by increasing its integration in the global economy. A central action plan of the NEPAD was to encourage the integration of the African equity markets on a regional basis around four central core markets: South Africa, Nigeria, Kenya and Egypt. In Chapter 4, Bruce Hearn and Jenifer Piesse document the considerable interest in Africa in attracting foreign investment capital from world markets, given the low levels of domestic savings and investment. Cross-border equity market integration is argued to increase the likelihood that African stocks would be included within institutional investors' global investment portfolios, and lead in turn to more analyst coverage of African markets and greater awareness of investment opportunities within Africa. Hearn and Piesse provide an empirical evaluation of the degree of price integration between eight African markets (i.e. Egypt, Kenya, Mauritius, Morocco, Namibia, Nigeria, South Africa and Tunisia), as well as between these African markets and two major international markets (viz. France and the United Kingdom). They find little evidence of significant price integration, with the exception of pair-wise integration between Namibia and South Africa, Egypt and Tunisia, and Egypt and France. Integration is found to be strongest between markets where investors are faced with similar levels of transaction costs, particularly information search and verification. They conclude that African countries should concentrate on strengthening levels of investor protection and the effectiveness of regulatory enforcement if they wish to attract greater inflows of foreign capital.

Corporate governance also has strong impacts on the process of strategy formation in firms. Some of those involved – such as the chief executive officer (CEO) and the senior managers – can be termed 'insiders', whilst others – such as block shareholders and partners – may be termed 'outsiders'. In Chapter 5, Simon Harris argues that the extent to which insiders and outsiders are involved in strategy formulation is related not only to the governance structure of the firm, but also to the national cultural characteristics of the firm's home country. He contrasts firms with two different types of governance structure (manager-owned and institution-owned), and suggests that outsiders will typically have a greater role in strategy formulation in the latter than in the former. However, Harris also suggests that different national cultural values may influence the kinds of people who are involved. Specifically, more people, and especially more insiders, will be involved in formulating strategy in countries with 'person-oriented' values, whilst fewer people will be involved in countries with more 'task-oriented' values. He examines these propositions through four matched case studies: two of the firms are manager-owned and the other two are institution-owned. One of each type of firm was from the 'person-oriented' Netherlands and from the 'task-oriented' United Kingdom. He concludes that both governance structure and cultural values are important influences upon participation in the strategy formulation process, and that both interact so that simple predictions based on just one of these factors are likely to be unreliable.

The introduction of new equity capital not only introduces new financial resources, but also has a number of other effects upon the corporate governance and strategy of the funded firms. In Chapter 6, Antonella Zucchella and Enrico Cotta Ramusino examine the experiences of four infant technology-based firms, and report that the arrival of new equity investors typically results in a reorganization of the firm's corporate governance structure, the introduction of new financial reporting procedures, and the acquisition of reputation benefits and greater networking opportunities. Furthermore, some investors take an active role in the decision-making of the business and, in particular, are instrumental in the internationalization process of the firms. Many technology-based firms are effectively obliged to internationalize early in their existence given the competitive dynamics of their industries, yet often the founders possess a scientific/technical background and do not have the requisite expertise in marketing and strategic management. The contribution of the equity investor may be crucial in such circumstances through the provision of the necessary resources and organizational capabilities. Thus, the role of the equity investors in the growth strategies of firms changes as corporate governance and finance evolve. Zucchella and Cotta Ramusino further describe the process of organizational learning within the funded firms by showing how the knowledge and skills of the investors are transferred to the firms and transformed into organizational routines.

As suggested by agency theory, corporate governance and associated institutions may impact corporate performance at the firm level. In Chapter 7, Andrei Kuznetsov, Rostislav Kapelyushnikov and Natalya Dyomina consider the concurrence of interest between dominant and minority shareholders in the context of transition economies and the associated challenges in institutionalizing effective forms of investor protection. In such settings, control becomes more important for the allocation of firm value than formal income rights, and opportunities exist for dominant shareholders to extract private benefits from their control of the firms. Such benefits include both non-pecuniary benefits (e.g. the social prestige of running the firm) that have no impact on profits, and also the extraction of material benefits ('tunnelling') through the transfer of assets at non-market prices, loan guarantees using the firm's assets as collateral, and a variety of other practices. The empirical context for their study is Russia, which has followed its own idiosyncratic approach of mass privatization as a method of economic restructuring and whose firms thus have distinctive ownership structures. Kuznetsov et al. find a negative relationship between the size of the dominant shareholding and various measures of firm performance. They point out that the Russian legal system offers inadequate legal protection to all shareholders, even those that hold majority stakes, making it difficult for shareholders to realize the value of their investments given the underdeveloped state of the Russian capital markets. Dominant shareholders are insecure about the future long-term status and security of their investments, and thus predisposed to extract wealth from the firm, even to the detriment of long-term growth prospects.

In Chapter 8, Zhonghua Wu takes up the role of dominant shareholders in more depth. She notes that ownership concentration in the hands of one large shareholder may have two offsetting effects on the incidence of tunnelling. On the one hand, a dominant shareholder may have the power to appropriate assets and resources for their private benefit. On the other hand, the dominant shareholder has a stronger incentive and more opportunity to monitor management and to improve corporate efficiency. She provides data from a sample of Chinese companies listed on the Shanghai Stock Exchange in 2005, and finds empirical support for a non-linear relationship between the likelihood of tunnelling and the equity stake held by the largest shareholder: the monitoring incentive is stronger at lower levels of shareholding, whilst the tunnelling effect comes through more strongly at higher levels of shareholding. Furthermore, she highlights two corporate governance mechanisms that might improve protection for minority shareholders in emerging markets where formal institutional mechanisms are generally weak. The first is through the composition of the compensation package for the CEO. In particular, the incidence of tunnelling is reduced when the CEO is remunerated with stock options and/or the package has pay-for-performance components. The second arises from the countervailing influence of other large shareholders. An active market for corporate control provides a check on the behaviour of controlling shareholders, although such markets seldom exist in emerging economies. The active involvement of other large shareholders provides a realistic deterrent to tunnelling by the controlling shareholder, as they can together potentially initiate a battle for corporate control.

Comparative corporate governance: diffusion and institutional adaptation

In Part II of the book, the various chapters develop comparative perspectives on corporate governance by looking more closely at institutions and their cross-national diversity. Comparative and institutional perspectives are rooted in critiques of agency theory, which point out its 'under-contextualized' nature and inability to accurately compare and explain the diversity of corporate governance arrangements (Aguilera and Jackson, 2003). This perspective emphasizes that no 'one best way' exists, but that different corporate governance systems may have different strengths and weaknesses, not just in resolving agency problems but also in supporting different types of firm strategies through stakeholder involvement or different types of incentive structures. Similarly, much of the resulting policy prescriptions enshrined in codes of 'good' corporate governance rely on universal notions of 'best practice', which often ignore how these will be or need to be adapted to the local contexts of firms or 'translated' across diverse national institutional settings (Ahmadjian and Robbins, 2005; Fiss and Zajac, 2004).

For IB scholars, institutional diversity raises a number of interesting issues related to the diffusion of MNE practices and strategic adaptation to the conflicting pressures of internationalization and local institutions. Internationalization raises questions concerning the extent to which best practice in governance regimes may be transported or transplanted from one national business system to another, spawning numerous studies on the prospects of international convergence. Institutional theory has tended to stress the barriers or undesirable nature of such diffusion, due to the likely absence of complementary institutions to support imported practices (Aoki, 2007; Hall and Soskice, 2001; Streeck, 1996). However, recent institutional approaches also emphasize the possibility of new combinations of practices and incremental adaptation of institutions. It remains to be seen whether this sort of cross-fertilization will lead to potentially effective new 'hybrid' forms of corporate governance (Aoki and Jackson, 2008; Kester, 1996) or undermine the distinctive advantages and social foundations of existing national models, particularly as ideologies of shareholder value erode strong stakeholder or employee involvement in some countries (O'Sullivan and Lazonick, 2000; Vitols, 2004).

By way of introducing the perspective of comparative institutional analysis, Chapter 9 summarizes a conference roundtable on the relationship of comparative analysis and IB scholarship. This chapter features short contributions from Mari Sako, Christel Lane, and Richard Hyman. From differing perspectives, the authors highlight the importance of looking at institutions in the context of comparing specific national cases. Sako explores how IB scholars may go beyond notions of 'institutional voids' (Khanna and Palepu, 2006) and better conceptualize the diversity of institutions across countries, particularly where those institutions are informal and underwrite non-market forms of coordination. Lane links institutional analysis with debates over global value chains, summarizing some of her empirical work on the United Kingdom, the United States and Germany that demonstrates how firms' strategic choices and the consequences of global value chains often differ greatly according to national context. Hyman compares the research agendas in comparative industrial relations and IB scholarship, and suggests that both fields of study are increasingly concerned with the impact of MNEs on local institutional settings. He argues that despite the necessity of comparing how institutions share and are shaped by internationalization, the task of comparison brings serious methodological difficulties, since the nature of institutional effects are highly contextual and to some degree 'incomparable' across different countries.

In Chapter 10, John Dunning examines the topic of corporate social responsibility (CSR) from an institutional perspective. While noting that IB scholarship has been largely focused on the creation of wealth in the physical environment, Dunning argues that changes in the human environment have made societal goals and also CSR practices more salient. While a congruence between private interests of firms and their contribution to societal interests is often seen as existing through the mechanisms of the market, several common types of market failures create an important gap for CSR *as an element of corporate governance* and consequently as an important research agenda for IB scholars. CSR is a way for firms to communicate, engage with, and guide their behaviour to be more consistent with societal values and interests. Dunning argues that such divergence may be reasonably addressed within a single nation-state, but becomes a great deal more problematic when firms cross national borders into different cultural and institutional environments. The resulting 'distance' of MNE activities from those environments exposes CSR to much broader sets of values in diverse local communities. A key question for IB scholars thus concerns to what extent MNEs may take on board the location-specific components of CSR, while capturing the economic benefits of a global coordination of value-added activities. Given the widely different ideologies, cultures and forms of capitalism, Dunning suggests that a consensus for a global standard of CSR seems extremely remote despite some progress within more voluntary frameworks. Rather, Dunning argues that the mechanisms for effectively promoting CSR are likely to be institutionally diverse across different societies, and should form an important part of future IB research.

In Chapter 11, Gregory Jackson and Hideaki Miyajima compare the growth in M&A markets in five countries: France, Germany, Japan, the United Kingdom and the United States. Using evidence on M&A transactions from 1991 to 2005, the chapter shows that despite the common trend towards growth in the number and value of transactions, the style and types of M&A transactions differ substantially across countries. Both the United Kingdom and the United States have historically very developed markets for corporate control. Here transactions are relatively arm's-length – bidding firms have little prior ownership ties with their target, public tender offers are common, and bidders usually buy stakes leading to 100 per cent control of the target firm. In the more 'coordinated' economies of France, Germany and Japan, M&A transactions tend to involve buying and selling of large share blocks among 'known' parties, frequently use private negotiation, and leave target companies independent, either as subsidiaries or within a network of firms grouped around the bidder. Japan is the most extreme case, reflected in the zero to negative takeover premium paid for shares. Jackson and Miyajima argue that, although a market for corporate control exists in all five countries, the nature and dynamics of these markets are still strongly influenced by the institutional legacies of corporate governance, ownership patterns and wider sets of institutions of their respective national business systems.

In Chapter 12, Mairi Maclean and Charles Harvey compare the recent changes in the UK and French systems of corporate governance. These two European economies have faced extensive corporate restructuring across national boundaries and responded to a growing focus by national and European policy-makers on issues of corporate responsibility, accountability and transparency. However, Maclean and Harvey show that these national systems are not converging, but undergoing adaptation that is deeply conditioned by their past institutions. They develop their argument through a quite novel focus on business elites, an area which has tended to be neglected in existing research. They examine the board memberships, structure and career pathways of managers in the top 100 companies in France and the UK respectively during the period 1998 to 2003. In particular, they compare the number and nature of challenges or interventions made against incumbent CEOs. Maclean and Harvey argue that corporate governance regimes are to a large extent self-reinforcing, restricting their capacity to adapt to new influences whilst not precluding change. As such their chapter looks at institutions not just at the level of regulation and organizational responses, but also at the wider ideological aspects of how top managers themselves interpret and enact institutions through their own ideas, ideologies and 'habitus'.

Chapter 13, by Tord Andersson, Colin Haslam, Edward Lee and Nick Tsitsianis constructs a 'financialized' account of recent changes in corporate governance. The chapter presents an innovative theoretical framework centred on how companies account for and deliver value to shareholders. In particular, Andersson et al. focus on the impact of 'fair value' accounting in the United States on corporate strategy and the market for corporate control. Fair value reporting blends stock market value (wealth accumulation) with current earnings in corporate sector financial accounts. During the recent period of high M&A activity, the authors argue that fair value accounting has pushed balance sheet capitalization ahead of cash earnings, thus putting a growing proportion of corporate value at risk. Looking at data from the S&P 500 firms, the authors find evidence to suggest that these firms are aiming to increase cash from operations and to modify the pattern of cash distribution towards equity investors to contain value at risk. The implications are that greater 'financialization' of corporate governance will drive firms to strategic arbitrage in product, procurement and labour markets, since firms will seek to modify contractual relations and settlements. Moreover, fair value accounting has wider international implications for changes in corporate governance. The International Accounting Standards Board (IASB) has taken fair value as a baseline principle, and fair value has now become the standard in European markets as well. Consequently, this chapter draws attention to some further consequences of the recent growth of M&A transactions in Europe, as noted by Jackson and Miyajima, in terms of creating similar distributive pressures in European firms and thus threaten the 'stakeholder' orientation of firms in continental Europe.

In Chapter 14, Trevor Buck and Amon Chizema look at the issue of 'transplanting' corporate governance practices in the interesting case of executive stock options (ESO) in Germany. Given the broad institutional differences between German and Anglo-American corporate governance practices, the ESO faces significant institutional resistance in Germany, since it may be opposed by large blockholders and banks, as well as employee representatives and some groups of management. ESOs may be expected to be rejected or at least 'translated' by German firms, to preserve their legitimacy, i.e. to suit the interests of salient stakeholders. Despite such inertia, however, German firms have certainly adopted ESOs in large numbers. The chapter draws on 'neo-institutional' theory to develop a series of detailed micro-level hypotheses about the constellations of stakeholders that may support or oppose adoption of ESOs. In testing these hypotheses with time-series data of the DAX-100 firms, Buck and Chizema find much support for their hypotheses. German firms with greater exposure to US markets through cross-listing or foreign institutional investors were more likely to adopt ESOs. Meanwhile, certain aspects of institutional embeddedness, such as employee power, decreased the likelihood of adoption. ESO was also associated with high levels of managerial discretion, such as high profitability and dispersed ownership. This result suggests the potential importance of managerial self-interest in driving change. Meanwhile, other findings suggest that large blockholders were likely to support adoption, rather than hinder it. The result suggests the potential importance of changes in actors' preferences over time to supporting new sets of practices. In their conclusion, Buck and Chizema raise some critical issues with regard to how these contradictory pressures for adoption and non-adoption may play out over time – such as a growing diversity of practices across firms, and most importantly, the potential 'translation' of Anglo-American practices into a more egalitarian, camouflaged variation on the American template (Buck and Shahrim, 2005).

In Chapter 15, Stephen Chen and Petra Bouvain link the theme of cross-national diffusion with the theme of CSR, discussed in the chapter by Dunning. Corporate social responsibility reporting is not mandatory in most countries, but has been adopted by many large companies around the world. Chen and Bouvain examine how corporate social responsibility reporting in different countries is related to national corporate governance systems by comparing the CSR reporting of leading companies in the United States, Germany and Australia. The chapter adopts an interesting methodological approach by analysing the CSR statements of each company using a content analysis software package called 'Leximancer' in order to inductively identify key themes in the reports of each company. The results show highly significant differences between countries in the relative importance of CSR concepts of community, social responsibility and sustainability but little difference in terms of employee and environment concepts. Thus, echoing the arguments of Dunning, this chapter substantiates the view that despite a global diffusion of CSR practices, companies based in different countries hold substantially different perspectives on how important it is to be perceived as socially responsible, and which CSR issues are most important.

The final chapter by Viola Makin, Ruth Clarke and Mark G. Albon touches on a number of themes from earlier chapters, such as transition economies, diffusion and comparative analysis. The authors examine the case of South Africa and how changing regulation impacts companies in South Africa both through the implementation of new corporate governance codes, and through growing exposure to US corporate governance rules, such as the Sarbanes-Oxley Act, through cross-listings on US stock exchanges. The political transformation of South Africa after 1994 and the opening of the economy has raised the salience of corporate governance, but leaves open different approaches to regulation based on voluntary codes or mandated requirements through law. The King II report of 2002 brought a voluntary approach based on codes to South Africa, but leaves open the possibility that companies may adopt dual-listings with American stock exchanges, where legally based approaches predominate. Based on interviews at five of the nine dual-registered firms in 2006, the authors find a strong sense of commitment and support for the indigenous and voluntary King II regulations. However, the chapter finds that the additional elements of the SOX regulations also suggest some potential improvements, provided that concerns with costs associated with implementation are ameliorated. This finding is suggestive for studying the issue of cost effective regulation in emerging economies, where the benefits of stronger legal regulation also come with associated costs that have strong effects on smaller market capitalized companies.

Conclusion

In this chapter, we suggested that corporate governance has not yet been a major topic for IB scholars, but that corporate governance and international business could be usefully linked in at least three ways. First, corporate governance institutions influence the attractiveness of host countries to inward investors, and hence have an impact upon flows of FDI (Globerman and Shapiro, 2003). Furthermore, institutional constraints in the home economy may also promote outward FDI (Witt and Lewin, 2007). The primary link here concerns the basic problems of agency between shareholders and managers, and the different formal and informal ways of resolving agency conflicts. Second, different groups of shareholders and stakeholders have different objectives (Lien et al., 2005; Filatotchev et al., 2007), and the diverse patterns of ownership, control and stakeholder involvement are likely to be reflected in the strategic decision-making of the firm, and its international-ization strategies in particular. These impacts thus go beyond questions of agency in a narrow sense, and concern the strategic resources and capabil-ities of firms. Third, the corporate governance systems in host economies are strongly influenced by the introduction of foreign capital and the activ-ities of MNEs. Internationalization constitutes a major driver of institutional change, although this change may be incremental and adaptive, leading to further differences rather than simple convergence. The chapters in this vol-ume explore these linkages in a variety of contexts, and together demonstrate the rich potential of this line of research for scholars of both international business and corporate governance.

Notes

1. For example, Aoki (2001) shows that in Japan insider-based corporate governance supports the formation of firm-specific skills and cooperative team-based pro-duction, which have contributed to firms' success in industries characterized by incremental innovation.
2. Formerly known as the Organization of African Unity (OAU).

Bibliography

Aguilera, R. V. and Cuervo-Cazurra, A. (2004). 'Codes of good governance worldwide: what is the trigger?' *Organization Studies*, 25(3): 415–44.
Aguilera, R. V., Filatotchev, I., Gospel, H. and Jackson, G. (2008). 'An organiza-tional approach to comparative corporate governance: costs, contingencies, and complementarities'. *Organization Science*, forthcoming.
Aguilera, R. V. and Jackson, G. (2003). 'The cross-national diversity of corporate gov-ernance: dimensions and determinants'. *Academy of Management Review*, 28(3): 447–65.
Ahmadjian, C. L. and Robbins, G. E. (2005). 'A clash of capitalisms: foreign sharehold-ers and corporate restructuring in 1990s Japan'. *American Sociological Review*, 70(3): 451–71.
Aoki, M. (2001). *Toward a comparative institutional analysis* (Cambridge, MA: MIT Press).
Aoki, M. (2007). 'Endogenizing institutions and their changes'. *Journal of Institutional Economics*, 3(1): 1–31.
Aoki, M. and Jackson, G. (2008). 'Understanding the emerging diversity of corpor-ate governance and organizational architecture'. *Industrial and Corporate Change*, forthcoming.
Barney, J. B. (1991). 'Firm resources and sustained competitive advantage'. *Journal of Management*, 17(1): 99–120.
Buck, T. W. and Shahrim, A. (2005). 'The translation of corporate governance changes across national cultures: the case of Germany'. *Journal of International Business Studies*, 36(1): 42–61.
Connolly, T., Conlon, E. J. and Deutsch, S. J. (1980). 'Organizational effectiveness: a multiple-constituency approach'. *Academy of Management Review*, 5(2): 211–17.

Davis, G. F. (2005). 'New directions in corporate governance'. *Annual Review of Sociology*, 31(1): 143–62.

Filatotchev, I. and Wright, M. (eds) (2005). *Corporate governance life-cycle* (London: Edward Elgar).

Filatotchev, I., Strange, R., Piesse, J. and Lien, Y.-C. (2007). 'FDI by firms from newly industrialised economies in emerging markets: corporate governance, entry mode and location'. *Journal of International Business Studies*, 38(4): 556–72.

Fiss, P. C. and Zajac, E. (2004). 'The diffusion of ideas over contested terrain: the (non)adoption of a shareholder value orientation among German firms'. *Administrative Science Quarterly*, 49(4): 501–34.

Gilson, R. J. (2000). 'The globalization of corporate governance: convergence of form or function'. Columbia Law School, Center for Law and Economic Studies, Working Papers no. 192.

Globerman, S. and Shapiro, D. (2003). 'Governance infrastructure and US foreign direct investment'. *Journal of International Business Studies*, 34(1): 19–39.

Gourevitch, P. A. and Shinn, J. (2005). *Political power and corporate control: the new global politics of corporate governance* (Princeton, NJ: Princeton University Press).

Hall, P. A. and Soskice, D. (eds) (2001). *Varieties of capitalism: the institutional foundations of comparative advantage* (Oxford: Oxford University Press).

Kester, W. C. (1996). 'American and Japanese corporate governance: convergence to best practice?' In S. Berger and R. Dore (eds), *National diversity and global capitalism* (Ithaca, NY: Cornell University Press).

Khanna, T. and Palepu, K. (2006). 'Strategies that fit emerging markets'. *Harvard Business Review*, 84: 60–9.

Lien, Y.-C., Piesse, J., Strange, R. and Filatotchev, I. (2005). 'The role of corporate governance in FDI decisions: evidence from Taiwan'. *International Business Review*, 14(6): 739–73.

Mahoney, J. T. and Pandian, J. R. (1992). 'The resource-based view within the conversation of strategic management'. *Strategic Management Journal*, 13: 363–80.

O'Sullivan, M. (2000). *Contests for corporate control: corporate governance and economic performance in the United States and Germany* (Oxford: Oxford University Press).

O'Sullivan, M. and Lazonick, W. (2000). 'Maximising shareholder value: a new ideology for corporate governance'. *Economy and Society*, 29(1): 13–35.

Pfeffer, J. and Salancik, G. R. (1978). *The external control of organizations* (New York: Harper & Row).

Roe, M. J. (2003). *Political determinants of corporate governance: political context, corporate impact* (Oxford: Oxford University Press).

Streeck, W. (1996). 'Lean production in the German automobile industry: a test case for convergence theory'. In S. Berger and R. Dore (eds), *National diversity and global capitalism* (Ithaca, NY: Cornell University Press).

Vitols, S. (2004). 'Negotiated shareholder value: the German version of an Anglo-American practice'. *Competition and Change*, 8(4): 1–18.

Whitley, R. (1999). *Divergent capitalisms: the social structuring and change of business systems* (Oxford: Oxford University Press).

Witt, M. A. and Lewin, A. Y. (2007). 'Outward foreign direct investment as escape response to home country institutional constraints'. *Journal of International Business Studies*, 38(4): 579–94.

Part I
Corporate Governance, Strategy and Performance

2
The Impact of Privatization on Company Performance in Transition Economies: an Evaluation

Saul Estrin

Introduction

It is nearly twenty years since the process of transition in Central and Eastern Europe (CEE) began, and more than fifteen since privatization began in earnest. There has been considerable hypothesizing in the literature that the mechanisms of corporate governance that pertain under private ownership are better than those under state ownership, and hence that privatization would lead to superior enterprise performance (Estrin and Perotin, 1991; Megginson and Netter, 2001; Megginson, 2005). Privatization has been nowhere so extensive nor so rapid as in the former communist countries, so these represent an important laboratory for us to test the impact of privatization on company performance. In this chapter,[1] I provide an overview of the findings from the huge economics literature that has emerged to explore this issue. I will concentrate on the former Soviet bloc but also consider the evidence that is now emerging from China.

This is not the first paper to address this question. Djankov and Murrell (2002) made a major attempt to survey this literature, applying a meta-analysis to the findings from a large number of diverse early studies and combining various indicators of performance (restructuring) into one composite measure. They found that privatization to outside owners resulted in 50 per cent more restructuring than privatization to insiders (current managers or workers). Privatization to workers had no effect in Central and Eastern Europe, and a negative effect in the Commonwealth of Independent States (CIS) that replaced most of the former Soviet Union. Investment funds, foreigners and other blockholders were found to produce more than ten times as much restructuring as diffuse individual ownership. Hardening of budget constraints (i.e. curtailing firms' access to formal or informal state subsidies) was also found to have a positive effect on restructuring. Among other factors, import competition had a positive effect on performance in CEE, but a negative effect in the CIS. Overall, the authors noted that the impact of privatization on company performance was typically positive and statistically significant in CEE, but statistically insignificant in the CIS. They explained this by the more widespread occurrence of insider ownership after privatization, and a weaker institutional environment leading to less effective governance by outside owners in the CIS countries. Finally, the authors noted that about one-half of the studies they surveyed did not take into account the endogeneity and selection issues associated with ownership and firm performance, and they urged future research to tackle this issue.

These surveys have not included much detail on China, perhaps because much of the private sector development has been either through foreign direct investment (FDI), entry *de novo*, or through unique Chinese ownership arrangements such as the township-village enterprises. However, since the mid-1990s, many large state-owned enterprises (SOEs) in China have been commercialized (made to operate as independent commercial entities) and shares in them have been sold, and private owners have gone on in some cases to obtain a majority stake or 100 per cent control.

We focus on total factor productivity (TFP) as our measure of company performance. Our results are somewhat different from those of the previous literature for two reasons. First, we are able to draw on a number of important and methodologically strong new studies as well as earlier analyses, and second we distinguish studies on the basis of their sample size, econometric methodology and indicator of performance in order to draw conclusions that take these characteristics explicitly into account. Ownership structures have evolved, leading to changes in control over firms, and so the emphasis in the literature has to some extent shifted from insider versus outsider, and concentrated versus dispersed, ownership to domestic as against foreign owners. We find that privatization to foreign owners raises efficiency relative to state-owned firms, although in China this result is less clear-cut and relatively more estimates suggest that private domestic ownership raises TFP. The effect of domestic private ownership is by and large also found to be positive in the CEE region and in Ukraine, but it is quantitatively much smaller than that of foreign ownership. Russia appears to be different in that the effect of domestic private and mixed ownership is found to be negative or insignificant. Concentrated (especially foreign) private ownership has a stronger positive effect than dispersed ownership in CEE and CIS, but foreign joint ventures rather than wholly owned foreign firms have a positive effect on TFP level in China. Worker ownership in either CEE or the CIS (and collective ownership in China) does not seem to have a negative effect relative to other forms of private ownership. Finally, data from CEE and the CIS suggest that new firms appear to be equally or more productively efficient than firms privatized to domestic owners, and foreign start-ups appear to be more efficient than domestic ones.

The chapter is organized as follows. First we briefly consider why reformers in transition economies placed such emphasis on privatization, summarizing the corporate governance arguments in favour of private ownership.

We go on to consider the unique characteristics of privatization in transition economies, notably its scale and the innovative privatization methods used. These may have influenced the way that privatization has affected company behaviour. The impact of privatization on company TFP is surveyed in the third section, drawing on some of the findings of Estrin et al. (2007). Conclusions are drawn in the final section.

Corporate governance in private and state firms: the reasons for privatization

It is normally argued that the fundamental difference between state-owned and private firms rests in their objectives: the latter focus exclusively on profit, which generates close attention to costs and to the demands of customers. State-owned firms may be interested in profits too, but they may be expected to meet politically determined targets as well, for example maintaining employment in economically depressed regions. In this situation, inefficiencies can emerge because they are not a central concern of the owner, and managers can exploit the lack of clarity in company objectives to ensure an easy life for themselves and employees (see Vickers and Yarrow, 1988; Shleifer and Vishny, 1994). But the problems of state ownership go beyond diffuse and non-commercial objectives. When a public-sector firm operates in a competitive market and the government tries to enforce an objective of profit maximization on its management, weaknesses in corporate governance can still cause inferior performance to what might be achieved under private ownership. The problem is centred on the asymmetry of information held by managers and owners; outside owners – private or state – can never have full access to the information about corporate performance that is in the hands of managers. Thus, it is hard for them to establish whether poor results are a consequence of unforeseen circumstances or managers exploiting firm profits for their own purposes. Whenever ownership and control are separated, firm-specific rents can be used to satisfy management's aim – for example, lower effort or managerial power, via the size of the firm – rather than profits. However, a private ownership system places more effective limits than does state ownership on their discretionary behaviour, via external constraints from product and capital markets (and perhaps also the market for managers, which will place value on previous performance) which largely operate through the market for corporate control, and through the internal constraints imposed via statutes and monitoring by the owners themselves (see Estrin and Perotin, 1991).

It is hard for the state to imitate these market-based constraints. State-owned firms are not subject to private capital market disciplines, so neither the competitively driven informational structure nor the market-based governance mechanisms can be substituted for in full. State employees are usually civil servants and often do not compete in the wider managerial market. Moreover, though the government's ownership stake is concentrated, the state is rarely directly represented on the boards of public sector companies and usually does not have the capacity in the supervisory ministries to undertake the necessary scale and quality of monitoring.

These arguments have particular resonance in transition economies. The problems of the socialist system were largely a result of the impact of state ownership and planning on investment allocation, incentives and efficiency (see Gregory and Stuart, 2004). Firms did not attempt to maximize profits, and productive efficiency was a low priority. Instead, weak monitoring of managers by the state as owner and the absence of external constraints gave management almost total discretion to follow their own objectives – rent absorption, asset stripping, employment and social targets. The softness of budget constraints (Kornai, 1990) that goes with the political determination of resource allocation was a further source of incentive problems, since managers did not have to bear the consequences of their own actions. Mistakes were condoned and losses were subsidized.

Privatization in transition economies

It is therefore clear why privatization was so important in the transition process. Nonetheless, reforming governments might in principle have left privatization until the track records of particular firms in the market environment had become firmly established and until the stock of domestic savings in private hands was sufficient to ensure the success of a competitive bidding process for the assets. But the state was probably not able to manage its firms effectively in the intervening period, and managers and workers began very rapidly to steal the assets (Canning and Hare, 1994). The collapse of communism had left state-owned firms with limited internal structures to handle the new demands of the marketplace and no mechanisms to monitor or enforce governance on state-owned firms (see Blanchard et al., 1991). The authorities had either quickly to create structures whereby the state as owner could control enterprise decisions, or face a gradual dissipation of the net worth of the enterprise sector by waste or theft. These stark alternatives persuaded many reforming governments to consider rapid privatization.

The sheer scale of privatization required in the transition economies posed considerable practical problems, however. The communist heritage meant that the majority of firms in all the transition economies needed to be privatized (Estrin, 2002). At the aggregate level, the stock of domestic private savings in these countries was too small to purchase the assets being offered. This led the reformers to innovate with privatization methods.

For selected firms, many countries used auction or public tender, as has been the norm in the West. Such sales could in principle be to domestic or foreign purchasers but, in practice, only Hungary and Estonia were willing or able to sell an appreciable share of former state-owned assets to foreigners.

Foreign capital ended up purchasing about 20 per cent of the privatized assets in Hungary and up to 50 per cent in Estonia. Foreign direct investment flows to the transition economies were modest in the early years, when privatization was taking place, and were highly concentrated towards Czech Republic, Hungary and Poland (Meyer, 1998). In practice, sales of SOEs were mainly to the countries' own citizens: either to external capital owners or to insider management–employee buy-outs. Managers and employees were the more common initial buyers.

To increase the pace of privatization, a number of transition countries began to experiment with 'mass privatization'. This entails placing into private hands nominal assets of a value sufficient to purchase the state firms to be privatized. To avoid the inflationary consequences of such wide-scale 'money' creation, the new assets had to be non-transferable and not valid for any transaction other than the purchase of state assets. This was largely achieved using the instrument of privatization vouchers or certificates. It was hoped that any deficiencies in the resulting corporate governance mechanism arising from the fact that the ownership structure was initially diffuse would be addressed by capital market pressures leading to increased ownership concentration (Boycko et al., 1995).

Mass privatization has been carried out in a number of different ways, but the differences can be summarized around two issues. The first was whether the vouchers or certificates were distributed on an egalitarian basis to the population as a whole or whether, as in Russia and many other countries of the former Soviet Union, management and employee groups received many of the shares, perhaps to diffuse potential opposition to privatization. Second, policy-makers needed to determine whether vouchers should be exchanged for shares in companies, or whether the vouchers should be in funds that own a number of different companies. In the Czech and Slovak Republics and in Russia, vouchers were exchanged directly for shares, although financial intermediaries soon developed in the market. In the Polish scheme, vouchers were exchanged for shares in government-created funds that jointly owned former SOEs.

Every country used a variety of privatization methods and everywhere different sorts of firms were sold in different ways. For example, in most transition economies small firms were usually sold to the highest bidder, and utilities were often floated on stock markets. However, it was possible by the time the bulk of privatization was completed in the late 1990s to discern the predominant method used in each country, and we report the widely used EBRD summary in Table 2.1. Mass privatization was the most common privatization method across the transition economies; nineteen of the twenty-five countries listed used some form of mass privatization as either a primary or secondary method. Moreover, management–employee buy-outs (MEBOs) also proved important, perhaps because transition governments sometimes did not have the authority to take on entrenched insiders in firms. Thus, nine

Table 2.1:   Methods of privatization in Central and Eastern Europe

	Primary method			Secondary method		
Country	Direct sales	MEBOs*	Vouchers	Direct sales	MEBOs*	Vouchers
Albania		+				+
Armenia			+		+	
Azerbaijan			+	+		
Belarus		+				+
Bulgaria	+					+
Croatia		+				+
Czech Republic			+	+		
Estonia	+					+
FYR Macedonia		+		+		
Georgia			+		+	
Hungary	+				+	
Kazakhstan			+	+		
Kyrgyzstan			+		+	
Latvia			+	+		
Lithuania			+	+		
Moldova			+	+		
Poland	+				+	
Romania		+		+		
Russia			+	+		
Slovak Republic	+					+
Slovenia		+				+
Tajikistan		+				+
Turkmenistan		+		+		
Ukraine			+		+	
Uzbekistan		+				

Note: *MEBO signifies management–employee buy-outs.
Source: EBRD, *Transition Report 1998*.

countries used MEBOs as their primary method, and six as their secondary method. Most transition economies therefore eschewed the conventional method of privatization, by direct sale. In fact, only five countries used this as their primary privatization method, though these were among the most developed transitional economies.

There was an extremely speedy ownership change in most transition economies. Few countries had contained a private sector of any significance in 1990 and the growth in the private sector share during the 1990s, reported in Table 2.2, is remarkable. As early as 1995, the private sector share was above 50 per cent in nine countries, though in eight former republics of the Soviet Union it remained below 30 per cent. By 2002, the private sector in thirteen additional nations had reached at least 50 per cent of GDP and in only two laggards, Belarus and Turkmenistan, was private sector activity still

Table 2.2: Private sector shares of GDP and of employment in Eastern Europe, 1991–2002

Country	Share of GDP			Share of employment		
	1991	*1995*	*2002*	*1991*	*1995*	*2001*
Albania	24	60	75	–	74	82
Armenia	–	45	70	29	49	–
Azerbaijan	–	25	60	–	43	–
Belarus	7	15	25	2	7	–
Bosnia and Herzegovina	–	–	45	–	–	–
Bulgaria	17	50	75	10	41	81
Croatia	25	40	60	22	48	–
Czech Republic	17	70	80	19	57	70
Estonia	18	65	80	11	–	–
FYR Macedonia	–	40	60	–	–	–
Georgia	27	30	65	25	–	–
Hungary	33	60	80	–	71	–
Kazakhstan	12	25	65	5	–	75
Kyrgyz Republic	–	40	65	–	69	79
Latvia	–	55	70	12	60	73
Lithuania	15	65	75	16	–	–
Moldova	–	30	50	36	–	–
Poland	45	60	75	51	61	72
Romania	24	45	65	34	51	75
Russia	10	55	70	5	–	–
Serbia and Montenegro	–	–	45	–	–	–
Slovak Republic	–	60	80	13	60	75
Slovenia	16	50	65	18	48	–
Tajikistan	–	25	50	–	53	63
Turkmenistan	–	15	25	–	–	–
Ukraine	8	45	65	–	–	–
Uzbekistan	–	30	45	–	–	–
Means	20	44	62			

Note: – signifies the figure is unavailable.
Sources: EBRD, *Transition Report 1999* and *Transition Report 2003*.

below 25 per cent of GDP. Thus the privatization process in the transition economies was in many countries effective in transferring the bulk of economic activity from state to private hands in the space of hardly more than a decade.

This remarkable performance should not conceal real concerns raised at the time about the quality of privatization, and therefore about its consequences for enterprise restructuring. First, there are questions about how real the privatization has been. In many transition economies, the state continued to own golden shares or significant shareholdings in companies. Evidence is provided in Table 2.3. For example, the Russian state retained more than a

Table 2.3:   Retained shareholdings in privatized firms in transition

Country	0%	1–30%	>30%
Albania	83.9	0	16.2
Armenia	97.1	2.9	0
Azerbaijan	94.1	5.9	0
Belarus	80.4	10.7	8.9
Bulgaria	30.8	61.6	7.7
Croatia	59.1	33.4	7.6
Czech Republic	100	0	0
Estonia	92.3	3.9	3.9
Georgia	79.3	7	13.8
Hungary	100	0	0
Kazakhstan	93.6	2.1	4.2
Kyrgyz Republic	91.2	1.8	7.1
Latvia	100	0	0
Lithuania	80.8	19.3	0
Macedonia (FYR)	92.9	0	7.1
Moldova	87.7	5.4	7.1
Poland	71.7	13.3	15.1
Romania	80	13.4	6.7
Russia	82.6	8.7	8.7
Slovak Republic	92.3	7.7	0
Slovenia	63	24.1	13
Ukraine	83.6	9.6	6.8
Uzbekistan	69.2	27	3.9
Total	80.9	11.8	6.3

Source: EBRD Survey.

20 per cent share in 37 per cent of privatized firms, and kept more than a 40 per cent share in 14 per cent of the firms that it privatized. Only in half of privatized firms did the Russian government sell its entire holding. Thus, the clean break between the state as owner and the enterprise sector has perhaps been more notional than real.

Moreover, the long 'agency chains' implicit in mass privatization may not provide appropriate incentives for corporate governance. Voucher privatization led to ownership structures that were highly dispersed (Coffee, 1996). Typically the entire adult population of the country, or all insiders to each firm, were allocated vouchers with which to purchase the shares of the company. The desire for equitable and politically acceptable outcomes dominated the need to create concentrated external owners who would have a large enough stake to be motivated to maintain oversight of management. However, it was possible that financial intermediaries could aggregate individual voucher holdings and carry out effective monitoring of management, and in Czech Republic, Poland, Slovenia and Slovakia some effort was made to ensure such concentrated intermediate agents did emerge. This was often associated with fraud and the outright theft of assets by managers to avoid their use by the new owners – so-called 'tunnelling' (Johnson et al., 2000).

The way that mass privatization was carried out in many countries also sometimes led to majority ownership that was not best suited to accelerate restructuring, for example by insiders. This was probably largely for political reasons, especially in countries where the pro-reform forces were politically weak. According to Earle and Estrin (1996), insiders held a majority share-holding in 75 per cent of firms in Russia immediately post-privatization (1994) and outsiders only 9 per cent. Insider ownership was predominantly in the hands of workers. However, this created little problem for manage-ment because worker ownership was so highly dispersed. Indeed Blasi et al. (1997) argue that control was effectively in the hands of management in Russian employee-owned firms. Outsider ownership is also typically highly dispersed, with much of it in the hands of banks, suppliers, other firms and an assortment of investment funds. In Russia, it appears from a variety of stud-ies (see Estrin and Wright, 1999 for a survey) that outside shareholding has increased at the expense of the state and insiders during the 1990s, but owner-ship is also becoming increasingly dispersed and the greater degree of outside ownership may largely represent the fact that former insider voucher-owners have left the firm but retained their shares.

This pattern of extensive employee ownership seems broadly consistent with the evidence for other CIS countries. In Ukraine, insiders owned 51 per cent of shares in all privatized firms in 1997 – managers 8 per cent and workers 43 per cent – while outsiders held 38 per cent and the state residue share was 11 per cent. In Ukraine, insiders have actually increased their shareholdings, while managers have been buying shares from workers. Thus, rather than evolving towards the structure of firms owned by a concen-trated group of outsiders, as was hoped by reformers, enterprises in the CIS appear to have remained primarily owned by dispersed groups of employees or outsiders. However, the situation appears to have been somewhat different in Central Europe, where many of the most important firms in the economies are now quoted on the relevant national stock exchanges or owned by large foreign firms. As we have seen, foreign ownership was predominant in Hungary; ownership by new entrepreneurs was common in Poland; while investment fund ownership initially predominated in the Czech Republic.

Despite these concerns about the impact of privatization methods on national economic performance, there is no evidence that mass privatization has had negative effects on growth in the long term. Indeed, the evidence suggests that the results go the other way. Thus Bennett et al. (2007) focus on privatization methods and use an expanded Solow-Barro empirical growth framework, in which GDP growth is associated with growth in factor inputs (capital, labour and human capital) and a number of other variables including capital market and private sector development. The authors use a panel data model and GMM estimation methods for almost all the transition economies (twenty-six countries) for the period from 1991 to 2003. They find that countries that used mass privatization actually enjoyed significantly higher growth post-privatization relative to pre-privatization compared to countries that used other privatization methods. They use a variety of alternative specifications as well as country-specific fixed effects to control for possible alternative explanations of their findings. Their study suggests that, as predicted by policy advisers at the time, the advantage of speed in privatization brought about by mass privatization may have yielded benefits in terms of economic growth.[2]

The impact of privatization on company performance

Previous economic surveys of firm-level studies examining the effects of privatization on firm performance in transition economies range from ones that find a large variation of outcomes but no systematically significant effect of privatization on performance (Bevan et al., 1999) to ones that are fairly confident that privatization tends to improve performance (Shirley and Walsh, 2001; Djankov and Murrell, 2002). This variation in the interpretation of results is brought about in part by the fact that the early studies had access to different and often somewhat limited data on firm ownership. For these reasons, many studies treat ownership as a relatively simple categorical concept and some are often unable to distinguish the exact extent of ownership by individual owners or even relatively homogeneous groups of owners.

Equally important, the diversity of interpretations and findings is generated by three types of interrelated analytical problems that may be expected in early studies in the context of the rapidly changing transition economies. First, the early studies rely on short time periods with observations concentrated immediately before and after privatization. Second, the early studies (a) use small and often unrepresentative samples of firms, (b) are frequently unable to identify ownership accurately because privatization is still ongoing or because the frequent post-privatization changes of ownership are hard to detect, and (c) often combine panel data from different accounting systems. Third, evaluating the impact of privatization correctly involves careful controlling for problems of endogeneity. For example, it may be that a subset of firms operate with higher levels of TFP, but for other reasons (location, management quality) that are firm-specific. If a government is interested in revenue, it will obtain a higher price from these firms, and thus sell them first. The better-performing firms are then the privatized ones, while the worse-performing firms remain in state hands. A simple regression analysis will infer that privatization increases efficiency but the conclusion would be incorrect. Even this simple example highlights the need to control for selection to avoid bias in the estimates of the effects of privatization.

In view of these problems, we have enlarged the survey of privatization studies reported by Djankov and Murrell (2002) with studies that have been published or circulated as working papers up to November 2006, and we have taken into account pertinent information about the data and econometric techniques used by the various authors. The overlap between the TFP studies of CEE and the CIS that we evaluate, and those covered by Djankov and Murrell (2002), is twenty-one studies. Since the studies are heterogeneous with respect to their methodologies and the nature of the data used, we classify studies as belonging to category 1, 2 or 3. Category 1 (C1) contains studies that employ at least fixed effects or use instrumental variables (IVs) to handle the selection/endogeneity problem in ownership, and have a relatively large sample size (which we define as at least 200 firms in large and medium-sized countries, or at least 75 firms in small countries such as Slovenia); category 2 (C2) includes studies that use fixed effects or IVs, but work with smaller sample sizes than studies in C1; and category 3 (C3) has studies that use OLS with any sample size. In our evaluation, we place emphasis on studies in C1 and to a lesser extent C2.

We have identified twenty-two studies that analyse the impact of ownership on TFP, or the rate of change of TFP, in the transition economies, using value-added, total product or sales revenues as the dependent variable and either dummy variables or percent share ownership as measures of different types of ownership: fourteen studies belong to C1, three to C2, and five to C3. A number of studies have simply examined the differential effect of state versus private ownership, while others examine the effects of other subcategories of ownership. The studies cover both the CEE and the CIS regions.

Once we focus our attention on the C1 and perhaps also the C2 studies, the confused results of the earlier literature are dispersed and some clear findings show through. With the possible exception of Russia, the effect of private relative to state ownership is found to be positive or non-negative. Moreover, studies that break private ownership into several categories show that the overall private versus state ownership dichotomy subsumes different private ownership effects. Virtually all suggest that privatization to foreign owners increases efficiency. This effect of foreign ownership is strong and robust across regions. The effect of domestic private ownership is by and large also found positive in the CEE region and in Ukraine, but it is quantitatively much smaller than that of foreign ownership (the quantitative effects are not shown in a tabular form). Russia appears to be different from Ukraine in that Sabirianova et al. (2005) and Brown et al. (2006) both find, with large datasets, the effects of domestic private and mixed ownership to be negative or insignificant. Similarly, Commander and Svejnar (2007) use a large firm-level dataset from twenty-six transition economies and find an insignificant average (across countries) effect of domestic private ownership relative to that of state ownership. In general, the effect of domestic private ownership appears to be more positive in the CEE region than in the CIS.

Compared to the Djankov and Murrell (2002) survey that found the effect of private ownership to be positive in CEE but insignificant in the CIS, we hence find a strong positive effect of foreign ownership in both the CEE and CIS regions, and a quantitatively smaller positive effect of domestic private ownership in CEE and in Ukraine (together with a negative effect in Russia). The reason for finding a stronger positive effect than Djankov and Murrell (2002) is in part the focus on C1 and C2 studies, but also that more of our studies cover recent years and privatization may take a few years to have an effect as strong owners take control and markets start to function. Finally, institutional development is a slow process and more recent data may pertain to a more developed legal and institutional setting in most of the transition economies.

Several studies examine concentration of ownership and find that it plays an important part, with majority private ownership having mostly positive effects on TFP. Primarily foreign-owned firms again drive the overall positive effect. The effect of majority domestic private ownership tends to be positive as well, but it tends to be smaller in magnitude. As before, the effect is found to be positive in Ukraine but negative in Russia. Overall, we hence find qualified support for the hypothesis that concentrated private ownership tends to increase efficiency more than dispersed ownership.

Two studies distinguish between privatized SOEs and newly created private firms. Sabirianova et al. (2005) use 1992–2000 firm-level data for almost all industrial firms in the Czech Republic and Russia, and find that foreign start-ups are less efficient than existing foreign-owned firms, but more efficient than domestic start-ups, which are in turn more efficient than existing domestic firms. This study hence suggests that new firms tend to be more efficient than firms privatized to domestic owners. Using 2002 and 2005 firm-level data from twenty-six transition economies, Commander and Svejnar (2007) find that domestic start-up firms are less efficient than foreign-owned firms but not significantly different from domestic privatized or state-owned firms. The two studies hence suggest that *de novo* firms are more productive than, or at least as productive as, SOEs privatized to domestic owners.

Studies that examine the dynamics of productive efficiency show that foreign-owned firms improved efficiency faster than domestic private and state-owned firms in the 1990s and early 2000s. This differential effect is not detectable, however, in the Commander and Svejnar (2007) 2002–5 panel data study of twenty-six transition economies. It is hence possible that foreign owners brought about a sizeable increase in efficiency in the period immediately after acquiring the local firms in the 1990s, but that later on the rate of change in efficiency has been on average similar in all the principal types of ownership of firms.

In view of the above results, the question naturally arises as to why the TFP effect of privatization to domestic owners has been much smaller than the TFP effect of privatization to foreign investors. Discussions with managers, policy-makers and analysts suggest three leading possible explanations. The finding may reflect in part the limited skills and access to world markets on the part of the local managers. Domestically owned privatized firms are also the ones where performance-reducing activities such as looting, tunnelling and defrauding of minority shareholders have been most frequent. Finally, in a number of countries, the nature of the privatization process initially prevented large domestic private owners from obtaining 100 per cent ownership stakes, and insiders or the state often owned sizeable holdings. It often took these large shareholders several years to squeeze out minority shareholders and, in the process, the large shareholders sometimes artificially decreased the performance of their newly acquired firms in order to squeeze out the minority shareholders at low share prices.

The existing privatization studies also provide information about the effect of employee (insider) ownership on efficiency. There has been a major debate about whether employee ownership and control are associated with lower or higher efficiency and excessive use of labour (labour hoarding).[3] We have found seven studies that examine the effect of employee ownership on TFP. Six estimates from both CEE and CIS countries are statistically insignificant, and one (Estonia) shows a positive effect of employee ownership on TFP. These results are different from those of Djankov and Murrell (2002), who find the overall effect of employee ownership on performance to be insignificant in CEE and negative in the CIS. One reason for this discrepancy may be the aforementioned limited overlap between our and the Djankov and Murrell (2002) studies in this area. Moreover, Djankov and Murrell (2002: 758) report that 'the results for managers and workers show a considerable degree of sensitivity to how selection bias is handled', while we focus on studies that handle the issue of selection (categories C1 and C2). Finally, Djankov and Murrell (2002) recalculate some estimates (e.g. in their Table 1) for the sake of comparability across studies, while we present the effects as reported in the original studies.

Simoneti et al. (2005) use Slovenian data to test for the effect of a firm being listed or not listed on a stock exchange, relative to being government-controlled. They find that the TFP effect of being listed is positive, while being privately controlled and non-listed has no significant effect relative to state control. This study hence supports the hypothesis that listing induces monitoring, better corporate governance and superior performance.

We have also surveyed the ownership-related studies that have been carried out on data from China. Probably because privatization is a relatively recent phenomenon in China, a number of studies, including Jefferson et al. (1996), address TFP issues with firm-level data but do not examine differences in TFP related to privatization or ownership. Studies that address these issues find diverse results, with the effect of non-state ownership being mostly positive but sometimes statistically insignificant and sometimes negative. Thus Jefferson and Su (2006) use a large sample of firms (N > 20,000) and show that the effect of private joint stock ownership on the level of TFP is positive. Hu et al. (2004) use a much smaller sample of firms in selected regions (N > 700), and find the effects of cooperative as well as domestic and foreign private ownership to have a positive effect on the level of productivity. Yusuf et al. (2006) use a relatively large sample of firms (N > 4,000), and find the effects of domestic private, collective and complete foreign ownership on the level of productivity to be statistically insignificant, the effect of foreign joint ventures to be positive, unreformed state ownership negative, and reformed state ownership positive. Finally, Dong et al. (2006) use firm-level data from Nanjing (N = 165) to examine the effect on the rate of change of TFP, and they find the effect of state urban ownership to be positive, while the effects of state rural and both private urban and private rural ownership are found to be insignificant.

The TFP studies of CEE, the CIS and China hence generate a variety of results. The CEE and CIS results suggest that privatization to foreign owners rather than domestic ones raises efficiency relative to state-owned firms. In China, this result is less clear-cut and relatively more estimates suggest that private domestic ownership raises TFP, though not the rate of change of TFP. Similarly, concentrated (especially foreign) private ownership has a stronger positive effect than dispersed ownership in CEE and CIS, but foreign joint ventures rather than wholly owned foreign firms have a positive effect on TFP level in China. Worker ownership in CEE and CIS (collective ownership in China) does not seem to have a negative effect relative to other forms of private ownership. Finally, the data from CEE and the CIS suggest that new firms appear to be equally or more efficient than firms privatized to domestic owners, and foreign start-ups appear to be more efficient than domestic ones.

Conclusion

The most impressive feature of privatization in the transition economies has been the speed and scale at which it occurred. The reforming governments of the late 1980s and early 1990s managed successfully to transfer the huge state-owned sector into largely private hands in a time period of hardly more than a decade, and to do so they had to use innovative privatization methods. However, this led them to introduce private ownership into situations where other crucial aspects of the business environment were not yet sufficiently developed to support the private economy. At the enterprise level, the effects of privatization have usually been positive, though the most serious problem for privatization as a policy has been its use in a weak legal and institutional environment. Perhaps because they are able to resolve the institutional weaknesses and resource constraints more effectively, we find that privatization to foreign owners raises efficiency relative to state-owned firms in the transition economies apart from China (where the results are less clear-cut). The impact of privatization to domestic owners is also usually positive, but it is quantitatively much smaller than that of foreign ownership. Russia appears to be different in that the effect of domestic private and mixed ownership is found to be negative or insignificant. Traditional governance issues are also relevant to understanding the variations in the impact of privatization: concentrated (especially foreign) private ownership has a stronger positive effect than dispersed ownership in CEE and the CIS, though foreign joint ventures rather than wholly owned foreign firms have a positive effect on the TFP level in China. Worker ownership in either CEE or the CIS (and collective ownership in China) does not seem to have a negative effect relative to other forms of private ownership.

In view of the above results, the question naturally arises as to why the TFP effect of privatization to domestic owners has been much smaller than the TFP effect of privatization to foreign investors. Discussions with managers, policy-makers and analysts suggest three leading possible explanations. The finding may reflect in part the limited skills and access to world markets on the part of the local managers. Domestically owned privatized firms are also the ones where performance-reducing activities such as looting, tunnelling and defrauding of minority shareholders have been most frequent. Finally, in a number of countries the nature of the privatization process initially prevented large domestic private owners from obtaining 100 per cent ownership stakes and insiders or the state often owned sizeable holdings. It often took these large shareholders several years to squeeze out minority shareholders and in the process the large shareholders sometimes artificially decreased the performance of their newly acquired firms in order to squeeze out the minority shareholders at low share prices.

Notes

1. This chapter was developed from the keynote address by the author at the 2007 conference of the UK & Ireland Chapter of the Academy of International Business, held at King's College London. The chapter draws on the work reported in Estrin et al. (2007). The author acknowledges useful discussion and comments from Keith Brothers, Klaus Meyer, Alan Rugman, Daniel Shapiro, Mike Wright and participants at the conference. Any errors remain his own responsibility.
2. The result may be due to an increase in ownership concentration following mass privatization that had strengthened control over firms.
3. In addition to the discussion above, see Hinds (1990), Earle and Estrin (1996) and Brada (1996).

Bibliography

Bennett, J., Estrin, S. and Urga, G. (2007). 'Privatization methods and economic growth in transition economies'. *Economics of Transition* (forthcoming).

Bevan, A., Estrin, S. and Schaffer, M. (1999). 'Determinants of enterprise performance during transition'. Heriott-Watt University, Centre for Economic Reform and Transformation, Working Paper 99/03.

Blanchard, O., Dornbusch, R., Krugman, P., Layard, R. and Summers, L. (1991). *Reform in Eastern Europe* (Cambridge, MA: MIT Press).

Blasi, J. R., Kroumova, M. and Kruse, D. (1997). *Kremlin capitalism: privatizing the Russian economy* (Ithaca and London: Cornell University Press).

Boycko, M., Shleifer, A. and Vishny, R. (1995). *Privatizing Russia* (Cambridge, MA: MIT Press).

Brada, J. C. (1996). 'Privatization is transition – or is it?' *Journal of Economic Perspectives*, 10(2): 67–86.

Brown, J. D., Earle, J. S. and Telegdy, A. (2006). 'The productivity effects of privatization: longitudinal estimates from Hungary, Romania, Russia, and Ukraine'. *Journal of Political Economy*, 114(1): 61–99.

Canning, A. and Hare, P. (1994). 'Privatization and regulation of utilities in economies in transition'. In S. Estrin (ed.), *Privatization in Central and Eastern Europe*, pp. 69–82 (Harlow: Longman).

Coffee, J. C. (1996). 'Institutional investors in transitional economies: lessons from the Czech experience'. In R. Frydman, C. W. Gray and A. Rapaczynski (eds), *Corporate governance in Central Europe and Russia*, pp. 111–86 (Budapest: Central European Press).

Commander, S. and Svejnar, J. (2007). 'Do institutions, ownership, exporting and competition explain firm performance? Evidence from 26 transition countries'. Mimeo.

Djankov, S. and Murrell, P. (2002). 'Enterprise restructuring in transition: a quantitative survey'. *Journal of Economic Literature*, 40(3): 739–92.

Dong, X.-Y., Putterman, L. and Unel, B. (2006). 'Enterprise restructuring and firm performance: a comparison of rural and urban enterprises in Jiangsu province'. *Journal of Comparative Economics*, 34(3): 608–33.

Earle, J. S. and Estrin, S. (1996). 'Employee ownership in transition'. In R. Frydman, C. W. Gray and A. Rapaczynski (eds), *Corporate governance in Central Europe and Russia: insiders and the state* (Budapest: Central European University Press).

Estrin, S. (2002). 'Competition and corporate governance in transition'. *Journal of Economic Perspectives*, 16(1): 101–24.

Estrin, S., Hanousek, J., Kocenda, E. and Svejnar, J. (2007). 'Effects of privatization and ownership in transition economies'. CERGE-EI Discussion Paper no. 2007-181. Available at: http://home.cerge-ei.cz/hanousek/jel-revised_06_04_2007.pdf

Estrin, S. and Perotin, V. (1991). 'Does ownership always matter?' *International Journal of Industrial Organization*, 9(1): 55–72.

Estrin, S. and Wright, M. (1999). 'Corporate governance in the former Soviet Union: an overview of the issues'. *Journal of Comparative Economics*, 27(3): 398–421.

European Bank for Reconstruction and Development (various years). *Transition Report* (London: EBRD).

Gregory, P. R. and Stuart, R. C. (2004). *Comparing economic systems in the twenty-first century* (Boston: Houghton Mifflin). Originally published in 1971.

Hinds, M. (1990). 'Issues in the introduction of market forces in Eastern European socialist economies'. In S. Commander (ed.), *Managing inflation in socialist economies in transition* (Washington, DC: World Bank).

Hu, Y., Song, F. and Zhang, J. (2004). 'Competition, ownership, corporate governance and enterprise performance: evidence from China'. Hong Kong Institute of Economics and Business, Strategy Working Paper 1111.

Jefferson, G. H., Rawski, T. G. and Zheng, Y. (1996). 'Chinese industrial productivity: trends, measurement issues, and recent developments'. *Journal of Comparative Economics*, 23(2): 146–80.

Jefferson, G. H. and Su, J. (2006). 'Privatization and restructuring in China: evidence from shareholding ownership, 1995–2001'. *Journal of Comparative Economics*, 34(1): 146–66.

Johnson, S., Porta, R. L., Lopez-de-Silanes, F. and Shleifer, A. (2000). 'Tunneling'. *American Economic Review*, 90(2): 22–7.

Kornai, J. (1990). *The road to a free economy. Shifting from a socialist system: the example of Hungary* (New York: W. W. Norton).

Megginson, W. L. (2005). *The financial economics of privatization* (New York: Oxford University Press).

Megginson, W. L. and Netter, J. (2001). 'From state to market: a survey of empirical studies on privatization'. *Journal of Economic Literature*, 39(2): 321–89.

Meyer, K. (1998). *Direct investment in economies in transition* (Cheltenham: Edward Elgar).

Sabirianova, K., Svejnar, J. and Terrell, K. (2005). 'Foreign investment, corporate ownership and development: are firms in emerging markets catching up to the world standard?' William Davidson Institute, Working Paper no. 734.

Shirley, M. and Walsh, P. (2001). 'Public versus private ownership: the current state of the debate'. World Bank Policy Research Paper no. 2420.

Shleifer, A. and Vishny, R. W. (1994). 'Politicians and firms'. *Quarterly Journal of Economics*, 109(4): 995–1025.

Simoneti, M., Damijan, J. P., Rojec, M. and Majcen, B. (2005). 'Case-by-case versus mass privatization in transition economies: initial owner and final seller effects on performance of firms in Slovenia'. *World Development*, 33(10): 1603–25.

Vickers, J. and Yarrow, G. (1988). *Privatization: an economic analysis* (Cambridge, MA: MIT Press).

Yusuf, S., Kaoru, N. and Perkins, D. H. (2006). *Under new ownership: privatising China's state-owned enterprises* (Washington, DC: World Bank).

3
Corporate Governance and the Composition of Foreign Equity Investment Inflows

Roger Strange and Jian Chen

Introduction

Many emerging and transition economies welcome inflows of foreign equity capital as a means of augmenting the funds available for domestic capital formation. There are three main channels though which such foreign capital may be introduced into the host economy: foreign direct investment (FDI), foreign portfolio investment (FPI), and the issuance of shares by domestic firms on overseas stock exchanges. However, the relative importance of these three sources of funds varies considerably between advanced and less developed economies, with FDI typically dominating inflows of foreign capital in the latter group whilst FPI and overseas share issues are more important for the former group (Cornelius and Kogut, 2003). These empirical observations raise two important questions. First, why is so little capital introduced through FPI and overseas share issues in less developed economies? Second, does this imbalance matter?

This chapter is structured as follows. We first explain in theoretical terms why the composition of foreign equity investment flows might be expected to vary with the level of economic development. Essentially the answer lies in the asymmetry of information between potential investors and domestic firms in emerging markets. In the following section, we look at the potential benefits and costs of inward equity capital flows through FDI, FPI and overseas share issues, in order to establish that the meagre inflows of capital through FPI and overseas share issues are an indicator of more fundamental corporate governance problems. Then we consider the case of China, and its record vis-à-vis corporate governance reform and the introduction of foreign capital. The final section summarizes the arguments, and draws policy conclusions.

The composition of foreign equity investment flows

The typical emerging economy is characterized by immature markets that are not competitive, inefficient economic institutions, a weak corporate governance system and an underdeveloped regulatory framework, and poorly functioning financial markets. Information problems are pervasive, and different economic agents have different information sets when they engage in transactions. These information asymmetries mean that different agents have different views about firms' performance and rates of return: a key asymmetry is that between the owners/managers who are able to monitor directly the performance of their firms and have privileged information, and potential outside investors who have to rely on incomplete information, imprecise signals and conjecture. Furthermore these agents are obliged to operate in an environment that is often subject to random disturbances, and their ability to do so is constrained by the information available. As Fausten (2004: 8) notes, 'market processes are therefore susceptible to opportunistic behaviour that may be incited, for instance, by moral hazard and adverse selection incentives.'

How do these considerations affect the composition of foreign equity investment? In the case of FDI, such asymmetries have a limited impact as, although the investment involves a transfer of capital and perhaps tangible and intangible assets (e.g. managerial and technical expertise, marketing know-how, property rights etc.) to the host economy, the foreign investor crucially retains control over the activities of the affiliate.[1] Thus FDI projects, although still subject to many risks, are not unduly susceptible to the information and agency problems highlighted above. They are thus not dependent upon the efficient functioning of local institutions and financial markets, notwithstanding the fact that additional capital is sometimes raised in the host country, or reliant on an effective local system of corporate governance.

Overseas share issues are a means by which domestic firms may raise additional capital, and typically at lower rates of interest than are available in the domestic financial markets. But information problems are very much an issue, and firms wishing to raise capital in this way will need to be able to reassure potential investors about the security of their investments and the health of their businesses. In particular, investors will require protection from expropriation by large investors and/or incumbent managers. Such overseas listings will therefore require the firms to adhere to the stricter reporting and disclosure requirements of the governance systems in the country of issue. These requirements will place an additional cost on such firms as compared to those firms which have raised capital on the domestic market. This additional cost may well be substantial, and is likely to be prohibitive to all but the largest and most efficient firms in emerging economies (Makin et al., this volume). Overseas share issues are thus unlikely to be a major source of finance for many firms from low-income emerging economies.

Whereas overseas share issues necessitate the firm(s) in question raising their standards of corporate governance, the attraction of FPI requires a more across-the-board improvement in the financial intermediation infrastructure within the host economy (Bekaert and Harvey, 2000). Capital inflows in the case of FPI are essentially stimulated by cross-border differences in expected returns in financial markets. As Fausten (2004: 5) points out, this requires 'reliable risk assessment and intensive monitoring on behalf of the financier. This requires appropriate financial institutions that are capable of managing the intermediation process effectively and reliably. Similarly, a regulatory-legal environment that maintains adequate disclosure standards and governance structures is an essential prerequisite for the viability of the various types of financial instrument (Razin et al., 2001).' Furthermore these capital inflows need to be transformed into capital formation by domestic firms, but the informational asymmetries in many emerging markets provide a major obstacle to the effective intermediation of loanable funds between investors and savers on terms that are mutually acceptable. Fausten (2004: 11) again reports that the 'prevalence of thin and highly regimented financial structures in emerging economics implies that domestic entrepreneurs do not have the wherewithal to achieve the bundling of finance and control. Potential domestic managers need to rely on outside finance to undertake capital formation, and savers do not possess the managerial skills to run enterprises.'

The implication of the above analysis is that, in emerging economies with weak corporate governance systems, foreign investment flows will be dominated by FDI with only limited finance provided by overseas share issues and FPI.

The costs and benefits of foreign equity investment inflows

Does it matter that capital inflows through overseas share issues and FPI are meagre in comparison to those through FDI? Or to put it another way, what are the potential benefits and costs of inward equity capital inflows through FDI, FPI and overseas share issues?

The potential benefits of inward FDI have been widely documented in the literature, and include not only the additional capital provided by the foreign investors but also technology transfers and productivity spillovers from the multinational companies (MNCs) to indigenous firms (Blomstrom and Kokko, 1998; Gorg and Strobl, 2001). These spillovers may occur through movements of skilled staff, demonstration effects, and/or the additional competition forcing indigenous firms to become more productive. There is also evidence that FDI flows from developed economies are positively correlated with FPI inflows (Soto, 2003), that 'FDI has an essential role to play in restoring the function of an equity market for capital investment' (Razin et al., 1997: 2), and that FDI improves the institutions of corporate governance in the host economy (Kogut and Macpherson, 2003). And FDI flows are less volatile than portfolio investments (Albuquerque, 2003). On the other hand, there is some evidence that MNCs, in raising capital in domestic markets, reduce the amount of credit made available to indigenous firms and thus crowd out domestic investors (Harrison and Macmillan, 2003).

What are the benefits of overseas share issues? From the issuing firm's point of view, the benefits are threefold. First, the firms gain access to additional and cheaper sources of capital which may be particularly important for firms from countries with thin financial markets. Second, the firms gain experience of management methods, accounting systems, laws and regulations in Western markets, and strengthen their contacts with Western firms. And third, there are the indirect competitive benefits that accrue through the adoption and implementation of better corporate governance practices although, as noted above, these come at a cost. These in turn encourage investors, both domestic and foreign, and result in higher company valuations and easier access to debt finance. And it is possible that there will be demonstration effects to other firms within the economy. Notwithstanding the potential benefits of FDI to the host economy, there are associated constraints notably the sizeable and indivisible nature of the resource commitments, and the relative illiquidity of the invested funds. This is the downside of the lack of volatility cited earlier. In contrast, funds raised through overseas share issues provide potential investors with a more liquid investment vehicle.

What is the empirical evidence of a link between foreign investment inflows and economic growth and/or development in emerging markets? Durham (2004) reviews the extant literature and suggests that the effects are contingent upon the financial and institutional absorptive capacity of the host economy. There is also the possibility of two-way causation: i.e. that growth in the host economy stimulates foreign capital inflows which, in turn, stimulate growth.

Corporate governance reform and foreign investment in China

It has been suggested above that foreign equity investment inflows into emerging economies will be dominated by FDI, and that FPI and overseas share issues will only increase substantially once the local corporate governance and financial systems have developed along with their associated social, legal and economic institutions. A corollary of this is that secular changes in the composition of foreign investment inflows provide an important indicator of the development of the host economy. These predictions will now be examined in the context of the Chinese economy. China had essentially tried to attract foreign investment though three main channels: FDI, equity FPI, and overseas share issues. The phenomenal inflows of FDI[2] into China since the initiation of economic reform in 1978 are well documented, and these flows have been particularly large since the celebrated southern tour of Deng Xiaoping in spring 1992. In contrast, there was no inward equity FPI or overseas share issues up to the early 1990s – indeed there was no such thing as a listed Chinese company, and most firms were either state-owned enterprises (SOEs) or collective-owned enterprises (COEs) though there was a small private sector.

In the early 1990s, the Chinese authorities embarked on a policy of creating a 'modern enterprise system'. During the ensuing decade, many thousands of small and medium-sized SOEs were sold off, mostly through employee buy-outs (EBOs) or management buy-outs (MBOs). According to Tenev and Zhang (2002: 27–8), 81 per cent of the 63,490 small SOEs that had been in existence at the end of 1996 had been sold off by the end of 2000. In contrast, the authorities pursued a policy of corporatization for the large SOEs. Wei (2002: 226) notes that corporatization had been suggested as a way of reforming the SOEs in the early 1980s, but that the ideological debate on its merits did not really begin until the latter part of the decade and the early 1990s. Several limitations of state ownership were highlighted in the course of this debate.[3] First, the state (or the people of the nation) is the ultimate owner of the SOEs, though the property rights are typically exercised by a government department or ministry. Decisions on the use and disposal of the enterprise's assets are made by salaried managers. The well-known principal-agent problem is attenuated in a private company by the shareholders exerting their authority through various monitoring and/or bonding mechanisms, or through selling their shares in the stock market. But it is not practicable for the people of the nation to monitor the management of the SOEs, nor can the state divest their interest in public enterprises. Second, the state undertakes several roles with regard to the SOEs, being not only the owner, the regulator, and also the major creditor, but also establishing the policy and institutional environment within which the SOEs operate. In such circumstances, it is perhaps inevitable that the commercial objectives of the SOE may become confounded with other social goals. Third, the managers of the SOEs have no incentive to maximize the wealth of their enterprises, as they are only salaried officials with no independent authority and no claims on residual cash flows.

In contrast, it was noted that the modern private corporation was an independent entity with clearly defined property rights. Managers were given appropriate incentives, there was an external market for corporate control, and individuals were able to buy and sell their shares freely. As a result, there was a greater alignment of the interests of owners and managers, so that agency costs would be substantially reduced with consequent benefits for the economic efficiency of the enterprise. That was the theory. The Chinese practice of 'corporatization' involved the conversion of selected SOEs into independent legal entities, with more diversified ownership structures including other institutional, corporate and individual shareholders. The intention was to create a 'modern enterprise system', where the participation of outside shareholders would both improve the performance of the enterprises and also (see below) provide additional sources of finance. The policy of corporatization was officially endorsed at the 14th National Congress of the CCP in 1993, and the initiative was broadened and accelerated after the 15th National Congress in the autumn of 1997 when the Party adopted the policy of 'grasping the large and letting go of the small' (*zhua da fang*).

The typical process of corporatization comprised a number of stages. For those SOEs selected for conversion,[4] the first stage involved the auditing and registration of the original capital. The 'owners' of the corporation were thus identified, and the assets allocated accordingly. For historical reasons, SOEs may have received finance from different state investors, through different channels, and for different objectives.[5] Representatives were assigned to the board from the respective owners, even if all the assets belonged to state agencies. The enterprises would then choose an appropriate corporate form which might, according to the 1994 Company Law,[6] be as a 'limited liability company' or as a 'shareholding corporation'. The former category consists of companies which are wholly state-funded, whilst corporations in the latter category may raise capital through issuing shares on the stock exchanges. Both corporate forms introduced governance structures within which multiple owners jointly share finance and control, but only the latter were able to introduce non-state capital. But even here the potential diminution of state control was initially limited because of the idiosyncratic restrictions on share ownership and trade in China.

China had become the first communist nation in the world to have a stock exchange with the formal organization of the Shanghai Stock Exchange (SHSE) on 26 November 1990.[7] Five companies constituted the first batch of firms listed on the SHSE, though the number rose to eight by the end of the year. The Shenzhen Stock Exchange (SZSE) was established on 11 April 1991, initially for the trading of the stocks of only two companies. Since then the numbers of companies listed on the two Exchanges has risen dramatically – see Table 3.1 – to 1,434 by the end of 2006. Listed companies are able to issue three different categories of shares: A-shares, B-shares, and shares denominated in foreign currencies. Shares in each category have, in principle, the same voting and cashflow rights, but they differ in the extent to which they may be exchanged.[8]

- A-shares are held by state agencies, Chinese individuals, or institutions registered in China, and are traded in local currency. Some A-shares are held by the state, either by the central government, or by local governments, and/or by state asset management companies (AMCs). Before April 2005, state shares were not tradable. Some A-shares are held by autonomous domestic institutions such as industrial enterprises or securities companies, though not commercial banks. These legal person (LP) shares are issued in return for the provision of assets and, before April 2005, were only tradable privately to other domestic institutions with the approval of the China Securities Regulatory Commission (CSRC).[9] In contrast, tradable A-shares have been issued to public investors since 1991

Table 3.1:   The development of the Chinese stock markets

End year	Number of listed companies	Market capitalization		Shares issued (bn)				
		Rmb (bn)	% of GDP	Total	Restricted A-shares	Tradable A-shares	B	Other
1992	54	104.8	3.9	7.4				
1993	183	353.3	10.2	36.9	24.8	5.7	2.4	4.0
1994	291	369.1	7.9	75.0	45.5	14.4	4.1	11.0
1995	323	347.4	5.9	89.2	54.1	17.9	4.6	12.6
1996	530	984.2	14.5	126.7	76.5	26.7	7.8	15.7
1997	745	1,752.9	23.5	146.5	61.1	44.3	11.7	29.4
1998	851	1,950.6	24.5	265.2	160.4	60.7	13.4	30.7
1999	972	2,647.1	31.8	323.9	195.7	81.0	14.2	33.0
2000	1,121	4,809.1	53.8	379.2	243.7	107.8	15.2	12.5
2001	1,136	4,352.2	45.4	521.8	340.5	131.8	16.3	33.2
2002	1,244	3,832.9	37.0	587.5	383.9	150.9	16.8	36.0
2003	1,268	4,030.6	29.7	642.8	414.4	171.5	17.5	37.8
2004	1,377	3,705.6	23.2	714.9	454.3	199.3	19.7	38.8
2005	1,381	3,243.0	17.7	763.0	471.5	228.1	21.8	41.6
2006	1,434	8,940.4	42.4	1,489.8	926.0	330.1	22.9	210.8

Notes:
(1) The figures for 'market capitalization' include A- and B-shares only.
(2) Of the 1,434 listed companies at the end of 2006, 1,293 had issued A-shares only, 23 had issued B-shares only, and 86 had issued both. 143 companies had issued H-shares, of which 108 had issued H-shares only, and 32 had issued both A- and H-shares.
(3) The 'restricted A-shares' refer to the state shares and the LP shares. The tradable shares comprise the tradable A-shares, the B-shares, and the H, N, L and S-shares.
Sources: China Statistical Yearbook 1999, 2006 (www.csrc.gov.cn).

when companies have made their initial public offerings (IPOs): at least 25 per cent of the outstanding shares must be tradable A-shares. In April 2005, the CSRC announced a new initiative (CSRC, 2005) to change the status of many state and LP shareholdings from non-tradable to tradable, and companies were encouraged to prepare plans to implement this policy. But the conversion would be subject to regulatory and shareholder authorization (Hovey and Naughton, 2007), and the state would retain controlling shares of companies (such as major banks, telecom and oil companies) that were of strategic importance.

- B-shares are also tradable, but were available exclusively to foreign investors before February 2001 (see below) and have typically accounted for only a small proportion of the total outstanding shares.
- Shares of PRC-registered companies denominated in foreign currencies. These include H-shares denominated in HK dollars and listed on the Hong Kong Stock Exchange, N-shares denominated in US dollars and listed on

the New York Stock Exchange, L-shares denominated in UK pounds and listed on the London Stock Exchange, and S-shares listed on the Singapore Stock Exchange. In addition, 'red-chips' are PRC companies registered and listed overseas.

The primary purpose of the Chinese stock markets was, and still is today, to raise capital for the SOEs. Through the 1990s, the fiscal revenues of the central government had become increasingly inadequate to meet the state's needs for financing new investment projects. This was partly due to the policy of decentralization (Lin and Liu, 2000) that had placed many individual enterprises under the aegis of local governments, partly due to the erosion of SOE profits with the ending of many monopolies, and partly due to the fact that tax reforms had not progressed rapidly enough to provide alternative sources of revenue (Mohan, 2004: 5). New sources of capital were required, as was common in many developing countries.[10] The pressure on scarce state resources, combined with China's imminent accession[11] to the World Trade Organization (WTO), meant that 'there was little alternative to privatising the small SOEs, and also allowing the injection of capital into the larger ones' (Mohan, 2004: 5).

Foreign equity capital was introduced through issuing shares to foreign investors on the B-share market. The first B-share offering was Shanghai Vacuum – a television tube manufacturer – in 1991, and the issue was greeted with wild enthusiasm (Green, 2003a: 50). But the enthusiasm soon waned, and only 109 firms had issued B-shares by the end of December 2006. The total funds raised were Rmb 35.5 billion, or only 1.86 per cent of the total equity raised domestically since 1990. The reasons for the lack of success of the B-share market are perhaps twofold (Green, 2003a: 52–3). On the one hand, most of companies listed on the B-share market were chosen by the Shanghai and Shenzhen governments up to 1996, and were of poor quality. Even some of the best performers produced disappointing financial results. On the other hand, the shares were illiquid, and thus foreign investors' demand for them was low. Furthermore, excess domestic demand for equity meant that B-shares always traded at a significant discount relative to 'equivalent' A-shares, whereas the shares that foreign investors are allowed to buy normally trade at a premium in most other emerging markets. As Green (2003a: 50–2) notes, the

choice of a category of share exclusively reserved for foreign investors was odd. In order to introduce foreign capital in an orderly and gradual fashion, most other emerging markets have established variations of the Qualified Foreign Institutional Investor (QFII) framework. In QFII, a small amount of foreign capital is remitted into the country (through a 'hole' managed by the central bank in the otherwise closed capital account), which is allowed to be invested in listed companies, with certain restrictions. Thus, although domestic and international capital use different accounts, they trade the same shares: there is one price and all shareholders are treated equally. When considering such schemes, however, China's policy makers had to cope with the legacy of communism. While FDI, which bought fixed assets and employed people, could just about be accepted, portfolio investment was still seen as intrinsically speculative and unproductive. It was only by keeping foreign portfolio separate and by setting up a separate authorisation system for companies who wanted to access to it, that ideological opposition could be neutralised. The B-share system also calmed the fears of those worried about the stability of the renminbi since no currency conversion would be required. The result was, despite official claims to the contrary, a market with shares with different prices and different rights to domestic shares.

The third of China's strategies for attracting foreign investment has been to raise capital through share issues by PRC companies on the Hong Kong, New York, London and Singapore Stock Exchanges. Green (2003a: 56–7) reports a 'gold-rush' for Chinese equity after Deng's southern tour of 1992, with investment banks and the world's major stock exchanges all trying to convince Chinese SOEs to make overseas listings. The first such listing was that of Brilliance China Automotive Holdings, which issued 5 million shares on the New York Stock Exchange in October 1992. Other PRC-registered companies quickly followed, and there were thirty-seven further listings during the remainder of 1992. But enthusiasm soon waned, before share issues of 'red-chip' companies were stimulated in 1996 by the forthcoming return of Hong Kong to Chinese sovereignty in July 1997. The annual amounts of money raised though these overseas share issues thus rose and fell during the 1990s, but at modest levels compared to the inflows of FDI (see Table 3.2). As Green (2003a: 49) notes, 'the government allowed only a few chosen firms – mostly SOEs – access to foreign capital markets, thus channelling foreign funds to its favourite firms, a highly inefficient means of allocating foreign capital.'

Developments since the turn of the century should be seen as responses to the twin pressures of a deteriorating government fiscal situation, derived in large part from the need to establish social security provision, and the prospect of increasing competition following WTO accession. Five initiatives, in particular, have significant potential for the inflow of foreign investment capital.

First, the domestic private sector expanded rapidly through the 1980s and 1990s, aided by the general policy measures on reform, modernization, and the opening of the Chinese economy to the outside world. But the capacity of domestic banks and investors to provide funds for this expansion was restricted. At the March 1999 meeting of the National People's Congress, the role of the private sector was legitimized when its status was upgraded to being 'an important component of the socialist market economy' and, since

Table 3.2: Foreign equity capital in China

Year	Capital raised from overseas share issues (H, N, L and S-shares) (US$ bn)	Capital raised from issue of B-shares (US$ bn)	FDI (US$ bn)	Capital raised from overseas shares and B-shares as % of FDI
1993	0.7	0.5	27.5	4.4
1994	2.3	0.5	33.8	8.3
1995	0.4	0.4	37.5	2.1
1996	1.0	0.6	41.7	3.8
1997	4.3	1.0	45.3	11.7
1998	0.5	0.3	45.5	1.8
1999	0.6	0.0	40.3	1.5
2000	6.8	0.2	40.7	17.2
2001	0.8	0.0	46.9	1.7
2002	2.2	0.0	52.7	4.2
2003	6.4	0.0	53.5	12.0
2004	7.8	0.3	60.6	13.4
2005	18.9	0.0	66.7	28.3
2006	39.5	0.0	69.5	56.8

Sources: China Securities Regulatory Commission (www.csrc.gov.cn).
Ministry of Commerce of China (www.mofcom.gov.cn).

then, many of China's private companies (p-chips) have sought permission to raise funds abroad (Green, 2003a: 64). The first private Chinese company to list overseas was Yuxing Technologies: the listing took place in January 2000 on Hong Kong's new Growth Enterprise Market. The authorities have since permitted many other p-chips to seek foreign capital in Hong Kong, Singapore and New York.

The second initiative was the issuance, in January 2002, by the CSRC and the State Economic and Trade Commission of a *Code for Corporate Governance for Listed Companies in China*. The Code was based on the *OECD Principles of Corporate Governance*, originally issued in 1999 and revised in 2004 (OECD, 2004). The Code recognized that corporate governance issues were critical to the success of capital market development and enterprise reform in China, and addressed a variety of issues including the protection of investors' rights and interests (Mallin, 2007: 232). There have since been a raft of other related reforms and initiatives, including a regular policy dialogue between the OECD and the Chinese authorities, aimed at promoting sound and transparent corporate governance policies, and attracting international investors. For instance, in February 2006, the Ministry of Finance released thirty-nine standards based on the International Financial Reporting Standards. This will move China towards convergence with global standards, and should improve disclosure and transparency, and boost investor confidence (Mallin, 2007: 235).

Third, in October 2002, the CSRC relaxed the restrictions on mergers and acquisitions (M&A) by foreign investors. The new regulations allowed foreign investors to engage in equity acquisitions not only in foreign-invested enterprises and domestic enterprises, but also in SOEs and listed companies. The transactions can be made in the form of stock exchange, in addition to traditional cash offers. The range of permissible targets has been greatly expanded though there are still some restricted sectors as listed in the *Catalogue for the Guidance of Foreign Investment Industries* (amended in 2004). There were also restrictions on foreign investment that could threaten economic security, such as might lead to the transfer of high-reputation brands to foreign investors.[12] All transactions require approval from the Ministry of Commerce, or equivalent Chinese authorities. As Green (2003a: 209) notes, 'this M&A market will be driven by interests different from the domestic M&A market. Domestic firms buy listed-company LP shares primarily in order to obtain a back-door listing and gain access to finance, but foreign firms are interested in gaining control of companies with assets that will be useful to them in expanding into China. Their favourite targets will be firms with clear shareholding structures, low debts and strategic assets.'

The fourth initiative was the liberalization of certain restrictions on trading shares on the stock exchanges.[13] As noted above, the Chinese authorities had initially limited foreign participation in domestic listed companies by the simple expedient of restricting foreigners to the purchase of B-shares and other shares listed on foreign exchanges. On 5 November 2002, the authorities announced a QFII scheme, under which approved foreign institutions[14] would also be permitted to buy and sell A-shares and bonds listed on the domestic exchanges. The scheme came into effect on 1 December 2002 and, at the end of 2006, fifty-three QFIIs shared a capped quota of US$10 billion. However, many other foreign institutional investors have applied for approval, and there is strong demand for higher quotas.

All four of these initiatives favoured the growth of FPI and/or overseas share issues. The fifth initiative was the new Corporate Income Tax Law that was promulgated in March 2007, and which took effect from January 2008. Under the previous tax regime, FDI projects received more favourable treatment than domestic enterprises and this had generated many problems including local governments offering tax incentives to potential FDI projects, and the well-known problem of 'round-tripping'. The new law will standardize the tax rate so that domestic and foreign enterprises both enjoy a 'level playing field' in accordance with WTO principles, and preferential treatment will henceforth only be industry-specific.

The effects of this fifth initiative are not yet apparent, but it is likely to have some marginal negative impact on inward FDI. In contrast, the first four initiatives should all facilitate the introduction of further foreign capital through the other channels. The data in Table 3.2 appear to confirm this, with capital raised through overseas share issues increasing dramatically from US$2.2 billion in 2002 (4.2 per cent of FDI inflow) to US$39.5 billion in 2006 – a figure that is well over half of the FDI inflow for that year. In addition, foreign investors have started to acquire interests in the tradable A-shares of listed companies through a variety of means, though the sums involved are still limited. First, there have been several instances of foreign firms buying stocks in the controlling shareholders of listed companies.[15] Second, there have been cases involving negotiated transfers of large blocks of shares to foreign investors.[16] Third, some listed companies have issued new shares specifically to selected institutions, many of which involve foreign shareholders.[17] All three forms of transactions typically take place at discounted prices.

Conclusions

The main argument put forward in this chapter is that the information and agency problems inherent in emerging economies lead to a bias in the composition of foreign investment inflows away from relatively liquid portfolio investment towards relatively indivisible and illiquid direct investment. Most emerging economies are characterized by inefficient institutions, weak regulatory frameworks, underdeveloped financial markets, and corporate governance systems that are neither reliable nor transparent. In such circumstances, potential foreign investors experience difficulties in assessing the real worth of indigenous companies, and may also be susceptible to opportunistic behaviour by the owners/managers. FDI alleviates these problems as the foreign investor has control (at least in part in the case of joint ventures) over the activities of the affiliate, and the opportunity to monitor directly the performance of the affiliate. In contrast, investors who simply purchase shares – either those traded domestically or overseas – in an indigenous company have to deal with incomplete information and imperfect market signals.

It is apparent that the composition of foreign investment flows in China has changed dramatically since the turn of the century, and that this change has been in large part brought about by the institutional/governance reforms introduced by the Chinese authorities. Foreign investors are increasingly 'buying into' rather than 'building in' the Chinese market. This change in the composition of foreign investment inflows, in turn, has had and will continue to have an impact on the development of financial markets within China, as has been the case in other emerging markets (Levine and Zervos, 1998; Soto, 2003). Indeed, the changing composition of the foreign investment inflows provides compelling testimony about the secular improvement in the governance regime in China, and in a way that no amount of statistics or official pronouncements can match. Furthermore, these changes also raise interesting questions (UNCTAD, 2006) about who controls the institutional investment funds that undertake equity FPI, and whether the strategic motivations of these institutional investors are different from those of the shareholders in the MNEs that undertake FDI. These questions merit study by students of international business.

Notes

1. This control may be partial if the affiliate is a joint venture, but still the foreign investor will have the opportunity to monitor directly the activities of the business.
2. In China, investment only counts as FDI if the foreign company takes at least a 25 per cent stake. Most FDI projects take the form of greenfield investments, with only a small proportion involving the acquisition of the assets of local firms (Green, 2003a: 207).
3. See also Clarke (2003).
4. Prior to corporatization, SOEs may be owned (managed) by different levels (state, province etc.) of the administrative hierarchy. The process of selection for conversion will be initiated at this level, though final approval will be required from higher administrative authority. The corporatization is then effected by the relevant department or bureau which has responsibility for the SOE. Branches of the state-owned Asset Supervision and Administration Commission have been set up at the different administrative levels to oversee the SOEs.
5. Some debt capital previously issued by state banks might be classified more properly as equity capital.
6. The Company Law was promulgated in 1993, and came into effect in July 1994.
7. Stock exchanges did exist in China before the establishment of the People's Republic in 1949, though on a very small scale. But soon afterwards, the Stock Exchange in Shanghai, and others in smaller cities, were abolished on the grounds that the joint-stock system was intrinsically contradictory to socialist ideas. Thereafter, anyone advocating the idea of a stock exchange was liable to serious punishment. After 1978, with the advent of greater freedom in decision-making, some pioneering non-state firms began to seek equity from 'private' investors, usually the firm's employees. Beijing Tiaoqiao Department Store was the first firm in China to issue 'equity' to its employees, although the 'shares' may be better understood as a bond-type security – the firm promised a guaranteed rate of return over five years and redemption of the initial investment at the five-year maturity date. The shares were not transferable before the maturity date nor did they have any associated voting rights, and the firm did not set up a board of directors. A more standard share issue was later made by Shanghai Feile Co. in that the shares had residual control rights, infinite maturity and voting rights, although they were non-transferable. The importance of these two pioneering firms was that they made people tolerate, then accept, the idea of a shareholding system. The policy-makers watched developments without significant obstruction. Other firms followed suit to issue equity or bond-type securities. But high returns were required by the investors because the lack of transferability increased the liquidity risk, and this raised the capital costs for the issuing firms. Some local non-banking financial institutions in Shanghai thus set up a trading room to facilitate the trading of shares. This was the embryo of the SHSE (Chen, 2005: 34–5).

8. Green (2003b: 3) reports that the owners of tradable shares generally have to be pay more for their shares than do the state and LP shareholders who are allocated their shareholdings prior to the IPO at prices close to net asset value.
9. The CSRC was set up in late 1992 to assert control over the stock markets following a number of scandals, but initially it proved ineffective (Green, 2003a: 157). It was not until the latter part of the decade that it was given any real powers.
10. In a survey of 59 countries around the world, Jones et al. (1999) report that the resolution of fiscal problems was the principal motivation for the implementation of privatization schemes.
11. Although China did not actually join the WTO until December 2001, the main obstacle had been overcome in November 1999 with the signing of its bilateral agreement with the United States on the terms of its accession.
12. These restrictions were introduced in September 2006, partly in response to the purchase by the private equity Carlyle Group of 85 per cent of Xuzhou Construction Machinery Co. Ltd., a leading Chinese construction machinery company. The case prompted a national debate in China on the potential threat of foreign control of key industries.
13. The strict segmentation of the 'A-share' and 'B-share' markets was relaxed when, on 19 February 2001, the CSRC allowed domestic investors to purchase 'B-shares' provided they met certain conditions and used foreign currencies.
14. These institutions were generally securities companies, fund management institutions, insurance companies, or commercial banks. Approval was subject to the foreign institutions satisfying certain capital and experience requirements.
15. In December 2006, for instance, Diageo Highlands Holding BV (a subsidiary of Diageo plc) acquired 43 per cent of the equity of Sichuan Chengdu Quanxing Group Co. Ltd. ('Quanxing') from Chengdu Yingsheng Investment Holding Co. Ltd. for Rmb 517 m. Quanxing holds 39.48 per cent of the equity in Sichuan SwellFun Joint Stock Co. Ltd., a firm listed on the SHSE and leading maker of premium Chinese liquor. The agreed price per share was significantly lower than the open market price, and led to concerns about the 'deal' between the managers and the foreign investors and about the unfairness to the existing shareholders.
16. For instance, Mittel Steel acquired 29.48 per cent of the equity in Hunan Valin Steel Tube & Wire Co. by direct placement.
17. In June 2007, for instance, a Beijing real estate company (Super Shine Co. Ltd.) issued 120 million new shares to Reco Shine Pte. Ltd., a Singaporean company controlled by the Singapore government, which thus became the largest shareholder with 29.12 per cent of the equity. The issue price of the new shares was Rmb 5.71, whilst the market price was Rmb 19.28 on the date of announcement.

Bibliography

Albuquerque, R. (2003). 'The composition of international capital flows: risk sharing through foreign direct investment'. *Journal of International Economics*, 61(2): 353–83.
Bekaert, G. and Harvey, C. R. (2000). 'Foreign speculators and emerging equity markets'. *Journal of Finance*, 55(2): 565–613.
Blomstrom, M. and Kokko, A. (1998). 'Multinational corporations and spillovers'. *Journal of Economic Surveys*, 12: 247–77.
Chen, J. (2005). *Corporate governance in China* (London: Routledge).

China Securities Regulatory Commission (2005). 'Circular on issues relating to the pilot reform of listed companies split share structure'. CSRC Circular no. 32 [2005]. Available at: http://www.csrc.gov.cn/n575458/n4001948/n4002120/4069838.html

Clarke, D. C. (2003). 'Corporate governance in China: an overview'. *China Economic Review*, 14(4): 494–507.

Cornelius, P. K and Kogut, B. (2003). 'Introduction: corporate governance and capital flows in a global economy'. In P. K. Cornelius and B. Kogut (eds), *Corporate governance and capital flows in global economy*, pp. 1–24 (Oxford: Oxford University Press).

Durham, J. B. (2004). 'Absorptive capacity and the effects of foreign direct investment and equity foreign portfolio investment on economic growth'. *European Economic Review*, 48(2): 285–306.

Fausten, D. K. (2004). 'Asymmetric information and the composition of foreign investment'. Monash University, Department of Economics, Discussion Paper 15-04.

Gorg, H. and Strobl, E. (2001). 'Multinational companies and productivity spillovers: a meta-analayis'. *Economic Journal*, 111(475): F723–F739.

Green, S. (2003a). *China's stockmarket: a guide to its progress, players and prospects* (London: Profile Books).

Green, S. (2003b). '"Two-thirds privatisation": how China's listed companies are – finally – privatising'. Royal Institute of International Affairs, Asia Programme Briefing Note (December).

Harrison, A. E. and Macmillan, M. S. (2003). 'Does direct foreign investment affect domestic credit constraints?' *Journal of International Economics*, 61(1): 73–100.

Hovey, M. and Naughton, T. (2007). 'A survey of enterprise reforms in China: the way forward'. *Economic Systems*, 31(2): 138–56.

Jones, S., Megginson, W. L., Nash, R. and Netter, J. (1999). 'Share issue privatizations as financial means to political and economic ends'. *Journal of Financial Economics*, 53(2): 217–53.

Kogut, B. and Macpherson, J. M. (2003). 'Direct investment and corporate governance: will multinational corporations "tip" countries towards institutional change?' In P. K. Cornelius and B. Kogut (eds), *Corporate governance and capital flows in global economy*, pp. 183–215 (Oxford: Oxford University Press).

Levine, R. and Zervos, S. (1998). 'Capital control liberalization and stock market development'. *World Development*, 26(7): 1169–83.

Lin, J. Y. and Liu, Z. (2000). 'Fiscal decentralization and economic growth'. *Economic Development and Cultural Change*, 49(1): 1–21.

Makin, V., Clarke, R. and Albon, M. G. (2008). 'Corporate governance challenges for dual-registered companies from emerging markets: focus on South Africa'. In R. Strange and G. Jackson (eds), *Corporate governance and international business*, pp. 280–300 (Basingstoke: Palgrave Macmillan).

Mallin, C. A. (2007). *Corporate governance*. Second edition (Oxford: Oxford University Press).

Markusen, J. R. and Venables, A. J. (1999). 'Foreign direct investment as a catalyst for industrial development'. *European Economic Review*, 43(2): 335–56.

Mohan, T. T. Ram (2004). 'Privatisation in China: softly, softly does it'. *Economic and Political Weekly* (6 November).

OECD (2004). *OECD Principles of Corporate Governance: 2004* (Paris: OECD).

Razin, A., Sadka, E. and Yuen, C.-W. (1997). 'Channelling domestic savings into productive investment under asymmetric information: the essential role of foreign direct investment'. NBER Working Paper no. 6338.

Razin, A., Sadka, E. and Yuen, C.-W. (1998). 'A pecking order theory of capital flows and international tax principles'. *Journal of International Economics*, 44(1): 45–68.

Razin, A., Sadka, E. and Yuen, C.-W. (2001). 'Why international equity flows to emerging markets are inefficient and small relative to international debt flows'. NBER Working Paper no. 8659.

Rodrigues-Clare, A. (1996). 'Multinationals, linkages and economic development'. *American Economic Review*, 86(4): 852–73.

Soto, M. (2003). 'Taxing capital flows: an empirical comparative analysis'. *Journal of Development Economics*, 72(1): 203–21.

Tenev, S. and Zhang, C. (2002). *Corporate governance and enterprise reform in China: building the institutions of modern markets* (Washington, DC: World Bank & IFC).

UNCTAD (2006). *World investment report 2006: FDI from developing and transition economies: implications for development* (Geneva: United Nations).

Wei, Y. (2002). 'Corporatization and privatization: a Chinese perspective'. *Northwestern Journal of International Law & Business*, 22(2): 219–34.

4

Equity Market Integration and the Implications for Foreign Investment in Africa

Bruce Hearn and Jenifer Piesse

Introduction

Africa's securities markets have seen unprecedented change over the last fifteen years with the rapid growth and development of existing bourses and the establishment of new markets. Despite this growth, very few of these markets and listed stocks have been included in popular investment benchmark indices (such as the Standard & Poor's frontier market range), demonstrating the marginalization of this region in terms of attracting much needed investment capital from worldwide flows. Historically, banking has dominated the economies of many of the countries within Africa, with stock markets only playing a sizeable and active role in financing in South Africa and Egypt. However, the role this has played in development finance has been limited by severe credit rationing from incomplete credit markets. Ironically, development is hindered not by a lack of funds within the banking sectors but rather an excess of liquidity caused by a lack of investment-grade opportunities in which banks are able to invest accumulated savings. Domestic investment is further hindered by the low savings rates in many countries, where investors prefer to invest in physical commodities or livestock in line with traditional beliefs, as well as uncertainty over the ability of savings to retain value due to macroeconomic mismanagement and instability.

Although many African countries outside South Africa and Egypt have had established stock markets from the early part of the twentieth century, these tended to be small and limited in their contribution to domestic financing. The combination of underdeveloped stock markets and constrained banking sectors caused many firms in the public and private sectors within the formal economy, as well as those in the burgeoning informal economy that exists in many of the countries in Africa, to look towards internal sources of capital for development and growth. The end of the Cold War, and the resulting shift in global capital flows away from ideological allegiances, caused a resurgence of interest across Africa towards the benefits of stock market financing. This was enhanced by the role of the international financial institutions in shaping policy within the developing countries of Africa towards privatization of former state-owned industries, with the desired goals of achieving greater internal managerial efficiency together with diversifying ownership and attracting much needed investment. Development policy has been directed towards the development of stock market infrastructure and institutions, largely because a stock market is an effective vehicle in the initial public offerings (IPOs) of newly listed former state-owned enterprises (SOEs) and the attraction of investment capital. The motivations behind IPOs of former SOEs significantly differ from those of private companies, as the former act as a source of well-known blue-chip stocks in attracting a wider ownership base while the latter seek primarily to raise new capital.

Almost all African markets have undergone financial liberalization and the removal of formal restrictions on foreign ownership (with the notable exception of the Dar Es Salaam Stock Exchange in Tanzania), as well as the abolition of capital gains tax and the dismantling of extensive capital controls. The combination of these measures greatly facilitates the repatriation of investment gains and enhances the attraction to overseas institutional portfolio investors. However, the potential benefits of these moves have been mitigated by ineffective regulation and by a lack of adherence to internationally recognized corporate governance standards. The lack of regulatory enforcement of effective corporate disclosure, and variable standards in financial reporting and accounting, are together responsible for investors being faced with considerable transaction costs in the form of substantial equity risk premiums. The lack of a coherent minority investor rights framework, together with limited corporate governance legislation in many of the continent's markets, further reduces transparency and increases information search and verification costs for investors. The presence of such uncertainty raises the cost of equity for firms listed on domestic markets, further reducing profits from project cash flow streams and making corporate investment less viable.

Given the emphasis of development policy on the privatization of former SOEs, and the urgent need to attract investment capital, there has been considerable importance placed on the role of stock markets as instruments to encourage development and growth. Owing both to the constraints on domestic supply of capital because of low savings rates and also the lack of domestic institutional investors, there is considerable interest in attracting foreign investment capital from world markets. Increasing the level of foreign investment in these markets would be a substitute for the low level of domestic investment, and would provide sufficient funds to achieve desired levels of output and economic growth. Cross-border equity market integration indicates that investors face similar levels of transaction costs (including search and verification costs as well as brokerage fees and deal related costs) between markets, which would increase the likelihood that they would be included within global institutional investment portfolios. The ability to span different integrated markets within cross-border institutional portfolios provides foreign investment capital, as well as deepening the market with greater demand for stocks and thus more liquidity. Furthermore, a virtuous circle is created where the increase in the number of analysts covering the market leads to greater general awareness of opportunities existing within the market and better monitoring and expectation of enforcement of internationally recognized corporate governance standards and regulation. Equity market integration across borders indicates the potential for markets and assets to be included in portfolios where premiums between substitutable instruments in different markets are close to zero and prices for similar assets are equal (Levy et al., 2006). Where this is the case, there is real potential for increased risk diversification in the investment portfolios of fund managers. The 'Law of One Price' for mutually substitutable identical assets traded in different markets is a fundamental law of economics, and is an effective measure of integration. The basic assumptions of the law are that purchasing power parity holds between markets; that markets are information efficient with prices reflecting all available information; that investors adhere to the rational expectations hypothesis; and that there are no restrictions on arbitrage trading between markets so that equilibrium is achieved through asset supply and demand (Lamont and Thaler, 2003).

In practice, however, perfect arbitrage rarely exists owing to transaction costs between markets. These include brokerage fees and commissions as well as payment, clearing and settlements costs, plus foreign exchange exposure where settlements commonly take three or more days. As such, arbitrage would be expected to take place within bands (Levy et al., 2006) where the premium 'lost' within the band is due to inter-market transaction costs. Foreign ownership, capital controls and costly information acquisition all hinder potentially seamless arbitrage between markets. However, liquidity and the inability to sell short are the most significant factors hindering overseas investors from equalizing prices across markets. This is particularly relevant in Africa, where short sales are forbidden due to the lack of sufficiently capitalized custodian banks and settlement systems as well as the liquidity impact of trades and consequent exacerbation of volatility (Pagano, 1989).

In order to resolve some of these problems and to increase the liquidity in the major markets, the New Partnership for Africa's Development (NEPAD) has proposed a policy framework to encourage integration of equity markets on a regional basis. This initiative envisages four central hubs: South Africa, Nigeria, Kenya and Egypt. This chapter considers whether the 'Law of One Price' holds for assets traded in the major markets in Africa. In particular, it identifies whether markets in Africa are price-integrated and, if so, what feedback mechanisms exist, plus whether these markets are integrated with the world equity market represented by London and Paris. The chapter proceeds as follows. The next section briefly discusses the characteristics of markets in Africa, followed by a description of the empirical methodology used in section 3. The characteristics of the price index and returns data are discussed in section 4, followed by the empirical results in section 5 which also includes a discussion of the implications for African financial markets and any policy recommendations. The final section concludes.

Securities markets in Africa

A significant improvement in Africa's securities markets has taken place during the last decade. Since 2001, the majority of stock exchanges have websites detailing operations, and almost all markets have adopted the internationally recognized International Security Identification Number (ISIN) system for asset identification. Additionally, there has been a widespread abolition of capital gains tax, and the harmonization of corporate and securities tax regimes and accounting standards across the Southern African Development Community (SADC). Former irregular and over-the-counter (OTC) market structures in many of the smaller markets have been overhauled and upgraded into well designed call-over auctions or open outcry trading floors, while larger markets such as Namibia, Johannesburg and Egypt now have computerized order matching systems. Market settlement systems have become increasingly compliant to internationally recognized G30[1] standards in order to reduce transaction costs, making individual markets more competitive in attracting order flow. The rapid pace of development of existing markets is matched by the more recent establishment of new markets in Mozambique (1999), Libya (2002), Cameroon and Gabon (2003) and Angola (2006).

However, despite these improvements, almost all African markets suffer from a persistent lack of liquidity, with few companies meeting stringent listings requirements, and low levels of market capitalization to GDP. Markets also lack completeness, with much having been established in some of the poorest countries in the world with high levels of poverty emasculating much of the local population. As such, there is little room for savings as income generated is spent immediately on consumption and longer-term institutional investment through pension funds is hindered by extremely low life expectancy due to HIV/AIDS (Piesse and Hearn, 2006). Stock market awareness is also a major issue where subsistence agriculture, micro-enterprises and the informal economy dominate the business environment and domestic savings preferences amongst the rural population often takes the form of heads of livestock or commodities, as opposed to either bank deposits or stock market investment. These preferences are rooted in traditional values and beliefs, as well as the fear of loss of value in monetary instruments where many countries have experienced hyperinflation and macroeconomic instability in recent history. Non-institutional and individual investors also tend to be reluctant to participate in markets, fearing a lack of small-investor legal protection (IMF, 2005).

The ratios of domestic savings and market capitalization in relation to GDP provide proxies of the size of stock market in relation to the overall economy, and are very low for most African countries with the exception of South Africa where levels of participation are approaching the levels of developed OECD countries. Although many countries have now formally passed foreign direct investment bills into law, and ratified securities market legislation in order to regulate the markets and provide effective investor protection, attracting foreign investors has been a persistent problem for the majority of markets in Africa. Again with the exception of South Africa and Egypt, many of the markets could benefit from better designed and more proactively enforced regulation in the light of weak judicial systems lacking the technical sophistication and expertise to handle complex corporate litigation issues. Poorly defined property rights and weak levels of legal and regulatory enforcement further exacerbate problems in attracting foreign investors to these markets. Equally the virtual non-existence of an investment banking industry in many markets, with activities such as coordinating primary market listings being handled by brokerage houses, both discourages domestic companies from listing and increases uncertainty in firms' stock values. A lack of comprehensive disclosure requirements at listing and the quality of the monitoring role undertaken by local analysts, together with a lack of liquidity in the secondary market, add further to foreign investor uncertainty in these markets. Foreign investor wariness of investment in sub-Saharan African (SSA) markets is highlighted in a 2003 World Bank report citing foreign equity investment in SSA (excluding South Africa) at only US$500 million, or only 3.5 per cent of worldwide flows valued at US$14.3 billion (*African Business,* 2005). Since the demise of the Morgan Stanley Africa Fund in 2002, only two prominent fund managers, Old Mutual (Bermuda) and Lazard Brothers (Luxembourg), retain investment funds specifically directed at Africa, and these are focused towards South Africa and Egypt respectively.

The supply side of African markets is hampered by a lack of listings and a paucity of investment opportunities. In 2001, the World Bank reported that 313 million people live on less than US$1 a day, and that subsistence agriculture and micro-enterprises tend to dominate the domestic business environment. Many companies lack the capital structure in order to meet listing requirements (World Bank, 2003; Marone, 2003), and most listings are the result of state-sponsored IPOs as part of the privatization of government holdings in parastatals. Privatizations have been a central theme in IMF and World Bank reform packages directed at governments in order to generate efficiencies in state-controlled institutions. However, the resulting new listings, and the subsequent increase in market capitalization, do not necessarily increase market liquidity, causing domestic companies to raise capital from overseas primary equity and ADR listings or to seek greater reliance on internal sources of finance.

In order to address the problems of African markets, the Committee of SADC Stock Exchanges (COSSE) members launched Project Thusanang in 1997. This initiative had the common objective of the integration of equity markets within the member states, with the trading system centred on the larger, more established and highly successful Johannesburg Stock Exchange. The motivation was to promote the deepening of secondary markets and increasing liquidity, both of which are essential to retain and attract further investment. SADC regional markets have already adopted South African listings and accounting standards, while retaining some autonomy necessary to reflect the concerns of their fragile domestic business environments. Markets in South Africa and Namibia have shared a trading system from 1998, prior to their joint migration to the London Stock Exchange Shares Electronically Traded System (SETS) in 2002. The platform of this system is located in London, and stocks from both markets benefit from inclusion in the FTSE Africa indices and from access to marketing opportunities on the London market. Zimbabwe and Zambia have expressed some commitment to upgrade their own domestic trading systems and associated hardware in order to move across to the common South African sponsored FTSE SETS platform, although only Zambia shows any signs of progress.

Integration of stock markets is thus progressing, with the first stage taking place amongst the regional hub markets of the Northern, Southern, Eastern and Western African trading communities. In the East African Community, listings and accounting standards are harmonized and cross-listings are taking place between Tanzania, Uganda and the dominant market of Kenya, and a common Central Securities Depository (CSD) will be based in Nairobi. There is a common trading area and a considerable degree of macroeconomic policy harmonization. Integration in North Africa has only taken place between the two Egyptian domestic markets in Cairo and Alexandria, which now form the Egyptian Stock Exchange. Memorandums of Understanding have been signed between many of the sub-region's markets, where there are high levels of infrastructure including electronic trading platforms and CSD. Integration amongst the countries in the more fragmented West African region has been frustrated by difficulties. These include the introduction of a common currency and harmonization of macroeconomic policy, but the process is also stalled by lack of agreement over common market regulation given the differences between Francophone countries' French civil law legal code and the English common law prevalent in Ghana and Nigeria.

The measurement of equity market integration

Three strands of the literature on the 'Law of One Price' are appropriate to the measurement of financial market integration. The first uses pricing models to measure premiums or discounts between markets. However, such pricing models assume the joint hypothesis of market efficiency, which states that security prices contain all information available and, for weak form efficiency, that prices reflect information to the point where the marginal benefits of acting on information do not exceed the marginal costs (Fama, 1991). As a direct result of this joint hypothesis, when pricing models produce unexpected results, it is difficult to apportion anomalous results due to hidden information (Fama, 1991). Pricing models are either variations of the capital asset pricing model (CAPM) or arbitrage pricing theory (APT). Both models are used to identify pricing or premium differences for similar asset classes across markets.

The second strand concerns correlations between index returns within markets with the benefits of portfolio diversification. Piesse and Hearn (2002) used cointegration to investigate financial integration based on the 'Law of One Price' between the markets of Namibia, South Africa and Botswana during the 1990s. Several papers have used the same methods for developed markets (for example Corhay et al., 1993), and a few papers have similarly studied the emerging markets of Asia and Latin America. All of these papers are subject to composition bias because of the different construction of national indices, which can only be resolved by considering closed-end country funds and the difference between fund value and the underlying held assets derived from net asset value of the fund. Another group of papers report the differences between American depository receipts (ADR) and general depository receipts (GDR) to their underlying assets (Lamont and Thaler, 2003). However, this is not appropriate in African markets as there are few liquid ADR or GDR instruments. Furthermore with the demise of the Morgan Stanley Africa Fund in 2002 (Bloomberg L.P., 2007), the only closed-end funds are currently restricted to Egypt or South Africa.

A third strand of literature uses threshold autoregressive (TAR) models, which focus on the equivalence of the inter-market equity premium outside the bands of no-arbitrage caused by market frictions and transaction costs. Levy et al. (2006) report that financial integration increases with increased liquidity while intuitively, capital controls increase the size of the threshold band of no-arbitrage and increase segmentation.

This study extends the earlier work of Piesse and Hearn (2002) in this area by assessing integration amongst a greater number of markets across the entire continent of Africa, rather than the simple subset of southern African markets (i.e. Botswana, Namibia and South Africa) undertaken previously. These three markets have a largely similar background, infrastructure and shared macroeconomic environment, underscored by Namibia and South Africa sharing the same underlying currency and trading arrangements. Furthermore this study extends the concept of integration amongst African equity markets, to that of integration with the world equity market represented by London and Paris and employs weekly data periodicity in contrast to the original use of monthly values. Following Harris et al. (1995) and Phylaktis (1999), three different methods are used in conjuction to assess the extent of form of cross-border equity market integration. However, before the three methods are applied, it is necessary to establish whether there is a presence of a stochastic unit root within each return's indexed time series. More formally, when a time series is mathematically broken down into its underlying component series, this test seeks to establish the presence of a random drift element amongst the components as opposed to purely deterministic elements. The approach commonly employed to undertake this analysis is the Augmented Dickey-Fuller (ADF) test (Piesse and Hearn, 2007). Those time series that possess a random drift element, or stochastic unit root, are then subjected to further analysis by three sets of empirical methods.

The first method involves bivariate vector autoregressive (BVAR) models, which centre on the analysis on each of the four principal markets (i.e. Egypt, South Africa, Kenya and Nigeria) against each of the other markets in the sample group. Cointegration tests based on Johansen trace statistics may then be used to reveal the existence, or otherwise, of a common long-term link, or vector, between pairs of market price indices. However, such tests on their own do not indicate the relative strength and direction of the price relationships between the markets and, at this stage, it would be customary to construct the vector error correction model (VECM) associated with the BVAR constructed earlier. This would assess the speed of return back to the common long-term trend, from short-term deviations of the evolving time series of errors generated from the BVAR that best 'fits' the index return time series. However, this study dispenses with this additional level of analysis in favour of the more sensitive autoregressive distributed lag (ARDL) models. The second method is to estimate the multivariate equivalent of the earlier constructed BVAR which uses the same sequence of methods to assess the number of common links, or cointegrating vectors, in a model containing any two of the principal or core markets and a third country between which it is hypothesized that the core markets are integrated. The third method is to use an ARDL model to assess potential price integration, as this is an accurate and sensitive way of analysing any feedback effects between markets where there is evidence of integration. The first stage of the ARDL method is to test the joint probability that all variables within the hypothesized long-run error correction relationship are significantly different from zero. This is done using an F-test, with a non-standard F-distribution inferring two critical bounds: a lower bound below which series are considered not to be related with no further ARDL testing necessary, and an upper bound above which series are automatically referred to the second stage of formal inclusion within the ARDL model. Test statistics falling between the two bounds are defined to be fractionally integrated and, as such, are subjected to individual unit root testing. The F-statistic of each market return series is included as a dependent variable in the levels within a bivariate error correction model, with the independent variable in first differences. A formal consideration of the three empirical methods and techniques employed here is given in Appendix 1 of Piesse and Hearn (2007).

Data and descriptive statistics

The sample has been selected on the basis of data availability, market size and relative level of development. The sample thus excludes the smaller and highly illiquid markets which exhibit strong first-order autocorrelation and severe price rigidity. Egypt, Kenya, Nigeria and South Africa are defined as markets at the centre of regional integration, reflecting NEPAD policy. The end-of-week nominal closing values of the indices are used, denominated in local currency units. The index data have been sourced directly from the local markets for Tunisia, Namibia, Nigeria and Mauritius, and the data for all the other markets are from Datastream. US$ exchange rates are from Datastream and Bloomberg. Background information on the markets was obtained from the IFC statistics database, Standard & Poor's Global Markets Factbook, media publications via the Internet, and the Nigerian Stock Exchange Factbook. The stock exchanges also provided significant amounts of supplementary information on regulation, market operations, listings and ownership.

Construction of the indices

The construction of the domestic indices and the trading systems and times are reported in Table 4.1. The trading times in all markets are largely synchronous, with all countries being either one hour less or two hours more than the South African time zone. The index data are converted to a US$ equivalent using same frequency US$ exchange rates. These are then expressed in natural logarithms, and differenced to create the final adjusted returns series. Transforming the series to US$ equivalents in value removes the effects of domestic inflation on domestic price levels, by substituting the more stable US inflation in its place. This is based on the assumption of purchasing power parity (PPP) between US$ and local currencies. In addition, time series denominated in US$ terms are easily recognized and commonly used by overseas investors for performing market analysis for cross-country portfolio investment.

Analysis of the index returns series

Emerging stock market returns series are usually regarded as being different from those of developed markets, and are characterized by significant departures from a normal distribution, particularly in measures of skewness and kurtosis. These data are no exception, and the choice of end-of-week closing values is justified given that it is of sufficiently high frequency to capture market movements whilst not giving rise to many additional complications inherent in very high frequency data such as daily or intra-daily. Table 4.2 reports descriptive statistics. Kenya and Namibia exhibit the highest levels of

Table 4.1: Summary of institutional and trading arrangements on African stock markets

Market	Trading hours	Trading arrangement	Index	Details of index construction
Egypt (Cairo and Alexandria)	Listed Securities Market (On the Exchange): 11.30 a.m.–15.30 p.m.	Electronic order matching system for Cairo and Alexandria Stock Exchanges (CASE) – The CASE Trading System, or CTS	Two Indices: 'CASE 30 Index' and 'Dow Jones CASE Egypt Titans 20 Index'	CASE 30 Price Index is designed and calculated by CASE. CASE started disseminating its index on 2 February 2003 via data vendors, its publications, website, newspapers etc. The start date of the index was on 2 January 1998 with a base value of 1000 points. CASE 30 Price Index includes the top 30 companies in terms of liquidity and activity. CASE 30 is a price index, i.e. it measures the return on investment from the change in market value of the stock (capital appreciation/depreciation) only. CASE 30 Price Index is weighted by market capitalization and adjusted by the free float. Adjusted Market Capitalization of a listed company is the number of its listed shares multiplied by the closing price of that company multiplied by the percentage of freely floated shares. For a company to be included in CASE 30 Index, it must have at least 15% free float. This assures market participants that the index constituents truly represent actively traded companies and that the index is a good and reputable barometer for the Egyptian market.
Kenya	10.00 a.m.–12.00 noon	Open Outcry (commenced by sounding of a bell)	NSE All Share and NSE 20 Share Index	NSE 20 Share Index: Geometric mean of the top twenty companies traded on exchange. Index recalculated according to algorithm at end of each trading session. NSE All Share is market capitalization weighted and takes account of all lines of stock on market.
Mauritius	9.00 a.m.–11.30 a.m.	Open Outcry	SEMDEX (All Share)	SEMDEX All Share: The SEMDEX reflects capitalization based on each listed stock that is weighted in accordance to its shares in the total market. In its computation, the current value of the SEMDEX is expressed in relation to a base period, which was chosen to be 5 July 1989, when Index was 100.

(Continued)

Table 4.1: (Continued)

Market	Trading hours	Trading arrangement	Index	Details of index construction
Morocco	9.00 a.m.–4.00 p.m.	Electronic order matching system	MASI® (Moroccan All Shares index) and MADEX® (Moroccan Most Active Shares Index)	**Two Main Indices:** The **MASI®** (Moroccan All Shares index), and the **MADEX®** (Moroccan Most Active Shares Index). Each are recalculated at the end of each trading session and are weighted in accordance to market capitalization.
Namibia	9.00 a.m.–4.00 p.m.	Electronic (JET) trading link	NSX All Share	**NSX All Share:** Capital weighted average with base period in 1992 at start of index – 100.
Nigeria	11.00 a.m. to 13.00 p.m.	Call Over trading system was replaced in April 1999 by Automated Trading System (ATS) which serves as an electronic order matching system	NSE All Shares Index	**NSE All Share Index:** The Exchange maintains an All Share Index formulated in January 1984. Only common stocks (ordinary shares) are included in the computation of the index. The index is value-relative and is computed daily.
South Africa	8.25 a.m.–9.00 a.m.: Pre-Opening electronic call auction. 9.00 a.m.–4.00 p.m.: Continuous Trading. 4.00 p.m.–6.00 p.m.: Run-Off.	JSE SETS Electronic Trading system (SETS trading system has been in place at the London Stock Exchange and replaced the former JET system in 2002)	JSE/Actuaries Index	**JSE/Actuaries Index:** The price index is formed as the total market capitalization divided by the market divisor. The market divisor is defined as the base value of capitalization, and is attached to all corporate actions on market in an attempt to adjust these actions to keep overall index constant. Any capital structure changes need to be accommodated in the index divisor. Indices are under effectively constant review in terms of potential corporate actions.
Tunisia	9.00 a.m. to 10.00 a.m.: Pre-Opening// 10.00 a.m.–11.30 a.m. Trading Session	Electronic order matching system	BVMT Index	**BVMT Index:** Market Capitalization weighted index of all companies traded on exchange.

Note: All trading hours quoted are in local time. Nigeria is 1 hour behind South Africa. Kenya and Mauritius are 1 and 2 hours respectively ahead of South Africa.
Source: The data were compiled by the authors from Datastream and from various national stock exchanges.

Table 4.2: Descriptive analysis of the returns on eight African stock markets, 1998–2006

Descriptive statistics	Kenya	South Africa	Mauritius	Namibia	Nigeria	Egypt	Morocco	Tunisia	UK (FTSE)	France (CAC 40)
Skewness	1.51577	-0.51501	0.48765	-0.38070	-0.00668	0.16860	0.27101	0.77442	0.22914	0.06306
Kurtosis	10.89512	1.34121	4.03929	5.27813	2.98123	2.99417	3.21346	2.36045	2.07111	1.24018
Std Dev	0.02629	0.03801	0.01356	0.04106	0.02766	0.04263	0.02170	0.01656	0.02177	0.02793
Max Value	0.20307	0.12783	0.06458	0.23588	0.09994	0.20972	0.10864	0.08027	0.08790	0.09824
Min Value	-0.11442	-0.13859	-0.06531	-0.21290	-0.12790	-0.19255	-0.08336	-0.04368	-0.10351	-0.10866
Mean	0.00023	0.00314	0.00102	0.00203	0.00182	0.00313	0.00106	0.00091	-0.00057	-0.00139
Median	-0.00246	0.00580	0.00004	0.00393	0.00060	0.00172	0.00023	-0.00017	-0.00300	-0.00360
Jarque-Bera Statistic	2,149.16	47.02	286.95	473.94	146.45	149.69	175.51	132.50	73.53	24.75

Correlation coefficients	Kenya	South Africa	Mauritius	Namibia	Nigeria	Egypt	Morocco	Tunisia	UK	France
Kenya	1.0000									
South Africa	0.0646	1.0000								
Mauritius	0.1266	0.0051	1.0000							
Namibia	0.0442	0.6391	-0.0651	1.0000						
Nigeria	0.0182	0.0231	0.1150	0.0067	1.0000					
Egypt	0.0387	0.1828	0.1112	0.1137	0.0252	1.0000				
Morocco	0.0243	0.1255	0.1553	0.0732	0.0142	0.1290	1.0000			
Tunisia	0.0178	0.1385	0.0840	0.0708	0.0322	0.0891	0.3023	1.0000		
UK (FTSE)	-0.0271	-0.0299	-0.0135	-0.0089	0.0150	0.0534	0.0525	0.0361	1.0000	
France (CAC 40)	-0.0428	-0.0332	0.0040	-0.0164	-0.0380	0.0235	0.0628	0.0488	0.8071	1.0000

Notes: The data refer to the end-of-week returns, and are expressed as the natural logarithm of the returns in US dollars.
The period covered is January 1998 to January 2006, and there are 422 observations.
Source: The data were compiled by the authors from various national stock exchanges.

kurtosis (10.89 and 5.27 respectively), which are much greater than that of a normal distribution (3). This departure from normality is confirmed by the Jarque-Bera statistics, which again are high for these countries (2,149.16 and 473.95). Kenya exhibits considerable skewness (1.51), and the overall departure from normality is explained by the presence of very large and significant outliers during the sample period. In a small, illiquid market, there is insufficient liquidity to absorb shocks that would be relatively insignificant to a more developed market with greater depth. For Namibia, the largest outlier is on 2 August 2002 (−0.2119), and is due to the move of trading and indices to the London Stock Exchange SETS. For Kenya, the largest outliers are caused by variation in the US$ exchange rate and can be explained by macroeconomic fluctuations and the trade balance affecting value, rather than by domestic corporate events in the market. In contrast, the other markets within the sample, including those of Paris and London, all have skewness values comparable to a normal distribution centred on zero, and the Jarque-Bera statistics are within the acceptable range. There are generally very low levels of correlation across the sample, with only a few notable exceptions. There are high correlations between the markets in Paris and London (>0.8) and between South Africa and Namibia (0.63), and a lower value between Tunisia and Morocco (0.3).

Empirical results and discussion

All index returns series were found to possess unit roots after having been subjected to testing.[2] As noted above, three different methods were used to analyse the data: the BVAR model, the multivariate vector autoregressive model, and the ARDL model. The results are reported below.

Bivariate tests of cointegration

BVAR models were generated for each of the four core markets (i.e. Egypt, South Africa, Kenya and Nigeria) with each of the other markets in the sample. Pulse dummy variables that may explain significant outliers have been excluded from any of the bi- or multivariate VAR and VECM models, to minimize the risks of pre-specification bias. The Johansen trace statistics are reported for each BVAR system in Table 4.3. These results indicate significant links between Egypt and Kenya, and between both and other markets, but far fewer relationships between South Africa and the other markets. Only two possible relationships are identified between Nigeria and the other markets. It should be noted, however, that these results do not indicate the relative strength and direction of the price relationships between the markets.

Multivariate tests of cointegration

Multivariate cointegration tests assess the presence of cointegration within VAR models containing any two of the core regional markets, with which

Table 4.3: The bivariate VAR tests for price integration between the African stock markets

	Johansen trace test statistics	
	$H_0: r = 0$	$H_0: r \leq 1$
Panel A: Comparisons with Egypt		
UK (1)	34.1492**	13.7209*
France (1)	32.6414**	13.5926*
Morocco (1)	30.6358**	3.0145
Tunisia (1)	31.0648**	8.3969
Nigeria (1)	29.4446**	9.4611
Kenya (2)	31.6918**	3.7247
Namibia (1)	29.7091**	10.6186*
Mauritius (1)	35.7949**	3.5654
South Africa (1)	30.0483**	11.9222*
Panel B: Comparisons with South Africa		
UK (1)	17.2526	1.7707
France (1)	20.8036	3.1437
Morocco (1)	15.1657	6.1791
Tunisia (1)	16.8542	3.2348
Egypt (1)	30.0483**	11.9222*
Nigeria (1)	17.8035	2.4343
Kenya (1)	24.1082*	4.5029
Namibia (2)	25.6031**	4.6747
Mauritius (2)	13.3012	5.4382
Panel C: Comparisons with Kenya		
UK (1)	40.8725**	6.6641
France (1)	37.6529**	9.2982
Morocco (1)	49.2144**	7.8252
Tunisia (1)	28.0860**	4.3301
Egypt (1)	31.6918**	3.7247
Nigeria (1)	25.7482*	7.5964
Namibia (1)	26.8607**	4.3851
Mauritius (2)	19.2143	4.8008
South Africa (1)	24.1082*	4.5029
Panel D: Comparisons with Nigeria		
UK (1)	14.6146	2.0422
France (1)	15.2110	2.0897
Morocco (1)	18.7351	5.6243
Tunisia (1)	16.7782	2.7262
Egypt (1)	29.4446**	9.4611
Kenya (1)	25.7482*	7.5964
Namibia (1)	17.7968	3.3043
Mauritius (1)	20.9345	7.8742
South Africa (1)	17.8035	2.4343

Notes: If r denotes the number of significant vectors, then the first column of Johansen trace statistics test the hypothesis that r is zero, whilst the second column test the hypothesis that r is at most one.
** indicates significance at 5% level. * indicates significance at 10% level.
The figures in parentheses indicate number of lags in the VAR models. The lag length of models is chosen on basis of the SBC informational criterion.

other markets are assumed to be integrated, plus a third market. Trivariate VAR models were set up with South Africa and Egypt, against South Africa and Kenya, against Kenya and Egypt, plus a third country in each case. The results are in Table 4.4. These results suggest that South Africa and Egypt together exhibit considerable integration when examined alongside a third market, and that this relationship is stronger than combinations of either South Africa and Kenya, or Egypt and Kenya, with a third market. Thus, the

Table 4.4: The multivariate VAR tests for price integration between the African stock markets

	Johansen trace test statistics		
	$H_0: r = 0$	$H_1: r \leq 1$	$H_0: r \leq 2$
Panel A. Group A: Egypt, South Africa, Additional Country			
UK (1)	49.3684**	25.4120**	10.9118*
France (1)	48.9803**	29.3566**	11.6793*
Morocco (1)	49.3145**	18.4479	3.6175
Tunisia (1)	48.5362**	25.8660**	11.0631*
Nigeria (1)	44.3173**	22.2840	9.4422
Kenya (1)	53.4745**	15.4807	2.6599
Namibia (1)	69.9551**	32.8279**	15.7148*
Mauritius (1)	63.3836**	20.7786	3.3468
Panel A. Group B: Egypt, South Africa, Tunisia, Namibia, UK, France			
Lag length: 1		95% Quantile critical values	90% Quantile critical values
$H_0: r = 0$	186.7896**	115.8500	110.6000
$H_0: r \leq 1$	110.5360**	87.1700	82.8800
$H_0: r \leq 2$	72.0591**	63.0000	59.1600
$H_0: r \leq 3$	45.0872**	42.3400	39.3400
$H_0: r \leq 4$	24.7079*	25.7700	23.0800
$H_0: r \leq 5$	7.5488	12.3900	10.5500
	Johansen trace test statistics		
	$H_0: r = 0$	$H_1: r \leq 1$	$H_0: r \leq 2$
Panel B. Group A: South Africa, Kenya, Additional Country			
UK (1)	60.5389**	23.1171*	9.3802
France (1)	53.3005**	23.2695*	6.7345
Morocco (1)	58.8650**	15.9463	4.3801
Tunisia (1)	43.4868**	19.1619	4.6056
Egypt (1)	53.4745**	15.4807	2.6599
Nigeria (1)	39.1693**	13.9960	6.2445
Namibia (1)	67.2022**	21.1540	5.5851
Mauritius (2)	33.3141	17.3174	5.0382

(*Continued*)

Table 4.4: (Continued)

	Johansen trace test statistics		
	$H_0: r = 0$	$H_1: r \leq 1$	$H_0: r \leq 2$
Panel C. Group A: Egypt, Kenya, Additional Country			
UK (1)	82.0320**	37.2788**	7.6445
France (1)	70.1340**	26.7727**	9.0540
Morocco (1)	77.4323**	26.3745**	5.0157
Tunisia (1)	57.8326**	14.6179	3.3935
South Africa (1)	53.4745**	15.4807	2.6599
Nigeria (1)	59.9907**	14.2921	4.0781
Namibia (1)	53.1309**	13.4357	2.6278
Mauritius (2)	44.4608**	12.8243	3.6606
Panel C. Group B: Egypt, Kenya, UK, France, Morocco			
Lag length: 2		95% Quantile critical values	90% Quantile critical values
$H_0: r = 0$	135.7298**	87.1700	82.8800
$H_0: r \leq 1$	75.7421**	63.0000	59.1600
$H_0: r \leq 2$	40.5133**	42.3400	39.3400
$H_0: r \leq 3$	19.8865	25.7700	23.0800
$H_0: r \leq 4$	6.5598	12.3900	10.5500

Notes: If r denotes the number of significant vectors, then the first column of Johansen trace statistics test the hypothesis that r is zero, whilst the second column test the hypothesis that r is at most one.
** indicates significance at 5% level. * indicates significance at 10% level.
The figures in parentheses indicate number of lags in the VAR models. The lag length of models is chosen on basis of the SBC informational criterion.

markets of North Africa and those of Southern Africa exhibit stronger levels of integration and statistical linkages than those of East Africa. The results of cointegration from the bivariate analysis reported in Table 4.3 concerning Nigeria are too inconclusive for this country to be further analysed within a multivariate context, and the West African market is considered to be segmented.

Augmented ARDL analysis

As noted above, the first stage in the ARDL method is to test the joint probability that all variables within the hypothesized long-run error correction relationship are different from zero. These results, prior to inclusion in the second stage of ARDL analysis, are in Table 4.5. The F-test statistic of each market return series is included as a dependent variable in the levels within an error correction model, with the independent variable in first differences given in Table 4.5. It is immediately clear that far fewer potential relationships are likely to exist between markets using this approach.

Table 4.5:   The ARDL tests for bivariate relationships with the four core African stock markets

	Dependent variable	Kenya	South Africa	Egypt	Nigeria
Kenya	----/---- >	–	–	–	–
	< ----/----	–	–	–	–
South Africa	----/---- >	4.6376[.032] (UB)**	–	–	–
	< ----/----	0.33205[.565]	–	–	–
Egypt	----/---- >	0.094201[.759]	0.75577[.385]	–	–
	< ----/----	2.7494[.098] (LB-UB)*	13.8290[.000] (UB)**	–	–
Nigeria	----/---- >	5.9221[.015] (UB)**	1.0414[.308]	11.6340[.001] (UB)**	–
	< ----/----	0.92378[.337]	0.23340[.629]	0.61074[.435]	–
Mauritius	----/---- >	0.96780[.326]	0.57325[.449]	12.8136[.000] (UB)**	0.13799[.710]
	< ----/----	0.44615[.505]	1.4091[.236]	0.72746[.394]	2.6084[.107]
Namibia	----/---- >	1.0481[.307]	2.8367[.093] (LB-UB)*	10.0900[.002] (UB)**	0.038027[.845]
	< ----/----	0.31842[.573]	4.4891[.035] (UB)**	0.40033[.527]	1.3455[.247]
Morocco	----/---- >	0.67252[.413]	0.31509[.575]	4.3640[.037] (UB)**	0.91266[.340]
	< ----/----	2.7993[.095] (LB-UB)*	4.7762[.029] (UB)**	0.80077[.371]	4.9692[.026] (UB)**
Tunisia	----/---- >	0.088067[.767]	0.86381[.353]	5.9513[.015] (UB)**	0.52903[.467]
	< ----/----	0.79568[.373]	2.6224[.106]	0.52586[.469]	0.32514[.569]
UK	----/---- >	6.5360[.011] (UB)**	0.65485[.419]	0.014730[.903]	0.65741[.418]
	< ----/----	4.8676[.028] (UB)**	4.0626[.044] (LB-UB)**	2.3567[.126]	1.6983[.193]
France	----/---- >	3.4187[.065] (LB-UB)**	0.40743[.524]	0.9149E-4[.992]	0.40598[.524]
	< ----/----	6.1880[.013] (UB)**	3.2127[.074] (LB-UB)**	3.2675[.071] (LB-UB)**	0.10008[.752]

Notes: UB represents the upper bound of the F-statistic critical values, LB represents the lower bound of the F-statistic critical values, and LB-UB represents a value falling between the two bounds.
In all cases, the lag length was three.
** indicates significance at 5% level. * indicates significance at 10% level.

All pairs of series exhibiting potential relationships in Table 4.5 are further analysed using bivariate ARDL models. The individual bivariate analyses focused on the relationships of the four regional market integration hubs (i.e. Kenya, Nigeria, South Africa and Egypt) and are shown in Figures 4.1 to 4.4. The arrows and direction are proportional to the underlying statistically derived relationship.

Discussion

Overall, the results of the ARDL model complement those of the earlier bivariate and multivariate VAR analyses. Nigeria is completely segmented

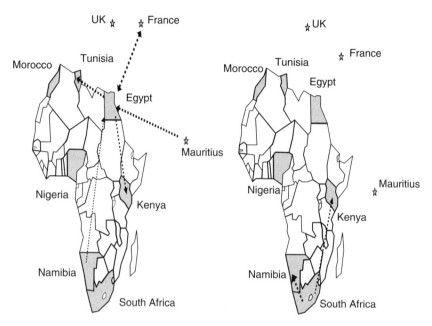

Figure 4.1: Egypt

Figure 4.2: Kenya

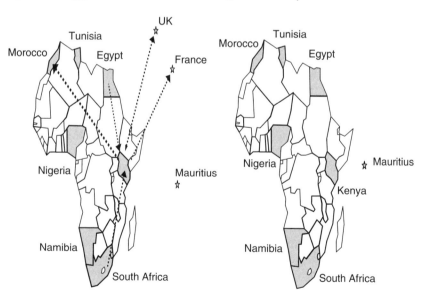

Figure 4.3: South Africa

Figure 4.4: Nigeria

Figures 4.1–4.4: Integration of the four core African stock markets

from the other African markets and the world capital markets, whilst the majority of relationships that Egypt and Kenya have with other markets are very weak. The principal exceptions are the strong relationships between Kenya and Morocco, Egypt and France, and Egypt and Tunisia. Thus, Kenya is weakly integrated and influenced by the world capital markets and has risk-adjusted premiums that are minimal comparable to those on the world capital market. This offers little opportunity for Kenya to attract investment capital that could increase domestic growth. Egypt is different in being more strongly integrated with France. Furthermore, other local markets in the region would benefit from trans-Mediterranean investment and close proximity to the European Union (EU). Egypt's close relationship to Tunisia reflects both geographical proximity and the similarities between the two markets, in terms of partial adherence to Shari'ya regulation and Islamic principles of finance as well as a common level of development and openness to foreign portfolio investment. Additionally the three markets of Egypt, Tunisia and France share a similar legal family origin based on the francophone civil code. Despite Egypt's colonial links to the United Kingdom, the francophone civil code had already been adopted prior to any significant legal influence by English common law. Interpreted in this way, this relationship could be indicative of a wider, more well-documented phenomenon in financial markets derived from the inherent differences between the French civil legal code and its English common law counterpart in Africa.

Although intuitively the strength of the relationships between Egypt and related markets is not surprising, it is harder to attribute reasons behind the direction of the price Granger-causality. The strength and direction of the relationship between Egypt and Tunisia is expected with the much smaller satellite market of Tunisia acting as a price-taker from its larger regional neighbour. The presence of a very weak relationship between Egypt and Kenya, with Egypt influencing prices in Kenya, would also be anticipated, given that Kenya is weakly integrated and hence weakly influenced by the two much larger neighbouring markets of Egypt and South Africa. It is also plausible that Egypt itself would be influenced by Mauritius due to the latter having a strong, well-developed institutional base, strong regulation and legal code derived from the French civil code inferring lower transaction costs in relation to the size of the market. However, the direction of the relationship with France is considerably harder to explain despite the size and strength being as expected, in line with the common institutional heritage and the significant degree of cross-listing and the general influence of the French market on Egyptian firms. Given that France is an established OECD developed market, the bi-directional nature of the relationship with Egypt, an emerging market, is likely to come from a significant degree of French ownership of Egyptian investment banks and brokerage houses as well as the relative importance of the French markets in relation to other EU markets for Egyptian exporting firms.

South Africa has a very close and well-documented relationship with Namibia (Piesse and Hearn, 2002). The results of this analysis (which uses a more recent sample period) would infer that this relationship has become stronger. The ARDL model demonstrates that a 1 per cent change in South Africa is followed by a 0.835 per cent change in Namibian index price levels. This is most likely to be the result of these markets jointly adopting the London Stock Exchange SETS electronic trading system in 2002, their common central depository system for clearing and settlement of trading, and the parallel macroeconomic arrangements that are a function of their membership of the Common Monetary Area (CMA). Both share almost identical institutional arrangements, and a common Roman-Dutch legal heritage and regulatory arrangements based on South Africa. Furthermore, over 70 per cent of Namibian stocks are dual-listed on the Johannesburg exchange (Irving, 2005), significantly enhancing the joint price discovery process. Thus, the size and direction of the price influences between South Africa and Namibia are not surprising. Equally, the weak relationship between South Africa and Kenya, with Kenya a 'price-taker' or influenced Granger-causally by the South African market, would be expected in terms of size, direction and relative strength as there is no cross-listing and little interaction between the two markets.

These results provide strong support that integration is taking place within distinct geographical regional hubs, notably Kenya, Nigeria, Egypt and South Africa. Smaller 'satellite' markets such as Namibia (in relation to South Africa) and Tunisia (in relation to Egypt) are price influenced Granger-causally through their relationships with the larger hub markets. Because of Egypt's position in the Mediterranean basin, this market is more strongly integrated with the world capital markets than Kenya. However, Kenya is unique in exhibiting a strong relationship with Morocco in the francophone north. This relationship, together with the relative strength found through other cointegrating relationships, is hard to explain given the different trading systems and the lack of cross-listed stocks. One explanation is that both markets share a similar level of development, but this is a fairly flimsy connection, and a more likely explanation for the relative strength of this relationship is that both markets happen to share a similar level of transaction costs in the form of information search and verification costs faced by investors. The proportionate levels of transaction costs between the two markets would be representative of the levels of institutional development and infrastructure within each respective market. Given a similar level of institutional development, regulation, number of listings and size of the two markets and the lack of interaction between Morocco and other markets, it is plausible that Kenya would affect Moroccan prices within the confines of a system considering only these two component markets.

Conclusions and policy implications

Overall, there is little evidence of significant price integration between the equity markets in Africa. The principal exceptions are between Namibia and South Africa, Egypt and Tunisia, and Egypt and France, where in each case both markets share similar macroeconomic and trade arrangements and a high degree of transparency inferred by strong and effective regulation. The relationships identified in this chapter exhibit the greatest strength between markets in which investors are faced with similar levels of transaction costs, and in particular, informational search and verification costs. As many African countries have weak legal systems, and market professionals that do not possess the necessary technical knowledge and experience to intervene in complex corporate litigation cases, the emphasis of development policy should be in promoting effective and well-designed regulation, which has the ability to sanction rules concerning disclosure and promote internationally recognized corporate governance standards. The strength of the relationships between Egypt, Tunisia and France, which are largely along the lines of similar levels of institutional arrangements, shared legal family origin, and mutual importance of the French markets for exporting firms, further demonstrates the benefits of establishing high levels of regulation and corporate governance standards. Markets that are price-integrated are better able to attract foreign investment to supplement lower domestic levels of investment and have a positive effect on development, making output growth targets more realistically attainable.

Countries with developed economy trading partners can benefit from enacting legislation promoting adherence to many of the corporate governance standards and regulations of the developed country; that is, import institutional best practice. However, considerable care should be taken to avoid falling into the trap of trying to achieve an ideal system of regulation, which may be too costly and burdensome on firms within the developing country and be ill-suited to the peculiarities of the African institutional environment, as opposed to well-designed and cost-effective regulation tailored to the individual countries' business environment. While Egyptian and Tunisian firms take inspiration from France and the wider European Union for their corporate governance codes and regulation, Namibia is more closely integrated to South Africa in sharing identical regulatory environment and corporate governance codes.

Development policy should be focused on strengthening and improving the regulatory regimes in most African countries and on enhancing corporate governance legislation. However, these measures will only prove effective when the countries have achieved some degree of macroeconomic stability which boosts investor confidence in national currencies, lowers currency premiums, and contributes to reducing total risk premiums and indirectly to the lowering of cost of equity capital. These measures would have the effect of facilitating price integration, increasing market depth and raising awareness amongst the global investment community. Deeper and more liquid markets, together with improved settlement and payment systems, would enable the relaxation of short sales constraints that are enforced in most African markets. This would further increase the opportunities for African markets to be included in foreign investor portfolios and enhance competitiveness of these markets in attracting investment from global capital flows.

Notes

1. The Group of Thirty encourages standardization and improvement in global securities administration. In 1989, the following recommendations were agreed:
   - Brokers should match trades on day after deal date (T + 1).
   - Trade confirmation on trade day plus 2 days (T + 2).
   - Central Depository for safe keeping of shares.
   - Net basis settlement of cash and stock.
   - Settlement takes place as delivery vs. payment or receipt vs. payment.
   - Settlement in same day funds.
   - Settlement effected on trade date plus 3 days (T + 3).
   - Securities lending should be permitted.
   - International securities numbering system must be adopted (ISIN code).
2. All index returns series were subjected to preliminary unit root testing following the procedure outlined in Piesse and Hearn (2007). The results show that all returns series possess a unit root at the 95 per cent confidence level with no lags in the underlying Augmented Dickey-Fuller test equation, with the sole exception of Kenya which has one lag. These results are available from the authors on request.

Bibliography

African Business (2005). *African Business* (London: IC Publications).

Bloomberg L. P. (2007). *Financial data vending system and news service* (New York: Bloomberg L.P.).

Corhay, A., Rad, A. T. and Urbain, J. P. (1993). 'Common stochastic trends in European stock markets'. *Economics Letters*, 42: 385–90.

Chemmanur, T. J. and Fulghieri, P. (1994). 'Investment bank regulation, information production, and financial intermediation'. *Journal of Finance*, 49(1): 57–79.

Dickey, D. A. and Fuller, W. A. (1979). 'Distribution of the estimators for autoregressive time series with a unit root'. *Journal of the American Statistical Association*, 74: 427–31.

Fama, E. F. (1991). 'Efficient capital markets: II'. *Journal of Finance*, 46(5): 1575–1617.

Harris, de B. F. H., McInish, T. H., Shoesmith, G. L. and Wood, R. A. (1995). 'Cointegration, error correction, and price discovery on informationally linked security markets'. *Journal of Financial and Quantitative Analysis*, 30(4): 563–79.

International Monetary Fund (2005). *Uganda: Selected Issues and Statistical Appendix*. IMF Country Report: 05/172 (Washington, D.C.: International Monetary Fund).

Irving, J. (2005). 'Regional integration of stock exchanges in Eastern and Southern Africa: progress and prospects'. IMF Working Paper WP/05/122 (Washington, D.C.: International Monetary Fund).

Johansen, S. (1989). 'Statistical analysis of cointegrating vectors'. *Journal of Economic Dynamics and Control*, 12: 231–54.

Johansen, S. (1991). 'Estimation and hypothesis testing of cointegrating vectors in Gaussian vector autoregressive models'. *Econometrica*, 59(6): 1551–80.

Kenny, C. and Moss, T. (1998). 'Stock markets in Africa: emerging lions or white elephants?' *World Development*, 26(5): 829–43.

Lamont, O. and Thaler, R. H. (2003). 'Anomalies: the Law of One Price in financial markets'. *Journal of Economic Perspectives*, 17(4): 191–202.

Levy, E., Sergio, Y. and van Horen, S. N. (2006). 'International financial integration through the Law of One Price'. World Bank Policy Research Paper 3897 (Washington, D.C.: World Bank).

Marone, H. (2003). 'Small African stock markets: the case of the Lusaka Stock Exchange'. IMF Working Paper WP/03/6 (Washington, D.C.: International Monetary Fund).

Pagano, M. (1989). 'Endogenous market thinness and stock price volatility'. *Review of Economic Studies*, 56(2): 269–87.

Pesaran, M. H. and Shin, Y. (1995). 'An autoregressive distributed lag modelling approach to cointegration analysis'. University of Cambridge, Department of Applied Economics, Working Paper no. 9514.

Pesaran, M. H., Shin, Y. and Smith, R. (1996) 'Testing for the existence of a long-run relationship'. University of Cambridge, Department of Applied Economics, Working Paper no. 9622.

Phylaktis, K. (1999). 'Capital market integration in the Pacific Basin region: an impulse response analysis'. *Journal of International Money and Finance*, 18(2): 267–87.

Piesse, J. and Hearn, B. (2002). 'Equity market integration versus segmentation in three dominant markets of the Southern African customs union: cointegration and causality tests'. *Applied Economics*, 34(14): 1711–22.

Piesse, J. and Hearn, B. (2006). 'Is there a role for micro-markets in sub-Saharan Africa? A study of the Swaziland stock exchange'. King's College London, Department of Management, Research Paper no. 44.

Piesse, J. and Hearn, B. (2007). 'A test of the Law of One Price: intra-regional equity markets in Africa and two major European markets'. King's College London, Department of Management, Research Paper no. 46.

World Bank (2003). *World Bank Annual Report 2003* (Washington, D.C.: World Bank).

5
Who Develops Strategy in Firms? Governance and National Values Effects
Simon Harris

Introduction

Corporate governance and strategic management research has found some empirical support for the proposition that diversity in the management team engaged in the strategy development process is of value for firms' long-term performance (e.g. Dalton et al., 1998, 1999; McNulty and Pettigrew, 1990). The management implications of differences in the formal mechanisms and structures within which firms are guided and controlled have been a recent focus of interest (see Daily et al., 2003).

Two clearly different types of governance mechanism have long been recognized in Western countries (Albert, 1994). In the 'Anglo-American model' associated with, for example, the United Kingdom (UK) and the United States (US), management and ownership are separated. The financial institutions that dominate the ownership of companies in these countries expect the senior managers they hire to work in their interests, to take qualified advice over major decisions, and they may appoint directors to the boards of control if they have sufficient power to do so (see Dalton et al., 2003). In many other countries, management and ownership are less often separated. In manager-owned firms, only the owner-managers may *formally* be able to determine strategy, though they may involve others according to local governance requirements, beliefs and values (Casson, 1996; Thomsen and Pedersen, 2000).

Here we propose that who develops strategy in firms may be a cultural phenomenon as well as an issue of governance system, because the choice as to who is involved in strategy formation takes place in a value-laden national cultural context. Many 'national values' are directly concerned with personal relationships at work, and these values vary between nations (Schein, 1985; Hofstede, 2001). Here we explore how those involved in forming firms' strategies may differ between nations, and the extent to which these differences might be associated with the corporate governance systems associated with those countries, and with the national cultural characteristics concerning relationships between people within those countries. We do this through the comparative case analysis of four firms, all of which we would expect to benefit considerably from wide participation in strategy formation, but in very different national cultural and corporate governance settings.

Participation in strategy formation

'Top-down' (or 'autocratic') processes of strategy formation have long been distinguished in the strategic management literature from 'participative' processes. Vroom and Yetton (1973) characterized 'autocratic' decisions to be those made by leaders, participative 'group' decisions to involve subordinates in a consensus-generating process, and 'consultative' decisions to reflect information and perspectives collected by leaders. The top-down process whereby chief executive officers (CEOs) and top managers set directions and make major decisions to be implemented by their staff (Andrews, 1980) has its advocates (e.g. Ireland et al., 1992), and is much reflected in normative management practitioner literature's avocations for business leaders to be tough, single-minded individualists (e.g. Pearson, 1988).

Corporate governance research has categorized a range of other types of people who can act as directors of firms (Anderson and Reeb, 2004; Daily et al., 2003; Lynall et al., 2003), and these are presented in Table 5.1. We will use these categories in our exploration of who contributes in strategy formation. But whilst corporate governance research tends to focus on those formalized as members of a supervisory board or as directors, our interest here is on all those involved in the strategy formation process, including those without a formal legal position but who are trusted and valued by the CEO and/or other senior managers.

'Insiders' include current employees: the CEO, other senior managers of the firm, other employees more widely in the firms, friends and family of the current employees, and former employees. Strategic management process research has typically seen participation in strategic thinking from inside the firm as enabling holistic and complete strategic visions to be developed which, through learning processes, lead to changed operational behaviour

Table 5.1: Potential contributors to strategy formation identified by corporate governance research

Insiders	Outsiders
CEOs/top leaders	Affiliated to blockholders
Senior management team	Affiliated through commercial activity
Other employees not senior managers	Interdependent
Friends and family of CEOs/top leaders	Independent
Former managers/employees	

(e.g. Pettigrew and Whipp, 1991). 'Teamwork' approaches tap inputs from different skills and points of perspective within an organization, integrate the perspectives and approaches of different functional specialists for better decisions in complex circumstances, and achieve agreed group-based courses of action (Baden-Fuller and Stopford, 1992). There is a danger here, however, of 'group think' (Janis, 1982) and of 'paralysis by analysis' (Ansoff, 1965), which lessen firms' ability for decisive and proactive strategic action. Only equivocal conclusions can yet be drawn from the empirical research on the relationship between participative decision-making and performance (Lam et al., 2002).

'Outsiders' can be affiliated or independent. If affiliated, they have an existing or potential business tie to the firm. Corporate governance research has been concerned with blockholding shareholders limiting the self-serving behaviour of the managers they employ (Dalton et al., 2003; Deutsch, 2005) by demanding management board representation to monitor and control the firm in their interest (Jensen and Meckling, 1976; Lynall et al., 2003). Affiliation can also arise from a commercial arrangement: for example a joint venture or other business collaboration, or a close customer or supplier relationship. Interdependent outsiders are appointed by the managers and may feel obligated to them and their strategies (Daily et al., 2003). Independent outsiders act as individuals, do not have agency roles with any other body, and provide their service only in the interests of the firm as a whole. They may come from the network of customers, potential customers, competitors, suppliers, distributors, industry experts and knowledgeable people in other firms, but may also be external advisers, such as business consultants, trusted counsels from whatever source: industrial associations, advisory organizations, accountants, lawyers, or industry experts.

Strategy, corporate governance and 'top echelon' research has also identified outsiders, particularly unaffiliated outsiders, to be a potentially valuable resource. Longitudinal studies highlight the need for a diversity of view and approach in those developing firm strategies, in order to allow and to generate appropriate strategic change (Grinyer and Spender, 1979; Zimmerman, 1989). Strategy process research highlights the value of an 'outsider perspective' (Johnson, 1987), and an openness to external influences (Pettigrew and Whipp, 1991) especially in transition periods (McNulty and Pettigrew, 1999). Outsiders are an organizational resource (Geletkanycz and Hambrick, 1997; Carpenter and Westphal, 2001; Carpenter et al., 2003) providing advice and counsel (Hillman and Dalziel, 2003; Zahra and Pearce, 1989), as well as linkages and legitimacy both to other shareholders and to external bodies generally (Hillman et al., 2000; Lynall et al., 2003). Their personal qualities and behaviour are important (Carpenter, 2002). Roberts et al. (2005) identify an independence of mind to be more important than independence of position, and a willingness and ability to be engaged, challenging and supportive in the strategy formation process.

The meta-analysis of Dalton et al. (1999) indicated an overall positive relationship between board size and diversity and firm performance, but the direction of causality is uncertain, and top management team (TMT) heterogeneity studies have produced ambiguous results (Finkelstein and Hambrick, 2001; West and Schwenck, 1996). But firm context, in the context and the nature of the decisions involved seems to be important (Vroom and Yetton, 1973). Management team diversity helps most in environmental and strategic complexity (Hambrick et al., 1996; Priem, 1990), particularly where international business activity is involved (Carpenter, 2002). Outside advice and counsel is especially linked to performance in smaller firms (Dalton et al., 1999), and in young and entrepreneurial firms (Daily et al., 2002; Filatotchev and Bishop, 2002; Lynall et al., 2003; Filatotchev and Wright, 2005). Our study here focuses on young entrepreneurial firms in fast-changing and complex technical contexts, and competing in global markets. Here, the resource of a diverse body helping in strategy formation would appear to be most important.

Firm governance structures and involvement in strategy formation

Divergent economic and institutional histories have led to different and sometimes complex patterns of governance structures in different countries (Albert, 1994), with different conventions, laws and regulations concerning the power and rights of different groups (Thomsen and Pedersen, 2000; Jackson and Aguilera, 2003). As a result, firms operate under different structures of ownership and governance that not only differ considerably within territories, but that also differ in other ways internationally. To begin to make sense of some of the consequences of these differences, here we will examine two sharply contrasting governance structures that have relevance and meaning in different countries. In one, firm ownership is concentrated in the hands of financial institutions; and managers are employed to steward the firms. In the other, ownership is concentrated in the hands of the managers themselves. We now propose who might be involved in strategy formation in 'institution-owned' compared to 'manager-owned firms'.

Participation in strategy formation in institution-owned firms

Even though younger and smaller firms are often owner-managed, and some large owner-managed firms remain, outside bodies and groups more often control and manage the ownership of companies in 'Anglo-American model' countries. Financial institutional structures have evolved that make for complex and distant agency relationships. Reflecting their history, UK and US company law asserts the controlling and exclusive power of owners and protects equal ownership interests (see La Porta et al., 1998, 1999). Stock market regulations concerning insider trading restrict the close involvement of owners in strategy formation.

As a result, owners' powers are mainly restricted to the employment or otherwise of the managers and governing board. Financial institutions are effectively the employers of the CEOs and senior managers, and their appointed board of directors will often include their own representatives as affiliated outsiders to protect their interests, and other non-executive inter-dependent and independent outsiders. Boards will typically propose outside directors for approval by owners, and managers can always appoint out-side advisers. The extent to which these individuals are actually engaged in strategy formation, however, may largely reflect their own personal qual-ities (Carpenter, 2002; Roberts et al., 2005). Those employing them, from the financial owners to the senior managers, however, will have beliefs and expectations concerning their participation in strategy formation, aware of the conventional wisdom that it improves firm performance. Appointments would be on the basis of experience, performance and independence of mind and not on the basis of personal or family relationships with the employed managers (Geletkanycz et al., 2001).

Participation in strategy formation in manager-owned firms

The simplest governance structure of the firm involves the owners of firms managing them themselves, as is found not only in entrepreneurial firms, but also in some of the world's largest and best established firms. In many European countries, financial institutions are less involved in the ownership of firms, and family companies predominate that in varying degrees combine management with ownership. But the regulations and conventions differ as well. In many countries (including France, the Netherlands and Germany), the focus of corporate law is less on the protection of equity rights and more on the duties of firms to take employees' (and in Germany local communi-ties') interests into account in their decision-making (La Porta et al., 1997). It is not only that these interests have (within larger firms at least) the right to representation on supervisory boards or committees, but that the structure and nature of corporate governance is undertaken with different underlying perspectives (Albert, 1994; Clarke and Bostock, 1994; Clarkham, 1994).

There may be no expectations or requirements that CEOs should involve, or even consult, others in the process of strategy formation and, if they do, it will be their own choice and reflect their own interests (Casson, 1996). From a resource perspective, owner-managers might consider it to be use-ful to involve those who have power in terms of control over important resources, whether from inside or outside the organization, in a participative way (Medcof, 2001). So even if manager-owned firms have financial support from institutions or other individuals, who may also be involved in deter-mining the firms' strategies, there will not be a governance requirement for them to do so.

So owner-managers might decide to determine strategy alone. If they feel a need to broaden the basis of their strategic counsel, they might choose to involve family members or personal friends who may have a personal interest in the success or failure of the firm. Indeed, there is strong evidence that it would be sensible for them to do so. Families and trusted friends, often having had lengthy involvement with the firm and having deep knowledge of it, can be particularly well-qualified to provide oversight (Anderson and Reeb, 2003). They can be sources of the valuable resources that have been noted above to contribute to effective strategy formation (Filatotchev and Bishop, 2002), as well as capital and human investments (McConaughy et al., 2001). This, however, is really only possible in manager-owned or family firms, because institution owners would not regard this as professional management practice.

Concerning these two sharply contrasting governance structures, therefore, we might expect to find affiliated outsiders, especially those reflecting financial shareholdings, to be involved in the strategy formation of institution-owned firms where they might not have a role in manager-owned firms. Similarly, reflecting the broader owner interests and their role in appointing boards, we would also expect more types of outsiders to be involved in the strategy formation of institution-owned firms than one would expect in manager-owned firms. On the other hand, whereas one would not expect the personal family and friends of CEOs and senior managers to be involved in the strategy formation of institution-owned firms, we could well expect this within manager-owned firms.

National values and involvement in strategy formation

One view of culture widely adopted in international business research is to see it as the shared meanings assigned by individuals to the world around them. Schein (1985) noted, for example, how managers of different national backgrounds can be expected to hold different underpinning values, different assumptions regarding the environment, and different expectations about relationships among people, and that these values, assumptions and expectations are resilient to change. Cross-cultural research, typically using structured questionnaires quantitatively to explore similarities and differences in attitudes between individuals in different countries, has catalogued a number of 'values' in different countries (Hofstede, 2001; Trompenaars and Hampden-Turner, 1997), and much of this has been subjected to repeated empirical validation and use in international business. These 'national values' indicate bodies of belief that people in nations tend to share, and reflect a national cultural environment to which firms are expected by people in them to adapt, even if the managers involved do not share those values (Smith et al., 2006).

Some of these value concepts are highly relevant to the issue of who is involved in the development of strategies within firms, and these may lead to differing beliefs not only about the appropriate forms of participation in the process of strategy formation, but also to the kind of people used in that participation. Few studies have studied an association between values and participation, but two recent studies of managers' perceptions of their own efficacy in participative decision-making within different cultures provide support for such an association. Gibson (1999) found an association between cultural variables and group-efficacy beliefs. A larger study of perceptions of the self-effectiveness of participation in decision-making among matched samples of US and Hong Kong employees in one organization found a clear association between national cultural background and beliefs about the value of participation (Lam et al., 2002).

Our attention now turns to the specific national cultural values of 'person orientation' that measure how relationships are developed and maintained in different countries. Hofstede (2001) defined a dimension which he called 'masculinity and femininity', which encompasses a range of social and inter-personal interactions and values which reflect ways of self-conceptualization (Inkiles and Levinson, 1969). In 'feminine' societies, people are expected to be concerned with people and relationships, and emphasize the importance of these in life. People in 'masculine' societies, by contrast, are expected to be more goal-focused, emphasizing decisiveness, assertiveness, ambition and toughness in a search for material success. In feminine societies, then, we would expect senior managers to be expected to seek greater involvement of other people, with whom relationships are held, in important decision processes. To research his dimensions, Hofstede undertook social-psychological research amongst IBM employees, work that has received substantial corroboration (e.g. Sondegaard, 1994), where subsequent studies have 'sustained and amplified his conclusions rather than contradicted them' (Smith and Bond, 1998: 56). They represent the most widely used basis for the standardized examination of national values.

Like his 'masculinity' and 'femininity' distinction, Hofstede's short-term and long-term orientation dimension is a more complex concept than its labels imply, in this case being developed from later work by researchers working with managers in China (Hofstede and Bond, 1988). 'Long-term' thinking reflects a desire for personal growth in its broadest sense, over and beyond the span of life, in which the fostering and development of valuable relationships over a long period of time is important. A 'short-term' orientation implies an outcome focus, for speedy achievement of less prosaic goals such as wealth. Top managers in 'long-term' cultures would be expected to develop their businesses through the development of skills, capabilities and good relationships. We can see an overlap here with some aspects of 'person orientation' noted earlier, and clear potential association with the extent that others might be brought in to participate in the process of strategy formation. In long-term cultures, we might expect firms to pay special attention to the nurturing and development of their relationships with their staff as well as their senior managers, and with all kinds of potentially useful relationships outside the firm. In short-term cultures, where a greater emphasis can be expected on the achievement of quick, material results, we would expect CEOs and senior managers to engage with fewer groups.

Using a similar approach to Hofstede, but with a larger and less homogeneous and standardized dataset, Trompenaars and Hampden-Turner (1997) also undertook research on orientations to time. Their distinction between 'person' and 'task' orientations was highly relevant. In person-oriented cultures, the needs and requirements of people as human beings in the workplace take precedence over the need to accomplish specified work tasks, whereas in task-oriented cultures, the job to be done takes precedence. In 'person-oriented' societies, then, we would expect firms to involve other groups of people more in their decision-making.

Combining these different but related notions of 'person-orientation', therefore, we can draw together a composite picture of the nature of participation in strategy formation that we could expect in countries with person-oriented values in comparison with countries which do not share these values. We would expect more people, and especially insider groups of the full senior management team and other employees who are not senior managers, to be involved in forming strategies in firms operating in person-oriented national cultures, much more than we would expect this in countries without these values.

Research approach

Our aim here is to explore who is actually involved in making major strategic decisions in firms. This points to the qualitative exploration of appropriate case entrepreneurs (Eisenhardt, 1989; Silverman, 1993; Yin, 1994), with the use of a 'fine grained' case study methodology that enables attention to important details and actions in relationship formation (Harrigan, 1983). Selecting countries and industries to study is not easy. We need to study firms in countries with different person-oriented values if we are to have the chance of finding any association that will be worthy of note, but we also need to find firms where the overall institutional backdrops are broadly similar. The United Kingdom and the Netherlands meet these requirements well. There are clearly many broad institutional and industrial differences between the two countries, although both are mature, democratic industrial nations with a number of common institutions and shared global corporations. Hofstede found the Netherlands to be one of the most 'feminine' and long-term countries in the world, and the United Kingdom to be one of the more 'masculine' and short-term. Hampden-Turner and Trompenaars found the Netherlands to be 'person-oriented', but found the United Kingdom to be more task-oriented.

The firms needed to be closely matched, except with regard to the governance differences under study. The businesses were all young, growing, and profitable small niche firms in a sub-segment within Standard Industrial Code 33.20/1, and developed and combined electronic hardware and software technologies to address the needs of global industrial customers. We therefore explore the issue of decision-making in four matched firms, two Dutch (which we here call *NE-man* and *NE-ins*) and two British (*UK-man* and *UK-ins*), with in each country, one being institution-owned (*NE-ins* and *UK-ins*) and one manager-owned (*NE-man* and *UK-man*).

Our starting point was the one category of person whom we could assume would always be involved in the strategy formation process: the CEO. We followed a highly structured 'native category' interview protocol, to access the interviewees' own perspectives of who they involved in the strategy formation process, as untainted as possible by suggestions as to who they 'should' involve. The interviews involved in-depth conversations around non-directive questions that enabled the CEOs – all of whom were electronics engineers – to describe fully how strategies developed in their firms (Harris, 2000).

While the data needed to come from the CEOs and not be driven by our questions, strict consistency and some structuring of the interview process were needed to direct discussion to relevant topics and to achieve equivalent data (Ericsson and Simon, 1985). The interviews started with the question 'What do you think about when you consider the future of your business?' After the explanation of each issue raised by the CEO himself, we asked 'Who do you discuss [this issue] with, or consult with?' This yielded a list of people who had direct involvement in the strategy formation process (Harris, 2000). We asked interviewees the same questions in the same order, deviating from this only to obtain clarification.

To assess the value of these different people in the strategy formation process, we then asked, for each issue: 'What do you seek when you discuss [the issue raised] with these people?' This was a difficult question for most interviewees to address, but it yielded rich and considered evaluations of the role of each party in the strategy formation process. It was necessary, however, to gain some finer-grained data concerning the origins, background, nature, function and outcomes of each relationship with which to triangulate and confirm the data that would be used in analysis. Later in the interview, the following set of questions were posed for each relationship that the CEO had highlighted: 'When and how did you meet?', 'How would you describe your relationship with them?', 'When and how do you discuss things?', 'How do you regard his/her views and opinions?', and 'How have they affected the business?' To ensure that no important relationships were missed, the CEOs were asked 'Are there, or have there been, other people important to you in the development of your business?' We conducted the interviews at the interviewees' own business premises, using the English language.

Each interview lasted between 90 and 150 minutes, and each interviewee was interviewed twice. The interviews were separated by about one year, in order to ensure some stability within the responses gained (Ericsson and Simon, 1985; Yin, 1994). Verbal protocol analysis (Ericsson and Simon, 1985) was used to help analyse transcripts and notes from the interviews, with the categories developed from the theoretical developments outlined above (in Table 5.1). Triangulation was achieved not only between the interviews undertaken, but also to other sources of data, including a historical record of annual reports and completed questionnaires from the inception of their firms to the date of the interviews (Eisenhardt, 1989; Yin, 1994).

Case findings

An ambitious Dutchman with six years' commercial experience in the United States with a major Dutch multinational, the CEO of *NE-ins* had approached a major clearing bank's industrial division expressing an interest in leading a management buy-in of an electronics firm. Seven months later he was in partnership with a venture capital consortium comprising that bank, a venture capital house, and three private individuals to replace the management of a firm manufacturing specialist printed circuit board (PCB) assemblies for major Dutch and foreign companies. In redirecting the company, he discussed the strategic issues extensively and regularly with members of his supervisory board, which comprised affiliated outsider directors from the bank and the venture capital house, and the private investors. Notably, he did not involve any other insiders, but this was not for want of trying. He had spent a lot of time trying to do this with the incumbent employees, but at the time of the case study, he believed: *'There is no one here to discuss these things with. Ultimately, there will be a complete management team here and my job is to develop this as well as to reorient the company.'* So he, and his other affiliated outsider directors, were not happy with the situation of his being unable to discuss strategy fully within the firm, and he diagnosed the failure to develop a management team and internal culture that would enable this as the main failing of the previous CEO.

The CEO of *UK-ins* had been recruited under similar circumstances four years ago, by the lead investor of a venture capital consortium. The firm, which made equipment based on new technologies for low-cost PCB manufacture, had been hit hard by a telecommunications crash. His chairman, an outside director appointed by the venture capital consortium, was his main source of strategic counsel, and he also regularly consulted with two other directors affiliated to investor companies, and he regularly discussed matters with his predecessor, the firm's founder, who remained a major shareholder. Unlike *NE-ins*, however, he held regular, open and wide internal discussion of matters with both the management team of five, and more widely with others within the firm:

> *We have worked hard to get the right team in place here ... it is a team effort ... We discuss all these things at our monthly operations review, which has quite a wide agenda. I have a fortnightly meeting with the chairman, as well as the monthly board meetings. But the opportunities are discussed all the time, and these discussions are driven by events and the outsiders, and we have, deliberately, quite an informal style within the company.*

The CEO of *NE-man* had started his firm, a specialist PCB designer and contract manufacturer, while working for a large international company, and it had grown well over the subsequent twelve years and was highly profitable. There was not a formal board of directors, but the senior management team were involved in all decisions, large and small: *'Yes we speak a lot; we have a meeting twice a week about what is happening and that means it is a triangle. We speak a lot to each and say OK this is right this is wrong.'* These other two internal directors, however, had been hand-picked following long experience. The CEO had recruited his production director as a young trainee soon after he had founded the company, and his operations director, who he had employed only for a couple of years, had been his boss at the large international company where his career had begun. While these were the main people involved in the decision process, he also believed that everyone in the firm was involved and participated in the process, but reflecting a general informality within the firm, this was done on an ad hoc and informal basis. Revealing the ownership structure and his pride that *'I owe nothing to anyone; when I bought a €400,000 machine last year I paid cash'*, he later revealed another de facto director: *'I talk to my wife and she is involved and has to agree to every decision, this is a team.'*

Of the four directors of *UK-man*, the strategic issues regarding the firm's future are only discussed by the two insider directors, who were the joint CEOs. These were the remaining co-founders of the firm, a specialist designer of electronic membrane based control panels, principally for the aeronautical industry. They had left an American multinational ten years earlier to form the firm, with the (minority) financial support of a regional venture capital company. These two were close friends, and the non-executive chairman and the director affiliated with the venture capital company received six-monthly reports, but no more. *'Most of the important issues are discussed and decided between Ken (co-CEO) and myself. We might discuss the things with the staff, things relevant to them.'* The CEOs also closely involved an industrial design consultant: an industry contact that they had known for many years (and with whom a strong friendship had developed) who had a strong global perspective of the dynamic changes at play in the industry, who *'brings a broader view of the market'*. While not a formal director of the company, he was clearly more important in its governance than even the chairman.

Discussion

Table 5.2 presents a summary of the findings concerning those involved in strategic decisions in the four firms, alongside the indications that we had developed from corporate governance and national values theory. It is clear that the governance structure of the firms has a clear and direct effect on behaviour: the sharpest differences between the firms are between the institution-owned firms that involve people who are affiliated to blockholders in their strategic decision-making, and the manager-owned firms that do not. The clearest indication of the force of influence here emerges with *UK-man*, who had a minority shareholder who was entirely powerless to influence strategy and who was barely informed of it, let alone consulted or involved. So the governance factors of the institution-financed firms demand involvement of more useful people in the strategy formation process, and specifically the involvement of insiders affiliated to the blockholding investors. It is no coincidence that corporate governance research has tended

Table 5.2:   Involvement in strategy decisions: expectations and findings from the case firms

National values	Governance structure	
	Institution-owned *Expectations:* Many others, especially affiliated to blockholders; Not friends/family or former managers/employees	**Manager-owned** *Expectations:* Few outsiders, Not affiliated to blockholders; Family & friends (insiders & outsiders)
Dutch *Expectations:* Many insiders especially senior management & other employees	*NE-ins* insiders: Wanted; awaits recruitment *NE-ins* outsiders: Affiliated to blockholders Independent	*NE-man* insiders: Senior management team Family Other employees *NE-man* outsiders: None
British *Expectations:* Not the full senior management team & not other employees	*UK-ins* insiders: Senior management team Other employees *UK-ins* outsiders: Affiliated to blockholders Independent	*UK-man* insiders: Some senior management Friend of leaders No other employees *UK-man* outsiders: Affiliated through commercial activity

to examine the participation on boards of different types of outsiders: this is clearly highly relevant.

But strategy formation is a serious business, and strategic management research has shown it to be an activity that does not, and should not, necessarily conform to formal structures. CEOs do it with the people they feel most comfortable doing it with, and with the people that they find most helpful, supportive and useful in their worlds. It can take place informally with people who are not necessarily charged with the role. Some CEOs are comfortable discussing their firms' futures with the lowliest of employees, and the employees expect it. Other CEOs are not, and the employees may not expect it either. 'Person-orientation' values do seem to be related to orientations here, but it takes a fine-grained approach to see it. While we saw this enacted within *NE-man*, we could see it only as an aspiration in *NE-ins* where this kind of participation in strategy formation was wanted, but could not be achieved. It appeared to be cultural values within the Netherlands, concerning a belief in a common community of interest, which placed cultural expectations that strategy would be discussed widely within the firm, expectations that were shared by the CEO and his supervisory board.

Conclusions

This study has made an attempt to address the difficult research challenge of separating the influences of governance structure from the national cultural factor of 'person-orientation' in explaining differences in possibly the most important senior management task, that of forming strategies for firms' future development. This case exploration has highlighted some difficulties faced in this research task. First, the dependent variable – who a firm involves in its strategy formation – is not easy to establish, and researchers need to spend time with firms to find out who is really involved. Nevertheless, developments in corporate governance research have helped to identify a number of coherent categories that seem to be of value in this task.

Second, the independent variables are complex and interconnected. Values are complex phenomena, and how they work in different countries is not straightforward, reflecting countries' unique histories and institutional structures, including their governance systems (d'Iribane, 1997). Governance structures are also complex, unique to each country, and also reflect their particular histories and contexts, including their national values. There are many other factors that affect both, and other independent variables as well.

When seeking to understand differences internationally, comparative management research has tended to polarize on explanations based either on institutional differences (particularly governance structures) or on cultural values. Unbundling the different factors is challenging, but this study has highlighted how both have their part to play, but in different ways.

Most clearly, the many studies that try to attribute behaviour to cultural values without taking governance structure into account are seriously deficient. Here, we see how governance structure can dictate involvement in strategy formation. Similarly, culture is also likely to be important, and we saw it influencing choice concerning who is involved. Both are important, the influences are not always obvious, and direct and simple predictions based on either cultural values variables or governance structure arrangements are likely to be unreliable.

Bibliography

Albert, M. (1994). 'Strategy styles and different blends of capitalism'. Keynote Address to the 14th Annual Conference of the Strategic Management Society, Paris, September.

Anderson, R. and Reeb, D. (2003). 'Founding-family ownership and firm performance: evidence from the S&P 500'. *Journal of Finance*, 53(11): 1301–28.

Anderson, R. and Reeb, D. (2004). 'Board composition: balancing family influence in S&P 500 firms'. *Administrative Science Quarterly*, 49(1): 209–37.

Andrews, K. R. (1980). *The concept of corporate strategy* (Homewood, IL: Irwin).

Ansoff, H. I. (1965). *Corporate Strategy* (New York: McGraw-Hill).

Baden-Fuller, C. and Stopford, J. (1992). *Rejuvenating the mature business* (London: Routledge).

Carpenter, M. A. (2002). 'The implications of strategy and social context for the relationship between top management team heterogeneity and firm performance'. *Strategic Management Journal*, 23(3): 75–284.

Carpenter, M. A., Pollock, T. G. and Leary, M. M. (2003). 'Testing a model of reasoned risk-taking: governance, the experience of principals and agents, and global strategy in high-technology IPO firms'. *Strategic Management Journal*, 24(6): 803–20.

Carpenter, M. A. and Westphal, J. D. (2001). 'The strategic context of external network ties: examining the impact of director appointments on board involvement in strategic decision-making'. *Academy of Management Journal*, 44(4): 639–60.

Casson, M. (1996). 'The comparative organisation of large and small firms'. *Small Business Economics*, 8: 329–45.

Clarke, T. and Bostock, R. (1994). 'International corporate governance'. In T. Clarke and E. Monkhouse (eds), *Rethinking the company* (London: Pitman).

Clarkham, J. (1994). *Keeping good company: a study of corporate governance in five countries* (Oxford: Oxford University Press).

d'Iribane, P. (1997). 'The usefulness of an ethnographic approach to the international comparison of organizations'. *International Studies of Management and Organisation*, 26(4): 30–47.

Daily, C., Dalton, D. and Rajagopalan, N. (2003). 'Governance through ownership: centuries of practice, decades of research'. *Academy of Management Journal*, 46(1): 151–8.

Daily, C., McDougall, P., Covin, J. and Dalton, D. (2002). 'Governance and strategic leadership in entrepreneurial firms'. *Journal of Management*, 28(3): 387–412.

Dalton, D., Daily, C., Certo, S. and Roengpitya, R. (2003). 'Meta-analysis of financial performance and equity: fusion or confusion?' *Academy of Management Journal*, 46(1): 13–26.

Dalton, D. R., Daily, C. M., Ellstrand, A. E. and Johnson, J. L. (1998). 'Meta-analytic review of board composition, leadership structure, and financial performance'. *Strategic Management Journal*, 19(2): 269–90.

Dalton, D. R., Daily, C. M., Johnson, J. and Ellstrand, A. E. (1999). 'Number of directors and financial performance: a meta-analysis'. *Academy of Management Journal*, 42(6): 674–86.

Deutsch, Y. (2005). 'The impact of board composition on firms' critical decisions: a meta-analytic review'. *Journal of Management*, 31(3): 424–44.

Eisenhardt, K. M. (1989). 'Building theories from case study research'. *Academy of Management Review*, 14(4): 532–50.

Ericsson, K. and Simon, H. (1985). *Protocol analysis* (New York: Sage).

Filatotchev, I. and Bishop, K. (2002). 'Board composition, share ownership and "underpricing" of UK IPO firms'. *Strategic Management Journal*, 23(10): 941–55.

Filatotchev, I. and Wright, M. (eds) (2005). *Corporate governance life-cycle* (London: Edward Elgar).

Finkelstein, S. and Hambrick, D. C. (2001). *Strategic leadership: top executives and their effects on organizations* (St Paul, MN: West).

Geletkanycz, M. A., Boyd, B. K. and Finkelstein, S. (2001). 'CEO compensation; executive networks; social capital; strategic leadership'. *Strategic Management Journal*, 22(9): 889–98.

Geletkanycz, M. and Hambrick, D. (1997). 'The external ties of top executives: implications for strategic choice and performance'. *Administrative Science Quarterly*, 42(5): 654–81.

Gibson, C. B. (1999). 'Do they do what we believe they can? Group-efficacy beliefs and group performance across tasks and cultures'. *Academy of Management Journal*, 42(1): 138–52.

Grinyer, P. H. and Spender, J. C. (1979). *Turnaround – managerial recipes for strategic success* (London: Associated Business Press).

Hambrick, D. C., Cho, T. S. and Chen, M. (1996). 'The influence of top management team heterogeneity on firms' competitive moves'. *Administrative Science Quarterly*, 41(4): 659–84.

Harrigan, K. R. (1983). 'Research methodologies for contingency approaches to strategy'. *Academy of Management Review*, 8(3): 398–405.

Harris, S. (2000). 'Reconciling positive and interpretative international management research: a native category approach'. *International Business Review*, 9(6): 755–70.

Hillman, A., Cannella Jr, A. A. and Paetzold, R. L. (2000). 'The resource dependence role of corporate directors: strategic adaptation of board composition in response to environmental change'. *Journal of Management Studies*, 37(2): 235–55.

Hillman, A. J. and Dalziel, T. (2003). 'Boards of directors and firm performance: integrating agency and resource dependence perspectives'. *Academy of Management Review*, 28(3): 383–96.

Hofstede, G. (2001). *Culture's consequences: comparing values, behaviors, institutions and organizations across nations.* Second edition (Thousand Oaks, CA: Sage).

Hofstede, G. and Bond, M. H. (1988). 'Confucius and economic growth: new trends in culture's consequences'. *Organizational Dynamics*, 16(1): 4–21.

Inkiles, A. and Levinson, D. J. (1969). 'National character: the study of modal personality and socio-cultural systems'. In G. Lindey and E. Aronson (eds), *Handbook of Social Psychology*. Second edition (Chicago: Rand McNally).

Ireland, R. D., Hitt, M. A. and Williams, J. C. (1992). 'Self-confidence and decisiveness: prerequisites for effective management in the 1990s'. *Business Horizons*, 35(1): 36–43.

Jackson, G. and Aguilera, R. (2003). 'The cross-national diversity of corporate governance: dimensions and determinants'. *Academy of Management Review*, 28(3): 447–65.

Janis, I. L. (1982). *Victims of groupthink*. Second edition (Boston: Houghton Mifflin).

Jensen, M. C. and Meckling, W. H. (1976). 'Theory of the firm: managerial behaviour, agency costs and ownership structure'. *Journal of Financial Economics*, 3: 305–60.

Johnson, G. (1987). *Strategic change and the management process* (Oxford: Blackwell).

La Porta, R., Lopez-De-Silanes, F. and Shleifer, A. (1999). 'Corporate ownership around the world'. *Journal of Finance*, 54(3): 471–514.

La Porta, R., Lopez-De-Silanes, F., Shleifer, A. and Vishny, R. (1997). 'Legal determinants of external finance'. *Journal of Finance*, 52(10): 1131–50.

La Porta, R., Lopez-De-Silanes, F., Shleifer, A. and Vishny, R. (1998). 'Law and finance'. *Journal of Political Economy*, 106(9): 1113–55.

Lam, S. S. K., Chen, X.-P. and Scaubroeck, J. (2002). 'Participative decision making and employee performance in different cultures: the moderating effects of allocentricism/idiocentricism and efficiency'. *Academy of Management Journal*, 45(5): 905–15.

Lynall, M. D., Goden, B. R. and Hillman, A. J. (2003). 'Board composition from adolescence to maturity: a multitheoretic view'. *Academy of Management Review*, 28(3): 416–31.

McConaughy, D., Matthews, C. and Fialko, A. (2001). 'Founding family controlled firms: performance, risk and value'. *Journal of Small Business Management*, 39(1): 31–49.

McNulty, T. and Pettigrew, A. (1999). 'Strategists on the board'. *Organization Science*, 20(1): 47–74.

Medcof, J. W. (2001). 'Resource-based strategy and managerial power in networks in internationally dispersed technology units'. *Strategic Management Journal*, 22(10): 999–1012.

Pearson, A. E. (1988). 'Tough-minded ways to get innovative'. *Harvard Business Review*, 66(3): 99–106.

Pettigrew, A. M. and Whipp, R. (1991). *Managing change for competitive success* (Oxford: Blackwell).

Priem, R. L. (1990). 'Top management team group factors, consensus, and firm performance'. *Strategic Management Journal*, 11(6): 469–78.

Roberts, J., McNulty, T. and Styles, P. (2005). 'Beyond agency conceptions of the work of the non-executive directors: creating accountability in the boardroom'. *British Journal of Management*, 16(1): 5–26.

Schein, E. H. (1985). *Organizational culture and leadership* (San Francisco: Jossey Bass).

Silverman, D. (1993). *Interpreting qualitative data: methods for analysing talk, text and interaction* (London: Sage).

Smith, P. B. and Bond, M. H. (1998). *Social psychology across cultures* (Harlow: Prentice Hall).

Smith, P. B., Bond, M. H. and Kağitçibasi, Ç. (2006). *Understanding social psychology across cultures* (London: Sage).

Sondegaard, M. (1994). 'Research note: Hofstede's consequences: a study of reviews, citations and replications'. *Organization Studies*, 15(3): 447–56.

Thomsen, S. and Pedersen, T. (2000). 'Ownership structure and economic performance in the largest European companies'. *Strategic Management Journal*, 21(6): 689–705.

Trompenaars, F. and Hampden-Turner, C. (1997). *Riding the waves of culture: understanding cultural diversity in business.* Second edition (London: Nicholas Brearly).

Vroom, V. and Yetton, P. (1973). *Leadership and decision-making* (Pittsburgh: University of Pittsburgh Press).

West, C. T. and Schwenck, C. R. (1996). 'Top management team strategic consensus, demographic homogeneity and firm performance: a report of resounding non-findings'. *Strategic Management Journal*, 17(7): 571–6.

Yin, R. K. (1994). *Case study research: design and methods* (Thousand Oaks: Sage).

Zahra, S. A. and Pearce, J. A. (1989). 'Boards of directors and corporate financial performance: a review and integrative model'. *Journal of Management*, 15(2): 291–334.

Zimmerman, F. M. (1989). 'Managing a successful turnaround'. *Long Range Planning*, 22(3): 105–24.

6

The Role of Equity Investors in the Internationalization Strategies of Infant Technology-based Firms

Antonella Zucchella and Enrico Cotta Ramusino

Introduction

The role of corporate governance issues in strategic decision-making and in building organizational capabilities is of considerable contemporary significance. According to Filatotchev (2006: 90), 'Corporate governance is not an exogenous mechanism that only provides checks and controls over the efficiency with which companies are run and whether managers make decisions in the interest of shareholders. It is also closely related to the distribution of power and experience among executive and non-executive board members.' In particular, the contribution of corporate governance to the process of internationalization decision-making and to performance is not explored sufficiently in the literature, and further dedicated research is required (Filatotchev, 2006; Carpenter et al., 2003).

Much of the recent debate on international entrepreneurship, international new ventures and early internationalizing firms has been devoted to the understanding of how these organizations could cope from their inception with foreign markets, and sometimes with a global scope, without any experiential learning and related organizational capabilities. Experiential learning (Kolb, 1984) is a construct which represents the cornerstone of the gradualist internationalization models based on stages (Johansson and Vahlne, 1977). The diffusion of *born global* firms (Oviatt and McDougall, 1994) challenges this interpretation. In our opinion, the phenomenon of early and instant firm internationalization is an inevitable corollary of the contemporary global economy, characterized as it is by higher interdependency between firms and more chances to identify and exploit opportunities on an international scale, and by the growing importance of industries and businesses where competitive advantage needs to be grounded in a global value chain from the establishment of the firm. It is thus possible to identify many features (related to precocity, speed and simultaneity) of the internationalization process of modern firms which contradict the gradualist stage models, but they do not necessarily conflict with the experiential learning construct. This consideration is supported by several studies which report that many firms may be born global, but their founders are not since they already had previous experience in international contexts (Zucchella et al., 2007). In addition to this, international experience may also be gained by hiring knowledgeable staff or through external advice.

A related perspective is provided by the role of equity investors in supporting the internationalization process of infant firms, and in building the necessary resources and organizational capabilities. In this work, the term 'equity investors' refers to the main categories of institutions which intervene in the financing of start-ups and young technology-based firms (TBFs): i.e. venture capitalists, private equity funds and 'business angels'. Business angels are frequently former businessmen who devote part of their capital and time to finance and manage new ventures, providing the needed competencies and relationships (Mason and Harrison, 1994). Venture capitalists (VCs) and private equity funds are financial intermediaries who raise funds and invest them in different companies characterized by high growth potential. The role of equity investors in the financing of companies across the globe has grown substantially in recent years (UNCTAD, 2006).

This chapter aims to develop, through exploratory research, an interpretative framework about the role of corporate governance issues in strategic and internationalization processes in infant TBFs, focusing on the role of equity investors in the building of organizational capabilities both in general management and specifically related to internationalization issues. Infant TBFs are frequently characterized by early internationalization, under the pressure of global competition and in the pursuit of global market opportunities. Internationalization at inception, or in the early years of life, is thus a key element in their strategic management. Corporate governance (with special attention to the role of equity investors), strategic management, and the internationalization process are the three interconnected core issues that provide the basis for the analysis in this chapter. In particular, the chapter addresses the following research questions. What value is added by equity investors to the setting of strategic decisions in new ventures? What is the role of equity investors in the decision to internationalize, and in the early management of internationalization activities in young firms, with special attention to infant TBFs?

Organizational learning and the internationalization of new firms

Two main problems are apparent at the infant stage of the firm. The first relates to the quality of the initial set of resources, with special emphasis on the founders and the management team. The second relates to the subsequent capacity of these people to take successful strategic decisions and develop organizational competencies. According to the resource-based view (Barney, 1991; Penrose, 1959), resources are the primary determinant of the competitive advantage of a firm. New firms often lack some critically important resources usually possessed by larger and more established companies (Teece, 1986). They also lack organizational capabilities, because the infant organization takes time to develop organizational routines for problem-solving and to develop the needed capabilities. From a knowledge-based and network perspective (Grant and Baden Fuller, 1995; Lorenzoni and Ornati, 1988), the exploitation of opportunities scanned by entrepreneurs requires complementary information, skills and competencies (Lipparini and Sobrero, 1994; Yli-Renko et al., 2001; Ravasi and Ruta, 2006) which can be accessed by developing partnerships with other organizations and professionals. Network relationships are a critical way to access, combine and develop knowledge, and networking might represent a distinctive organizational capability (Lorenzoni and Lipparini, 1999). Among the interpersonal and interorganizational relationships, the one between the start-up firm and the equity investors is a key vehicle for the firm to access not only financial resources but also complementary information, knowledge and managerial competencies.

TBFs provide an interesting field for the study of the above-mentioned problems (Robinson and McDougall, 2001; Zahra et al., 2000). TBFs are frequently founded by young entrepreneurs, who mostly possess a scientific/technological background and are missing adequate experience in firm management. These firms represent one of the main areas of intervention of private equity, due to their high-growth potential and a risk profile which is consistent with the operating spectrum of equity investors (Bagley and Dauchy, 1999). The financial commitment and the risk profile (Watson et al., 1998; Gaskill et al., 1993) of the funded firms call for an active role of private equity in the young TBF management, through 'participation in strategic-decision making, placement of directors on the board, recruitment of key executives, determination of ownership structure and mobilisation of other valuable resources via their network of contacts' (Carpenter et al., 2003: 805). From this perspective, the role of equity investors in the corporate governance of young TBFs also involves an influence on the firms' strategic management in two main, and not mutually exclusive, forms: via managerial roles (the placement of directors on the board, the hiring of executives) and via direct participation in strategic decision-making and implementation.

The exploration and exploitation of foreign market opportunities is frequently a key strategic decision. Young TBFs are confronted by the internationalization challenge, which is often a 'pursue or perish' dilemma. Recent studies provide evidence that pursuing internationalization at the firm's inception can enhance legitimacy, technological learning, and sales growth (Autio et al., 2000; Lu and Beamish, 2001; Zahra et al., 2000). For some firms, being global from the beginning is the natural condition of their business: this is the case with 'deep niche firms' which need to sell on a global scale to break even (Zucchella, 2001), or of many internet-based businesses. But operating in multiple countries, with foreign customers, increases the complexities of doing business and the related firm risk. This is particularly true when the internationalization effort is poorly planned and/or managed, as may happen frequently in very young firms (Mitchell et al., 1992; Hitt et al., 1997). In new international ventures, the liability of newness (Freeman et al., 1983) is associated with the liability of foreignness: both are related to lack of knowledge – predominantly tacit, experience-based and problem-solving oriented – regarding a new context, either running a business from scratch or entering a new foreign market. The firm governance and management (which frequently overlap in infant firms) might mitigate the joint effect of these liabilities. The entrepreneur and/or management team bring into the new venture their prior knowledge, and apply it to a more or less known context. In particular, knowledge based on prior experience is very important.

Two main processes are involved in overcoming the liabilities of newness and foreignness for any infant firm. First, there is obtaining access to the needed experience-based knowledge through a variety of alternative means, which differ from the established firm's intra-organizational learning processes based on own experience. Second, there is the pursuit of organizational learning, by which the former knowledge and skills are 'transferred' to the organization and 'transformed' into organizational routines. Learning is considered reactive in the Uppsala model, due to a focus on the acquisition of more knowledge about already identified solutions to solve the internationalization problem (Forsgren, 2002; Yli-Renko et al., 2002). But it is considered proactive in international entrepreneurial firms, and the main thrust of research has been directed towards identifying the antecedents of organizational learning (Autio et al., 2000; Sapienza et al., 2005; Yeoh, 2004; Yli-Renko et al., 2002; Zahra et al., 2000).

Top management's prior experience moderates the effect of international diversity on learning (Yeoh, 2004). Conversely, age at first international entry has a negative relationship with a firm's international learning effort (Sapienza et al., 2005). The younger the firm when it internationalizes, the more learning about internationalization occurs. Young firms may not have developed organizational routines that could hinder the process of learning international marketing and internationalization knowledge, whilst older more established firms might have (Knight and Cavusgil, 2004). Finally, a firm's entrepreneurial orientation and social capital also have a positive impact on learning about international markets (Sapienza et al., 2005, Yli-Renko et al., 2002). Other forms of learning relevant to the internationalization process of these firms are the acquisition of experiential knowledge through hiring knowledgeable staff (grafting), the imitation of other firms that have internationalized successfully (vicarious learning), searching for international market knowledge through consultants, and congenital learning, i.e. learning brought into the organization by founders (Saarenketo et al., 2004; Bengtsson, 2004).

It has often been stated that the start-up firm is an extension of the founders (Chandler and Jansen, 1992; Dyke et al., 1992), who determine the resources and the capabilities set at the beginning of the venture. On the one hand, the quality of the management is a critical factor in financing decisions (Goslin and Barge, 1986; MacMillan et al., 1987) whilst, on the other hand, financing can also provide some needed managerial competencies. It is widely recognized that equity investors bring both financial and managerial resources to the start-up firm. Equity investors are a 'very powerful governance mechanism since they are (1) risk seeking, (2) actively participate in and monitor management and strategy setting, and (3) have a significant amount of experience in risk-taking' (Carpenter et al., 2003: 806). A number of empirical studies highlight the positive effect of venture capital funding on firms' performance (Wijbenga et al., 2003). Most of this research is descriptive (MacMillan et al., 1989; Rosenstein, 1988; Fried and Hisrich, 1995) whilst another stream adopts the perspective of agency theory to explain the value created by the equity investor in terms of the mitigation of the potential opportunism of entrepreneurs (Amit et al., 1990; Barry et al., 1990). The value-adding role of equity investors has been pointed out by Hellmann and Puri (2000), Sapienza (1992), Gompers and Lerner (1999) and Hellmann (2000), but the roots of this value added[1] have not been sufficiently explored or explained (Hugo and Garnsey, 2005; Maula and Murray, 2000). But there are not many studies that try to open the 'black box' and explain why this happens and, in particular, which strategic decisions are taken (and which capabilities are developed) thanks to equity investors' support (Arthurs and Busenitz, 2006).

In particular, there are only a few studies on the role of equity investors in shaping the internationalization decision and in building the needed capabilities for consolidating an internationalization process (Carpenter et al., 2003; Van den Berghe and Levrau, 2002; Gabrielsson et al., 2004). The decision to go abroad and the capacity to manage international activities are key strategic factors in young TBFs, and significantly influence the prospective risk-return and growth profile of the new venture. In general, these studies hypothesize a positive relationship between venture capital commitment and firm internationalization. For instance, Van den Berghe and Levrau (2002: 131) suggest that 'due to international experience, the VC can judge the success or failure of similar scenarios (and) . . . keep the venture from making professional mistakes.' In fact equity investors are likely to be involved in decisions and capabilities building (mostly by supporting hiring of qualified staff) regarding internationalization.

The few empirical studies on the subject report apparently conflicting findings. Carpenter et al. (2003) adopt a 'reasoned risk-taking' approach, whereby the internationalization risk undertaken depends on the interaction of governance mechanisms and stakeholders' characteristics. The role of the equity investor is predicted to be positive in determining the foreign sales orientation, but they find in their empirical survey that technology-based

IPO firms are less likely to have relevant foreign sales intensity when backed by an equity investor. Investor backing needs to be complemented by previous international experience of their board appointees, top management team members, or both to determine a positive impact on foreign sales. These results might appear rather contradictory with respect to the hypotheses based on the reasoned risk-taking construct, but they are consistent with the key role of experiential learning in internationalization processes (Johansson and Vahlne, 1977). Moreover, these results depend on the different management styles of the equity investor, and the competencies brought in to the funded companies. Gabrielsson et al. (2004) consider the role of venture capitalists in supporting a born global attitude. In their study the role of venture capitalists is confirmed to be positive in providing the needed initial vision and experience to enter foreign markets from the firm's inception.

The theoretical framework: a tentative modelling

Equity investors may contribute to firms in several forms, as we have tried to summarize in Figure 6.1 in which four main areas of contribution have been identified. The first area of contribution is obviously the provision of financial resources. The second area may be referred to as 'reputation building'. Reputation is a rent-generating asset (Barney, 1991) according to the resource-based view of the firm. The fact of having received external financing – particularly from equity investors who are well known in the market – means that the firm has passed a sort of severe exam: its vision, its business model, its resources and capabilities have been judged good enough to attract the involvement of an experienced player who has decided that the firm was worth a bet. The relationship between the young TBF and the equity investor is thus a form of interorganizational endorsement (Maula and Murray, 2000). In particular, venture capitalists certify the quality of the ventures going public, thus reducing information asymmetries between insiders and outside investors (Barry et al., 1990; Brav and Gompers, 1997).

The other two aspects of investors' contribution are, however, the most relevant for the purposes of our research. The third area of contribution is networking, which encompasses both 'social' and 'interorganizational' networking (Yli-Renko et al., 2001). Generally speaking, the investor can offer the funded firm the possibility of entering the system of relationships he has, in the course of time, developed (MacMillan et al., 1989). According to Carpenter et al. (2003: 806), 'VCs also bring a large network of contacts that can further reduce the perceived and actual risk accompanying global operations.' This system of relationships typically includes:

- Other investors (equity investors with whom the main investor is used to cooperating on the basis of reciprocity, banks, and other financial institutions).

- Other firms with whom the investor has already operated in the past or is operating at the moment. This aspect is especially important for those investors who hold stakes in a large number of firms. In such circumstances, it is possible to give the funded firm access to new clients and/or new suppliers.
- Public agencies, universities, and research centres etc.
- People. Investors, making reference to their own social network, may be able to find men and women who can be hired by the funded firm.

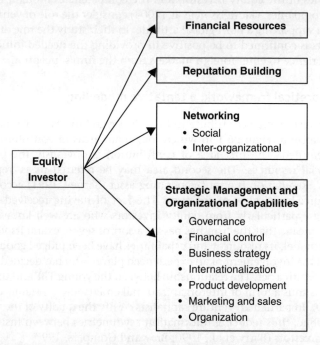

Figure 6.1:   The contributions of equity investors to funded firms

The fourth area of contribution rests in the improvement of the strategic management and organizational capabilities of the funded firms. This is the main focus of our research, and there are seven broad ways in which the investor can exert influence: governance, financial control, business strategy, internationalization, product development, marketing and sales, and the organization of the firm.

The need to monitor the development of the funded firm encourages investors to take part in the *governance* process (Filatotchev and Bishop, 2002; Filatotchev, 2006). Contracts stipulated before the acquisition of the stake generally regulate the participation of investors in the life of the firm, giving them the desired decision power. Investors typically intervene in the firm by participating in its board of directors, and through the appointment of members who are in charge of protecting investors' interests. On some particularly relevant issues – those which can influence the life and the development of the firm – the members appointed by investors might have a right of veto. But usually the main task of these members is to monitor economic and financial results. Other forms of intervention may be found in cases in which investors decide to take an active part in the management of the funded firm by choosing managers to cover relevant positions. The exploitation of this possibility largely depends on the investors' style of investment, discussed in the next paragraphs.

The most commonly used instrument to monitor the funded firm is *financial control* (Gompers and Lerner, 1998). Investors base their decision on whether or not to buy a stake in the firm on a deep, careful and structured evaluation process. The investor and the management of the firms agree upon a business plan which identifies the objectives and the forecast results of the firm. After the acquisition of the stake, the first priority of investors is to verify whether these results are progressively achieved or not. From the entrance of the investor in the firm, the latter is typically obliged to develop structured and highly detailed reporting systems (normally on a monthly basis).

Investors who decide to buy a stake in a firm normally support the existing business model, share the same vision about market evolution, and support the strategy the firm wants to pursue. But exceptions might be found. There are situations in which investors actively intervene in order to change some aspects of the *business strategy* of the funded firm in order to enhance their potential returns (Maula and Murray, 2000).

One of the ways in which investors may contribute to firms' strategy is in the field of *internationalization*. Generally speaking, equity investors support or even push the internationalization of funded firms as a way to boost their revenues (and revenue increase is the basis for value creation). The issue of internationalization is deeply connected with general strategic management since, for young TBFs, international markets are the natural endeavour both for selling and for purchasing (Autio et al., 2000). The credibility of the infant firm business plan is often dependent upon the presence of an international vision and of the capacity to pursue effectively an internationalization process. When the founders do not provide some of these elements, equity investors intervene to enhance these activities and competencies in the firm (Carpenter et al., 2003; Gabrielsson et al., 2004; Van den Berghe and Levrau, 2002). Investors may support the internationalization of funded firms in different ways, such as identifying experienced people in the international job market to cover key organizational roles, supporting the firm in the research of foreign partners that may contribute to product development and/or foreign sales development and helping the firm along the different dimensions of the internationalization process (viz. sourcing, marketing and financing).

It is widely known that the 'cultural background' (studies and professional experience) of equity investors is both financial and industrial. As a consequence, they are in the condition to help firms in the process of *product development* (Mason and Harrison, 1994). Again, this support may be offered in different ways, according to investors' style. On the one hand, it is commonly the case that investors – relying on their industrial experience – understand the technological problems of the firms, and, believing that the product is good, simply find the money to help the firm to complete its development. On the other hand, we have observed cases in which investors have intervened in this area more actively, either directly (business angels coming from the high-tech world) or bringing new people on board for the completion of the process (this aspect is closely linked to networking).

Increasing revenues is generally seen as the prior condition to foster firms' development and create the basis for value creation (for the firm itself, of course, but especially for investors). In young and non-structured firms, it is rare to find skilled resources in the areas of *marketing and sales*. Similarly, in high-tech start-ups created by young scientists, the resources devoted to these functions are very small, if any. The intervention of equity investors brings with it important investments in this area (Hsu, 2000). These functions may be created – if non-existing – or dramatically improved by hiring people from the outside.

As is apparent from the above, the intervention of equity investors often brings about a dramatic change in the *organization* of the firm. New functions are created, and the organizational structure is thus modified. New organizational mechanisms are introduced to give the firm discipline and rationality, and new personnel are hired, both at the managerial level – especially in key functions – and at the operating level. Much attention is devoted by equity investors to the progressive introduction of appropriate routines to detect problems (reporting) and to solve them (managerial practices), in order to build progressively organizational capabilities, which could better support the firm growth and consolidation after the equity investors' exit.

Research methodology

The purpose of this research is to identify the ways in which equity investors (as defined in the introduction) contribute to the process of strategic management (where internationalization is a key issue) in the funded firms. The research methodology is based on a qualitative approach, and the purpose of this study can be described as mainly exploratory and, to some extent, descriptive. Our aim is 'to build a rich description of complex circumstances that are unexplored in the literature' (Marshall and Rossman, 1999: 33). The aims of the project are twofold. First, we want to confirm the usefulness of our framework (see Figure 6.1) for the examination of the main areas of investors' contribution to the funded firms. Second, we want to classify equity investors' style of intervention in the funded firms according to their contributions to the firms' management.

Four high-tech firms have been selected for the case studies, and the analysis is based on a number of interviews with investors and their funded firms. Eight in-depth interviews were undertaken: two equity investors, two business angels, and the founders of each of the four companies. All the funded firms were in high-technology industries because we wanted to focus on those companies which represent the main area of intervention of VCs and business angels. They are characterized by a scarcity of both financial and managerial resources, and lack adequate knowledge and experience in strategic management. They are pressured to enter foreign markets early by the dynamics of their industries (Franko, 1989), even though they lack the necessary previous experience in these operations (Hitt et al., 1997; Mitchell et al., 1992). The interviews permitted us to make some general considerations about the management style and approach of private equity institutions, while the selected company cases permitted us to further analyse the role of equity investors in strategic management and in the internationalization process.

The case studies were selected according to their relevance in relation to the research guidelines. They are compared in order to find similarities and differences. The research objective requires that the problem is approached from different perspectives: that of the equity investor, and that of the funded company. From the former point of view, we aim to assess the background of the equity investor in order to understand which competencies s/he can bring into the company and how they have been developed. From the point of view of the infant firm, we aim at understanding how strategic management and the internationalization process take place and how organizational capabilities have been progressively built.

Table 6.1 summarizes some key facts and figures of the selected firms. Three out of the four companies belong to the software development industry, while the fourth is in the scientific publishing field. The similarities in the industry profiles enable a better comparison among the cases. Two of the four companies have been sold to multinational groups after their initial development of export activity. Most of the companies developed a global value chain, from sourcing to selling abroad. To these companies, the activity of strategic international sourcing (research and development partnerships, knowledge, patents, rights acquisition) appears even more important than developing foreign sales.

The case study firms

This section provides brief details of the internationalization experiences of the four TBFs used for the case studies.

Table 6.1: Key facts and figures for the selected infant technology-based firms

Firm	Business	Year founded	Year of internat	Investor intervention	Revenues	Founder/s	Main location	Internationalization stage
A	Open-source software for the wireless industry	2004	2004	First round 2004 Second round 2005 Two VCs from the start: one Italian and one US (major). The US VC has two board members	US$1m in 2004 US$1m in 2005	35-year-old Italian engineer	Silicon Valley	Export plus a foreign subsidiary 15% foreign sales/sales. Relevant number of foreign customers all over the globe. Research relationships with universities in US and Italy
B	Software for telecoms	2002	2005	One BA with an equity stake of 30% bought in 2003	€0.5 m before BA intervention; €2.5 m after BA exit (2005)	Italian diversified entrepreneur with software development skills	North-east Italy	Export (large global TLC companies). The firm has been sold to a multinational software company in 2005. Spin off and sold to another multinational group in 2006
C	Software for mobile phones and TV decoders	2005	2005	Participation (25%) in the company holding internationally registered patents	No revenues	Young scientist with deep skills in software development	Milan	Export, licensing, patent selling (global customers). The foreign company which held the international patent was sold to a Singapore producer
D	Editing of scientific journals	1993	2005	Participation in the company (% stake not available)	€0.1 m before the investor (2003); €8 m after his exit (2005)	Diversified entrepreneur	North of Italy	Import: acquisition of publishing rights from international medical journals

Case study A

The firm was established in Silicon Valley by a young Italian engineer in 2004, and provides open-source software for the wireless industry. Two venture capitalists, characterized by two different management styles, invested in the company from the beginning. The Italian VC had the lower equity commitment, and adopted a pure asset management approach with little investment in the first round, a larger investment in the second round, but with no involvement either in close monitoring through governance mechanisms or in strategic organizational decisions. In contrast, the US investor followed a classical venture capital approach: high commitment, high monitoring, two board members, information flows from the company have to be regularly provided according to a well-detailed schedule, organizational procedures are structured according to the VC's guidelines, and the VC requires professional head-hunting for some managerial roles. There was no direct intervention in strategic decisions, which are left to the founder. A company manager declared:

> They evaluate a business project and a management team which has to implement it. If they don't like the strategic guidelines, including internationalization, they either do not finance the venture or change the management.
>
> They intervene frequently and regularly in monitoring, through ex ante and ex post financial reporting. They imposed rules about organizational and managerial procedures and about selection of key managerial roles. But they never said something about markets, products or customer selection and management.

The internationalization decision was grounded on the previous experience of the founder, who had worked for some years in Hewlett Packard USA, after graduating in Italy. In the USA, he developed both professional (technical and managerial) experience and personal (social) contacts with customers. The decision to start the venture in Silicon Valley depended upon the previous experience of the founder, and upon the awareness that in the open-source software business '*you have to be where the main business, software developers and customers are.*' Business contacts with customers are mainly rooted in the Silicon Valley, though a growing percentage of customers are spread all over the world. The US sales still account for around 85 per cent of total revenues, but foreign customers have a higher weight if measured as a percentage of total customers. The social network of the entrepreneur is fundamental for establishing business contacts in the USA and abroad, especially in the start-up phase. The internationalization of the firm was characterized by exporting, coupled with the establishment of a foreign subsidiary in Italy.

Case study B

The firm operates in the production of software – namely products used by operators to optimize the short message service (SMS) with clients – which had been sold, until the arrival of the investor, only to large telephone carriers. Prior to the investment in 2003 by the equity investor, the firm – created the previous year in the north-eastern region of Italy by an entrepreneur with previous experience in other fields, but always in software production – had revenues of about €0.5 m, had reached the break-even point, and employed twenty people mainly engaged in software production. The organizational structure was a very simple one, the only managers being the chief executive officer (CEO) and the chief operating officer (COO).

The success of the firm was due to a good product, but growth was very slow because of two reasons. First, there was nobody in charge of marketing and sales activities. The second reason was strategic: the firm was not aware of the fact that – relying on its own resources and partly changing some features of its product – it would have been possible to enter the larger and most attractive corporate market, selling its software directly to business firms. These business firms would have found it useful to use the software to interface the carrier.

The equity investor – a 38-year-old engineer based in Milan with skills in the high-tech sector and long job experience in Italy and abroad – appreciated the opportunities open to the firm and decided to invest, buying a 30 per cent equity stake. He did not assume any direct role in the firm, but operated as a 'direct consultant' of the CEO. He told us: '*I worked in that firm for 1–2 days a week for one year and a half, directly cooperating with the CEO.*' But the contribution of the investor was very important. First, he brought new people on board, in order to enhance the firm's resources and organizational structure. He declared '*I brought with me a sales manager from Milan, and two engineers coming from abroad (one from Sweden and one from the UK), with whom I had already worked in my past experience.*' The former was in charge of developing clients' relationships at a global level, especially in the corporate segment, while the latter had the task of contributing to the development of the product in order to make it suitable for corporate clients. All the new people brought into the firm had already worked in the past with the investor, both in Italy and abroad. The changes to the organization of the firm were completed, with the COO asked to assume, in practice, the role of general manager so that the CEO could devote his whole time to strategic issues. Within a year and a half, there was been a substantial increase in the revenues of the firm (from €0.5 to 2.5 million with earnings before interest, depreciation and taxes of about 20 per cent). In 2005, a multinational group made a bid to buy the firm; the sale was completed in the course of the same year, and production of the firm has since been addressed to foreign clients. In 2006, the firm was spun off by the first investor and sold to another multinational group.

Case study C

This case is different from the previous two, although the firm is also involved in software production, namely products to be used in mobile phones and television decoders. The entrepreneur was a 36-year-old scientist with a deep knowledge of software development, working as his main activity as a consultant to a large multinational group. In parallel with this activity, he also worked with a partner to develop software which was registered outside Italy. The two men started looking around for equity financing, once they had progressed with the development of the product. Their idea was to create a new firm, giving it a structured organization and hiring people to finish the development of the product. They also intended to hire some engineers and a sales manager to develop relationships with clients.

The equity investor came in contact with the two men, and evaluated the possibility of intervention. He was impressed with the product that the firm was developing, and decided to take a 25 per cent equity stake in the newly created company. However, he soon realized that, although development of the product was proceeding satisfactorily, the firm had no structure at all and a great deal of effort was required to achieve the founders' objectives. In particular, huge additional investments were required, especially in terms of new personnel. In addition, there was the risk of losing their technological advantage, if they spent time establishing the firm and completing the product. An alternative solution was sought. The investor told us: '*I was in contact with many firms operating in the software development business, some of them large enough to support the activities of the founders.*' He contacted a large company from Singapore, and discussed with it the possibility of cooperation with the Italian promoters. The Singaporean company decided to buy the patents registered by the founders, hiring them as partners for the final development of the software and for its integration in its system. The founders accepted, sold their patent to the Singaporean company and worked with the buyer to complete the development of the product. The investor worked with the firm for 3–4 days a week for two months, the time he needed to organize the deal with the Singaporean company.

Case study D

This case refers to a company which edits a scientific review in the field of medicine, having physicians as the main clients. The firm was founded many years ago, but its evolution had been unsatisfactory in recent years with no growth and poor profitability. Before the arrival of the equity investor, the revenues were about €0.1 million and growth prospects were low. The investor came in touch with the company through his social network, and realized that development was possible only by changing fundamentally the business model of the firm. He bought a stake in the firm, providing fresh money for investments which could create growth opportunities. The idea was to buy from high-ranking American scientific reviews the rights to publish in Italy the articles of leading authors. Both the investor and the other partners in the firm believed that a market for these articles existed. A new programme for the permanent training of physicians in Italy had been introduced at the time the investment was made: the programme was based on a credit system, and the reviews officially recognized by the Ministry of Health are bought by physicians for their training.

The investor worked directly for the new project, searched for the contacts with the most highly rated reviews, negotiated the prices for the publishing rights, and signed the contracts. The new business model produced a dramatic increase in the firm's revenues from €0.1 million to 0.8 million. The investor sold his stake and the firm continues to operate according to the new model.

Discussion

The four firms analysed in the case studies provide an interesting range of experiences regarding young TBFs, and the roles played by equity investors in their strategic decisions. In all four cases, internationalization was central to the development of the firms, even though the internationalization process in each case had different dimensions. For three of the four companies, serving foreign customers was not an option but an essential feature of their businesses as their markets consisted of a few global players. Some of these firms viewed international sourcing as crucial: the cooperation with foreign universities for product development, the purchase of foreign technologies, copyrights and patents, all affected significantly their competitive positioning. The firm in case study A developed international customers thanks to the prior experience of the founder and his personal social network. Furthermore, the decision to open a foreign subsidiary in Italy was motivated by similar factors (the founder took his degree in Italy and maintained personal relationships with the research units at his alma mater). The American venture capitalist did not directly influence strategic decisions, and financed the company on the basis of their existing business plan. The main investor has representatives on the board, requires frequent financial reporting, and supported the hiring of independent managers.

In contrast, the firms in the other three case studies were subject to direct interventions by the equity investor in the firms' management: in two cases, the investors explicitly defined themselves as 'business angels' whilst, in the third case, the investor preferred the label 'venture capitalist'. Notwithstanding the labels, the investors devoted a significant part of their time to the company management in all three cases, contributing to strategic decisions and, in particular, developing business contacts abroad. Internationalization was seen as a core part of strategic decision-making and management. The investors typically seemed most concerned with the development of business contacts abroad, leveraging on their personal networks and on their knowledge of the industry, while they supported the hiring of qualified technical staff for product development, another critical issue for TBFs.

The contributions of the equity investors thus vary significantly in terms of the value added to the firm's activities. In some cases, the investors shape the marketing function, contact customers, and contribute to product development and operational activities. In other cases, the investors monitor the business closely, but without assuming direct control over strategic decisions. In short, the investors in all four firms intervened in the governance and in the financial control systems, and frequently influenced/determined the hiring of key managers. But some investors also provided a direct contribution in the other areas mentioned in Figure 6.1. This exploratory analysis allows us to categorize different management 'styles', according to the ways in which the equity investors managed their stakes in the funded firms. Generally speaking, we can highlight two extreme positions. On the one hand, we have investors – which we will label 'selection-oriented' – who put all their efforts into the selection of the firm in which to place their investment, but little or no energy into the running of the company following the acquisition of the stake. On the other hand, there are more 'management-oriented' investors, who take an active interest in the firm following their investment.

The basic ethos of the 'selection-oriented' investors is that it is important to identify a good investment, but that there is then little need of intervention to improve the performance of the funded firm. This approach is quite common for investors who hold stakes in a large portfolio of firms: in such situations, the investors' skills are concentrated on choosing 'good picks' especially when the management team is made up of a small number of people.[2] 'Selection-oriented' investors subsequently monitor their investments through financial reporting, and through participation on the board of directors. The impact of the investors on the funded firms is quite soft and, as long as economic and financial targets are achieved, the firms continue to operate with a high degree of independence. One investor told us: *'When we decide to buy a stake in a firm, it means that we appreciated its strategy and valuated its resources and capabilities, finding coherence between the former and the latter. After the investment we just monitor the evolution of the firm with little or no intervention.'*

Notwithstanding the lack of direct intervention, the 'selection-oriented' investor makes a number of contributions to the funded firm. The first contribution may arise from the selection process itself, which can provide valuation information for the firm. Even if the investor subsequently declines to acquire an equity stake, the decision may reveal to the firm its areas of weakness. But even a 'selection-oriented' investor will make several other important contributions if s/he does provide finance. First, the arrival of an equity investor produces an evolution in the firm, which is compelled to become more structured (establishment of a board of directors; redefinition of key managerial positions), and increased managerial control. Second, the need for the investor to monitor his/her investment requires the firm to develop reporting standards which had previously been absent. The firm thus acquires capabilities in the area of financial planning and control, which can be useful for the whole system of relationships it maintains with other stakeholders. Last but not least, the firm can take advantage of the investors' network of relationships and, at the same time, benefit from an enhanced reputation having obtained outside investors' financing.

In contrast, the ethos of 'management-oriented' investors leads them to take a more active interest in the funded firm. For them, the acquisition of the stake in the developing firm is considered only as the first step in the process which leads to value creation. Subsequent steps include taking part in the management of the funded firms in different ways: business contacts at an international level, developing relationships, strategic international sourcing, product development, and the hiring of personnel. These investors may also devote part of their weekly time to work inside the firm, together with managers and founders.

Such 'management-oriented' investors, of course, carry out a selection process as in the case of the 'selection-oriented' investors; the difference is that, in many cases, these investors accept firms which other investors might refuse because they believe that the 'gaps' that they have identified can be filled through their direct intervention. The activities of this category of investors are particularly relevant for the purposes of our research. Our exploratory research confirms the width and depth of their involvement: their contribution takes various forms, involving all the areas – including strategic management – identified in Figure 6.1.

Conclusions

Equity investors provide a substantial contribution to the firms in addition to financial resources: 'selection-oriented' investors typically have an impact upon firm governance, financial control, and organization, whereas 'management-oriented' investors also contribute to strategic decision-making and management issues. In both cases, though in the second more than in the first, it is possible to observe an organizational learning process at the firm level, through which individual knowledge becomes part of the organizational knowledge. The ability to retain what the investor has brought as a contribution gives a clear idea of the learning process the firm has experienced, and the extent to which capabilities have been really transferred into it from the investor. Thus, in answer to the two research questions raised in the introduction, our exploratory study confirms that the contribution of equity investors to the development of the funded firms' resources and capabilities is considerable, even if it takes place in different forms, according to the particular features of the investors and of the firms.

The internationalization decisions were considered as crucial strategic decisions in the case studies: TBFs cannot escape from the imperative to go abroad and, very early in their lives, have to develop international business relations, both on the sourcing and on the selling side. Infant TBFs are frequently founded by people who have technical/scientific know-how, but who may have difficulties in developing from scratch a global vision of their market and a sufficient knowledge of potential customers and international opportunities. The contribution of equity investors can be fundamental from this point of view, because they can bring to the company their networks of contacts, their industry knowledge, and their international experience. If the investors are 'management-oriented' and spend part of their time in the company, they will establish the conditions for organizational learning in international operations. On the other hand, 'selection-oriented' investors retain faith in the founders and their capacity to develop international operations, but may influence these decisions and their subsequent management through the control they exercise regularly on the business plan achievements.

As for the funded firms, we can say that the contribution they receive depends on their specific features, in terms of stage of development, sector, initial portfolio of resources and capabilities, etc. Young high-tech firms seem to need more support than more mature firms operating in more traditional business areas. They are often founded by young scientists or researchers and need more help in order to identify the market for their business ideas. In contrast, more mature firms – with more established business frameworks – often need financial help to implement their strategic plans, and some support in terms of planning and control, financial discipline and networking. In the first case, the equity investors help founder(s) to 'build the company'; in the second they, more simply, accompany the firm in the growth of investment and revenues. The work reported in this chapter has provided a deeper understanding of the role of equity investors in the strategic management of infant TBFs, and will form the basis for the development of more refined research hypotheses to be tested subsequently through large-scale surveys and statistical analysis.

Acknowledgements

The authors would like to acknowledge the financial support of the Italian Ministry for Education, Universities and Research (FIRB, Project RISC – RBNE039XKA: 'Research and entrepreneurship in the knowledge-based economy: the effects on the competitiveness of Italy in the European Union').

Notes

1. Bygrave and Timmons (1992) describe venture capital as having a catalytic role in the entrepreneurial process, and Hellmann (2000) defines venture capital as 'professionally managed, equity like financing of young, growth-oriented companies'. Gompers and Lerner (1999) go beyond these definitions, describing venture capital as a process which starts from raising funds and proceeds through monitoring and adding value to the firm. In our opinion, for an infant firm much of this

value-adding activity lies in the contribution to the development of strategic decision-making and the related organizational capabilities.
2. The selection process typically involves a number of phases for the potential equity investor: the leverage of contacts to generate a range of possible investment projects; a first 'paper selection' round made on the basis of the business plan supplied by the entrepreneurs in the firms seeking funding; a second round of selection made on the basis of meetings with the entrepreneurs selected in the first round; and the drafting of the contract.

Bibliography

Amit, R., Glosten, L. and Muller, E. (1990). 'Does venture capital foster the most promising entrepreneurial firms?' *California Management Review*, 32(10): 102–11.

Arthurs, J. D. and Busenitz, L. W. (2006). 'Dynamic capabilities and venture performance: the effects of venture capitalists'. *Journal of Business Venturing*, 21(2): 195–215.

Autio, E., Sapienza, H. J. and Almeida, J. G. (2000). 'Effects of age at entry, knowledge intensity and imitability on international growth'. *Academy of Management Journal*, 43(5): 909–24.

Bagley, C. and Dauchy, C. (1999). 'The entrepreneurial venture'. *Venture Capital Journal*, 41(3): 126–39.

Barney, J. B. (1991). 'Firm resources and sustained competitive advantage'. *Journal of Management*, 17(2): 99–120.

Barry, C. B., Muscarella, C. J., Peavy III, J. W. and Vetsuypen, M. R. (1990) 'The role of venture capital in the creation of public companies: evidence from the going public process'. *Journal of Financial Economics*, 27(1): 447–71.

Bengtsson, L. (2004). 'Explaining born global: an organisational learning perspective on the internationalisation process'. *International Journal of Globalisation and Small Business*, 1(1): 28–41.

Brav, A. and Gompers, P. A. (1997) 'Myth or reality? The long run underperformance of initial public offerings: evidence from venture and non-venture capital-backed companies'. *Journal of Finance*, 52(5): 1791–1821.

Bygrave, W. D. and Timmons, J. A. (1992). *Venture capital at the crossroads* (Boston, MA: Harvard Business School Press).

Carpenter, M. A., Pollock, T. G. and Leary, M. M. (2003). 'Testing a model of reasoned risk taking: governance, the experience of principals and agents, and global strategy in high technology IPO firms'. *Strategic Management Journal*, 24(6): 803–30.

Chandler, G. N. and Hanks, S. H. (1994). 'Founder competence, the environment and venture performance'. *Entrepreneurship: Theory and Practice*, 18(3): 129–38.

Chandler, G. N. and Jansen, E. (1992). 'The founder's self assessed competence and venture performance'. *Journal of Business Venturing*, 7(3): 223–36.

Dyke, L. S., Fischer, E. M. and Reuber, A. R. (1992). 'An inter-industry examination of the impact of owner experience on firm performance'. *Journal of Small Business Management*, 30(4): 229–41.

Filatotchev, I. (2006). 'Effects of executive characteristics and venture capital involvement on board composition and share ownership in IPO firms'. *British Journal of Management*, 17(1): 75–91.

Filatotchev, I. and Bishop, K. (2002). 'Board composition, share ownership and underpricing of UK IPO firms'. *Strategic Management Journal*, 23(4): 941–55.

Forsgren, M. (2002). 'The concept of learning in the Uppsala internationalization process model: a critical review'. *International Business Review*, 11(3): 257–77.

Franko, L. G. (1989). 'Global corporate competition: who's winning, who's losing, and the R&D factor as one reason why'. *Strategic Management Journal*, 10(5): 449–74.

Freeman, J., Carroll, G. R. and Hannan, M. T. (1983). 'The liability of newness: age dependence in organizational death rates'. *American Sociological Review*, 48(2): 692–710.

Fried, V. H. and Hisrich, R. D. (1995). 'The equity investor: a relationship investor'. *California Management Review*, 37(2): 101–13.

Gabrielsson, M., Sasi, V. and Darling, J. (2004). 'Finance strategies of rapidly growing Finnish SMEs: born internationals and born globals'. *European Business Review*, 16(6): 590–604.

Gaskill, L., Ricketts, A., Van Auken, H. E. and Manning, R. A. (1993). 'A factor analytic study of the perceived causes of small business failure'. *Journal of Small Business Management*, 31(4): 18–31.

Gompers, P. and Lerner, J. (1998). 'The determinants of corporate venture capital success: organisational structure, incentives and complementarities'. National Bureau of Economic Research, Working Paper no. 6725.

Gompers, P. and Lerner, P. (1999). *The venture capital cycle* (Cambridge, MA: MIT Press).

Goslin, L. and Barge, B. (1986). 'Entrepreneurial qualities considered in venture capital support'. *Frontiers of Entrepreneurship Research*, 7(1): 327–38.

Grant, R. and Baden-Fuller, C. (1995) 'A knowledge-based theory of interfirm collaboration'. *Proceedings of the American Academy of Management Conference*.

Guba, E. G. and Lincon, Y. S. (1994). 'Paradigmatic controversies, contradictions and emerging confluences'. In N. K. Denzin and Y. S. Lincoln (eds), *Handbook of qualitative research*. First edition (Sage Publications).

Hellmann, T. (2000). 'Equity investors: the coaches of Silicon Valley'. In W. Miller, C. M. Lee, H. Gong and H. Rowen H (eds), *The Silicon Valley edge: a habitat for innovation and entrepreneurship* (Stanford, CA: Stanford University Press).

Hellmann, T. and Puri, M. (2000). 'Venture capital and the professionalisation of start-up firms: empirical evidence'. *Journal of Finance*, 41(2): 821–34.

Hitt, M., Hoskisson, R. and Kim, H. (1997). 'International diversification: effects on innovation and firm performance in product diversified firms'. *Academy of Management Journal*, 40(4): 767–98.

Hsu, D. (2000). 'Do venture capitalists affect commercialisation strategies at start ups?' MIT Sloan School of Management, Working Paper 00-009.

Hugo, O. and Garnsey, E. (2005). 'Problem solving and competence creation in new firms'. *Managerial and Decision Economics*, 26(1): 139–48.

Johansson, J. and Vahlne, J.-E. (1977). 'The internationalization process of the firm: a model of knowledge development and increasing foreign market commitment'. *Journal of International Business Studies*, 8(2): 23–32.

Knight, G. A. and Cavusgil, T. (2004). 'Innovation, organizational capabilities, and the born-global firm'. *Journal of International Business Studies*, 35(4): 124–41.

Kolb, H. (1984). *Experience as the source of learning and development* (Englewood Cliffs, NJ: Prentice-Hall).

Lipparini, A. and Sobrero, M. (1994). 'The glue and the pieces: entrepreneurship and innovation in small-firm networks'. *Journal of Business Venturing*, 9(2): 125–40.

Lorenzoni, G. and Lipparini, A. (1999). 'The leveraging of interfirm relationships as distinctive organisational capability: a longitudinal study'. *Strategic Management Journal*, 20(4): 317–38.

Lorenzoni, G. and Ornati, O. (1998). 'Constellations of firms and new ventures'. *Journal of Business Venturing*, 21(3): 41–57.

Lu, J. W. and Beamish, P. W. (2001). 'The internationalization and performance of SMEs'. *Strategic Management Journal*, 22(1): 565–86.

MacMillan, I. C., Kulow, D. M. and Kholian, R. (1989). 'Venture capitalists' involvement in their investments: extent and performance'. *Journal of Business Venturing*, 4(1): 27–47.

MacMillan, I. C., Zemann, L. and Subba Narasimha, P. N. (1987). 'Criteria distinguishing successful from unsuccessful in the venture screening process'. *Journal of Business Venturing*, 2(2): 123–37.

Marshall, C. and Rossman, G. B. (1999). *Designing qualitative research*. Third edition (Sage Publications).

Mason, C. and Harrison, R. (1994). 'The role of informal and formal sources of venture capital in the financing of technology based SMEs in the UK'. In R. Oakey (ed.), *New technology based firms in the 1990s*, pp. 104–24 (London: Chapman).

Maula, M. V. J. and Murray, G. (2000). 'Corporate venture capital and the creation of US public companies: the impact of sources of venture capital on the performance of portfolio companies'. In M. A. Hitt, C. Lucier and R. D. Nixon (eds), *Creating value: winners in the new business environment* (Oxford: Blackwell).

Mitchell, W., Shaver, J. M. and Yeung, B. (1992). 'Getting there in a global industry: impacts on performance of changing international presence'. *Strategic Management Journal*, 19(2): 97–114.

Oviatt, B. M. and McDougall, P. P. (1994). 'Toward a theory of international new ventures'. *Journal of International Business Studies*, 25(1): 45–64.

Penrose, E. T. (1959). *The theory of the growth of the firm* (New York: John Wiley).

Ravasi, D. and Ruta, D. (2006). 'Integrating external contributions in the innovation process of entrepreneurial firms'. *IECER, 4th Conference Proceedings*, Rengensburg.

Robinson, K. C. and McDougall, P. P. (2001). 'Entry barriers and new venture performance: a comparison of universal and contingency approaches'. *Strategic Management Journal*, 22(4): 659–85.

Rosenstein, J. (1988). 'The board and strategy: venture capital and high technology'. *Journal of Business Venturing*, 3(2): 159–70.

Saarenketo, S., Puumalainen, K., Kuivalainen, O. and Kylaheiko, K. (2004). 'Dynamic knowledge-related learning processes in internationalizing high-tech SMEs'. *International Journal of Production Economics*, 89(3): 363–78.

Sapienza, H. J. (1992). 'When do equity investors add value?' *Journal of Business Venturing*, 7(1): 9–27.

Sapienza, H. J., Clercq, D. D. and Sandberg, W. R. (2005). 'Antecedents of international and domestic learning effort'. *Journal of Business Venturing*, 20(4): 437.

Teece, D. J. (1986). 'Profiting from technological innovation: implications for integration, collaboration, licensing and public policy'. *Research Policy*, 15(2): 285–305.

UNCTAD (2006). *World Investment Report 2006* (Geneva: United Nations).

Van den Berghe, L. A. A. and Levrau, A. (2002). 'The role of equity investor as a monitor of the company: a corporate governance perspective'. *Corporate Governance: an International Review*, 10(1): 124–35.

Watson, K., Hogarth-Scott, S. and Wilson, N. (1998). 'Small business start-ups: success factors and support implications'. *International Journal of Entrepreneurial Behavior & Research*, 4(3): 217–38.

Wijbenga, F. H., Postma, T., Van Witteloostuijn, A. and Zwart, P. (2003). 'Strategy and performance of new ventures: a contingency model of the role and influence of the equity investor'. *Venture Capital: an International Journal of Entrepreneurial Finance*, 5(3): 231–50.

Yeoh, P.-L. (2004). 'International learning: antecedents and performance implications amongst newly internationalizing companies in an exporting context'. *International Marketing Review*, 21(4): 511–35.

Yli-Renko, H., Autio, E. and Sapienza, H. J. (2001). 'Social capital, knowledge acquisition and knowledge exploitation in technology-based young firms'. *Strategic Management Journal*, 22: 587–613. Special issue on entrepreneurial strategies and wealth creation in the 21st century.

Yli-Renko, H., Autio, E. and Tontti, V. (2002). 'Social capital, knowledge and the international growth of technology-based new firms'. *International Business Review*, 11(3): 279–304.

Zahra, S. A., Ireland, D. R. and Hitt, M. A. (2000). 'International expansion by new venture firms: international diversity, mode of market entry, technological learning and performance'. *Academy of Management Journal*, 43(5): 925–50.

Zucchella, A. (2001). 'The internationalisation of SMEs: alternative hypotheses and empirical survey'. In J. H. Taggart, M. Berry and M. McDermott (eds), *Multinationals in a new era*, pp. 47–60 (Basingstoke: Palgrave Macmillan).

Zucchella, A., Palamara, G. and Denicolai, S. (2007). 'The drivers of the early internationalisation of the firm'. *Journal of World Business*, 42(2): 268–80.

7
Ownership Concentration and Firm Performance in a Transition Economy: Evidence from Russia

Andrei Kuznetsov, Rostislav Kapelyushnikov and Natalya Dyomina

Introduction

This chapter looks at the impact of ownership structure on the performance of firms in Russia and identifies, within the domain of corporate governance theory, the factors that may explain any revealed differences in such performance and that of their counterparts in other industrialized countries. When market reforms started in Russia, it was anticipated that mass privatization would create 'responsible' owners and, as a result, produce a foundation on which economic reconstruction and growth would flourish. These expectations have on the whole failed to materialize. Restructuring in privatized firms has been slow, fixed production assets show a significant rate of wear, and innovation activity is low as is the competitiveness of domestic goods. Significantly, the inability of new owners to lead the firms forward has been consistently identified by experts as one of the causes of the poor economic performance of Russian companies (Nellis, 1999; Desai and Goldberg, 2000).

It is appropriate to see the emerged ownership structure as a part of the problem. Privatization was intended to create widely dispersed ownership along the lines of the Anglo-American model. In fact, a quite different pattern of ownership and control has established itself: (a) ownership is highly concentrated; (b) dominant (blockholder) owners seek direct control over the firm by assuming managerial and board positions; (c) insiders prevail among the dominant shareholders. Theory makes a number of predictions regarding the performance of companies as a reflection of their ownership structures and the allocation of control. It is argued that concentrated ownership is likely to reduce the classical owner-manager problem, but at the same time to increase the possibility of an agency conflict between controlling shareholders and minority shareholders, in particular when legal protection of outside investors is weak and transparency is low, in other words when firms operate in a weak institutional environment (Fama and Jensen, 1983; Shleifer and Vishny, 1997; Burkhart et al., 2003).

Building on this analysis, we argue in this chapter that contemporary Russia provides a case of a weak institutional environment and set out to evaluate the impact of ownership structure on firm performance in such conditions. Specifically, we seek to appraise quantitatively the performance of blockholder controlled firms in Russia. To preview our findings, we find evidence of a negative association between the size of the dominant owners' shareholding and such performance parameters as profitability, investment and capacity utilization. These results are in contradiction to a substantial body of the literature that has established a positive link between ownership concentration, in particular in the guise of a family firm, and performance. At the same time, in line with Bennedsen and Wolfenzon (2000), we establish that control structures with multiple large shareholders increase efficiency. We believe that our findings reflect the insecurity of dominant shareholders in Russia, where the legal system offers inadequate protection of legitimate owners, even if they hold majority stakes.

The chapter is organized as follows: in the next section we review the literature on corporate governance and ownership relevant to our research question and present some stylized facts on corporate ownership in Russia. The subsequent sections outline data and methodology. The last section summarizes the findings and draws conclusions.

Literature review

There is substantial empirical literature on the impact of blockholder ownership on firm efficiency (Morck et al., 2000; Anderson and Reeb, 2003; Burkhart et al., 2003; Caselli and Gennaioli, 2003; Bartholomeusz and Tanewski, 2006; Villalonga and Amit, 2006). The findings, however, are not conclusive and the spectrum of results is quite wide. Using US data, both Demsetz and Villalonga (2001) and Holderness (2003) revealed no relationship between ownership structure and performance, whilst Anderson and Reeb (2003) were able to identify noticeable gains from concentrated ownership in family-controlled firms. Maury (2006), using a sample of 1,672 non-financial firms from thirteen Western European countries, shows that family control is responsible for 7 per cent higher valuations and 16 per cent higher profitability (return on assets), compared to firms controlled by non-family owners. In contrast, Kirchmaier and Grant (2005) maintain that concentrated ownership is not the form of ownership that is associated with best performing companies, at least for Germany, Spain and France.

Despite the ambiguity of the results from the empirical studies, there seems to be general agreement that the degree to which the interests of blockholder owners are aligned with the interests of minority shareholders, their resolution to maintain control over the firm, the forms in which they seek to extract private benefits of control, and their commitment to the firm would depend on the environment in which they operate, in particular the institutional settings and capital markets. For a long time, the impact of legal arrangements on ownership concentration and corporate governance was prioritized in research (La Porta et al., 1997, 1998, 1999). Recently, however, there has been growing recognition that the legal framework, important as it is, is only one of the manifestations of a more inclusive category, which may be characterized as the institutional context (see Castaneda, 2006, for more details). This approach implies that investors' decisions are shaped by the institutional environment and therefore differ from one economy to another. Institutions are action frameworks (laws, regulations, traditions, routines, customs, etc.) which constitute the procedures and practices that facilitate the resolution of economic conflicts and thus offer a solid and cost-effective foundation for market transactions by providing economic actors with universal and explicit rules that allocate responsibility and set up behavioural boundaries (North, 1990). If the mechanisms of conflict resolution are well evolved, the presence of large shareholders may be beneficial for small shareholders and increase the returns on investment and the value of the firm. In principle, firms with large dominating shareholders may achieve closer monitoring of managers' performance because, on the one hand, the cost of monitoring per share is low compared to small shareholders whilst, on the other hand, they are more likely to associate their own interests with the interests of the firm they control. Also, when blockholders are unable to dilute their holdings, there are strong incentives to 'supervise' in a manner consistent with shareholders' long-term commitments (Burkhart et al., 2003).

A weak institutional context can break this concurrence of interests of small shareholders and blockholders. The advantages that domination gives to blockholders will not be balanced any more by the protection that strong institutions offer to small shareholders, encouraging dominant owners to engage in expropriating behaviour. The ways in which the benefits of control are extracted offer a good example of the link between institutional provisions and owners' behaviour. Such benefits come in two forms (Burkhart et al., 2003; Kirchmaier and Grant, 2005). One has to do with the 'amenity potential' of control and refers to the non-pecuniary private benefits, like the social prestige of running a firm, that do not come at the expense of profits. The other is known as 'tunnelling' and involves using control to extract material benefits through the direct expropriation of outside investors and minority shareholders. This may range from transactions with related parties and transfer prices to outright theft (Johnson et al., 2000), and is possible in a systematic form only if outside investors and minority shareholders do not have adequate legal protection and the rules regarding the transparency and monitoring of business are either feeble or not enforced. In other words, 'tunnelling' thrives in economies besieged with institutional failings.

The literature indicates further that in such economies formal income rights become less important for the allocation of value than control (Shleifer and Vishny, 1997; Modigliani and Perotti, 1997). Furthermore, the market for corporate control becomes less important than internal dealings (Mayer, 1999). A weak institutional context both encourages dominant owners to internalize moral hazard, and offers prospects to insulate them from disciplinary sanctions. This is best achieved if dominant shareholders either occupy managerial and board positions themselves or entrust these positions to close associates. At the same time, by internalizing moral hazard, tightly held firms may get a relative performance advantage in economies in which the limitations of institutional settings make it difficult to arrange transactions on the basis of 'generalized trust' rather than 'particularized trust', to use the terms pioneered by Yamigichi and Yamigichi (1994). Institutions create the environment in which participants in a transaction have reasonable trust in most people, rather than only the people they know personally. This reduces transaction costs in as much as confidence in the ability of institutions to enforce contracts and enforce property rights makes unnecessary the cost of building specific relationships of trust between individual members of the society, organizations and firms (Uzzi, 1997). If, however, institutions perform poorly, then 'particularized trust' grows in importance at the expense of 'generalized trust'.

One implication particularly relevant to transition economies is that a lack of 'generalized trust' pushes most control transactions outside the official exchanges (Berglöf and von Thadden, 1999). This effect is multiplied by the fact that capital markets in such economies are relatively undeveloped. They are small in size, have liquidity problems, and do not offer a great variety of investment opportunities. These constraints severely limit the strategic options available to blockholders, especially their motives and ability to disinvest (Bhattacharya and Ravikumar, 2001; Caselli and Gennaioli, 2003). First, undeveloped markets make it problematic and costly to pull large investments out of the firm and diversify a portfolio. Second, the owner may find it difficult to sell stock if he wants to transfer some of his wealth from shares into cash, so may maintain the stock and use his position of control to transfer company assets into cash through 'tunnelling'.

In institutionally weak economies, the interests of large owners and small owners are likely to be disentangled. A lack of generalized trust and ineffective provisions for conflict resolution will stimulate blockholders to impose tight control over the firm, and become directly involved in management in order to create the conditions for realizing the benefits of control (entrenchment). They may not be particularly concerned with the market value of the firm because of the inefficiency of capital markets. Instead they may choose straightforward asset expropriation. This analysis gives some pointers regarding the likely behavioural pattern of blockholders in economies like Russia, but falls short of answering the question whether or not blockholders would be interested in improving firm performance. In principle, their choice would depend on the strength of commitment that they hold towards their investment. It is not inevitable that institutional inefficiencies should necessarily undermine that commitment. There is a body of literature that points out that supposedly inefficient ownership structures can in fact be efficient in the context of their specific institutional environment (Bebchuk and Roe, 1999; Roe, 2002; Stulz, 2005). Ineffective market mechanisms are likely to be detrimental to the welfare of market-trading shareholders and their willingness to provide financing, but blockholders may be nonetheless sufficiently interested in keeping and increasing their private benefits to become concerned with the long-term growth of the firm. In fact, research points out that inadequate institutions and failures in financial markets contribute to ownership concentration and the longevity of certain forms of tightly held firms such as family firms (Castaneda, 2006; Thomsen et al., 2006). In particular, the recent literature on blockholding shows that a more equal distribution of votes among large blockholders has a positive effect on firm value (Lehman and Weigand, 2000; Maury and Pajuste, 2005). Faccio et al. (2001) show that the presence of multiple large shareholders reduces expropriation in Europe (due to monitoring), but exacerbates it in Asia (due to collusion).

There is a sizeable body of literature scrutinizing the conceptual aspects of corporate governance in Russia (Aukutsionek et al., 1998; Berglöf and von Thadden, 1999; Black, 2001; Brown, 1998; Fox and Heller, 1999; Franklin, 2005; Krivogorsky, 2000; Kuznetsov and Kuznetsova, 2003; Muravyev, 2003; Perotti and Gelfer, 2001), but empirical evidence is conspicuously scarce. In this chapter, our aim is to evaluate the effects of ownership concentration on firms' performance in Russia. Specifically we will seek to corroborate two main hypotheses suggested by our literature review:

Hypothesis 1: In transition economies, the larger the shareholding held by the largest shareholder, the poorer will be firm performance.

Hypothesis 2: In transition economies, the larger the shareholding held by the second largest shareholder, the better will be firm performance.

The business environment in Russia

Russia provides a vivid example of a business environment which makes control more important than formal income rights, because of the weak legal protection of shareholders, underdeveloped capital markets, and the restricted role of institutional investors (Vasilyev, 1999). Throughout the immediate post-privatization period, shares did not bring any real benefits to most shareholders as they had low liquidity and dividends were not paid. In addition, corporatization coincided with a period of a profound economic crisis in the country, which had as its most notable manifestations demonetization and barterization of the economy. Both circumstances had a long-lasting impact on corporate governance and set preconditions for blockholder ownership. First, it diluted the strength of monetary signals and incentives, and hampered the informational content of prices, making it difficult for both shareholders and investors to determine the value of shares or identify the investment potential of individual firms. Open market competition for financial resources was unfeasible and the investment markets were extremely depressed. Second, these circumstances provided incentives to substitute networking and other informal arrangements for the market. Managers had to rely on successful networking, as they sought to compensate the poor performance of formal institutions with arrangements based on personal contacts. The role of networks was controversial. On the one hand, the informal relations created zones of trust within the general environment of distrust, thus reducing transaction costs. On the other hand, in the context of the economic crises and weak institutional arrangements, networking often pursued the goal of conspiring against outsiders and avoiding legal control over financial and other transactions, rather than obtaining better knowledge of business partners and their needs (Radaev, 1998).

Corporate ownership in Russia has been influenced by the bias in the allocation of shares built into the privatization programme: originally the majority of equity (51 per cent) was distributed among workers and managers of privatized enterprises. According to the Russian Economic Barometer (REB) data, insiders remained the largest shareholder group, controlling 47 per cent of all outstanding shares as late as 2003. However, this does not mean that the configuration of shareholding had remained unaltered during this period: ownership has shifted from workers to managers; from insiders to outsiders; from the state to private owners. Managers have come out as the biggest winners. Their equity stake has increased from less than 10 per cent in 1994 to over 30 per cent at present. REB statistics demonstrate that, by 2003, managers had accumulated more shares on average in industrial firms than the rest of employees together and, by 2007, they are expected to control 40 per cent of all shares against 14 per cent held by workers. Even these impressive figures, however, are believed to underestimate the degree of concentration of ownership in the hands of managers. The secretive nature of the Russian corporate world makes it very difficult to quantify the structure of ownership. According to expert evaluation, senior management is in control of no less than 50 per cent of firms because many shareholder-outsiders are just a façade for managers (Dolgopyatova, 2001; Sizov, 2004). The proportion of firms that have their senior manager as the largest shareholder increased from 24 per cent in 1999, to 39 per cent in 2005. It is also typical that the stake of the largest shareholder tends to grow (currently it is close to 50 per cent of the average authorized capital). As far as outsiders are concerned, an important feature of the modern ownership structure, from the point of view of corporate governance, is that the shareholders are mostly industrial firms and individuals. The share of banks, financial companies, investment funds, etc. remains stable and low at about 10 per cent.

A considerable volume of shares has been transferred between the people who received their shares as members of working collectives during mass privatization, and those who bought or received their shares from the original owners at a later stage. Some of the latter have managed to consolidate their acquisitions into blocks that allowed them to dislodge the old 'red director' and step into his place. According to our estimates, among those firms controlled by top managers in 2005, 44 per cent were controlled by their former 'red directors' whilst 56 per cent were controlled by the teams who arrived after privatization. The relative proportions were 36 per cent and 64 per cent among firms in which the CEO was the largest shareholder.

In most countries of the world, companies with concentrated ownership grew and developed as family firms, often from entrepreneurial origins. In Russia, in which private ownership of industrial assets has its origins in mass voucher privatization, medium and large firms neither originated with some innovative ideas of the founder-owners, nor could they become a family affair. Nonetheless, the majority of them are tightly held firms: shares are usually concentrated in the hands of a few (e.g. 2–7) individuals tied with informal links and common background. Indeed, the owners of such firms usually go back a long time together. Often they knew each other professionally before the market reforms started, they took their first steps as businessmen together, and they now own comparable stakes in the firm. This model of ownership may be found in the most successful Russian companies. It also facilitates an important feature of the Russian corporate scene, namely the deliberate complexity of ownership rights with the aim to conceal the true identity of owners. Often this is a reaction to the poor protection that the legal system offers to legitimate owners. The non-transparency of property rights is artificially maintained by the owners of many companies as a barrier against possible interference of the state or capture by market raiders (Pappe, 2002).

Data and methodology

This section contains details of the survey data used for the empirical analysis, the dependent and explanatory variables used in the regression models, and the estimation techniques and tests performed.

The sample data

The data are generated by regular microeconomic surveys organized by the Russian Economic Barometer (REB), an independent research centre located in Moscow. REB is probably the only regular source of survey data on the evolution of ownership in Russia. REB's respondents are executive managers of 700 industrial enterprises in almost all regions of Russia. The usual response rate is close to 30 per cent. The REB sample is reasonably representative of the

Table 7.1:   Distribution of enterprises in the REB surveys by industry (%)

Industries	1995 REB	1997 REB	1999 REB	2001 REB	2003 REB	1999 Goskomstat*
Power	4	2	1	1	–	1
Fuels	6	2	3	2	1	1
Metals	4	2	6	6	4	2
Machinery	29	28	29	26	25	36
Chemicals	3	5	7	6	3	4
Woodworking, pulp-and-paper	7	8	14	12	13	13
Construction materials	13	17	12	11	12	6
Light industry	12	13	12	21	17	12
Food	17	20	15	15	21	14
Other industries	5	3	1	1	2	10

Note: * Goskomstat – the official data of the State Statistics Committee of the Russian Federation.

Table 7.2:   Distribution of employees in the REB surveys by industry (%)

Industries	1995 REB	1997 REB	1999 REB	2001 REB	2003 REB	1999 Goskomstat*
Power	7	3	1	>0	0	7
Fuels	12	2	3	1	1	6
Metals	8	4	3	11	14	9
Machinery	27	36	37	31	43	36
Chemicals	6	7	21	16	6	6
Woodworking, pulp-and-paper	3	5	13	16	12	8
Construction materials	9	17	7	4	7	5
Light industry	13	8	7	12	6	7
Food	11	10	6	8	8	11
Other industries	3	18	1	2	3	6

Note: * Goskomstat – the official data of the State Statistics Committee of the Russian Federation.

whole population of Russian medium- and large-size industrial enterprises (see Tables 7.1 and 7.2) in terms of firm size, sector affiliation and methods of privatization. Every two years since 1995, REB has conducted specialized surveys dedicated to the issues of ownership and corporate governance, effectively covering the period from the completion of mass privatization till the present. From 1997, the bi-annual survey has contained a question on the largest shareholder and, from 2003, a question on the second largest shareholder. We were thus able to construct an unbalanced panel covering three years (1999, 2001, 2003) to test hypothesis 1 about the impact of the largest shareholder. But we could only use a cross-section to test hypothesis 2 about the impact of the second largest shareholder. Finally, it should be noted that the numbers of observations are not the same for every regression for two reasons: (a) not all variables were included in all three surveys, and (b) certain respondents chose to ignore some of the variables included in the survey whilst providing information on other variables.

The dependent variables

Many studies investigating the links between performance and ownership focus on net profit, average accounting profit rate, stock market returns, and cash flow as measurements of performance. This approach relies on the use of various accounting ratios, as 'performance' is calculated on the basis of the income generated by the firm and available for distribution among the various claimants to the firm (Clark and Wójcik, 2005). As far as transition economies are concerned, experts question the reliability of traditional performance measures (Hoskisson et al., 2000). In the Russian context we have found it more appropriate to replace accounting ratios with other parameters: first, because only about 10 per cent of Russian firms use GAAP/IAS rules in accounting (Guriev et al., 2003: 16) and second, because traditional accounting measures tend to be either unavailable or unreliable in Russia as a result of chronic income underreporting, payments in kind and barter transactions. Furthermore, many companies in the REB sample are not listed, and so the use of stock market performance indicators such as ROE (return on equity) or Tobin's Q is not feasible. Instead, we have chosen six alternative measures of performance:

- Capital investment in equipment or technology as a share of total capital stock in the previous year (INV). This is an important synthetic indicator of restructuring behaviour within the firm (Sim, 2001).
- The percentage of investment financed from external sources (EXT). One specific feature of Russian banking is that local banks are notoriously reluctant to invest in industrial projects. Consequently we interpret a greater share of external finance as some sort of acknowledgement by creditors of the growth record/potential of the firm.
- An index of productive capacity (CAP), which reflects changes in productive capacity and thus reflects aggregate performance.
- The profit margin (PM), a measure commonly used in the literature (Filatotchev et al., 2001) but reported by only a few firms in the sample.
- A binary variable (PROFIT), which equals 1 if the firm declared profits in the previous year, and 0 otherwise (Filatotchev et al., 2001).
- The capacity utilization rate (UR), defined as the share of actual production compared to perceived maximum production.

We felt it necessary to use multiple parameters because of the acknowledged problems in applying any single measures to processes in transition

Table 7.3: Descriptive statistics and pairwise correlation coefficients for the six dependent variables

	Mean	Std	UR	PM	INV	EXT	CAP	PROFIT
UR	62.81	29.05	1.0					
PM	3.25	9.72	0.23	1.0				
INV	44.47	48.79	0.28	0.18	1.0			
EXT	17.57	31.34	0.18	−0.08	0.13	1.0		
CAP	97.12	12.48	0.33	0.17	0.38	0.11	1.0	
PROFIT	0.59	–	0.19	0.38	0.24	−0.11	0.17	1.0

economies (Buck et al., 2003). Descriptive statistics and pairwise correlation coefficients for the dependent variables can be found in Table 7.3.

Explanatory variables and controls

We measure ownership concentration as the percentage of shares held by the largest shareholder (CON1). Following this definition, every firm in our sample has a largest shareholder because we do not assign a minimum value to CON1: if the largest shareholder owns just 1 per cent of shares, CON1 takes the value of 0.01. We further make a distinction between different categories of blockholders. REB data include eleven different categories of owners. We have grouped them into four categories: 'insiders' (INS): employees, managers and firms owned by managers; 'non-financial outsiders' (NONFIN): individuals and firms not affiliated with the company they own; 'financial outsiders' (FIN): banks, investment funds, holding companies and foreign investors; and 'the state' (STATE). In the regression analyses, the NONFIN category was taken as the reference group.

To deal with the possibility that a variety of factors can jointly affect performance and ownership variables and thus induce spurious correlations, we introduced a number of control variables. Firm-size factors are widely acknowledged as driving the performance of the firms (Boubakri et al., 2005; Wincent, 2005). We therefore introduce the control variable SIZE, measured by the total number of employees in the firm. A number of authors suggest that managerial opportunism and entrenchment may be associated with the firm maturity and age (Morck et al., 1988). Accordingly, we establish a control variable AGE, measured as the number of years since the firm was founded. We use industry dummies to control for industry effects (the reference category was 'other industries'), and dummies for the calendar years when the surveys were conducted. Finally some enterprises may be more seriously affected by the break-up of the centrally planned economy and disintegration of the former system of production and distribution than others. To control for this systemic factor, we introduced a control variable ORDER, that measures the number of orders the firm received in a particular year as a percentage of the previous year.

Methodology

We applied several estimation techniques that were robust to different descriptions of the error structure. In addition to OLS (or logit regressions for models with binary dependent variables), we used random and fixed effects estimation techniques, which allowed us to control for unobserved individual (firm-specific) effects. We employed the Hausman test to establish which of the fixed or random effects specifications was preferable. We tried various specifications of piecewise and polynomial regressions to account for a possible non-linear relationship between firm performance and ownership structure (Morck et al., 1988). However, these non-linear specifications did not improve the explanatory power of the models, so only the results for the linear specifications are reported below.

Econometric analysis

The results of the panel regressions to test hypothesis 1 are presented in Table 7.4; only four of the dependent variables (i.e. INV, UR, PM and PROFIT) are used. The Hausman test showed that the random effects specification was the best for the continuous dependent variables so only these results are reported.[1] Binomial logit analysis was used when PROFIT was the dependent variable.

We focus first on performance as measured by capital investment in equipment or technology (INV). The analysis demonstrates that ownership concentration is negatively and very significantly ($p < 0.01$) associated with INV. But the variables related to the identity of the blockholders (i.e. INS, FIN, and STATE) were all insignificant. In terms of the control variables, the regression coefficient for SIZE is positive and significant. This is a sign that large firms have better investment capabilities. The firm's AGE has proved to be insignificant, suggesting that investment activity in new firms is not higher than in old ones. However, there is a strong and significant ($p < 0.01$) positive relationship between investment and the level of orders. This is expected, as the level of orders may be considered as a proxy for the firm's competitive position and financial health in general. Most of the industry dummies are, surprisingly, insignificant. This pattern of relationships between the investment and control variables is generally consistent with results reported elsewhere (see, for example, Filatotchev et al., 2001).

Table 7.4 further reports the relationship between ownership concentration and three of the other performance proxies (UR, PM, PROFIT) – the results using the percentage of investment financed by external sources (EXT) and productive capacity (CAP) are not included. The regression coefficients for the largest single shareholding are negative and significant for all three performance proxies, and are also negative but insignificant for EXT and CAP. This consistency suggests that, other things being equal, the larger the block of shares held by the largest owner the less the capacity utilization, the

Table 7.4: The effect of ownership concentration on firm performance in Russia, 1999–2003

Explanatory variables	Dependent variables			
	INV	UR	PM	PROFIT
Ownership variables				
CON1	−0.52***	−0.20***	−0.18***	−0.03**
	(0.18)	(0.08)	(0.07)	(0.01)
INS	−0.47	−7.70**	−0.22	0.51
	(9.40)	(3.81)	(3.14)	(0.62)
FIN	−0.49	0.73	0.86	−0.36
	(12.25)	(4.87)	(7.17)	(0.86)
STATE	5.86	1.29	1.95	−0.01
	(14.65)	(6.45)	(7.22)	(0.75)
Control variables				
SIZE	8.38*	2.17	0.51	0.23
	(4.51)	(2.31)	(3.18)	(0.32)
AGE	0.09	−0.10	0.00	0.25
	(0.13)	(0.07)	(0.11)	(0.40)
ORDER	0.37***	0.52***	0.15*	0.03**
	(0.14)	(0.06)	(0.08)	(0.01)
2001	10.31	2.57		0.24
	(8.45)	(2.32)		(0.53)
2003	10.22	3.29	−0.83	−0.41
	(9.83)	(3.54)	(2.31)	(0.62)
Industry dummies	yes	yes	yes	yes
Constant	−196.87	217.15*	−10.73	−1.21
	(249.20)	(131.61)	(268.25)	(17.28)
Number of observations	155	169	54	163
Number of firms	63	71	27	69
Hausman statistic	4.2	27.2***	5.5	
R^2 (pseudo for logit)	0.24	0.46	0.13	0.17

Notes: Random effects panel estimation.
The figures in brackets are the standard errors of the regression coefficients.
*** indicates significance at 1% level; ** indicates significance at 5% level; and * indicates significance at 10% level.

smaller the profit margin and the higher the probability of loss-making. These results are also robust to alternative regression specifications.[2] The regression coefficients for the identity variables are insignificant for almost all performance proxies. Only in the regression with capacity utilization (UR) as the dependent variable does the coefficient for insider ownership (INS) become significant ($p \leq 0.05$) and have a negative sign. This result implies that enterprises in which the largest block of shares belongs to insiders (virtually to managers) tend to have greater spare capacity. SIZE is significant only in the model with fixed effects for capacity utilization while the firm's AGE remains

Table 7.5: The effect of ownership concentration on firm performance in Russia, 2003

Explanatory variables	Dependent variables					
	INV	UR	PM	PROFIT	EXT	CAP
Ownership variables						
CON1	−0.36*	−0.27**	−0.01	−0.026*	−0.45*	−0.11*
	(0.19)	(0.12)	(0.06)	(0.014)	(0.26)	(0.06)
CON2	1.11	0.52*	0.10	0.008	1.08*	0.33**
	(0.80)	(0.32)	(0.12)	(0.03)	(0.61)	(0.16)
Control variables						
SIZE	6.63	−0.16	1.24	0.353	9.08**	−0.05
	(4.16)	(2.67)	(0.80)	(0.26)	(1.25)	(1.25)
AGE	0.15	−0.27*	0.03	0.008	−0.18	−0.10*
	(0.22)	(0.14)	(0.04)	(0.06)	(0.29)	(0.06)
ORDER	4.48	0.45***	−0.02	0.016	0.19	0.09**
	(9.33)	(0.11)	(0.04)	(0.01)	(0.24)	(0.04)
Industry dummies	yes	yes	yes	yes	yes	yes
Constant	−303.87	563.58**	−60.11	−16.08	338.35	294.65
	(460.41)	(267.10)	(92.48)	(27.72)	(563.92)	(126.46)
Number of observations	65	66	58	66	46	63
R^2 (pseudo for logit)	0.22	0.40	0.08	0.19	0.35	0.25

Notes: Cross-section estimation.
The figures in brackets are the standard errors of the regression coefficients.
*** indicates significance at 1% level; ** indicates significance at 5% level; and * indicates significance at 10% level.

insignificant in all tests. The level of orders is strongly and positively associated with performance, indicating that firms that managed to preserve their traditional trade relationships are generally performing better. And again we have found that in most cases random effects estimators are preferable to fixed effects ones.

As the literature suggests that control structures with multiple large shareholders may act differently compared with firms with just one large owner (Bennedsen and Wolfenzon, 2000), we ran an additional series of regressions employing the independent variable (CON2) which measures the percentage of shares held by the second largest shareholder. We had to use cross-section regressions because only the 2003 survey contained a question on the second largest block of shares. The results of this exercise are provided in Table 7.5, which reports the results for all six dependent variables including the proportion of investment financed from external sources (EXT) and the index of capacity utilization (CAP). The table shows that the regression coefficients for the largest single shareholding (CON1) in most specifications are significant and have a negative sign, and that the regression coefficients for the second largest single shareholding (CON2) are significant but have a positive sign! It thus appears that the first and the second largest stakes exert opposite and statistically significant impacts on performance. In other words, sizeable stakes held by the second largest shareholders appear to encourage investments, create better opportunities for external financing, stimulate expansion of existing capacities, raise capacity utilization and provide positive effects on profitability (the coefficients for the second largest block of shares are positive but insignificant in the regressions with both PM and PROFIT as the dependent variable). We omit the discussion of effects of control variables, which are similar to the results obtained from the panel data.

Having established a statistical association between multiple ownership and performance, we are nonetheless unable to maintain with certainty that the former is the cause of the latter on the basis of the data available to us. It might be hypothesized that successful firms are more attractive to investors and therefore they are more likely to be controlled by a group of large shareholders. Yet we are inclined to think that, in Russia at least, it is multiple ownership that drives performance for the simple reason that equity issuance is used only very rarely as a means to raise new capital. Consequently, the premise that efficient firms are more likely to become owned by a group of significant owners lacks credibility.

Discussion

This chapter analyses the effects of ownership concentration on the performance of firms in Russia. In our opinion, our findings are relevant not only for Russian privatized firms but for corporations with concentrated shareholdings operating in economies with a weak institutional environment in general. In this respect they have implication for potential foreign investors considering doing business in transition, emerging and developing economies.

Our results may be summarized in two broad conclusions. First, our study establishes that there may be a negative impact of ownership concentration on firm performance. In doing so, our results conform with the theoretical model by Castaneda (2006) which suggests that when minority shareholders are not well-protected, markets are not very liquid, share prices do not convey the information needed to improve efficiency in allocation, and legal and political institutions that protect the rights of all stakeholders are weak, ownership concentration will result in controlling owners choosing low-risk, low-productive projects if they feel that their position is threatened. A similar view is expressed by Desai and Goldberg (2000), who argue that the problem of corporate governance in countries like Russia is not limited to protecting minority shareholders or other financiers. Rather it is the problem of insufficient incentives for owner-managers to restructure the firms and maximize their value over the long run. Desai and Goldberg (2000) relate this to two aspects of Russian reality. On the one hand, firm performance reflects the insecurity of dominant shareholders as they feel threatened by the general instability and uncertainty regarding property rights, inheritance rights, contract law, judicial protection, personal safety, etc.[3] On the other hand, the underdeveloped state of the Russian capital markets makes it difficult for owners to realize value accumulated in shares. In fact, Pappe (2005) maintains that the only legal way of doing this is by trading the shares of Russian firms on international stock markets. This, of course, is not possible for the majority of Russian companies. As a consequence of these constraints, controlling owners are more likely to be engaged in 'tunnelling' and asset stripping rather than increasing the long-term value of the firm.

The second broad conclusion is that, in a certain institutional environment, a coalition of several significant owners might have a favourable impact on the performance of the firm. We have obtained positive empirical evidence that coalitions can provide a governance mechanism that would minimize combined costs associated with both managerial and majority shareholder opportunism. Our results find support in the literature. Bennedsen and Wolfenzon (2000) argue that a coalition of owners internalizes the costs of its actions, resulting in less extraction of costly private benefits. Similarly, Brunello et al. (2003) obtain results that multiple non-CEO controlling shareholders are a governance mechanism that provides a substitute for outside members on boards of directors in lowering agency costs. Our own interpretation of our empirical findings is similar. In Russia it is very difficult for shareholders excluded from the narrow circle of owners who actually run the firm to exert any influence. However, the members of such a circle are likely to be in a position to organize effective monitoring and control both over the firm's managers and over each other. A more balanced configuration of property rights might contribute to the maximization of corporate wealth. Unfortunately, our current knowledge of coalitions between significant shareholders in Russian firms (their formation, stability and roles allocation within the coalition) is still very limited. Further research is needed to provide informed advice to both Russian policy-makers and foreign investors willing to invest in the Russian corporate sector.

In this chapter, we have identified two tendencies in the Russian corporate sector. Both are related to the same underlying cause. The poor state of the institutional framework puts a pressure on large shareholders to keep increasing their stake. As a result their control over the firm increases. However, the same institutional inadequacies make this category of shareholders feel insecure about the future of their investment. This undermines their commitment to the firm they own/control, and encourages them to 'tunnel' wealth out of companies. Evidently, these are the signs of an unhealthy situation that endangers the long-term restructuring and growth of the Russian economy.

Notes

1. The OLS and fixed effects regressions produced similar results: these are available from the authors.
2. The regressions using these alternative specifications are also available from the authors.
3. The Russian legal system offers inadequate protection to legitimate owners, even if they hold majority stakes. In the West, hostile takeovers are feasible when shares of the target company are widely available and easily purchased. In Russia, hostile takeovers rely on the abuse of the rights of shareholders and the exploitation of legalistic hitches and corruption in the judicial system. One of the common tricks is to obtain a judicial decision that bans the current owners of the firm from using their right to vote in the shareholders general meeting, or to take a position on the board of directors. Another ploy is to make the court requisite the registry of shareholders, the only legal proof of ownership, and then replace it with an alternative registry with a different composition of shareholders (Sizov, 2004). One notorious incident involved Krasnoyarsk Aluminium, which deleted from its share register a 20 per cent stake held by the British Trans World Group, effectively wiping out its holding (Mileusnic, 1996).

Bibliography

Anderson, R. C. and Reeb, D. M. (2003). 'Founding-family ownership and firm performance: evidence from the S&P 500'. *Journal of Finance*, 58(3): 1301–28.

Aukutsionek, S., Filatochev, I., Kapelyushnikov, R. and Zhukov, V. (1998) 'Dominant shareholders, restructuring, and performance of privatized companies in Russia: an analysis and some policy implications'. *Communist Economies and Economic Transformation*, 10(4): 495–517.

Bartholomeusz, S. and Tanewski, G. A. (2006). 'The relationship between family firms and corporate governance'. *Journal of Small Business Management*, 44(2): 245–67.

Bebchuk, L. A. and Roe, M. J. (1999). 'A theory of path dependence in corporate ownership and governance'. *Stanford Law Review*, 52(1): 127–70.

Bennedsen, M. and Wolfenzon, D. (2000) 'The balance of power in closely held corporations'. *Journal of Financial Economics*, 58(1–2): 113–39.

Berglöf, E. and von Thadden, E.-L. (1999). 'The changing corporate governance paradigm: implications for transition and developing countries'. University of Michigan, William Davidson Institute, Working Paper no. 263.

Bhattacharya, U. and Ravikumar, B. (2001). 'Capital markets and the evolution of family businesses'. *Journal of Business*, 74(2): 187–220.

Black, B. (2001). 'Does corporate governance matter? A crude test using Russian data'. *University of Pennsylvania Law Review*, 149: 2131–50.

Boubakri, N., Cosset, J.-C. and Guedhami, O. (2005). 'Postprivatization corporate governance: the role of ownership structure and investor protection'. *Journal of Financial Economics*, 76(2): 369–99.

Brown, A. N. (1998). 'Worker share ownership and the market for corporate control in Russia'. Stockholm Institute of Transition Economics and Centre for Economic Policy Research, Working Paper no. 133.

Brunello, G., Graziano, C. and Parigi, B. M. (2003). 'CEO turnover in insider-dominated boards: the Italian case'. *Journal of Banking & Finance*, 27(6): 1027–51.

Buck, T., Filatotchev, I., Demina, N. and Wright, M. (2003). 'Insider ownership, human resource strategies and performance in a transition economy'. *Journal of International Business Studies*, 34(6): 530–49.

Burkhart, M., Panunzi, F. and Shleifer, A. (2003) 'Family firms'. *Journal of Finance*, 58(5): 2167–202.

Caselli, F. and Gennaioli, N. (2003) 'Dynastic management'. CEPR Discussion Paper no. 3767.

Castaneda, G. (2006). 'Economic growth and concentrated ownership in stock markets'. *Journal of Economic Behaviour & Organization*, 59(2): 249–86.

Clark, G. L. and Wójcik, D. (2005). 'Financial valuation of the German model: the negative relationship between ownership concentration and stock market returns'. *Economic Geography*, 81(1): 11–29.

Demsetz, H. and Villalonga, B. (2001). 'Ownership structure and corporate performance'. *Journal of Corporate Finance*, 7(3): 209–33.

Desai, R. and Goldberg, I. (2000). 'Stakeholders, governance, and the Russian enterprise dilemma'. *Finance & Development*, 37(2): 14–18.

Dolgopyatova, T. (2001). 'Modeli korporativnogo kontroliya na rossiiskikh predpriyatiach'. *Mir Rossii*, 10(3): 12–24.

Faccio, M., Lang, L. and Young, L. (2001). 'Dividends and expropriation'. *American Economic Review*, 91(1): 54–78.

Fama, E. and Jensen, M. C. (1983). 'Separation of ownership and control'. *Journal of Law and Economics*, 26(2): 301–25.

Filatotchev, I., Kapelyushnikov, R., Dyomina, N. and Aukutsionek, S. (2001). 'The effects of ownership concentration on investment and performance in privatized firms in Russia'. *Managerial and Decision Economics*, 22(6): 299–313.

Fox, M. B. and Heller, M. A. (1999). 'Lessons from fiascos in Russian corporate governance'. University of Michigan Law School, Working Paper 99-012.

Franklin, A. (2005). 'Corporate governance in emerging economies'. *Oxford Review of Economic Policy*, 21(2): 164–77.

Guriev, S., Lazareva, O., Rachisnky, A. and Tsukhlo, S. (2003). 'Corporate governance in Russian industry'. CEFIR Working Paper, Moscow.

Holderness, C. G. (2003). 'A survey of block-holders and corporate control'. *Economic Policy* Review, 9(1): 51–63.

Hoskisson, R. E., Eden, L., Lau, C. M. and Wright, M. (2000). 'Strategy in emerging markets'. *Academy of Management Journal*, 43(3): 249–67.

Johnson, S., La Porta, R., Lopez-de-Silanes, F. and Shleifer, A. (2000). 'Tunnelling'. *American Economic Review Papers and Proceedings*, 90(2): 22–7.

Kirchmaier, T. and Grant, J. (2005). 'Corporate ownership structure and performance in Europe'. *European Management Review*, 2(3): 231–45.

Krivogorsky, V. (2000). 'Corporate ownership and governance in Russia'. *International Journal of Accounting*, 35(3): 331–53.

Kuznetsov, A. and Kuznetsova, O. (2003). 'Corporate governance: does the concept work in transition countries?' *Journal for East European Management Studies*, 8(3): 244–62.

La Porta, R., Lopez-de-Silanes, F., Shleifer, A. and Vishny, R. (1997). 'Legal determinants of external finance'. *Journal of Finance*, 52(3): 1131–50.

La Porta, R., Lopez-de-Silanes, F., Shleifer, A. and Vishny, R. (1998). 'Law and finance'. *Journal of Political Economy*, 106(6): 1113–55.

La Porta, R., Lopez-de-Silanes, F. and Shleifer, A. (1999). 'Corporate ownership around the world'. *Journal of Finance*, 54(2): 471–517.

Lehman, E. and Weigand, J. (2000). 'Does the governed corporation perform better? Governance structures and corporate performance in Germany'. *European Finance Review*, 4(2): 157–95.

Maury, B. (2006). 'Family ownership and firm performance: empirical evidence from Western European corporations'. *Journal of Corporate Finance*, 12(2): 321–41.

Maury, B. and Pajuste, A. (2005). 'Multiple large shareholders and firm value'. *Journal of Banking & Finance*, 29(7): 1813–34.

Mayer, C. (1999). 'Corporate governance, competition and performance'. OECD, Economic Department Working Paper no. 164 (Paris: OECD).

Mileusnic, N. (1996). 'The great boardroom revolution'. *Moscow Times* (16 July).

Modigliani, F. and Perotti, E. (1997). 'Protection of minority interest and the development of security markets'. *Managerial and Decision Economics*, 18(7–8): 519–28.

Morck, R., Shleifer, A. and Vishny, R. (1988). 'Management ownership and market valuation: an empirical analysis'. *Journal of Financial Economics*, 20(3): 293–316.

Morck, R. K., Stangeland, D. A. and Yeung, B. (2000). 'Inherited wealth, corporate control, and economic growth: the Canadian disease?' In R. K. Morck (ed.), *Concentrated Corporate Ownership*, pp. 319–69 (Chicago: University of Chicago Press).

Muravyev, A. (2003). 'Turnover of senior managers in Russian privatized firms'. *Comparative Economic Studies*, 45(2): 148–72.

Nellis, J. (1999). 'Time to rethink privatization in transition economies?' International Finance Corporation, Discussion Paper no. 38 (Washington, D.C.: World Bank).

North, D. C. (1990). *Institutions, institutional change and economic performance* (Cambridge: Cambridge University Press).

Pappe, Y. (2005). 'Rossiiskii krupnyi biznes kak ekonomicheskii fenomen: spetsificheskie cherty modeli ego organizatsii'. *Problemy prognozirovaniya*, 2: 83–97.

Perotti, E. C. and Gelfer, S. (2001). 'Red barons or robber barons? Governance and investment in Russian financial-industrial groups'. *European Economic Review*, 45(9): 1601–17.

Radaev, V. (1998). *Formirovanie novykh rossiiskikh rynkov: transaktsionnyje izderzhki, formy kontrolia i delovaia etika* (Moscow, CIPE/Tsentr politicheskikh tekhnologij).

Roe, M. J. (2002). 'Can culture ever constrain the economic model of corporate law?' Harvard Law School, Research Paper no. 36.

Sim, K. L. (2001). 'An empirical examination of successive incremental improvement techniques and investment in manufacturing technology'. *International Journal of Operations & Production Management*, 21(3): 373–99.

Sizov Y. (2004). 'Novyi vitok korporativnykh konfliktov. *Aktsionernoe obshestvo: voprosy korporativnogo upravleniia*'. Available at http://www.sovetnik.orc.ru/texts/sizov.htm

Shleifer, A. and Vishny, R. (1997). 'A survey of corporate governance'. *Journal of Finance*, 52(2): 737–83.

Stulz, R. (2005). 'The limits of financial globalization'. *Journal of Finance*, 60(4): 1595–638.

Thomsen, S., Pedersen, T. and Kvist, H. K. (2006). 'Block-holder ownership: effects on firm value in market and control based governance systems'. *Journal of Corporate Finance*, 12(2): 246–69.

Uzzi, B. (1997). 'Social structure and competition in interfirm networks: the paradox of embeddedness'. *Administration Science Quarterly*, 42: 35–67.

Vasilyev, D. (1999). 'Corporate governance in Russia: are there any chances of improvement?' Paper presented at the OECD Conference on Corporate Governance, Moscow, June.

Villalonga, B. and Amit, R. (2006). 'How do family ownership, control and management affect firm value?' *Journal of Financial Economics*, 80(2): 385–417.

Wincent, J. (2005). 'Does size matter? A study of firm behaviour and outcomes in strategic SME networks'. *Journal of Small Business and Enterprise Development*, 12(3): 437–53.

Yamigichi, T. and Yamigichi, M. (1994). 'Trust and commitment in the United States and Japan'. *Motivation and Emotion*, 18(2): 129–66.

8
Exploring the Impact of Ownership Structure and CEO Compensation Arrangements on Controlling Shareholders' Tunnelling Behaviour

Zhonghua Wu

Introduction

In recent years, corporate stakeholders and academic scholars have expressed increased concern about the expropriation of minority shareholders by controlling shareholders (La Porta et al., 1999). Johnson et al. (2000) define the term 'tunnelling' as the transfer of assets and profits out of firms for the benefit of their controlling shareholders. Tunnelling can take various forms, such as outright theft or dilutive share issues that discriminate against minority shareholders. These activities are perceived to be particularly serious in companies with concentrated ownership structures and where there is a weak market for corporate control. Dyck and Zingales (2004) find that the private benefits of control are larger in countries where the capital markets are less developed, ownership is more concentrated, and privatizations are less likely to take place. Furthermore, they find a negative association between the degree of statutory protection for minority shareholders and the level of private benefits of control. And Nenova (2003) concludes that over two-thirds of the cross-country variation in the value of private benefits is explained by differences in the legal environments, law enforcement, investor protection, takeover regulations and power-concentrating corporate charter provisions.

The cash-flow rights of the controlling shareholders not only give them the incentive to discipline the top management, but also provide them with discretionary power to tunnel firm resources for their own benefits. The corporate governance and financial economics literature has started to explore the effectiveness of institutional mechanisms in preventing controlling shareholders from engaging in tunnelling activities. Nevertheless, only a few studies have examined the effectiveness of particular governance mechanisms, such as CEO incentive arrangements, in preventing the tunnelling behaviour of the controlling shareholders. Some researchers consider long-term incentive for CEOs as an appropriate mechanism to induce the CEOs to make decisions which are consistent with long-term value maximization for the shareholders (Beatty and Zajac, 1994). However, the legitimacy of shareholder return as a core value in governing corporations is questionable when there is a controlling shareholder. As the incentive arrangements for the CEOs can be heavily influenced by the controlling shareholder, an associated question is what kind of incentive arrangements will motivate the CEOs to prevent controlling shareholders from engaging in tunnelling activities, or obligate the CEOs to turn a blind eye on such behaviour. This chapter addresses two related questions. First, under what conditions will the cash-flow rights of the controlling shareholders accentuate their tunnelling activities, or give them more incentives to monitor the management? Second, what is the effectiveness of various corporate governance mechanisms (including CEO compensation arrangements), checks and controls from other large shareholders, and political control in preventing the incidence of the controlling shareholders' tunnelling behaviour?

The institutional setting

China offers an informative setting in which to analyse these research questions. The Chinese stock market was initially established by the government to partially privatize its state-owned enterprises (SOEs), and so raise capital and improve performance. Since its inception in 1991, the Chinese stock market has grown exponentially to become the eighth largest in the world with 1,377 domestically listed companies and a market capitalization of Rmb 3,137 billion by October 2005.

The shares of these listed companies are classified according to the residency of their owners, as domestic or foreign shares. Although all shares have the same voting and cash flow rights by law, most shares are subject to trading restrictions. The majority of domestic shares are owned by the government or its agencies, and are not tradable. Shares that are subject to trading restrictions are classified according to the identity of their owners into state shares, legal person (LP) shares, and employee shares. State shares are held by government agencies which are authorized to invest on behalf of the state or solely held by SOEs. The state shares suffer from the separation of ownership held by the general public and control held by the bureaucracy, and their transfer must be approved by numerous government agencies, including the China Securities Regulatory Commission (CSRC) and the Ministry of Finance in China. LP shares are held by domestic institutions, or legal entities such as non-financial institutions and SOEs that have at least one non-SOE shareholder. LP can be transferred to domestic corporations with the approval of the CSRC. Employee shares can be purchased by individual employees of listed companies, and can be sold to the open market after a period of up to twelve months, again subject to the approval of the CSRC.

Notwithstanding the progress in improving the regulatory environment of corporate governance of Chinese listed companies in recent years (Chapter 2, this volume), there are several weaknesses in the regulatory framework. First, the CSRC lacks both the necessary resources and the power of investigation and prosecution, with the result that its rules and regulations are ineffectually executed. Due to the high cost and complexity involved in filing a civil claim, individual investors are often unable to sue in the courts for suspected infringements. Second, access to stock listings in China is strictly administered by the authorities, and the regulations are asymmetrically in favour of the SOEs or firms with close ties to the government. As a consequence, the ownership of listed companies is highly concentrated in the hands of the government. Third, the CSRC issued guidelines for introducing independent directors in 2001, and 90 per cent of listed companies had introduced at least two independent directors by 2002. Since the state or state-like legal persons are normally the largest shareholders of the listed companies, the state representatives dominate the boards of directors in practice, which greatly compromises the independence of the boards.

Theoretical background and hypotheses

The agency approach to corporate governance has attempted to explore ways to align the interests of the shareholders and of the professional managers. In recent years, however, attention has been diverted to consideration of the expropriation of minority shareholders by the controlling shareholders (La Porta et al., 1999). In companies where the ownership structure is highly concentrated, the controlling shareholders have substantial power and incentives to expropriate corporate resources for their own benefits (La Porta et al., 1999; Claessens et al., 2000). The purpose of this chapter is to identify corporate governance mechanisms that can help prevent the incidence of the controlling shareholders' tunnelling activities. Four potential influences on tunnelling behaviour are identified: the level of ownership of the largest shareholder, the compensation arrangements for the CEO, the shareholdings of other large shareholders, and the extent of political control.

Ownership of the largest shareholder

Concentration of ownership and power in the hands of the largest shareholder is prevalent in countries with weak investor protection (La Porta et al., 2000). Ownership concentration may result in two competing effects on the incidence of the controlling shareholder's tunnelling behaviour. The tunnelling view argues that a concentrated ownership structure accentuates the tunnelling problem by giving the largest shareholder too much discretionary power over allocating corporate resources, and then the largest shareholder serves its own interest at the expense of other shareholders and stakeholders (Fama and Jensen, 1983; Burkhart et al., 1998; Bennedsen and Wolfenzon, 2000). When a significant proportion of equity is held by the largest share-holder, who often has many affiliates, it may become feasible and profitable for the largest shareholder to transfer resources from the focal company to itself or its other affiliates.

In contrast to the tunnelling view, the monitoring view states that the largest shareholder has much stronger incentives and more opportunities, compared to small investors, to monitor managerial misbehaviour and improve corporate efficiency. If the ownership structure is initially widely dispersed, the emergence of a large shareholder may help overcome the free-rider problem in monitoring the management, and the cash-flow rights of the largest shareholder can reduce its incentives for expropriation and increase incentives to pay out dividends (Jensen and Meckling, 1976). La Porta et al. (1998) argue that ownership concentration is a substitute for legal protection in countries with poor regulatory investor protection, because only large shareholders in this environment can hope to receive the return on their investment.

Integrating the insights from these two views, I argue that challenges from the CEO, the board of directors and other large shareholders make it hard for the largest shareholder to initiate tunnelling activities, when the largest shareholder has only a low equity stake in the firm. In this case, the monitoring incentive dominates the tunnelling incentive. However, as the level of the largest shareholder's equity stake increases, the shareholder obtains more control over the board and the executives through nomination and other processes, whilst other large shareholders have relatively low voting rights to challenge the decisions of the largest shareholder. Although both the monitoring and tunnelling incentives of the largest shareholder become stronger, the tunnelling incentive increases more strongly and dominates the monitoring incentive. In sum, a non-linear relationship is expected between tunnelling behaviour and the ownership level of the largest shareholder. When the largest shareholder's ownership level is low, the impact of the monitoring incentive dominates the impact of the tunnelling incentive; but when the largest shareholder's ownership level is high, the impact of the tunnelling incentive dominates the impact of the monitoring incentive. Thus:

Hypothesis 1: There is a U-shaped relationship between the ownership stake held by the largest shareholder and the likelihood of tunnelling behaviour by this shareholder.

Compensation arrangements for the CEO

Compensation packages for CEOs typically include a number of compo-nents, including some linked to outcome measures. Jensen and Meckling (1976) introduced the notion of using incentive arrangements to align the interests of managers with the interests of shareholders to reduce moral hazard. Most agency theorists nowadays recommend corporations to use equity-based incentives, such as stock options as a supplement to board monitoring (Jensen and Murphy, 1990; Gomez-Mejia, 1994). The previous literature has found that CEOs prefer a compensation package with a lower weight of outcome-based components, and are reluctant to give up decision-making autonomy to the board of directors (Zajac and Westphal, 1994; Westphal and Zajac, 1998). Furthermore, outcome-based compensation arrangements create significant risks for the CEOs in the event of negative financial news or related-party transactions which are recognized as illegal by the regulatory authority. The impact of uncontrollable changes in stock market and investor expectations on market value is significantly stronger than the impact of the operating decisions controllable by the CEOs (O'Connor et al., 2006).

However, outcome-based compensation arrangements do motivate the CEOs to monitor corporate transactions with the largest shareholder (or its affiliates). CEOs will not welcome a public announcement from the regulatory authority about fund misappropriation by the largest shareholder (or its affiliates), as this will have a negative impact upon the value of their outcome-based compensation package and their personal reputation. Thus when the weight of the outcome-based component in the CEO compensation package is high, the CEOs tend to be more careful in selecting risky investment projects and be more likely to prevent the largest shareholders from expropriating corporate resources.

Hypothesis 2: There is a negative relationship between the weight of the outcome-based component in the CEO compensation package and the likelihood of tunnelling behaviour by the largest shareholder.

Ownership by other large shareholders

An active market for corporate control plays an important role in facilitating an efficient allocation of resources. For example, the market for corporate control enables capable managers to obtain control of sufficient shares in a short period to remove inefficient managers. However, in most emerging economies, an external merger and takeover market for corporate control seldom exists. Instead, in these economies, checks on the activities of the largest shareholder may be provided by other substantial shareholders.

When control rights are dissipated among several large shareholders, one single large shareholder may not be able to control corporate decisions without obtaining agreement from the others. If, for example, the largest shareholder wants the company to repay its own debt or investment costs, the other large shareholders in the company might together seek to obtain enough control rights to prevent such transactions (Bennedsen and Wolfenzon, 2000). Compared to small investors, large shareholders have stronger incentives and capabilities to restrain the over-influence of the largest share-holder, and become an obstacle to potential tunnelling activities by the largest shareholder. Furthermore, if the largest shareholder wants to expropriate corporate resources for its own benefits, the efficiency of the market for corporate control can be enhanced if the other large shareholders can initiate a fight for corporate control or assist an outsider's fight for control (Bai et al., 2004a). I use the combined share ownership of the second, third, fourth and fifth shareholders as a proxy for the degree of control exercised by the 'other' large shareholders in corporations in emerging economies, and expect this power to constrain tunnelling behaviour by the largest shareholder.

> *Hypothesis 3: There is a negative relationship between the combined sharehold-ing of other large shareholders and the likelihood of tunnelling behaviour by the largest shareholder.*

The role of political control

Although increasing the weight of the outcome-based compensation component for the CEOs will help to decrease the incidence of tunnelling activities initiated by the controlling shareholder, the legitimacy of shareholders' return as the core value governing corporations might be questioned (Child, 2002; Kochan, 2002). Other corporate stakeholders can also exert influences over the incidence of the controlling shareholder's tunnelling activities. Here I focus on the complicated role of political control over Chinese listed companies.

Politicians may hold non-profit maximizing objectives, but they still have incentives to prevent controlling shareholders and managers from engaging in behaviour that reduces the amount of resources over which they have discretion (Brada, 1996). Many Chinese listed companies have developed from state-owned enterprises, and there are three major sources of political control in the corporate governance system: state ownership, regulatory authorities, and local party committees (Chang and Wong, 2004).

The regulatory authorities (including the Shanghai and Shenzhen Stock Exchanges and the CSRC) are expected to have non-differential impact on all domestically listed companies. The state is the ultimate controlling share-holder in many listed companies, and it obtains equity control either directly or indirectly. The dominant position of the state not only enables it to encourage the companies to generate more employment opportunities and tax revenues at the expense of corporate value maximization, but also weakens considerably the market for disciplinary takeovers. The local party committees are the grassroots-level organizations of the Chinese Communist Party, and they have influence over most Chinese firms, including newly formed private and foreign join ventures. My survey results show that the local party committees are actively engaged in major corporate decisions, especially decisions on management turnover. When the largest shareholder is directly or indirectly controlled by the state, the largest shareholder and the local party committee share some political objectives. In this case, the local party committee will not impose an additional political cost over these companies; instead, it will facilitate the initiation of the controlling shareholder's tunnelling activities. When the largest shareholder is a private company or an individual, the local party committee will exert its political control over corporate decisions, and prohibit the largest shareholder from initiating tunnelling activities, because such activities will prevent the realization of the social and political objectives of the local party committee. Thus:

> *Hypothesis 4: There is a negative relationship between the power of the local party committee and the likelihood of tunnelling behaviour by the largest shareholder in companies which are not controlled by the state.*

Data and methodology

The sample

The sample frame consisted of the 837 companies listed on the Shanghai Stock Exchange at the end of 2004. A questionnaire was distributed to the board secretaries of all these companies, and 323 valid responses were completed by November 2005: i.e. a response rate of 40 per cent. The questionnaire requested data on compensation arrangements for the CEOs, and on political control. Multiple response formats are used to reduce response bias, and items measuring each construct are scattered throughout the survey (DeVellis, 1991). In addition, data on ownership structure, board composition, and CEO characteristics of the final sample of 323 firms were obtained from corporate annual reports. Data on corporate performance, size and industry category were gathered from the databases of the CSRC and SINA Corporation.

The dependent variable

The dependent variable is the incidence of tunnelling activities by the largest shareholder. The previous literature tends to measure tunnelling behaviour indirectly. For example, when analysing tunnelling transactions within Indian business groups, Bertrand et al. (2002) trace the propagation of earnings shocks from firms in which the controlling shareholders hold low cash-flow rights to firms in which they hold high cash-flow rights, and they find that such propagation takes place through items on non-operating earnings. Claessens et al. (2002) use the deviation of cash flow from control rights as a proxy for the incidence of tunnelling, and find that Tobin's Q is positively related to cash-flow rights held by the controlling shareholder, and negatively related to the divergence between cash-flow and control rights. La Porta et al. (2000) use dividend payouts as a proxy for tunnelling, and suggest that companies make lower dividend payouts in countries which have poor legal protection for minority shareholders.

In this study, tunnelling is measured more directly by whether or not the largest shareholder (or its affiliated companies) has appropriated capital from the listed company for non-operational purposes in 2005. A 'fund misappropriation' is defined as a capital transfer from a listed company to its largest shareholder or other affiliates of the largest shareholder. There are five forms of non-operational fund misappropriation identified by the CSRC[1] (see Appendix). Among other things, the CSRC Notice prohibits listed companies from paying salaries, benefits, insurances or advertising costs, or providing loans, securities or repaying debt for the largest shareholder or affiliates of the largest shareholder. All listed companies are required to report the details of fund misappropriation transactions to the local agencies of the CSRC for investigation and are required to hire an independent audit firm to disclose the transactions in the latest annual report as material issues. For companies in which the fund misappropriation transaction takes place, the board of directors needs to set up feasible plans to ensure that the misappropriated funds decrease at a rate of at least 30 per cent annually. The dependent variable 'fund misappropriation' is a binary variable (TUNNEL), and does not take account of the size of the appropriation.

The explanatory variables

The full list of explanatory variables is provided in Table 8.1. There are two ownership variables, measuring respectively the shareholdings of the largest shareholder (SH1) and the next four largest shareholders (SH25). The squared value of SH1 (SH1Q) is also included to capture the possible non-linear effect of ownership on the incidence of tunnelling behaviour. Four variables relate to the compensation arrangements for the CEO: one (SHCEO) measures the shareholding of the CEO; the second is a dummy variable (PFP) which takes the value of one if part of the CEO compensation is linked to the performance of the firm; the third is another dummy variable (LTP) which takes the value of one if the compensation package includes any long-term incentive arrangements such as stock options; and the fourth variable is the CEO salary (SAL). The extent of political control is captured by an index, which equally weights the three items assessing the local party committee's control over management turnover and key decision-making activities (see the Appendix).

Finally there are seven control variables. The first measures the age of the firm (AGE) in years since the firm was first listed on the stock exchange. Corporate complexity (COM) is an index which equally weights the intensity of two related corporate strategies: corporate acquisition and divestiture. Acquisition intensity and divestiture intensity are measured as the ratios of asset value acquired and asset value divested respectively during the year to total assets at the end of year. CEO duality (DUAL) is coded as one if

Table 8.1:   The explanatory variables used in the binomial logit regression

Explanatory variables	Description	Measurement
Ownership		
SH1	Shareholding of the largest shareholder	%
SH25	Combined shareholding of the second to the fifth largest shareholders	%
CEO compensation		
SHCEO	Shareholding of CEO	100%
PFP	CEO pay-for-performance compensation component	Dummy
LTP	CEO long-term incentive plans	Dummy
SAL	CEO salary in 2005	Million yuan
Political control		
PC	Control by local party committee	
Control variables		
AGE	Years since listing	As till 2005
COM	Corporate complexity	See text
DUAL	CEO duality	=1 if CEO and chairman are the same person; =0 otherwise
IND	Board independence	Ratio of independent directors to executive directors
LIQ	Firm liquidity	Ratio of current assets to current liabilities
SIZE	Firm size	Log (sales in 2005), million yuan
ROE	Return on equity in 2004	%

the CEO and the board chair positions are served by the same person, and zero otherwise. Board independence (IND) is measured as the ratio of independent non-executive directors to executive directors. Corporate liquidity (LIQ) is the ratio of current assets to current liabilities. Firm size (SIZE) is measured by the logarithm of total sales. And firm performance is measured as the return on total equity (ROE) in 2004. Table 8.2 provides descriptive statistics and correlations between all the variables. As it shows, 29 per cent of the sample had exhibited some tunnelling behaviour. Firms in the sample range from single-product firms to highly diversified conglomerates. The mean value and standard deviation of the Herfindal index for diversification are 0.241 and 0.237 respectively. Firm assets range from Rmb 7 million to Rmb 557 billion (around US$73 billion).

Table 8.2: Descriptive statistics and Pearson correlation coefficients

Variable	Mean	S.D.	TUNNEL	SH1	SH25	SHCEO	PFP	LTP	SAL	DUAL	IND	PC	AGE	COM	SIZE	LIQ	ROE
TUNNEL	0.29	0.45															
SH1	0.41	0.16	-0.03														
SH25	0.17	0.13	-0.09	-0.62													
SHCEO	0.26	1.66	-0.06	-0.19	0.15												
PFP	0.68	0.47	-0.11	0.06	0.01	-0.10											
LTP	0.31	0.46	-0.06	-0.02	-0.05	-0.05	-0.03										
SAL	0.25	0.24	-0.14	-0.08	0.10	0.04	0.16	-0.02									
DUAL	0.13	0.33	-0.12	-0.05	0.10	0.05	0.04	-0.04	0.07								
IND	0.35	0.05	-0.02	-0.08	0.01	0.07	-0.02	-0.01	0.02	0.06							
PC	0.33	0.29	0.00	0.22	-0.09	-0.11	0.08	0.11	-0.03	-0.02	-0.03						
AGE	9.44	3.61	0.06	-0.27	-0.02	-0.11	-0.08	-0.04	0.02	0.02	0.09	-0.16					
COM	0.01	0.04	0.14	0.01	0.01	-0.03	-0.11	0.00	-0.03	0.02	-0.03	-0.02	0.03				
SIZE	12.09	1.12	-0.11	0.22	-0.16	-0.07	0.12	0.03	0.45	-0.06	0.03	0.20	-0.08				
LIQ	1.45	1.50	-0.08	0.00	0.02	0.06	-0.13	0.08	-0.04	0.01	0.08	-0.01	-0.05	-0.08	0.07		
ROE	-0.42	7.52	0.02	0.10	-0.09	0.01	0.08	0.04	0.05	0.02	-0.07	0.03	-0.09	0.01	0.22	0.06	

Note: There are 323 firms in the sample. All correlation coefficients equal to or greater than 0.11 are significant at the 5% level.

Empirical results

Table 8.3 provides the results for the logit models predicting the incidence of the controlling shareholder's tunnelling activities. The results support the view that the largest shareholder's equity stake (SH1) significantly influences its incentive to initiate tunnelling activities. Consistent with Hypothesis 1, the findings indicate that SH1 has a U-shaped relationship with the incidence of its tunnelling transactions (TUNNEL).

I also find considerable support for the importance of incentive arrangements for the CEOs as a mechanism for preventing the initiation of controlling shareholders' tunnelling behaviour. The results show significant coefficients for the existence of pay-for-performance compensation (PFP) component for the CEO, and the level of ownership (SHCEO) held by the CEO (Hypothesis 2). However, the coefficient is insignificant for the effect of long-term incentive plans (LTP). In sum, these findings indicate that some of the incentive arrangements for the CEO affect the incidence of tunnelling activities initiated by the largest shareholder. I find support for Hypothesis 3 regarding the impact of checks and balances from other large shareholders, which posits that the level of ownership by the next four largest shareholders (SH25) is negatively related with the likelihood of fund misappropriation (TUNNEL).

Table 8.3: Results of the binomial logit regression

Explanatory variables	*Model 1*	*Model 2*
SH1	−7.82** (3.21)	−8.68*** (3.38)
SH1Q	6.34** (3.21)	7.21* (4.11)
SH25	−2.93* (1.55)	−4.97*** (1.98)
SHCEO	−0.14* (0.08)	−0.14* (0.08)
PFP	−0.47** (0.22)	−0.58* (0.36)
LTP	−0.33 (0.26)	−0.29 (0.48)
SAL	−1.00 (0.76)	0.07 (0.93)
DUAL	−0.98*** (0.40)	−0.73* (0.47)
IND	−0.60 (3.22)	0.55 (4.58)
PC	0.30 (0.46)	0.90 (0.82)
AGE	0.01 (0.04)	−0.02 (0.05)
COM	7.80** (3.53)	7.48 (6.85)
SIZE	−0.25* (0.15)	−0.64*** (0.25)
LIQ	−0.21** (0.10)	−0.43** (0.18)
ROE	0.03*** (0.01)	0.04*** (0.01)
Constant	5.59*** (2.02)	10.54*** (3.97)
N	323	186
Wald χ^2 statistic	267***	99***
pseudo log likelihood	−175	−99

Notes: Robust standard errors are in parentheses. *** indicates significance at 1% level; ** indicates significance at 5% level; and * indicates significance at 10% level.

Hypothesis 4 suggests a negative relationship between the political control of the local party committee and the likelihood of fund misappropriation initiated by the largest shareholder (or its affiliates) in companies which are not controlled by the state directly or indirectly. This is not supported either when the model is estimated with the full sample (Model 1), or with a sub-sample of companies which are not controlled by the state through equity ownership (Model 2). In both cases, the coefficient of the control of local party committee (PC) is insignificant. Thus Hypothesis 4 is not supported.

Regarding the control variables, CEO duality (DUAL), which is recognized as an indicator of CEO power (Finkelstein and Hambrick, 1996), is negatively related to the incidence of the controlling shareholders' tunnelling behaviour. CEOs with greater power have stronger capabilities to ensure that maximization of corporate value is foremost, and are more likely to prevent the controlling shareholder from tunnelling corporate resources. The complexity of corporate strategy (COM) is positively related to the dependent variable. Finally, the models show a positive and significant correlation between the return on equity in the previous year (ROE) and TUNNEL. One possible explanation is that it is easier and more possible for the largest shareholders to expropriate resources from profitable listed companies than from unprofitable companies.

Discussion

In this chapter, I examine two competing perspectives about the incentives of the largest shareholders in companies where the ownership structure is highly concentrated, the monitoring view and the tunnelling view. I show that, when the ownership level of the largest shareholders is low, the monitoring incentive dominates the tunnelling incentive, and the largest shareholders are more likely to take actions to monitor managerial slack and improve corporate performance. On the other hand, when the ownership level of the largest shareholder is high, the tunnelling incentive dominates the monitoring incentive, and the largest shareholders tend to expropriate corporate resources. These findings generate important implications for further extensions to theoretical and empirical research on tunnelling in companies in emerging economies.

Although my analysis only considers one particular form of tunnelling, in which capital transfers are made from the listed company to the parent company, it helps to answer a major puzzle about tunnelling. If minority shareholders know that neither corporate governance mechanisms nor laws protect them from expropriation by the controlling shareholders, then why are they willing to buy stocks of these firms? The answer is that, even in emerging markets which have poor legal protection for minority shareholders, there exist some corporate governance mechanisms which provide *de facto* protection.

The first mechanism is linked to the incentive arrangements for the CEO. My empirical findings show significant and positive impacts of CEO stock ownership and pay-for-performance CEO compensation arrangements in preventing the largest shareholders from tunnelling corporate resources. This finding is consistent with the arguments in principal-agent theory, and suggests that compensation incentives motivate CEOs to safeguard the interests of all shareholders. However, the impact of the existence of long-term incentive plans is insignificant. One explanation is that such long-term incentive arrangements have not been implemented in China until recently, and the effects of such arrangements are far from satisfactory. In a survey of 208 respondent companies conducted by the Shanghai Stock Exchange in April 2004, only 127 considered that long-term incentive arrangements should be granted to the board of directors and the management team. When asked about the major impediments to the initiation and implementation of stock option plans, 94 per cent of the respondents selected the unsound legal environment, 59 per cent suggested the poor governance system of their corporations, while 28 per cent respondents cited the inefficient financial market. Only 55 per cent of the respondents considered that long-term incentive plans for senior executives had, or would have, significant impact if such plans could be implemented in their companies in the future.

The second mechanism relates to the power of other large shareholders. The ownership structures of many listed Chinese companies are highly concentrated, with a few large shareholders. Of the 323 firms in the sample, the average shareholdings of the largest, the next four largest, and the second to tenth largest shareholders, were 41 per cent, 17 per cent, and 20 per cent respectively at the end of 2005. These empirical findings show that the market for corporate control is strengthened by the existence of multiple large shareholders. In other words, the incidence of the tunnelling behaviour of the largest shareholder can be lowered if other large shareholders share a commitment to prevent the incidence of such behaviour.

This chapter also proposes political control as a mechanism to prevent the initiation of the largest shareholder's tunnelling behaviour. However, the hypothesis is not supported. One possible explanation is that I only consider the influence of formal political control. However, informal political control, especially in firms where the state is not the controlling shareholder, might play a significant role. The previous literature provides some indirect support for Hypothesis 4. For example, Morck et al. (1988) argue that the partial privatization of SOEs, in which a minority of shares is transferred to individual investors while the government is allowed to retain majority control, creates entrenchment incentives for the controlling owners to expropriate minority shareholders. Bai et al. (2004b) find that Chinese firms with large controlling shareholders, and firms where the state is the largest shareholder, trade at a discount compared to other firms. One implication from these studies is that the development of the Chinese stock market should not only concentrate on allowing SOEs to leverage the market to attract more capital, but should also focus on how to improve the legal protection for investors to allow the listed companies to attract money from outsiders. It is clear that a market-oriented governance model should eventually be put in place in China, but how can China adapt its corporate governance practices from a political control-based model to a market-oriented model? The causality and dynamics between corporate governance practices and institutional constraints deserve further research.

This study has some limitations that must be kept in mind. First, the sample consists of listed companies in a single country for one specific year. The total number of enterprises in China was around five thousand times that of the domestically listed companies at the end of 2004. The findings are more applicable to large firms or listed firms, than to all enterprises in China, and especially to the private enterprises. Private enterprises have typically not established sound corporate governance systems, and their largest shareholders often take executive positions and receive stricter monitoring from other investors than in listed companies. Furthermore, as the CEOs in listed companies are subject to disciplinary forces from the stock market and regulatory authorities, they may have stronger incentives to protect the interests of minority shareholders than their counterparts in private enterprises. Second, future research might compare the compensation arrangements for the CEOs in China with those in other countries. CEOs in China typically receive a larger fraction of their compensation in the form of salary, and a lower fraction in the form of long-term incentive options, compared to the CEOs in developed economies.

Notwithstanding these limitations, the results of this study offer important implications for researchers and practitioners. For researchers, the findings suggest that the effects of governance mechanisms on the behaviour of controlling shareholders are more complex than have been hypothesized. Some scholars have noted the limitations of considering individual governance mechanisms independent of each other and have advocated examining joint or substitution effects (e.g. Agarwal and Knoeker, 1996). My findings indicate that simple substitution is not enough. Instead, future research should focus on the joint effects of the power relationships among the CEO, the controlling shareholders and the board of directors, and examine the impact of different types of incentive mechanisms on the behaviour of the controlling shareholder. Furthermore, although this chapter focuses on the incentives for, and the powers of, the CEO, future research might examine the effect of compensation arrangements for the board of directors and other core decision-makers.

I also have important advice for practitioners. First, although the political control implemented by state owners and the local party committee imposes political costs on the focal company, it can mitigate agency conflicts between the controlling shareholder and other investors. Therefore, the influence of political control on corporate decision-making and corporate outcomes is far from conclusive. Second, by aligning the incentives of the CEO with those of the shareholders in general, outcome-based CEO compensation arrangements can effectively prevent the incidence of the controlling shareholder's tunnelling activities. However, incentive arrangements do not all perform effectively if they are not monitored properly or if they are not applicable to the governance structure of the company. Third, although the separation of the CEO and board chair positions is strongly advocated and demanded by institutional investors, an overlap of the two positions can produce symbolic benefits if the CEO is strongly motivated to monitor the agency conflicts between the controlling shareholder and other investors. Finally, my results indicate that an ownership concentration in the largest shareholder may not lead to tunnelling activities, if their cash flow rights are not large enough to dominate over the board of directors, senior executives and other large shareholders.

Appendix: Data obtained from the questionnaire survey and annual reports

1. **Fund misappropriation behaviour**

   Five forms of non-operational fund misappropriation by the largest shareholder (or its affiliated companies) are addressed:

   - Appropriate fund freely to pay advertising, salary and welfare expenses
   - Borrow money from the company directly or indirectly
   - Defraud capital injection into the company
   - Have the company pay back debt, expenses and investment costs
   - Obtain bank loans by cashing commercial bills in the name of the company

2. **Outcome-based compensation arrangement for the CEO**

   - CEO ownership level
   - Whether or not the CEO compensation is linked with firm performance
   - Whether or not long-term incentive plans are provided for the CEO

3. **Political control**

   - Whether or not the current CEO is appointed by the state
   - Whether or not the board chair is appointed by the state
   - The number of functions implemented by the local party committee which supervises your company:
     - Participate in decision-making on operation issues
     - Recruit or remove senior executives or directors of the boards
     - Monitor the performance of directors and executives

- Motivate employees
- Coordinate the interaction between the top management team and the employees

Note

1. See the 'Notice Concerning Some Issues on Regulating the Funds between Listed Companies and Associated Parties and Listed Companies' Provision of Guaranty to Other Parties', promulgated in 2003 by the CSRC Assets Supervision and Administration Commission of the State Council.

Bibliography

Agarwal, A. and Knoeker, C. R. (1996). 'Firm performance and mechanisms to control agency problems between managers and shareholders'. *Journal of Financial and Quantitative Analysis*, 31(3): 377–97.

Bai, C., Liu, Q. and Song, F. (2004a). 'Bad news is good news: propping and tunneling evidence from China'. University of Hong Kong, CCFR Working Paper 1094 (www.hiebs.hku.hk/working_paper_updates/pdf/wp1094.pdf).

Bai, C., Liu, Q., Lu, J., Song, F. M. and Zhang, J. (2004b). 'Corporate governance and market valuation in China'. *Journal of Comparative Economics*, 32(4): 599–616.

Beatty, R. P. and Zajac, E. J. (1994). 'Managerial incentives, monitoring and risk bearing: a study of executive compensation, ownership and board structure in initial public offerings'. *Administrative Science Quarterly*, 39(2): 313–35.

Bennedsen, M. and Wolfenzon, D. (2000). 'The balance of power in closely held corporations'. *Journal of Financial Economics*, 58(1): 113–39.

Bertrand, M., Mehta, P. and Mullainathan, S. (2002). 'Ferreting out tunneling: an application to Indian business groups'. *Quarterly Journal of Economics*, 117(1): 121–48.

Brada, J. C. (1996). 'Privatization is transition – or is it?' *Journal of Economic Perspectives*, 10(2): 67–86.

Burkhart, M., Gromb, D. and Panunzi, F. (1998). 'Why higher takeover premia protect minority shareholders'. *Journal of Political Economy*, 106(1): 172–204.

Chang, E. C. and Wong, S. M. L. (2004). 'Political control and performance in China's listed firms'. *Journal of Comparative Economics*, 32(4): 617–36.

Child, J. (2002). 'The international crisis of confidence in corporations'. *Academy of Management Executive*, 16(3): 145–7.

Claessens, S., Djankov, S., and Lang, L. H. P. (2000). 'The separation of ownership and control of East Asia corporations'. *Journal of Financial Economics*, 58(1–2): 81–112.

Claessens, S., Djankov, S., Fan, J. P. H., and Lang, L. H. P. (2002). 'Disentangling the incentive and entrenchment effects of large shareholders'. *Journal of Finance*, 57(6): 2741–71.

DeVellis, R. F. (1991). *Scale development: theory and applications* (Newbury Park, CA: Sage).

Dyck, A. and Zingales, L. (2004). 'Private benefits of control: an international comparison'. *Journal of Finance*, 59(2): 537–600.

Fama, E. F. and Jensen, M. C. (1983). 'The separation of ownership and control'. *Journal of Law and Economics*, 26(2): 301–25.

Finkelstein, S. and Hambrick, D. C. (1996). *Strategic leadership: top executives and their effects on organizations* (Minneapolis: West).

Gomez-Mejia, L. R. (1994). 'Executive compensation: a reassessment and a future research agenda'. In G. R. Ferris (ed.), *Research in personnel and human resources management*, pp. 161–222 (Greenwich, CT: JAI Press).

Jensen, M. C. and Meckling, W. H. (1976). 'Theory of the firm: managerial behaviour, agency costs, and ownership structure'. *Journal of Financial Economics*, 3(4): 305–50.

Jensen, M. C. and Murphy, K. J. (1990). 'Performance pay and top-management incentives'. *Journal of Political Economy*, 98(2): 225–63.

Johnson, S., Porta, R. L., Lopez-de-Silanes, F. and Shleifer, A. (2000). 'Tunneling'. *American Economic Review*, 90(2): 22–7.

Kochan, T. A. (2002). 'Addressing the crisis in confidence in corporations: root causes, victims, and strategies for reform'. *Academy of Management Executive*, 16(3): 139–41.

La Porta, R., Lopez-de-Silanes, F., Shleifer, A. and Vishny, R. (1998). 'Agency problems and dividend policies around the world'. NBER Working Paper (http://mba.tuck.dartmouth.edu/pages/faculty/rafael.laporta/publications/LaPorta%20PDF%20Papers-ALL/Agency%20Problems.pdf).

La Porta, R., Lopez-de-Silanes, F. and Shleifer, A. (1999). 'Corporate ownership around the world'. *Journal of Finance*, 54(2): 471–517.

La Porta, R., Lopez-de-Silanes, F., Shleifer, A. and Vishny, R. (2000). 'Investor protection and corporate governance'. *Journal of Financial Economics*, 58(1–2): 3–27.

Morck, R., Shleifer, A. and Vishny, R. (1988) 'Management ownership and market valuation: an empirical analysis'. *Journal of Financial Economics*, 20(1): 293–315.

Nenova, T. (2003). 'The value of corporate voting rights and control: a cross-country analysis'. *Journal of Financial Economics*, 68(3): 325–51.

O'Connor, J. P., Priem, R. L., Coombs, J. E. and Gilley, K. M. (2006). 'Do CEO stock options prevent or promote fraudulent financial reporting?' *Academy of Management Journal*, 49(3): 483–500.

Westphal, J. D. and Zajac, E. J. (1998). 'The symbolic management of stockholders: corporate governance reforms and shareholder reactions'. *Administrative Science Quarterly*, 43(1): 127–53.

Zajac, E. J. and Westphal, J. D. (1994). 'The costs and benefits of incentives and monitoring in the largest U.S. corporations: when is more not better?' *Strategic Management Journal*, 15(special issue): 121–42.

Part II
Comparative Corporate Governance: Diffusion and Institutional Change

9

Dialogue on Comparative Institutional Analysis and International Business

Gregory Jackson, Mari Sako, Christel Lane and Richard Hyman

Gregory Jackson

Scholars of international business (IB) know that 'institutions matter', but how they matter remains a hotly contested question. Multinational enterprises (MNEs) operate in different business environments and face challenges in strategically locating themselves and adapting to the diversity of institutions across countries and regions. MNEs bring different home country endowments in the way of routines, standard practices and capabilities, but operate in diverse host country environments where very different sets of institutional constraints and opportunities may exist. MNEs' experience in emerging markets, including Central and Eastern Europe, has highlighted the importance of institutions for understanding business strategy and performance across national borders.

The theoretical and methodological approaches to studying institutions remain diverse, and draw variably from different fields of social science, such as economics (Aoki, 2001; North, 1990), sociology (Powell and DiMaggio, 1991; Streeck and Thelen, 2005) and political science (Immergut, 1998; Thelen, 1999). Indeed, the very meaning of institutions remains contested and despite much interdisciplinary cross-fertilization, institutional theory remains characterized by an eclectic set of approaches. IB scholars have studied institutions in terms of how diverse regulatory rules and legal norms impact transaction costs for MNEs (Brouthers, 2002) or expose firms to politically related hazards (Delios and Henisz, 2000). Institutions offer different degrees of support for market exchange (e.g. between advanced capitalist economies and transition or emerging economies) by securing property rights or protecting investors (Djankov et al., 2003). Institutions also create uncertainty for MNEs due to the 'distance' between home and host country institutions (Kostova, 1999) or cultures (Hofstede, 1980). IB scholars have thus stressed how institutions create incentives and constraints on MNEs' strategic choice, as well as linking MNEs' success with the adaptation of their strategy or structure to the institutional environments in diverse host countries (e.g. Wan, 2005). While institutions matter, the view of institutions in IB tends to be 'thin' and reliant on summary measures of the degree of institutional development or distance. In short, IB research has devoted surprisingly little attention to *comparing* the topography of institutional landscapes and understanding their diversity (Deeg and Jackson, 2008).

At a Special Roundtable session at the 2007 Conference of the UK & Ireland chapter of the Academy of International Business, scholars from a variety of disciplines were invited to comment on the potential contribution of comparative institutional analysis to the study of international business. This chapter features short contributions from Mari Sako (Professor of Business Studies, Oxford), Christel Lane (Professor of Sociology, Cambridge) and Richard Hyman (Professor of Industrial Relations, London School of Economics). From differing perspectives, the authors highlight the importance of looking at institutions in the context of comparing specific national cases. Sako stresses the importance of moving beyond descriptions of 'institutional voids' (Khanna and Palepu, 2006) to understand the diversity and function of various informal institutions across countries. Lane links institutional analysis with debates over global value chains, summarizing some of her empirical work on the United Kingdom, the United States and Germany that demonstrates how firms' strategic choices and the consequences of global value chains often differ greatly according to national context. Hyman stresses some commonalities between the research agendas in comparative industrial relations and IB scholarship, but suggests that the task of comparing how institutions affect, and are affected by, internationalization brings serious methodological difficulties precisely because the nature of those challenges and effects are highly contextual and to some degree 'incomparable' across different national environments. In sum, these interventions suggest both the challenges and benefits for future research in IB that will look much more closely at institutions from a comparative perspective.

Mari Sako

There is much that International Business Strategy (IBS) and Comparative Institutional Analysis (CIA) can learn from each other. IBS has traditionally adopted an 'inside-out' perspective, focusing on how multinational enterprises make strategic decisions about global expansion in diverse regions and countries. Among various factors that affect firms' location decisions, IBS has recently identified institutions (or their absence, i.e. 'institutional void') as important constraints as well as opportunities for firms operating in emerging markets. This brings the major concern of IBS closer to that of CIA, which, with its 'outside-in' perspective, compares how different national institutional contexts shape corporate strategy and structure.

However, the concept of 'institutional void' is narrowly defined as the absence of formal regulative institutions, and would benefit from a fuller understanding of what is meant by institutions in broader social sciences. In doing so, we also shed light on CIA's recent preoccupation with institutional change of an incremental sort. This short note elaborates this line of argument.

Many interesting research questions may be posed in IBS with the rise of emerging markets including Brazil, Russia, India and China. For example, what alternative strategies are available to foreign firms when they consider entering China with its relative absence of intellectual property rights protection? How do foreign firms formulate a strategy to change the institutional context of a host country rather than adapt its strategy to existing institutions? Emerging markets are typically defined as low or medium income countries facing rapid growth and undergoing institutional reform to become free-market economies. Rapid growth makes emerging markets highly attractive prospects for market entry by foreign firms. At the same time, institutional reform has taken various shapes and forms, creating 'institutional voids' that pose serious risks in entering such markets.

Khanna and Palepu coined the phrase 'institutional void' to refer to the absence of certain types of institutions that facilitate the well-functioning of markets (Khanna and Palepu, 1997; Khanna et al., 2005). They argue that foreign firms have a choice of either avoiding by not entering the market, adapting their business models, or working towards changing the institutional context when they encounter institutional void. Khanna and Palepu see institutions as offering both constraints and opportunities for strategic action. By institutions, they refer to such things as regulatory systems, specialized intermediaries and contract-enforcing mechanisms. Because of their focus on the functioning of markets, these are closest to the sort of institutions for property rights and investor protection taken up by law and finance scholars (La Porta et al., 1998). As is evident, these are a narrower set of institutions than is normally captured in institutional analysis. In particular, Douglass North saw institutions as both formal *and* informal rules of the game (North, 1990), but 'institutional void' is the absence of primarily formal rules only. So if a multinational enterprise identifies one institution as a formal rule in a home country setting (typically the United States), then the absence of the same formal rule in the host country amounts to an institutional void. But if we extend the definition of institutions to include informal rules, then the firm may identify alternative informal rules in host countries, making it harder to identify a void against a single home country benchmark. Rather than a blinkered vision seeing many voids, however, IBS would do well to recognize informal rules, for example governing mutual help and bribery, in host countries.

Moreover, institutions according to Khanna and Palepu are primarily regulative, and not normative nor cultural-cognitive using the schema of Scott (1995). Ignoring the normative and cultural-cognitive dimensions of institutions is likely to lead to an under-appreciation of the variety of ways in

154 Corporate Governance and International Business

which markets may function well. For example, Comparative Institutional Analysis distinguishes among different configurations of institutions in product, capital and labour markets that lead certain countries' markets to be more coordinated than others (Amable, 2003; Crouch, 2005; Hall and Soskice, 2001; Whitley, 1999). Thus, CIA pushes IBS away from identifying separate institutional voids in the political and social system, product, labour, and capital markets, towards understanding how different institutions fit together at the national level. Thus, the notion of 'institutional void' may be extended to, or complemented by, the idea of institutional mismatch in a particular country.

By stretching, but not destroying, the notion of institutional void in these ways, IBS offers CIA a clear perspective of actors acting strategically towards institutions to change the latter. Up until recently, a conventional treatment of institutions in CIA emphasized their stability and complementarity in nationally based capitalist systems (Hall and Soskice, 2001; Whitley, 1999). Consequently, a high degree of institutional fit implied little scope for strategic action, pointing to exogenous shocks as the only mechanism for bringing about radical change in institutions. For example, in a classical Japanese business system, the main bank system and cross-shareholding provided 'patient capital', whilst lifetime employment enabled multi-skilling to provide functional flexibility (Aoki et al., 2007). These institutions in financial and labour markets in turn complemented long-term relational contracting in horizontal and vertical *keiretsu* corporate groups.

More recently, not least due to the apparent disintegration and transformation of business systems in previously well-performing economies such as Germany and Japan, CIA has begun to analyse the mechanisms for bringing about incremental institutional change (Streeck and Thelen, 2005). For example, institutions may change in an incremental manner because of *layering*, a case of new institutions co-existing with old institutions. It may happen also due to *conversion*, namely the redeployment of old institutions for new goals, functions or purposes. In Japan, the financial markets have been transformed since the late 1990s due to the layering of new stock exchanges onto a bank-based system and the conversion of venture capital from loans to syndicated investment funds. In labour markets, similarly, there has been a layering of non-standard contingent workers onto lifetime employment, and the conversion of Shunto wage bargaining to legitimize pay dispersion (Sako, 2007). In all these instances, company-level agency accounts for much of incremental institutional change.

In conclusion, scholars in IBS and CIA should work more closely to further our understanding of institutional change. This note argued that IBS may learn from CIA by extending the notion of 'institutional void' through a fuller appreciation of what is meant by institutions, whilst keeping its focus on actors acting strategically to bring about institutional change. This latter perspective helps CIA in its preoccupation with agency as one mechanism for bringing about incremental institutional change.

Christel Lane

This brief presentation is about what is variously called global commodity chains (GCC), global value chains (GVC) or global production networks (GPN) and the processes of outsourcing and offshoring involved. Building a GPN involves the fragmentation of the value-creation process and the geographical relocation of particular functions/processes to nominally independent supplier/contractor firms, on a global scale. Firms' objective in building GPNs is often to escape national institutional constraints, such as high social payments, or to seek alternative institutional arrangements, more compatible with changes in strategic objectives, such as seeking access to a specific type of knowledge, not available in the home country.

The building of GPNs and the process of offshoring has become more prevalent during the last decade or so, due to both new global opportunities and pressures. New opportunities have been created by both liberalization of international trade and geopolitical transformation, bringing many more newly industrialized and transition economies into the trading network. New pressures flow from intensified global competition and, for listed companies, further pressure to increase shareholder value which offshoring can facilitate. Also outsourcing has spread from externalization of mainly simple manufacturing processes, to highly knowledge-intensive ones and to service operations of increasing levels of complexity.

Lead firms in GPNs are very different from multinational companies (MNCs), the main object of study in International Business. Although IB scholars have examined global networks internal to companies and the varying social influences of home and host institutional environment (e.g. the several studies by Ferner et al.), GPNs have received comparatively little study, particularly from a social-institutional perspective, associated with the study of comparative capitalisms. Building a GPN involves no capital investment and no ownership of the firms, executing functions/processes vital to the lead firm's final product. This means that inter-firm ties are more shallow and less durable, and footlooseness often forms an integral part of firm strategy. Control of outsourced functions becomes more problematic, and last but not least, offshoring represents a more pronounced social disembedding from the home country.

GPNs do not exist in an anonymous global space but remain territorially embedded, albeit in multiple locations and at several geopolitical levels. Hence the question of how firms and their GPNs interact with specific varieties of capitalism, in both countries of origin and destination, as well as with overarching international rule systems, has informed my comparative research of GPNs. Three specific questions have been addressed.

First, are GPNs still shaped by the national origin of lead firms and, if so, to what extent? Second, given that firms build GPNs to escape specific constraints of their home environment and enjoy much greater chances of 'regime shopping' than do MNCs, do they become the autonomous strategic actors that many globalization theorists envisage? If so, to what extent and in what circumstances? Third, how do the activities of lead firms in GPNs impact on their home countries? Do they reinforce or disrupt the institutional arrangements of a given variety of capitalism? Do they consolidate or impair its comparative advantage?

My answers to these questions draw on empirical findings from a study of GPNs in two industries – clothing and pharmaceuticals – in three countries (the United Kingdom, the United States and Germany). These two industries are in no way representative of processes of offshoring but are best seen as polar opposites. Clothing firms externalize a simple and low-technology manufacturing process and pharmaceutical companies, amongst other processes, the knowledge-seeking process or research function. The work has been informed by two sets of theory, namely the theory of global value chains/global production networks and the variety of capitalism/comparative capitalisms approaches.

Global commodity/value chains versus global production networks

Gereffi (1994), who developed the thesis of GCCs since 2005 renamed as GVCs (Gereffi et al., 2005), adheres to a linear conception of the relations between buyer and supplier firms, linking firms at the economic centre with those at the periphery or semi-periphery. He focuses on the different nodes in the value chain and on the process of value extraction that takes place at each node. His emphasis is on power relations and whether power emanates from buyers (retailers) or producers (manufacturers). He has shown less interest in how the competitive advantage of firms, and the degree of power derived from this, are constituted by social-institutional bases in different locations. In contrast, Dicken (2003) and various co-authors (Henderson et al., 2002) prefer the concept of GPN which invites identification of sets of firms, linked in multi-level relationships, resulting in network formation. Although they insist on the social embeddedness of networks, their empirical work does not strongly develop this insight. Both sets of theorists view firms as relatively autonomous, strategically oriented actors, pursuing their competitive advantage. They thus differ from scholars in the comparative capitalism field who dwell on the social-institutional constitution of competitive advantage and emphasize the divergence of the latter with respect to different types of capitalism.

Varieties of capitalism/comparative capitalisms

The work of Hall and Soskice (2001) on varieties of capitalism – contrasting a 'liberal market' economic type with one of 'co-ordinated market economy' – remains very inward-looking: i.e. it is mainly concerned with firms' co-ordinating activities and resulting competitive advantage in their domestic context. Nevertheless, their notion of 'institutional arbitrage' shows some engagement with the activities of global firms, though less with the impact of the latter on their domestic economy. More recent work on comparative capitalisms (e.g. Deeg and Jackson, 2008) explores such interaction effects more fully, albeit only focusing on MNCs. But there is lack of agreement among scholars in this paradigm about the effects of firms' global activities on home countries. One set of theorists argue that firms' global activities only reinforce existing domestic institutional arrangements and even inten-sify concentration on specific industries or market segments, supported by societal institutions. Another group of scholars, in contrast, argue that MNCs may challenge and even alter existing institutional arrangements. The cumu-lative impact may be to undermine or even destroy distinctive institutional sub-systems.

GPNs in the pharmaceutical and clothing industries

My own position is that lead firms in GPNs have varied effects which, in some circumstances, supports the first set of analysts, and in other circum-stances agrees with the claims of the second set of theorists. What are these circumstances? Three different sets of circumstances will be elaborated, draw-ing on empirical data from the two industries studied. They are connected both with industry environment and, to a lesser extent, the firms' country of origin. They concern first and foremost the nature of the global market, i.e. the market in which firms source and the kind of GPN that evolves in this market environment. This may be illustrated by reference to the two industries studied.

In the pharmaceutical industry where there exists an oligopolistic inter-national market for 'sourcing'/in-licensing new drug candidates, firms adhere to global 'best practice'. Hence the innovation networks they establish, mainly in the US, do not differ fundamentally between lead firms from dif-ferent national origins (Lane and Probert, 2007). In order to gain timely access to new knowledge about drug candidates, networks become deeply embedded in knowledge-rich regions, which leads simultaneously to signifi-cant dis-embedding from the home country that may impair the working of a domestic innovation system. In the globally highly fragmented clothing industry, by contrast, relatively simple assembly operations are outsourced with the effect that networks have greater global reach and are more unstable.

Suppliers' expertise receives relatively low evaluation, making them more easily substitutable one by another in a predominantly price-oriented global market for sourcing. No global 'best practice' evolves. In this context, firms perpetuate the product paradigms and manufacturing practices, shaped by their domestic institutional environment.

This behaviour is further reinforced by a second set of circumstances, namely the market environment in which firms sell the clothes they make. Due to lasting national differences in consumption practices and retail organization, clothing firms remain predominantly oriented to domestic markets for their sales and, indeed, display a considerable dependence on domestic retailers. This, in turn, influences how they organize their GPNs which become a conduit for the 'exporting' of practice, associated with specific varieties of capitalism. In pharmaceuticals, in contrast, where markets for drugs are highly international and regulatory systems have become increasingly homogenized, domestic institutional environments have far less influence on firms' practices in innovation networks.

However, the influence of markets is still mediated by national institutional effects. These are particularly active in the clothing industry where nationally shaped firm structures and production paradigms – German diversified quality production versus British and American diversified mass production – strongly mediate institutional influences of supplier countries (for details, see Lane and Probert, 2007). Network relations of firms from liberal market economies have a greater 'market' character than is the case for those of German 'coordinated market economy' firms. However, 'market' type arm's length relations and footloose behaviour were found to be a good deal more prevalent in American than British firms, demonstrating that the 'liberal market' type does not always capture the differences between the two main economies allocated to this type in the literature. In the pharmaceutical industry, in contrast, network relationships were not noticeably structured by institutional influences of lead firms' country of origin, although the extent of externalization of the research function was considerably less for a subset of German, as compared with British firms. German firms, with some notable exceptions, are still less prepared to relocate research operations and scientists to the US than are UK firms.

A final question to address is whether global sourcing and the external networks developed for this purpose reinforce or undermine the institutional architecture and the comparative institutional advantage derived from lead firms' home country. In the clothing industry, at first sight, retention of traditional production paradigms, forming the basis of comparative advantage, tend to strengthen it. At second sight, however, the nearly total reliance on labour in low-wage countries, now prevalent in this industry, creates a negative feedback loop which particularly undermines the traditional institutional specificity of relationships between capital and labour in Germany, commonly characterized as one of negotiated consensus. The practice of foreign sourcing has not remained confined to this industry, but, over time, this avoidance of domestic institutional constraint has seeped out into other industries, 'contaminating' the whole sub-system of industrial relations. In the pharmaceutical industry, where external sourcing of knowledge was embraced to stem decline of firms' competitive advantage, in a transformed global industry now based on radical innovation, negative feedback has been more pronounced. In Germany it is gradually transforming the industry, which is traditionally based on incremental innovation. In both Britain and Germany, it is siphoning off vital human and financial capital resources. This transfer of resources is simultaneously serving to enrich the innovation system of the United States and impoverishing that of the two European competitor countries.

Thus, in conclusion, the recent expansion of outsourcing, in both volume and spread of functions entailed, has very complex and differentiated effects on globalizing firms and their home countries. It calls for a renewed examination of the tenets of the comparative capitalisms literature. It also may persuade scholars of International Business to pay more attention to the study of firms' external global networks and the way institutional environments of both home and host countries mediate such network building and utilization.

Richard Hyman

I write very much as an outsider to this forum. Indeed I have a strong research interest in comparative institutional analysis, but I have never studied international business beyond paying some attention to key developments in the literature. My own main area of expertise is in the study of trade unions, and more generally the institutions of employment regulation (industrial relations). Theoretically I am concerned to explore the ways in which labour, always a 'fictitious commodity' (Polanyi, 1944), is subject to further 'decommodification' (the rather ugly term invented by Esping-Andersen, 1990) through institutional mechanisms such as law, collective bargaining and the internal organizational practices of employers. My aim in this brief contribution is to sketch some potential complementarities between industrial relations and international business and some common analytical problems.

In terms of empirical focus, there is evidence of increasing areas of overlap between the two fields of study (I hesitate to say 'disciplines'). The key point of intersection involves the impact on employment regimes of the growing internationalization of trade, production chains and company ownership. While in the past, students of industrial relations may have been concerned primarily with the bargaining activities of trade unions (and in some countries, the mechanisms of labour law), the last quarter century has seen a shift in research and analysis to employers as industrial relations actors. This reflects the extent to which, cross-nationally, management has become the key driver of change – in some cases, successfully challenging central features of the 'social models' which were firmly entrenched for the first several post-war decades. Even where such encompassing models of employment regulation persist, there has been an advance of company-specific labour regimes within the framework of macro-level standard-setting.

Associated with this shift in focus is a growing attention to the impact of business policies on company-level employment regimes. In the past, corporate personnel and industrial relations practices and functions could be seen as relatively autonomous from other areas of management. The 'human resource management' revolution has involved an integration and subordination of employment policies with broader managerial priorities. Industrial relations scholars have been compelled to look 'upstream' in order to understand the dynamics of employment regulation.

Economic internationalization (or, as it is commonly described, 'globalization') – and the related processes of European economic integration – presents analytical and methodological challenges to students of industrial relations which parallel the concerns of international business scholars. How does the internationalization of product markets, corporate identity and investment decisions affect, and how is it affected by, the complex institutional architecture of employment regulation constructed at national level – and the national 'business systems' (Whitley, 1992) of which these are an integral component?

There is a well-worn argument within the industrial relations literature – often linked to ideas of convergence – that common economic and technological pressures necessarily erode idiosyncratic national institutional arrangements. Others, drawing on the 'varieties of capitalism' school (Hall and Soskice, 2001b), insist that the functional interconnectedness of different elements of national systems represents a source of inertia.

By now it is widely accepted that neither thesis is well founded. Some national industrial relations systems have indeed changed radically over recent decades, at least in part as a result of the international restructuring of business. Kochan et al. (1986) described as a systemic transformation the virtual collapse of the New Deal institutions of employment regulation in the United States. The same might be said of Britain: in 1980 the majority of employees were trade union members, today the proportion is little more than one in four, and the coverage of collective bargaining has fallen in parallel. In some other Anglophone countries (Australia, New Zealand) the trend has been similar. Yet this experience is far from universal. In Germany, though native observers regularly write of the collapse or at least radical erosion of the institutional framework (Hassel, 1999), from the outside the stability of multi-employer collective bargaining and company-level codetermination seems more notable. In Sweden, many commentators in the 1990s questioned whether a series of challenges to the post-war 'model' posed a terminal threat, but more recent experience has suggested a consolidation of macro-institutional regulation. In neighbouring Denmark, the major recent study of industrial relations (Due et al., 1994) is entitled 'the survival of the Danish model'. In many southern European countries, the predominant trend seems to be a new institutionalization (or, as the French employers like to term it, *refondation*) of employment regulation. Hence the key analytical question becomes: why are some industrial relations systems more resilient than others? What are the *endogenous* sources of stability and change? Does relative resilience relate, for example, to distinctive forms of corporate governance which are certainly not immutable but are nevertheless not easy to transform (Gospel and Pendleton, 2004; Streeck and Thelen, 2005)?

How do institutions matter?

I turn now to some more general issues and problems. It has become commonplace for comparative researchers to insist that institutions matter: but which institutions, and how? More fundamentally, what do we mean by an institution; and how can we identify one when we see it? In his frequently quoted definition, North (1990: 3–4) states that 'institutions are the rules of the game in a society or, more formally, are the humanly devised constraints that shape human interaction'; they are not, he insists, the same as organizations. Yet he also argues that the same rules can have contrasting effects in different national settings because of different enforcement mechanisms and norms of behaviour. But is this to say that not all rules are 'really' rules? Or else, perhaps, that the constraining effect of first-order rules depends on higher-order rules/institutions? Does this offer the prospect of an infinite regress? At least there is a risk of circularity if we wish to argue the causal significance of institutions: the capacity to constrain human behaviour seems both a defining characteristic of institutions and a theoretical proposition about social organization.

Such issues are of crucial importance for the analysis of the changing nature of markets – a question of major concern in the fields both of industrial relations and of international business. Part of Polanyi's argument – certainly of relevance for more recent debates over globalization – was encapsulated in his distinction between a 'market economy' in which markets were subordinate or complementary to other social and political institutions, and a 'market society' in which they had become hegemonic. Yet it is essential to insist that markets are *themselves* social and political institutions, and that they can never function independently of other such institutions – as Durkheim famously declared with his maxim that contracts are binding only if they rest on social norms which are non-contractual.

Yet if markets are themselves institutions, and operate only through their interconnections with other institutions, the geometry of these interconnections is nevertheless highly variable. This, in essence, was Polanyi's point. His thesis that markets were traditionally 'embedded' within broader regulatory institutions – a concept which has lately become increasingly fashionable – pointed to a hierarchical ordering which in his view became overturned with the rise of modern capitalism but was reconstituted politically in the twentieth century as the 'freeing' of markets provoked a political reaction.

Much recent debate over globalization points to a novel process of 'disembedding'. This involves at least three aspects of change. First, the 'embedding' of markets was in the past nationally structured: a fact particularly evident in the case of labour markets, which were regulated by a diversity of national industrial relations systems. The internationalization of economic activity seems to threaten the regulatory capacity of such national regimes, without providing an adequate infrastructure for effective compensatory supranational regulation. Second, a new hierarchy among markets seems to have emerged. Polanyi wrote of land, labour and money as 'fictitious commodities' because their production and consumption were not commensurable to the production and consumption of cloth or potatoes. In particular, the 'money market' was a somewhat esoteric appendage to the material economy. Today, the priorities have been reversed: financial markets (dealing in ever more exotic forms of quasi-commodities) exercise hegemony over the 'real' economy. In the realm of industrial relations this means, for example, that the vagaries of private equity institutions determine not only the employment conditions of real workers, but whether their jobs continue to exist. Third, there has been a reshaping of behavioural norms. Dore (2003) speaks of the triumph of a 'market mindset': the belief that the hegemony of market (including financial) institutions is right and proper. Part of this mindset is the assumption that all market processes are equivalent. This is a bizarre belief. My local fruit and vegetable market is in important respects incommensurable to the New York Stock Exchange. To regard tomatoes and derivatives as analogous objects of market exchange is to succumb to the fetishism of fictitious commodities.

Models and systems: do they exist?

Comparativists always face the problem of generalization. Given the multiplicity of national cases (27 now just within the European Union), how can we simplify in order to make analytical sense? The solution has to involve typification: reducing diversity to a limited number of 'models' or ideal-types by abstraction of what are regarded as key characteristics and suppression of more complex aspects of differentiation. Such a process is necessary but treacherous: simplification inevitably involves over-simplification. So, for example, it is common to speak of a 'European social model' of corporate governance and industrial relations; but national systems of employment protection, labour market regulation, employee representation and social welfare are so diverse that all attempts to 'harmonize' on a standard pattern have proved futile (Ebbinghaus, 1999).

In typification there is always a trade-off between accuracy and parsimony (Przeworski and Teune, 1970) – for this reason I do not accept the argument of Crouch (2005: 40) that a simpler model is preferable to a more complex one only if there is no loss of explanatory power. To my mind, this counsel of perfection entails a veto on any kind of theory. The issue has to be: what is gained and what is lost with a specific parsimonious account of complex reality? And costs and benefits have to be judged in terms of the actual purpose of a researcher's modelling. The dichotomy proposed by Hall and Soskice (2001b) between 'liberal' and 'coordinated' market economies is for most purposes woefully inadequate, offering idealized accounts of the USA and Germany as exhaustive alternatives within which national diversity can be encompassed (Crouch, 2005; Deeg and Jackson, 2008). Yet this simplistic presentation of varieties of capitalism remains popular because of its heuristic value in demonstrating starkly that market economies can indeed be organized according to very different institutional logics.

What is important though – a point which Crouch (2005) makes cogently – is to avoid conflating analytical abstractions with empirical descriptions. To speak of models of capitalist variety, to repeat my earlier remark, is to offer schematic (over-)simplifications of complexity. For example, when La Porta et al. (1998) refer to 'French civil law countries' in their study of the effects of corporate governance rules they do not pretend to give a full and precise description of the company law regimes in all countries grouped under this label (perhaps not even France) but to highlight, one-sidedly, features central to their analytical purpose. (This was of course Weber's intention when devising the concept of ideal types.)

As a corollary, the tendency of many current researchers to write of 'hybridization' is deeply suspect. A mule is a hybrid of a donkey and a mare, two empirically existing animals. By contrast, a 'hybrid' business system or employment regime is a case, which cannot usefully be attributed to any category within a classificatory scheme. To say, for example, that France or Germany is hybridizing really means simply that there are important changes going on in the real world and that our analytical abstractions fail to capture these. No more and no less.

One reason references to hybridization are so common is that ideal types, models and systems are frequently viewed as internally coherent and functionally integrated. It is assumed that institutions are 'tightly coupled with each other' (Hollingsworth and Boyer, 1997: 3), giving rise to what Dore (2000: 45–7) calls 'institutional interlock'. Functional integration in turn makes incremental change difficult if not impossible. Where change undeniably does occur, the explanation must be that social-systemic mares and donkeys somehow manage to combine what are at first sight incompatible institutional elements to construct a new coherent amalgam.

Such analytical stratagems are unnecessary, as Crouch has shown, if we abandon the idea that socioeconomic systems through some process of

natural selection evolve complementary institutional elements. His thesis is that economic institutional complexes typically display contradiction
and incoherence, opening possibilities of 'recombination' of the constituent
elements; and that this is why change is possible and persistent. This said,
however, we need to recognize that some socioeconomic systems *are* more
systemic than others. How and why 'tight coupling' occurs in some national
contexts but not others is a major analytical issue.

What does it mean to compare?

My concluding thoughts address a core problem for comparativists: to clarify
what is meant by cross-national comparison and how it can be accomplished.
I have explored these questions elsewhere (Hyman, 2001) and wish here only
to offer some very brief remarks.

Comparison, as I understand it, means the *systematic* cross-case analysis of
phenomena displaying both similarities and differences. It both contributes
to and is informed by theory and generalization. Hence: how and why are
institutional differences between countries reflected in different outcomes?
Or – to revisit North's argument cited previously – how do differences in regulatory context affect the effects of what are superficially the same institutions?

In my own field of trade union studies, this question has been provoca-
tively discussed by Locke and Thelen (1995). Ostensibly similar issues, they
argue, vary markedly in significance for trade unions according to national
circumstances and traditions; while apparently dissimilar issues may have
similar implications across countries. More specifically, the historical formation of distinctive national union identities shapes those issues which
are likely to provoke visceral conflict and those which are not. Hence, they
suggest, the task for researchers must be to develop 'contextualized comparisons' which involve in each national case the choice of issues which present
equivalent challenges to union identities. 'By focusing on the way different
institutional arrangements create different sets of rigidities and flexibilities,
we can identify the range of possible "sticking points"... We find that those
that generate the most intense conflicts are those which are so bound up with
traditional union identities that their renegotiation in fact sets in motion a
much deeper and fundamental reevaluation of labour's "project"' (Locke and
Thelen, 1995: 338).

This argument has much in common with the call by Geertz (1973) for
'thick description': behaviour can be properly understood only in terms of
the social context which gives it meaning. In the fields both of international
business and industrial relations, the meaning of institutions seems to vary
with national context. Yet this entails, as Locke and Thelen propose by the
title of their article, that cross-national comparison is a dubious process of
comparing apples and oranges. How can we *make* institutions comparable
despite contextual variation? Alas, it is questionable how far 'contextualized

comparisons' are in fact comparative. Rather, the logic of the approach which Locke and Thelen advocate would seem to be that each context is unique and that the dynamics of each national institutional configuration must be analysed in its own terms.

The underlying paradox, to my mind, is that comparative analysis is essential but perhaps impossible. Less dramatically, one might say that comparative research is an art rather than a science. As comparative researchers, our main contribution to understanding lies in our ability to tell a plausible and elegant story, one which illuminates both our own national context and that of the 'other'. Our concern with the unfamiliar (together with our willingness to perceive what is strange in the familiar) can indeed assist us in unearthing new and important types of evidence. How we move from this to comparative argument and explanation will always involve a certain alchemy.

Bibliography

Amable, B. (2003). *The diversity of modern capitalism* (Oxford: Oxford University Press).

Aoki, M. (2001). *Toward a comparative institutional analysis* (Cambridge, MA: MIT Press).

Aoki, M., Jackson, G. and Miyajima, H. (eds) (2007). *Corporate governance in Japan: institutional change and organizational diversity* (Oxford: Oxford University Press).

Brouthers, K. D. (2002). 'Institutional, cultural and transaction cost influences on entry mode choice and performance'. *Journal of International Business Studies*, 33(2): 203–21.

Crouch, C. (2005). *Capitalist diversity and change: recombinant governance and institutional entrepreneurs* (Oxford: Oxford University Press).

Deeg, R. and Jackson, G. (2008). 'Comparing capitalisms: understanding institutional diversity and its implications for international business'. *Journal of International Business Studies* (forthcoming)

Delios, A. and Henisz, W. J. (2000). 'Japanese firms' investment strategies in emerging economies'. *Academy of Management Journal*, 43(3): 305–23.

Dicken, P. (2003). *Global shift: reshaping the global economic map in the 21st century* (London: Sage).

Djankov, S., Glaeser, E., La Porta, R., Lopez-de-Silanes, F. and Schleifer, A. (2003). 'The new comparative economics'. *Journal of Comparative Economics*, 31(4): 595–619.

Dore, R. (2000). *Stock-market capitalism, welfare capitalism: Japan and Germany versus the Anglo-Saxons* (Oxford: Oxford University Press).

Dore, R. (2003). 'New forms and meanings of work in an increasingly globalized world'. ILO Social Policy Lectures. Available at: http://www.ilo.org/public/english/bureau/inst/download/dore.pdf

Due, J., Madsen, J. S. and Petersen, L. K. (1994). *The survival of the Danish model: a historical sociological analysis of the Danish system of collective bargaining* (Copenhagen: Jurist- og Økonomforbundets Forlag).

Ebbinghaus, B. (1999). 'Does a European social model exist and can it survive?' In G. Huemer, M. Mesch and F. Traxler (eds), *The role of employer associations and labour unions in the EMU*, pp. 1–26 (Aldershot: Ashgate).

Esping-Andersen, G. (1990). *The three worlds of welfare capitalism* (Cambridge: Polity Press).

Ferner, A., Quintanilla, J. and Sanchez-Runde, C. (eds) (2006). *Multinationals, institutions and the construction of transnational practices* (Basingstoke: Palgrave Macmillan).

Geertz, C. (1973). *The interpretation of cultures: selected essays* (New York: Basic Books).

Gereffi, G. (1994). 'The organization of buyer-driven global commodity chains: how US retailers shape overseas production networks'. In G. Gereffi and M. Koreniewicz (eds), *Commodity chains and global capitalism*, pp. 95–122 (Westport: Praeger).

Gereffi, G., Humphrey, J. and Sturgeon, T. (2005). 'The governance of global value chains'. *Review of International Political Economy*, 12(1): 78–104.

Gospel, H. and Pendleton, A. (eds) (2004). *Corporate governance and labour management* (Oxford: Oxford University Press).

Hall, P. and Soskice, D. (2001a). 'An introduction to varieties of capitalism'. In P. Hall and D. Soskice (eds), *Varieties of capitalism: the institutional foundations of comparative advantage*, pp. 1–72 (Oxford: Oxford University Press).

Hall, P. and Soskice, D. (eds) (2001b). *Varieties of capitalism: the institutional foundations of comparative advantage* (Oxford: Oxford University Press).

Hassel, A. (1999). 'The erosion of the German system of industrial relations'. *British Journal of Industrial Relations*, 37(3): 484–505.

Henderson, J., Dicken, P., Hess, M., Coe, N. and Yeung, H. (2002). 'Global production networks and analysis of economic development'. *Review of International Political Economy*, 9(3): 436–64.

Hofstede, G. (1980). *Culture's consequences: international differences in work-related values* (Beverly Hills, CA: Sage).

Hollingsworth, J. R. and Boyer, R. (1997). 'Coordination of economic actors and social systems of production'. In J. R. Hollingsworth and R. Boyer (eds), *Contemporary capitalism: the embeddedness of institutions*, pp. 1–47 (Cambridge: Cambridge University Press).

Hyman, R. (2001). 'Trade union research and cross-national comparison'. *European Journal of Industrial Relations*, 7(2): 203–32.

Immergut, E. M. (1998). 'The theoretical core of the new institutionalism'. *Politics and Society*, 26(1): 5–34.

Khanna, T. and Palepu, K. G. (1997). 'Why focused strategies may be wrong for emerging markets'. *Harvard Business Review* (July–August).

Khanna, T. and Palepu, K. (2006). 'Strategies that fit emerging markets'. *Harvard Business Review*, 84 (June): 60–9.

Khanna, T., Palepu, K. G. and Sinha, J. (2005). 'Strategies that fit emerging markets'. *Harvard Business Review*, 83(6) (June): 63–76.

Kochan, T., Katz, H. C. and McKersie, R. B. (eds) (1986). *The transformation of American industrial relations* (Ithaca: ILR Press).

Kostova, T. (1999). 'Transnational transfer of strategic organizational practices: a contextual perspective'. *Academy of Management Review*, 24(2): 308–24.

Lane, C. and Probert, J. (2007). 'Domestic capabilities and global production networks in the clothing industry: a comparison of German and UK firms' strategies'. *Socio-Economic Review*, 4(1): 35–68.

La Porta, R., Lopez-de-Silanes, F., Shleifer, A. and Vishny, R. W. (1998). 'Law and finance'. *Journal of Political Economy*, 106(6): 1113–55.

Locke, R. M. and Thelen, K. (1995) 'Apples and oranges revisited: contextualized comparisons and the study of comparative labor politics'. *Politics and Society*, 23: 337–67.

North, D. C. (1990). *Institutions, institutional change and economic performance* (Cambridge: Cambridge University Press).

Polanyi, K. (1944). *The great transformation* (New York: Rinehart).

Powell, W. W. and DiMaggio, P. J. (eds) (1991). *The new institutionalism in organizational analysis* (Chicago: University of Chicago Press).

Przeworski, A. and Teune, H. (1970). *The logic of comparative social inquiry* (New York: Wiley).

Sako, M. (2007). 'Organizational diversity and institutional change: evidence from financial and labour markets in Japan'. In M. Aoki, G. Jackson and H. Miyajima (eds), *Corporate governance in Japan: organizational diversity and institutional change* (Oxford: Oxford University Press).

Scott, R. (1995). *Institutions and organizations* (London: Sage Publications).

Streeck, W. and Thelen, K. (2005). *Beyond continuity: institutional change in advanced political economies* (Oxford: Oxford University Press).

Thelen, K. (1999). 'Historical institutionalism in comparative politics'. *American Review of Political Science*, 2: 369–404.

Wan, W. P. (2005). 'Country resource environments, firm capabilities, and corporate diversification strategies'. *Journal of Management Studies*, 42(1): 161–82.

Whitley, R. (ed.) (1992). *European business systems* (Oxford: Oxford University Press).

Whitley, R. (1999). *Divergent capitalisms: the social structuring and change of business systems* (Oxford: Oxford University Press).

10
Corporate Social Responsibility: an Institutional Perspective
John H. Dunning

Introduction

Over the past two decades much has been written on the subject of corporate social responsibility (CSR). From an international business perspective, several papers in a recent focused issue of the *Journal of International Business Studies* (JIBS) reviewed some of the firm-specific organization and strategic managerial issues and challenges posed by them (Eden et al., 2006). A more multifaceted and interdisciplinary approach is taken by van Tulder and van der Zwart (2006). They view CSR as part of a business–society management nexus, which has become more varied and complex as a result of globalization.[1] The ethical implications of CSR have been addressed by several scholars, such as Sethi (2003a, 2003b), van Marrewijk (2003), Kolk and van Tulder (2004) and Garriga and Mele (2004). In this chapter, we shall attempt to integrate these alternative approaches to CSR by relating each to the 'big picture' now emerging in international business (IB) scholarship. In so doing we shall suggest that this can best be done by embracing a more institutional perspective on the subject.

The big picture

The unique issue addressed by IB scholars, from each of the disciplines comprising this distinctive field of study, relates to the determinants of the cross-border value-added and transactional activities of firms; the strategies of such firms in identifying and pursuing these activities; and the effects which such activities may have on their objectives and those of other actors affected by their actions. Such activities may take the form of trade, foreign direct investment (FDI) and a host of alliances and network-related ventures.

While this brief has not changed over time, its contents may and do differ. So indeed do the critical questions arising from, and pertinent to, IB. Thus, as a result of globalization, technological advances, and the emergence of new economies in the international arena, perhaps the main question in the early twenty-first century is how best to reconcile the economic benefits of globalization with the social needs and cultural aspirations of local communities. Such a question is being primarily addressed in the context of the changing *human environment*, which embraces both economic and non-economic goals sought by individuals and organizations, and the institutions underpinning and effecting the achievement of these goals.[2]

For much of the last two or more decades, the attention of IB researchers has focused on how wealth creation and the efficient deployment of resources and capabilities can be enhanced by multinational enterprises (MNEs) operating in the global marketplace. The strong assumption has been that the main ingredient of wealth creation is knowledge enhancement. Such enhancement may take the form of upgrading either human or physical capital. Both, however, imply the efficient management of such assets by private or public organizations to increase the quantity, variety and quality of goods and services, and so improve the *physical environment* in which people live.[3] Drawing on an impressive range of data showing that knowledge-intensive societies are generally materially richer and/or the faster growers of GNP per capita, IB and other scholars have examined the implications of these facts for the strategies of MNEs and the geography of their activities, as well as for the welfare of communities of which they are part.[4] Resource based and evolutionary theories of the firm, as well as those focusing on the financial and marketing decisions of firms, largely address themselves to issues relating to the *physical environment*.

In its way, this research has yielded highly useful results – and continues to do so. As the current main modality of international commerce (UNCTAD, 2006), FDI is essentially an instrument for the transfer of information and knowledge, whether that information and knowledge take the form of technology, managerial or organizational competencies, or access to markets. In the 1970s, some countries placed objectives other than increasing GNP per capita (via FDI) at or near the top of their economic and social agenda, and a great deal of attention was paid to issues of national sovereignty and cultural identity. Yet, for the most part, firms and countries from market economies tended to pursue, and indeed were sometimes encouraged to pursue, explicit and single-minded objectives. Both goals were assumed to be achieved by upgrading the *physical environment* in which they operated. In the former case this was assumed to be the pursuit of profits (Friedman, 1983), and in the latter case to improving their GNP per head and their international competitiveness.

What then has changed? The answer is that the *human environment* in which firms do business across border has changed. And it has done so in three main ways. The first is that the goals and/or their prioritizations by individuals and organizations – both individually and collectively – have become more multifaceted. Essentially, as countries have become richer, as more data have become available on the relationship between human well-being and economic performance (Oswald, 1997; Layard, 2005), and as issues relating to health, safety, the environment, social safety nets and security become more valued for themselves as intrinsic goods (Donaldson, 2001), the content and significance of their *human* as well as their *physical environment* changes. Not only this. Globalization has increased awareness of the fact that the *human environment* of countries varies as much as, if not more than, their *physical environment*; and that the former is often more resistant to change (North, 2005; Dunning, 2007a).

Second, the behaviour of individuals is being increasingly influenced by the institutions of society of which they are part.[5] These institutions comprise a bevy of formal and informal incentive structures and enforcement mechanisms, which, between them, determine the understanding, attitudes, motivation and behaviour of individuals and organizations. While institutions of a regulatory, cognitive or normative kind[6] have always influenced the conduct and character of the activity of firms, the *physical* and *human environment* in which they operate has become more complex, volatile and uncertain. Consequently, the need for more and stronger institutions to mitigate or counteract the accompanying rise in transaction costs has become more urgent (North, 2005). Again, these institutions vary markedly across national boundaries. How do the MNEs take account of them (Husted and Allen, 2006)? And how far does their widening geographical spread help induce a global mindset and facilitate the cross-border transfer of new institutional capabilities (Dunning, 2007b)?

Hence our contention is that, since societal goals are becoming more multifaceted, and as issues relating to human welfare spread beyond the material and extend to those of fairness, sovereignty, security and the environment, so the incentive structures and enforcement mechanisms initiated by, or imposed on, particular MNEs, have become a more important ingredient of their contribution to the upgrading of the *human environments* in which they operate.

It is not the purpose of this chapter to describe in detail why, or how, the formal and informal institutions affecting IB activity have changed over the last two decades or more; nor why and in what respects IB scholars are giving more attention to them. Our main point of emphasis is that such institutions are essentially part of the *human environment*. The values and belief systems underpinning them are likely to vary more across, rather than within, national or regional boundaries.[7] As they are essentially devised and implemented by human beings, they critically affect the motivation and behaviour of wealth-creating entities and hence deserve more careful attention by IB scholars for these reasons. Of course, for many years, culture and human resource management – to mention just two areas of IB dealing specifically with the *human environment* – have made important contributions to our thinking about the determinants of the international activities of firms, and their impact on the countries in which they operate (Graham, 2000). But, all too frequently, these contributions – apart perhaps from those of Geert Hofstede – have been sidelined and undervalued by mainstream IB scholars.[8] But recent events have catapulted several of them to centre stage in IB teaching and research.

A new approach to evaluating corporate social responsibility

So what are the implications of the big 'picture', as it has evolved over the past two or three decades, for IB scholarship? How, in theory or practice, do issues relating to the demands by society that corporations should behave in a particular – what we will define as a responsible – way affect our understanding of the determinants of IB activity, the ways in which it is organized, and the response of governments and other extra market actors to it?

We shall concentrate our remarks on CSR viewed primarily from the perspective of *firms* and *national governments*. This in no way belittles the importance of other social-cum-ethical issues. Take corruption, for example, which is dealt with by Senior (2006) and several authors in the JIBS focused issue mentioned earlier.[9] Corruption is a very human activity! Corruption is shown to affect FDI; it does so in varying degrees according to (a) other *push* and *pull* factors, e.g. attraction of markets, availability of natural resources and lower costs of production; (b) the extent of, and attitudes of, firms and home governments towards corruption; and (c) the institutions affecting the cognition, motivation and behaviour of the individuals and organizations of home and host countries, which display the extent and content of corruption, and the response of firms to it. However, although very important in some countries, sectors and areas of decision-taking, it remains a *relatively* small part of the changing *human environment* in which MNEs operate.

This is not so in the case of CSR, which is a topic which often generates more heat than light! From the point of view of an economist and IB scholar, we would like to offer a rather different (but we believe complementary) view on the role of CSR in affecting the motivation and strategy of MNEs, and on business–society management, to that taken by most contributors to the debate. In doing so, we would like to start with the proposition (which itself may be somewhat contentious) that the *business and responsibility of corporations is to engage in value added activities and the transactions associated with them, in a way that best satisfies the objectives of the society of which they are part.* These needs may extend well beyond the creation of material wealth, and include a range of desirables such as security, food safety and environmental protection. In most contemporary capitalist societies it is accepted that firms operating within the discipline of the market offer the best opportunity for achieving this goal. The challenge of national governments, however, on the part of the constituents they represent, is to ensure that the outcome of decisions and actions taken by firms in pursuit of their private goals produces results that best coincide with societal needs.[10]

In received neo-classical economics, and in conditions of perfect markets, this congruence of interests of firms and society is completely and uniquely met. But the assumptions underlying this congruence are very strict. These include no extra-market consequences of market activities, no monopolistic or structural distortions, the absence of uncertainty, and complete freedom of entry and exit of firms. In such an institutional setting, firms can only make normal profits if they behave in a socially responsible way, and Pareto optimality exists.

In practice, this situation has never accounted for other than a relatively small proportion of the activities of firms in most economies. Today, monopolistic competition and oligopoly are the dominant market structures. There are two reasons why in the early twenty-first century (with one or two notable exceptions)[11] it is less applicable than it has ever been. The first is the growth of public goods which are not produced or sold in the open market. The second is that, due *inter alia* to the growing uncertainty, volatility and complexity of contemporary economic activity, market failure abounds.

In our present context, we shall identify three main types of market failure, in which corporate behaviour *may* not satisfy the needs of society. The first is where the structure of the market is itself distorted, and the participating firms have the option to engage in socially irresponsible practices. Such a failure may be the outcome of an increased (relative) size and economic power of firms (Hymer, 1976); but, more usually, it is a reflection of opportunism, moral hazard and information asymmetries (Buckley and Casson, 1976). At worst, such failure can result in corporate malfeasance, the abuse of human rights and in the exploitation of child labour in some of the poorer developing countries (Kolk and van Tulder, 2004). But, normally, the opportunities for the practice of corporate social irresponsibility (CSI) are less blatant than these. *Inter alia* they range from bribery, lack of transparency, tax evasion and environmental degradation, to poor working conditions and a failure to provide information about the safety or health implications of the products being sold.

The second type of market imperfection relates to externalities. These market 'spillover' effects of the activities of firms may be beneficial or disadvantageous to society. Examples of the former include the externalities of the training and innovatory activities of firms, and, of the latter, the discharge of pollution of one kind or another. Corporations may or may not be aware of these externalities. Sometimes, they may act as trailblazers – especially where regulations and standards are higher or more stringent in the home country and are transferred to a host country. But more often than not, corporations have been accused of externalizing whatever costs they can. Indeed, one author (Bakan, 2004) claims that such actions are one of the most virulent forms of CSI.

The third type of imperfection arises because, in practice, both individuals and organizations have differing cognitive abilities and mindsets, and different interpretations of the contents of CSR. As Maitland and Nicholas (2003) have observed, the uncertainties, volatility and complexity of the contemporary global economy combine to create a *human environment* in which corporate decisions are taken in conditions of bounded rationality and information asymmetries, and where moral hazards abound. Such conditions may open up a new set of behavioural options to firms. Some of these, if deployed, could widen the gap between private and social behavioural responsibilities; others might help to lessen it. Taking a rather different perspective, Levy et al. (2007) point to cross-border differences in managerial mindsets and intentions which, they argue, may inhibit the global strategies and operational flexibility of MNEs.

It is critical to acknowledge that the content of CSR (and CSI) is likely to be highly contextual over both time and space. In the United Kingdom and the United States, for example, the current values attached to environmental protection, working lifestyles, health and product safety are generally much less than those voiced a century ago; while these same ingredients of human welfare are today accorded a lower priority in most developing countries than in developed countries (UNCTAD, 1999a: Chapter 12). This means that the likelihood of a divergence between corporate private and social interests is likely to be particularly marked where First World MNEs are investing in Third World countries, and where Third World MNEs are investing in First World countries (UNCTAD, 1999b, 2001, 2006). It is also the case that some processes and products are likely to generate more social and economic externalities than others. Similarly, the extent and content of mindsets and external or internal institutional incentives necessary to promote CSR are likely to fluctuate over time and space.

We accept that, in pursuing this line of argument, we are in danger of going beyond the normal interpretations of 'responsibility'; and that expressions such as 'conduct', 'acceptability' or 'net benefits' may be more appropriate. At the same time, the boundaries and definitions of the scope and content of CSR vary a great deal, while the borderline between the 'responsible' and 'neutral' corporate actions of firms are frequently very blurred.[12]

One answer to this conundrum is to introduce the moral or ethical dimension.[13] Obviously not all differences between corporate and societal interests are value laden. Clearly too, in some cases, to align the two sets of interests where the expected social net benefits are likely to exceed the expected private net benefits, it is up to society to provide the formal or informal institutions which encourage or compel firms to produce the products or engage in the processes it requires at minimum social costs. At the other extreme, it is also patently obvious that some actions by firms *are* value laden, and have considerable moral or ethical implications. Corporate malfeasance (e.g. corruption, dishonesty, fraud, deliberately withholding information, false or misleading advertising) may each be regarded as completely unacceptable to societal well-being. Other practices may be similarly criticized, such as providing deliberately opaque information concerning the content of particular health or food products, the financial viability of the company, its subcontracting procedures, its labour practices, or its marketing techniques. It is such practices – and the motivation and belief systems behind them – which are not in accordance with societal values that most scholars interpret as being irresponsible. CSR, on the other hand, is viewed as firms not only possessing a mindset and behaving in a way consistent with societal objectives and values, but in some cases, acting as spearheads in advancing these objectives and values.

Let us summarize our thoughts up to this point. We have identified the content of CSR as the cognition, belief systems, motivations and behaviour of firms, as articulated in their production and transactional activities, which are consistent with the goals of society, as interpreted by the leading opinion formers and decision-takers of that society.[14] In a capitalist economic system it is accepted that privately owned corporations are not only the main wealth creators of society but, left to their own devices and within the legal framework set by governments, they will pursue their own goals, or those of their shareholders. Likely differences between the role of market institutions and extra market actors, and between private and societal needs, can be proxied by the content and the degree of market and hierarchical failure. Such failures may reflect a variety of structural market distortions, and/or various forms of intrinsic market imperfections, including positive and negative externalities and information deficiencies or asymmetries. Action taken consequential to, or influencing, such failures may be induced either by firms or by extra market actors. Often these may result in a divergence between the private and social good that may or may not be value laden. Ways and means of aligning these goals and practices (and the mindsets behind them) with the received theories of the firm are at the heart of any scholarly discussion of CSR (McWilliams and Siegel, 2001).

Within a single nation-state, these divergences may be (reasonably) easily identified and dealt with between firms and society.[15] However, when firms cross national borders into different value and institutional regimes, the problems of reconciling corporate and social goals and attitudes are likely to intensify. This is primarily because, by one means or another, a nationally oriented firm is likely to internalize the culture of society of which it is part, and the mindsets of its peoples. Where, however, it engages in international transactions, and, in particular, where it engages in FDI, a firm is compelled to relate its CSR to a different and often broader set of values, and to the goals and expectancies of the communities in which it locates its activities.

While globalization and technological change have exposed huge differences between countries in their *physical and human environments*, it is those of the latter which are currently commanding increasing attention, and posing the greatest challenges for global commerce (Sethi, 2003a; Garriga and Mele, 2004; van Tulder and van der Zwart, 2006). This is partly because of the huge transaction costs of reaching any consensus about common standards of CSR, but more we suspect, the lack of will or desire to do just this. It is this challenge of coordinating organizational learning, and reconfiguring the institutions underpinning the *human environment* so they can best facilitate and capture the benefits of globalization while protecting (where appropriate) the belief systems embedded in local cultures and social mores. We would assert that this challenge is equally, if not more, demanding than the creation and better use of resources to improve the *physical environment*.

So what can be done? A possible agenda for IB research

There continues to be much disagreement among scholars and practitioners on how the perceptions, goals and actions of corporations may accord with, or differ from, those of the societies of which they are part. Yet we believe this pales into insignificance when compared with the appropriate set of actions that might be taken to reconcile the two. That, of course, is one of society's critical and most demanding challenges. By contrast, the corporation in any given situation faces a challenge of 'how best to reconcile its CSR with that of its main and unique task in society, viz: the efficient production of goods and services, as demanded by the market, and which best meets the objectives of its stakeholders?'

Upgrading CSR in a globalizing world: a societal perspective

Let us first tackle the first question. Here there are two diametrically opposing views. The first is that it is entirely up to the actors in the wealth creation process – viz. both market (e.g. shareholders, consumers, and labour unions) and extra market actors (e.g. non-government organizations (NGOs) and governments) – to set the objectives to firms, and determine the legal, economic and institutional framework in which they operate. It is, then, the responsibility of the firm to do what it is intended to do to satisfy its stakeholders in the best way possible (Donaldson and Preston, 1995). In other words, the upgrading of CSR (whether or not one takes a value laden approach) is dependent on the choice, contents and effectiveness of extra-firm incentive structures and enforcement mechanisms.

Activism among the extra firm market participants to influence the mindsets and behaviour of corporations may come from three main sources. The first is pressures from shareholders for the firms in which they invest to engage in (what they interpret to be) socially responsible behaviour (e.g. by not investing in countries which have a bad human rights record, or are governed by racist regimes), even if this can only be achieved at the expense of profits or capital growth. Second, there may be actions by consumers to boycott the purchase of goods or services from corporations perceived to be acting in a unethically unacceptable way (e.g. MNEs subcontracting to foreign firms in apartheid regimes, or employing child labour). Third, labour unions in home countries of MNEs may use their influence and advocacy to help ensure that the rights of workers in the Third World are adhered to.

But most of the ways in which firms are influenced to be more socially responsible in their behaviour is by the content and enforcement mechanisms of extra-market institutions. Some of these may be informal (e.g. much of the advocacy of NGOs and of international agencies such as the United Nations) but, most certainly, the more widespread and effective are those of national governments. These too, may range along a spectrum ranging from constitutional reform, through a bevy of legal, regulatory requirements and policies, to example and moral suasion.

Such institutions include statutory requirements for financial reporting and the setting of accounting standards, the outlawing of illicit payments, and of minimum wages legislation. They also embrace effective competition policy, intellectual property right protection, a range of fiscal incentives and penalties, and the setting of food safety, health and environmentally friendly standards. Each of these institutions is, to some extent, value laden. Each varies in its ethical content. Each reflects a particular mindset of its initiator. Each has its own array of enforcement. Each has its own set of enforcement mechanisms. Each is intended to set the conditions under which firms might pursue their legitimate strategies of creating wealth in a cost efficient and quality enhancing way.

Much of this, of course, is well known to IB scholars. However, in respect of our current debate on the growing significance of the *human environment* in affecting IB activity and the consequential strategy of MNEs, it is worth emphasizing that the events of the last two decades – and especially that of globalization, e-commerce and the exposure of several high profile acts of corporate malfeasance[16] – have caused governments to focus increasingly on extra-market institutions as the modality for enhancing CSR (UNRISD, 2004). Whether or not this is the most cost effective way is open to question! But there is some evidence to suggest that developing and transition economies which are demanding higher CSR standards from their firms, are those which are among the most competitive and attractive to inbound foreign investors (Swift and Zadek, 2002).

The alternative view to the one just expressed is that corporations themselves should take the lead and make themselves more socially responsible; and that many of the actions implemented by them should be spontaneously and voluntarily undertaken (Utting, 2005). Chief among the institutions for encouraging such behaviour are self-generated codes of conduct or guidelines to 'good' behaviour by which individual firms, or groups of firms, agree to abide. There are literally hundreds of such codes initiated by, or addressed to, MNEs; and they cover virtually all aspects of corporate behaviour. These range from the UN Global Compact, which identifies nine principles of behaviour to which all firms are invited to subscribe (Kell and Ruggie, 1999), and the UN norms of responsibilities of transnational corporations and business enterprises with regard to human rights (UN, 2002);[17] through incorporating CSR provisions into bilateral or international investment agreements (UNCTAD, 2001), to a variety of informal incentive structures initiated and implemented by international agencies or MNEs (OECD, 2000, 2001). Again these actions vary from those designed to promote both socially acceptable behaviour and the (long-term) self-interest of corporations – and often these corporations act as trailblazers in advancing social objectives – to those which are purely altruistic in intent.

Once again, however, the attitudes of corporations to their own rights and responsibilities for acting in accord with societal values are highly contextual. They are likely to vary between (and in some cases within) firms (e.g. according to their objectives, size, corporate culture, form, and the geography of their internationalization strategies), the market structure in which they compete, the type and range of products they supply, the processes they engage in, and their relationships with their stakeholders, other firms and extra-market entities.

Most certainly, it is difficult to generalize as to the most effective way of promoting more CSR by firms – and particularly by MNEs. Husted and Allen (2006) have examined the tradeoffs between an institutional and a strategic approach to CSR, and conclude that such a choice is likely to be highly contextual. Our own belief is that, only an integrated and multifaceted approach will come near to achieving this goal. In some cases, *top-down* legislation and enforcement mechanisms, or *bottom-up* activism on the part of consumers, investors and special interest groups may help to produce the desired results (but at what cost?). In others, the belief systems and culture of the corporation itself – and more especially that of the key decision-takers within the corporation – may be the spontaneous and pro-active agent for change. As already stressed, so much depends on the particular context in which CSR is being examined. Questions such as what do different national governments expect of their corporations, and what is the quality and authority of their institutions? What particular aspects of CSR are most in need of upgrading? What should be the respective role of informal and formal incentive structures and enforcement mechanisms in influencing the attitudes and conduct of firms? How does the balance between such structures vary between societies, industries and type of corporations? To what extent should CSR be regarded as an integral part of the stakeholder theory of the firm and related to sustainable value creation (Pitelis, 2004)? And in the case of MNEs, how may they harmonize their value-added activities to meet the (often) very different goals of the societies in which they operate in a way which is consistent with their own legal obligations[18] and global strategies?

A corporate perspective

As long as a firm is making at least the returns on any given investment equal to its opportunity cost (i.e. the next best investment alternative) it will continue to abide by any formal rules or informal codes of behaviour placed upon it by either market or extra-market actors – and especially those of national governments. If, however, the meeting of these demands reduces its profits to below that level, it will either exit from some, or all, of its current value-added activities or reconfigure these and/or its strategic focus in a way which reduces the gap between its private and societal interests. Again, the MNE (and its affiliates) might respond in several ways when faced with diverse interpretations of what is expected of it by different national governments. These may range from a complete exit from countries imposing such responsibilities, particularly where the company is fighting for its commercial survival, to a simple absorption of the costs involved, when it is making above normal profits. Yet very little is known about the reactions of foreign investors to the various institutional measures which might be initiated by host governments to induce or enforce responsible behaviour by their subsidiaries: or, indeed, on how this response might depend on the types of incentive structures implemented (e.g. moral persuasion and tax breaks compared with regulatory measures). As a result, it is extremely difficult to generalize on how extra market attempts to inject more CSR into the strategy and conduct of firms – especially MNEs with their wider options – will be successful, and at what cost, both to the firm and society.

Of course, corporations may also be pro-active instruments in advancing CSR (Sethi, 2003a). In many cases (e.g. in the environmental, health, safety and security areas, in financial reporting, and in reducing information asymmetries), some have actively sought to invest in and/or promote more socially acceptable or higher product standards. While, in the short run these might reduce profits, in the long run they may regain or increase their market share, as they are flagged as good corporate citizens. Moreover, the introduction of higher standards, improved working conditions and more responsible advertising may, at least over time, be cost and/or market effective; and entirely consistent with the social legitimacy and legal obligations of the corporation.

One thing is, however, quite clear. As issues relating to the *human environment* have become more important; as and when corporations incorporate these into their agenda; as and when corporations extend or deepen their international operations; and as and when they become conduits for transferring mindsets, institutions, resources and capabilities across the world – CSR is likely to demand more attention of scholars as a component of IB activity and a factor influencing the competitiveness of firms.

Are global codes of behaviour standards the answer?

In the course of this chapter, we have alluded to the problem that the reconciliation of the goals and strategies of firms which operate outside their national boundaries, with those of the societies of which they are part is made difficult because those of the latter vary over time and space, and because the global *human environment* is becoming more complex, volatile and uncertain.

The solutions offered to this dilemma stretch along a continuum between two extremes. The first is to try and harmonize or standardize institutions and the incentive structures of countries participating in international commerce. After that, the global challenge of ensuring MNEs behave in a socially acceptable way would be similar to that of reconciling the values and actions of national corporations to those of the societies of which they are part. This implies that it is both possible and desirable to design and implement a cosmopolitan mindset among corporate managers, and, too, a universally acceptable set of standards, incentive structures and enforcement mechanisms. In the current situation in which the global *human environment* is made up of widely different ideologies, cultures and forms of capitalism, this kind of consensus to upgrade the CSR of firms seems extremely remote. A contemporary example is the very different perceptions on the content and desirability of CSR, taken by the Chinese and most Western governments as implemented by their own MNEs.[19]

At the same time, there is evidence to suggest that some types of global institutions can be very effective – particularly as they help advance a socially acceptable *physical environment*.[20] But even in such an environment human beings are inherently more value-oriented and idiosyncratic than are other assets; and a global consensus about competition policy, the environment, labour standards, social disorder and information disclosure is likely to be more difficult to achieve, than that to do with promoting an acceptable patent system, the regulation of air transport, or the implementing of common product norms. Yet, some values and virtues are not only essential to the efficient conduct of international business but are respected by each of the cultures in which MNEs operate. Such values and virtues have been variously named as 'fundamental', 'cardinal,' 'basic' and 'cosmopolitan'. They are what Donaldson and Dufee (1999) refer to as hypernorms. Even though such values as basic human rights, human dignity, truthfulness, honesty, reciprocity and forbearance are inevitably subject to different interpretations, these ingredients of CSR, and the institutions underpinning and guiding their implementation are likely to generate more consensus between societies than the second order or subordinate values. These latter values are more likely to reflect differences in improved localized institutions such as social norms, traditions and belief systems. However, over time, as cross-border economic integration progresses, not only is it likely there will be some convergence of these, but as Kwok and Tadesse (2006) and Ozawa (2005) have shown, the MNE may be an important agent in linking national with extra-national institutional frameworks.

Once again the globalization versus localization debate over CSR yardsticks is a highly contextual one. So is the debate over the extent to which the incentive and/or regulating structures initiating, implementing and monitoring such yardsticks should be formal or informal. Over the last decade, some progress has been made on reaching international agreement on some of the main technical issues relating to CSR such as environmental standards, financial transparency, intellectual property rights and corporate accountability, as well as towards the establishment of a global compact on corporate behaviour and embedding CSR into international investment agreements (Sethi, 2003b; Kolk and van Tulder, 2005). It has been claimed that because most of these initiatives are informal institutions and do not bind corporations to abide by their provisions, they can never be fully effective. However, it is difficult to see how, in today's world, and at a global level, more formal mechanisms for encouraging CSR can be effectively enforced.[21]

With respect to more specific issues, and most noticeably in tackling deliberate anti-social behaviour by firms (e.g. in the area of human rights, monopoly or exploitative labour practices), there is a case for strengthening both national and international regulations and enforcement mechanisms for harmonizing mindsets and ensuring that common CSR standards are effectively policed. Indeed, there is a growing consensus among countries about the need to devote more societal resources to reducing the social 'bads' of economic activity, and/or to encourage corporations to internalize the extra market costs they impose on society. But for the many grey areas where society is forced to choose between advancing economic efficiency and a variety of social 'goals', differences between the institutions and values of firms and governments are likely to persist. In such cases, the IB scholar is compelled to take a very pragmatic approach to evaluating the net benefits of producing any particular combination of welfare-enhancing products, not to mention the way in which they are produced and the ways in which the resulting benefits are distributed. In the end, we believe that, given the knowledge and values it has, society has to decide both on the choice of options to adopt, and on the ways in which that choice is implemented.

Conclusions

One of the features of contemporary global capitalism is the belief by democratic governments that, although they, on behalf of the constituents they represent, should set the agenda for the creation and sustenance of economic and social well-being, and the institutional framework for its achievement, much of the responsibility for delivering the desired well-being, and the way it is delivered is being increasingly delegated to, or shared with, private firms. This, of course, has always been so in the production of goods and services, the optimum amount, quality and price of which are determined by market forces. But, today, corporations are having to factor in both extra-market considerations and new societal values into their attitudes, strategies and behaviour, either voluntarily or by decree. This development sets the broad-brush framework for analysing CSR and its various components which embrace the perspective of both corporations and the other stakeholders in global capitalism.

In this chapter, we have sought to identify both the conditions under which firms may be prompted to upgrade their CSR; and why, when operating in very different *human environments*, each with its own particular cultures and institutions, the MNE is faced with a number of additional unique challenges. Foremost among these is the reconciliation of the benefits of a globally accepted CSR with the very specific economic and social needs, resources, capabilities and institutions of the countries in which they operate. A key component of any agenda for research by IB scholars concerns whether and to what extent it is possible to take on board the location-specific components of CSR, while capturing the economic benefits of a global coordination of value-added activities. And, what exactly does this mean for the cognitive sensitivity of corporate managers, and the institutional strategy of firms and of governments? How far, and in what respects, is it in their best interests, and that of the societies in which they operate, for firms – and MNEs in particular – to spontaneously and voluntarily upgrade their CSRs? When (and where) are *top-down* incentive structures and enforcement mechanisms desirable, and when (and where) are *bottom-up* initiatives likely to be more effective? How far are these institutions likely to be country-, industry- or firm-specific? How far too by acting as a link between national and extra-national institutional environments can MNEs help to make known and encourage the acceptance of best practice CSR?

These are partly positive and partly normative questions. But each (and many others) needs to be addressed if IB scholars are to construct a 'big picture' of how the growing attention paid to CSR and related topics are affecting the determinants and impact of IB activity; and the strategies of firms and the policies of governments in implementing them. The agenda open to scholarship is, indeed, a daunting one, but it is one which, we believe, offers considerable intellectual and societal rewards.

Notes

1. See also a review of some of the reactions of extra-market actors (e.g. governments and civil society) to CSR in UNCTAD (1999a).
2. Elsewhere (Dunning, 2007a) we have identified the contents of the *human environment* as embracing all the elements affecting the cognition, belief systems, motivation and behaviour of individuals and organizations engaging in the *physical environment* of which they are part.
3. I am indebted to the work of Douglass North (2005) from where I have abstracted the terms *physical and human environment*. For the purposes of this chapter, we define the *physical environment* as the ways in which firms create and deploy the scarce resources and capabilities available to them, and their accessing and exploitation of input and output markets. For an extended review of this concept and its relevance to and for IB scholarship see Dunning (2007a).

4. Some of these studies are reviewed in Chapter 10 of Dunning and Lundan (2008). See also the *Economist* (2005).
5. For some reviews of the meaning and type of institutions see Henisz (2000), Williamson (2000), Xu and Shenkar (2002), Maitland and Nicholas (2003), Mudambi and Navarra (2002), and Rodrick et al. (2004).
6. In a recent contribution, Rondinelli (2005) has classified institutions into seven groups: i.e. those assisting economic adjustment, those perfecting private property, those facilitating freedom of enterprise, those promoting competition, those strengthening economic motivation, those promoting social equity and access to opportunity, and those setting rules and offering societal guidance. It is the last four which are especially relevant when considering the content and effectiveness of the *human environment*.
7. The term 'institutional distance' has been recently coined in the literature *inter alia* by Xu and Shenkar (2002).
8. As evidenced, for example, by the limited citations to such contributions.
9. Notably by Yadong Luo, Chuck C. Y. Kwok and Solomon Tadesse, Utz Weitzel and Sjors Berns, Alvaro Cuervo-Cazurra, and Eden et al. (2006).
10. We accept that included in our interpretation of CSR, is the presumed compliance of corporations to formal rules and regulations set by national governments. Yet institutions which cause firms to behave in a socially acceptable way include a galaxy of informal and persuasion instruments including those which might be spontaneously initiated by the firms themselves. For a survey of the ways in which the CSR of corporations may be affected by formal institutional mechanisms see Abrahams (2004).
11. These primarily represent a reduction in transaction costs due to advances in communications technology.
12. David Henderson, who is highly critical of the doctrine of CSR, at the same time believes that 'businesses should behave responsibly'. His concept of the scope of CSR, however, is particularly broad and embraces measures to affect some perceived negative aspects of globalization, which not all commentators, including myself, would accept (Henderson, 2001).
13. Dealt with by various scholars, cited earlier, writing particularly in the *Journal of Business Ethics*.
14. We appreciate that, in practice, such goals may be manipulated by powerful groups within society.
15. Although some nation-states (e.g. Japan) are more culturally and institutionally homogeneous than others (e.g. the United States).
16. As for example are documented in Dunning (2003).
17. This document treats human rights as including those relating to equal opportunity and non-discriminatory treatment, to security of persons, to the rights of workers, to respect for national sovereignty, to obligations with respect to consumers and environmental protection. In short they are nearly as broad in scope as our own interpretation of CSR.
18. In this connection, Joel Bakan (2004) points out that corporations are 'created by law' and that 'law dictates what their directors and managers can do, what they cannot do and what they must do' (p. 35). Bakan goes on to say that in the United States and other industrialized countries 'the corporation, as created by law ... compels executives to prioritise the interest of their companies and shareholders above all others' (p. 35). In this sense at least, corporate officials, as stewards of their shareholders' money, have no legal obligation to undertake social

or any other actions which are not in the interest of their shareholders (Bakan, 2004: 37).

19. Compare, for example, the social responsibility practices by Chinese MNEs in sub-Saharan extractive industries with those of traditional First World foreign investors. This is one of the topics currently being pursued by UNCTAD in preparation of the *World Investment Report* for 2007.

20. Witness a huge array of international organizations in the scientific, technological, medical, air transport and communication domains; and in a variety of social activities, e.g. health and education, cooperation in the detection/reduction of crime, promotion of tourism, etc.

21. However, cross-border cooperative efforts to enforce intellectual property rights (IPR), and combat intellectual property crime (IPC) taken by the G8 countries at the St Petersburg summit in July 2006, might (if successful) serve as a template for an international approach to fostering CSR (Jamieson, 2007).

Bibliography

Abrahams, S. (2004). *Regulating corporations: a resource guide* (Geneva: UNRISD).

Bakan, J. (2004). *The corporation: the pathological pursuit of profit and power* (London: Constable and Robinson).

Buckley, P. J. and Casson, M. (1976). *The future of the multinational enterprise* (Basingstoke: Macmillan).

Donaldson, T. (2001). 'The ethical wealth of nations'. *Journal of Business Ethics*, 31(1): 25–36.

Donaldson, T. and Dufee, T. W. (1999). *Ties that bind: a social contracts approach to business ethics* (Boston: Harvard Business School Press).

Donaldson, T. and Preston, L. O. (1995). 'The stakeholder theory of the corporation: concepts, evidence and implications'. *Academy of Management Review*, 20(1): 65–91.

Dunning, J. H. (ed.), (2003). *Making globalization good* (Oxford: Oxford University Press).

Dunning, J. H. (2007a). 'A new zeitgeist for international business and scholarship'. *European Journal of International Management*, 1(4): 278–301.

Dunning, J. H. (2007b). *Space, location and distance in IB activities: a changing scenario.* Reading and Rutgers Universities (mimeo).

Dunning, J. H. and Lundan, S. (2008). *The multinational enterprise and the global economy* (Cheltenham: Edward Elgar).

Economist (2005). 'A survey of corporate social responsibility'. 22 January: 3–18.

Eden, L. Hillman, A., Rodriguez, P. and Siegel, D. (eds) (2006). 'Three lenses on the multinational enterprise: politics, corruption and corporate social responsibility'. *Journal of International Business Studies*, 37(6): 733–46.

Friedman, M. (1983). 'The social responsibility of business'. In T. L. Beauchamp and N. E. Bowie (eds), *Ethical theory and business* (New Jersey: Prentice Hall).

Garriga, E. and Mele, D. (2004). 'Corporate social responsibility theories: mapping the territory'. *Journal of Business Ethics*, 53(1–2): 51–71.

Graham, E. M. (2000). *Fighting the wrong way: antiglobal activists and multinational enterprises* (Washington, D.C.: Institute for International Economics).

Henderson, D. (2001). *Misguided virtue* (London: Institute of Economic Affairs).

Henisz, W. J. (2000). 'The institutional environment for international business'. *Journal of Law, Economics and Organisation*, 162: 334–64.

Husted, B. W. and Allen, D. B. (2006). 'Corporate social responsibility in the multi-national enterprise: strategic and institutional approaches'. *Journal of International Business Studies*, 37(6): 838–49.

Hymer, S. (1976). *The international operations of national firms: a study of direct foreign investment* (Cambridge, MA: MIT Press).

Jamieson, P. (2007). 'G8's prioritization of IPR enforcement a positive step'. *The Times: Intellectual Property Supplement* (21 February).

Kell, G. and Ruggie, J. G. (1999). 'Global markets and legitimacy: the case of the "global compact"'. *Transnational Corporations*, 9(3): 101–20.

Kolk, A. and van Tulder, R. (2004). 'Ethics in international business: multinational approaches to child labor'. *Journal of World Business*, 39(6): 49–60.

Kolk, A. and van Tulder, R. (2005). 'Setting new global rules: TNCs and codes of conduct'. *Transnational Corporations*, 14(3): 1–29.

Kwok, C. C. Y. and Tadesse, S. (2006). 'The MNC as an agent of change for host-country institutions: FDI and corruption', *Journal of International Business Studies*, 37(6): 767–85.

Layard, R. (2005). *Happiness: lessons from new science* (London: Allen Lane).

Levy, O., Beechler, S., Taylor, S. and Boyacigiller, N. A. (2007). 'What we talk about when we talk about "global mindset": managerial cognition in multinational corporations'. *Journal of International Business Studies*, 38(2): 231–58.

Maitland, E. and Nicholas, S. (2003). 'New institutional economics: an organizing framework'. In J. Cantwell and R. Narula (eds), *International business and the eclectic paradigm*, pp. 47–73 (London & New York: Routledge).

McWilliams, A. and Siegel, D. (2001). 'Corporate social responsibility: a theory of the firm perspective'. *Academy of Management Review*, 26(1): 117–27.

Mudambi, R. and Navarra, P. (2002). 'Institutions and international business: a theoretical overview'. *International Business Review*, 11(6): 635–46.

North, D. C. (2005). *Understanding the process of economic change* (Princeton: Princeton University Press).

OECD (2000). *The OECD guidelines for multinational enterprises: revision 2000* (Paris: OECD).

OECD (2001). *Making codes of corporate conduct work: management control systems and corporate responsibility* (Paris: OECD).

Oswald, A. J. (1997). 'Happiness and economic performance'. *Economic Journal*, 107: 1815–31.

Ozawa, T. (2005). *Institutions, industrial upgrading and economic performance in Japan* (Cheltenham: Edward Elgar).

Pitelis, C. (2004). '(Corporate) governance, (shareholder) value and (sustainable) economic performance'. *Corporate Governance*, 12(2): 210–23.

Rodrick, D., Subramanian, A. and Trebbi, F. (2004). 'Institutions rule: the primacy of institutions over geography and integration in economic development'. *Journal of Economic Growth*, 9: 131–65.

Rondinelli, D. A. (2005). 'Assessing government policies for business competitiveness in emerging market economies: an institutional approach'. In R. Grosse (ed.), *International business and government relations in the 21st century*, pp. 395–420 (Cambridge: Cambridge University Press).

Rondinelli, D. A. and Behrman, J. N. (2000). 'The institutional imperatives of globalization'. *Global Focus*, 12(1): 65–78.

Senior, I. (2006). *Corruption: the world's big C* (London: Institute of Economic Affairs).

Sethi, S. P. (2003a). 'Globalization and the good corporation: a need for pro-active existence'. *Journal of Business Ethics*, 43(1–2): 21–31.

Sethi, S. P. (2003b). *Setting global standards: guidelines for creating codes of conduct in multinational corporations* (Hoboken, NJ: John Wiley and Sons).

Swift, T. and Zadek, S. (2002). *Corporate responsibility and the competitive advantage of nations* (Copenhagen: The Copenhagen Centre for Accountability).

UNCTAD (1999a). *World investment report 1999: foreign direct investment and the challenge of development* (New York and Geneva: United Nations).

UNCTAD (1999b). *The social responsibility of transnational corporations* (New York and Geneva: United Nations).

UNCTAD (2001). *Social responsibility*. UNCTAD series of issues in international investment agreements (New York and Geneva: United Nations).

UNCTAD (2006). *World investment report 2006: FDI from developing and transition economies – implications for development* (New York and Geneva: United Nations).

United Nations (2002). *The human rights responsibilities of companies* (New York: United Nations).

UNRISD (2004). *Corporate social responsibility and development: towards a new agenda* (Geneva: United Nations Research Institute for Social Development).

Utting, P. (2005). 'Rethinking business regulation from self regulation to social control'. *Technology, Business and Society*, no. 15 (Geneva: United Nations Research Institute for Social Development).

van Marrewijk, M. (2003). 'Concepts and definitions of CSR and corporate sustainability: between agency and communion'. *Journal of Business Ethics*, 44(2): 95–105.

van Tulder, R. and van der Zwart, A. (2006). *International business–society management: linking corporate responsibility and globalisation* (London and New York: Routledge).

Webley, S. and Le Jeune, M. (2005). *Corporate use of codes of ethics: 2004 survey* (London: Institute of Business Ethics).

Williamson, O. (2000). 'The new institutional economics: taking stock, looking ahead'. *Journal of Economic Literature*, 38: 595–613.

Xu, D. and Shenkar, O. (2002). 'Institutional distance and the MNE'. *Academy of Management Review*, 27(4): 608–18.

11

A Comparison of Mergers and Acquisitions in Japan, Europe and the United States

Gregory Jackson and Hideaki Miyajima

Introduction

A large social science literature has emerged on the role of mergers and acquisitions (M&A) in corporate strategy. Yet the frequency, motivation and type of takeover activity across countries are strongly influenced by various institutional characteristics of the national business system (Goergen et al., 2005; Hall and Soskice, 2001; Rossi and Volpin, 2003). In the United States and the United Kingdom, the level of M&A is high and hostile takeovers are seen as being common (or at least a realistic possibility). In Japan and other continental European countries such as France or Germany, the level of M&A activity has been much lower prior to the 1990s. Moreover, hostile takeovers were extremely infrequent or even perceived as being impossible to implement.

This difference in the role of the market for corporate control reflects a central distinction among diverse national systems of corporate governance (Aguilera and Jackson, 2003; Baums, 1993; Höpner and Jackson, 2001; Kester, 1990). In the United States and the United Kingdom, takeovers represent a central market-based mechanism for corporate governance. In Japan and Germany, corporate governance involves banks that undertake long-term relational lending and stable equity ties with industrial companies (Aoki and Patrick, 1994; Baums, 1993; Hoshi and Kashyap, 2001; Vitols, 2001). Likewise, both countries have strong inter-firm groups bound by horizontal cross-shareholding arrangements or pyramidal blockholding. These features of stable ownership and banking monitoring effectively prevent hostile takeovers. France does not have a strictly bank-based system, but corporate governance also involves large blockholdings and interlocking directorates among financial, business and government elites (Goyer, 2003). The *absence* of takeovers in these countries may help prevent 'breach of trust' and support firm-specific or relationship-specific investments by different stakeholder groups (Armour et al., 2003; Deakin et al., 2002; Höpner and Jackson, 2001).

Nonetheless, the diversity of national corporate governance systems has changed in recent years and M&A activity has increased globally. In particular, bank–firm relations and inter-firm cross-shareholding arrangements have eroded. Other legal changes have facilitated mergers and acquisitions by liberalizing share swaps, spin-offs and holding companies. Japan has experienced a small number of unsolicited hostile takeover attempts that have a high symbolic importance. Other coordinated market economies, such as France or Germany, have also seen a growth in levels of M&A and a growing 'hostility' of takeover activity. The hostile takeover of Mannesmann by Vodafone represents a watershed change towards a growing international market for corporate control (Höpner and Jackson, 2006).

This chapter will examine the implications of the global market for corporate control by comparing the characteristics of M&A deals in five countries: France, Germany, Japan, the United Kingdom and the United States. The comparative analysis draws data from the Thomson Banker One 'Deals' database, and relates to all deals in Japan, France, Germany, the United Kingdom and the United States that were completed between 1991 and 2005. The United States and the United Kingdom both have relatively developed takeover markets, but approach takeover regulation in quite different ways in terms of defensive tactics and mandatory bids. Meanwhile, Germany and France have undergone institutional changes similar to Japan in terms of changing ownership patterns, as well as legal reforms towards more 'open' takeover markets. The chapter asks what similarities and differences exist in the ways the M&A market operates across countries? The central hypothesis is that despite some convergence towards increasing M&A, significant differences exist in the type of market transactions found within different national 'varieties of capitalism' (Hall and Soskice, 2001). This hypothesis is explored with respect to a number of deal characteristics: takeover bids, the size of stakes purchased, the prior stakes held, the use of private negotiation, degree of hostility, and takeover premium.

These aspects of transactions reflect different sociological characteristics of markets, such as their social embeddedness (Podolny, 2001; White, 2002). The analysis suggests that in countries with 'coordinated' market economies, M&A displays greater social embeddedness in ongoing business relations reflected in greater 'coordination' of transactions. As such, the market for corporate control does not necessarily entail a convergence of national business systems, but a pattern of change influenced by strong continuities.

The rise of M&A in comparison

Comparative data on M&A activity was drawn from the Thomson Banker One 'Deals' database. The database tracks all mergers and acquisitions of both

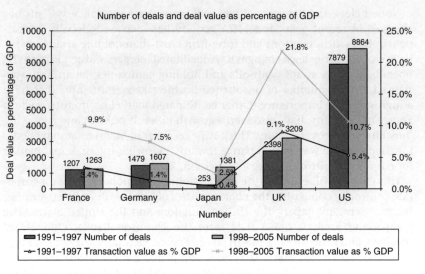

Figure 11.1:   Volume of M&A deals, 1991–1997 and 1998–2005

publicly listed and private companies based on public or media disclosure. Deals for each country are counted here to include:

- domestic deals (In-In);
- deals with foreign buyers and domestic targets (Out-In);
- deals with domestic buyers and foreign targets (In-Out).

The section presents a comparison of the volume and characteristics of M&A deals. The section aims to show the rise of M&A particularly in Japan, France and Germany, and explore the factors driving M&A in terms of economic growth strategies in new industries and restructuring in declining industries.

Figure 11.1 reports a summary comparison of average annual deal volume in the periods 1991–7 and 1998–2005. All five countries show moderate to large increases in the number of deals, and large increases in deal value relative to GDP. The United Kingdom notably has the highest level of deal activity at roughly 21 per cent of GDP. Meanwhile, deal value in France and Germany in the 1998–2005 boom period totalled 8–10 per cent of GDP. Deal value in Japan totalled only 2.5 per cent of GDP during the boom period, and thus remains substantially lower than the other four countries.

Much of the existing literature suggests that takeovers come in 'waves' that have common characteristics. The period from 1993 is sometimes considered the fifth major historical wave of M&A, following waves of the early 1900s, the 1920s, the 1960s and the 1980s. According to the historical precedents, the increase in M&A in recent years has been influenced by a variety of causes (Martynova and Renneboog, 2005):

- excess industrial capacity in particular sectors;
- technological innovation and new growth opportunities in particular sectors;
- deregulation of markets in previously regulated sectors or through regional integration of markets that either increase pressures for restructuring or open new growth opportunities (e.g. EU integration);
- change in the supply of finance (e.g. changes in the availability of finance or high stock market valuations utilized in share swaps, etc.); or
- reduction of institutional barriers towards M&A (e.g. holding company, share swaps, etc.).

No one factor explains the increase in M&A activity across all five countries. M&A activity was found in both growing and consolidating sectors, and these patterns were intensified by deregulation and cross-border market integration. Finance also played a role through the stock market boom of the late 1990s and growing use of share swaps to finance transactions. In institutional terms, France, Germany and Japan all removed some important barriers to M&A transactions and helped them narrow the gap in M&A activity with the United States and the United Kingdom. Despite these strong common trends across countries, the weight of these various factors differed between Japan, Europe and the USA. Sectoral consolidation and restructuring was somewhat more important in Japan, whereas high-growth industries were more important in the United States. European countries saw a dramatic increase in cross-border M&A that reflects the growing liberalization and integration of European markets.

Institutional diversity and takeover markets

The previous section noted the 'catching up' of Japan, Germany and France to levels more similar to the United States and the United Kingdom. Besides the possible 'demand side' factors for M&A, important changes occurred in the 'supply side' of target firms and their institutional characteristics, particularly in Japan, France and Germany. Japan, Germany and France are all broadly considered to be 'coordinated market economies' (CMEs) where corporate ownership, finance, inter-firm relationships and industrial relations all display higher degrees of coordination based on relationship-specific assets and long-term cooperation ties (Amable, 2003; Hall and Soskice, 2001; Yamamura and Streeck, 2003). Meanwhile, the US and UK are considered 'liberal market economies' (LMEs) where transactions are more market-driven and arm's length. For example, differences in ownership concentration mean that M&A must be negotiated with key blockholders, banks or other stable shareholders in the case of CME countries. Likewise, German and Japanese banks have also tended to support management against hostile bids. Given the different contexts of market-based and bank-based financial systems, few groups of investors have emerged in Germany or Japan, who are willing and skilled in providing specialist finance for risky or aggressive takeovers oriented at corporate restructuring.

In the past, these institutional differences contributed to the higher levels of M&A in the United States and the United Kingdom, and lower levels in France, Germany and Japan. But the growth of M&A among CME countries raises an interesting set of questions as to whether this growth reflects institutional change towards more liberal sets of institutions (Hall and Thelen, 2005; Howell, 2003; Paunescu and Schneider, 2004). An alternative view may be that M&A has become situated within and at least partially adapted to past sets of institutions in a 'path dependent' manner (Aoki, 2001; Deeg, 2005; Mahoney, 2000). Put another way, to what extent do past institutional differences still shape the M&A market across countries? Do distinct varieties of capitalism also lead to varieties of takeover markets? The differences in ownership and legal rules may be reflected in the more 'organized' or 'coordinated' nature of the market for corporate control in Germany, France and Japan.

Changes in the institutional barriers to M&A

Institutional factors are important in explaining cross-national variation in takeover activity (Rossi and Volpin, 2003). First, M&A is higher where investor protection is greater, reflected in shareholder rights or good accounting standards. Second, M&A is also higher in countries with concentrated ownership, since transfers of control may be easier. However, ownership concentration acts as a major barrier against hostile takeovers and may generally only facilitate M&A during periods of time when concentrated owners may be willing to sell (Burkhart and Panunzi, 2006). Finally, M&A may be facilitated in countries where legal protection for employment (e.g. rights regarding dismissal) are low (Pagano and Volpin, 2005). To what extent have these types of barriers to M&A transactions decreased in the last decade?

In terms of shareholder rights, we compare changes in a six-point index of shareholder rights between the years 1990 and 2000 (La Porta et al., 1998; Pagano and Volpin, 2005). While the United Kingdom and the United States score 5 out of 6 during both time periods, France increased from 3 to 4 points, Germany from 1 to 3 points, and Japan increased from 4 to 5 points. The three coordinated economies have moved towards greater shareholder rights, although only Japan equals US levels. Meanwhile, firms in France and Germany have increasingly moved to the use of international accounting standards that are more market-oriented and based on the notion of a true and fair view of company value. Similarly, Japan has introduced market-based valuation and consolidated accounting into its accounting rules in the late 1990s, which particularly affected the valuation of cross-shareholdings among Japanese companies. Consolidation has reduced some of the accounting benefits to having complex group structures, since losses cannot be easily hidden off balance sheet in subsidiary firms. These accounting rules and corresponding tax reforms have also made it easier to merge companies.

Changes in corporate ownership have also influenced the level of M&A. In the United States and the United Kingdom, institutional investors are generally receptive to takeover bids as a way to realize share price premiums. By contrast, concentrated blockholders in Germany and France or cross-shareholding in Japan effectively limited M&A activity, especially hostile bids. Banks have been at the core of these stable shareholding arrangements, and have tended to defend management against hostile bids (Baums, 1993). However, these ownership patterns have changed substantially in the past decade. In Germany, the density of the core inter-firm network has been weakening (Höpner and Krempel, 2003). In Japan, cross-shareholding levels have also declined rapidly (Kuroki, 2003). Much of the unwinding of shares has been between banks and firms during the banking crisis. Likewise, French firms began to loosen and then consolidate patterns of cross-shareholding since the early 1990s.

As a very broad comparative measure, the Thomson Banker One database reports a figure for the percentage of 'closely held shares' among listed companies. The figure includes a wide variety of different owners, including families, inter-corporate holdings or even shares held by directors as being closely held. As such, the data are very vulnerable to disclosure practices across countries. For example, the Japanese figure reports the aggregate share of the top ten shareholders in a given year, since this information is available in company reports. These figures show that the percentage of closely held shares was 29 per cent among UK and US listed firms in 1997, and gradually increased to 33 per cent in 2005. Meanwhile, the same figure was 69 per cent in Germany, 61 per cent in France and 48 per cent in Japan in 1997. However, levels of closely held shares declined to 60 per cent in Germany, 58 per cent in France and 41 per cent in Japan in 2004/5. These data suggest some unwinding or erosion of tightly held share ownership in Europe and Japan, which may help to explain the growing exposure of firms to M&A.

The attitudes among stable shareholders have also begun to change. In Japan, stable shareholders increasingly consider potential share price performance and might be tempted or need to justify to their own shareholders if they decline a bidder offering a large premium. Likewise, German banks have shifted strategy overtly and dramatically towards UK or US-style investment banking (Hackethal et al., 2005, Vitols, 2005). Some banks have now played important roles in *supporting* hostile bids (Höpner and Jackson, 2001). Japanese main banks still play a more influential role in protecting group companies, but also increasingly broker M&A transactions by offering LBO-type finance and making introductions among friendly firms. Finally, the French system of state-led credits and inter-corporate shareholding has slowly collapsed and led to a more arm's-length relationship between French banks and large firms (Cieply, 2001; Hancké, 2002).

A final set of barriers to M&A concerns the role of employees. It is often noted that takeover gains in the US and UK are associated with corporate restructuring and rationalization of costs, often through reducing levels of employment (Conyon et al., 2001, 2002; Deakin et al., 2002; Schnitzer, 1995). This type of rapid employment adjustment is difficult to implement in France, Germany and Japan due to a variety of factors such as employment protection laws, employee participation and firm-specific human capital. In broad comparative terms, these institutions have remained stable relative to the other changes in ownership discussed above (Jackson, 2005).

In sum, institutional barriers to M&A have become weaker in France, Germany and Japan. The legal infrastructure has become more market-oriented, ownership has become less concentrated, and banks play a less openly defensive role. Nonetheless, these institutions have not converged on the same legal rules, ownership patterns or role of stakeholders as found in the United States or the United Kingdom. This raises an interesting question as to how these past institutions shape the characteristics of M&A transactions across countries. The remainder of this section explores these issues by comparing some key characteristics of M&A transactions across countries. Differences in coordination are explored in terms of the following:

- forms of transactions;
- use of takeover bids (TOBs);
- ties between acquirer and target firms;
- the importance of hostile bids.

Forms of transactions

The forms of M&A deals are shown in Table 11.1. Deals are classified as mergers when a combination of business takes place or 100 per cent of the stock of a public or private company is acquired. By contrast, acquisitions fall into various different categories where a majority or minority stake of the target company is acquired. Here some interesting differences emerge. Among

Table 11.1: Mergers and acquisitions of listed firms, by form of transaction, 1991–2005

	France	*Germany*	*Japan*	*UK*	*USA*
Acquisition of majority interest	23%	30%	13%	6%	6%
Acquisition of partial interest	52%	55%	68%	46%	45%
Acquisition of remaining interest	17%	8%	7%	3%	3%
Merger	8%	7%	12%	45%	45%
Number of transactions	2000	1110	2256	2715	13398

deals where the targets were publicly listed firms, mergers were the most common form of deals in the United States and the United Kingdom (45 per cent), but mergers were relatively uncommon in Japan, France and Germany (7–12 per cent). Acquisitions of majority interests were relatively common in France and Germany (23–30 per cent), less common in Japan (13 per cent) and rare in the United Kingdom and the United States (6 per cent). Meanwhile, the acquisition of partial interests was the most common in Japan (68 per cent), followed by Germany and France (52–55 per cent) and then the United States and the United Kingdom (45–46 per cent). These figures show the greater importance of acquisitions where the target firm remains independent in Japan, France and Germany than in the UK and US. In Japan, this may reflect the desire to retain firm-specific employment systems across different companies. More generally, the firm may be seen as an organic community, rather than a collection of assets, which can be transferred between communities. Overall, the importance of majority and partial acquisitions reflects the more coordinated nature of inter-firm groups in Japan, France and Germany (Hall and Soskice, 2001).

Public takeover bids

Another indicator of market coordination is given by the relative importance of public takeover bids. Use of a public bid is a key aspect of market-oriented transactions, since the bid is public and open to all shareholders. As such, it often reflects high degrees of ownership dispersion since target firm shareholders are not known individually. Likewise, TOBs represent a strong element of shareholder rights in deciding the outcome of a takeover. Table 11.2 shows the number of takeover bids (TOBs) based on tender offers for target companies. Notably the number of TOBs in Japan has increased in the last five years from 5 to 44 per year. TOBs are most common in the United Kingdom, which has strict mandatory bid rules, resulting in 43 per cent of deals using TOBs where target firms are listed. In France, the use of TOBs has increased from 27 per cent to 41 per cent of deals with public targets. Rates of TOB usage remain much lower in the US (15 per cent of deals with publicly listed targets), Germany (11 per cent) and Japan (12 per cent). Notably, the role of TOBs may differ across countries. For example, Japanese TOBs are used among foreign buyers or buy-out funds acquiring controlling stakes, as well as for within-group transactions, such as when parent firms take majority stakes in listed subsidiary companies or take those firms private. For example, Matsushita Electric Industrial launched a TOB when it increased its stake in Matsushita Electric Works from 34 per cent to 51 per cent. Looking at all Japanese TOBs, only 7 per cent involved mergers whereas 53 per cent involved acquisitions of majority stakes, 33 per cent partial stakes and 6 per cent remaining stakes. France and Germany are similar to Japan in that only 12 per cent of TOBs involved mergers, but 44 per cent involved acquisitions

Table 11.2:   Average numbers of takeover bids, 1991–1999 and 2000–2005

	1991–9	2000–5
Average number of TOBs per year		
France	57	51
Germany	8	13
Japan	5	44
UK	109	77
US	153	120
Percentage of deals when target firm is publicly listed using TOBs		
France	27%	41%
Germany	9%	11%
Japan	10%	12%
UK	38%	43%
US	10%	15%

of remaining interests, which suggests a consolidation of listed subsidiary firms within inter-company groups.

Relations between target and acquirer

Further evidence regarding coordination can be found by showing the percentages of shares previously held by acquiring companies and the size of stakes acquired during M&A. Figure 11.2 shows the percentage held by the acquiring firm before the M&A transaction and the average percentage acquired during the transaction. These data are restricted to publicly listed target firms only. Acquiring firms in the United States and the United Kingdom usually start with very low levels of shareholding, under 5 per cent of the target firm shares, and acquire very large stakes, averaging 65–75 per cent of target firm shares. In France or Germany, acquirers start with larger blocks of 10–25 per cent, and typically acquire roughly 30 per cent of target firm shares. This pattern is consistent with the high proportion of deals for majority or minority participations found in Figure 11.2. In Japan, acquirers held roughly 4 per cent of target shares during the early 1990s, but this figure has dramatically increased to nearly 11 per cent after 1998. This suggests that Japanese target firms are increasingly members of existing business groups or have some other relationship to the acquiring company prior to the bid. Likewise, the average size of stake purchased during M&A deals is 25–30 per cent. This pattern is again consistent in showing a very high proportion of Japanese deals involve acquisitions of partial interests.

Likewise, Figure 11.3 shows the percentage of deals involving acquisitions of large stakes. Here Japan has the highest level of large stake purchases at between 30 per cent and 45 per cent of deals. Notably, the trend is towards lesser involvement of stake purchases during the last two or three years.

Average stake held by acquirer prior to the deal, listed target firms

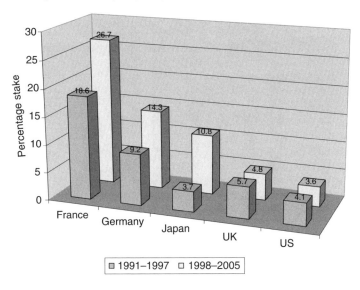

Average percentage stake acquired during M&A transaction

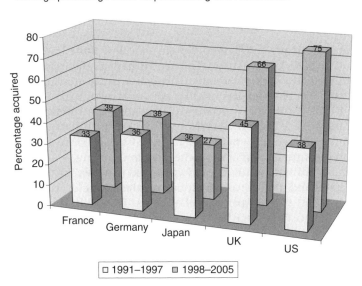

Figure 11.2: Average stakes held by acquirers prior to deals, 1991–1997 and 1988–2005

Percentage of deals involving acquisition of block stake from third party

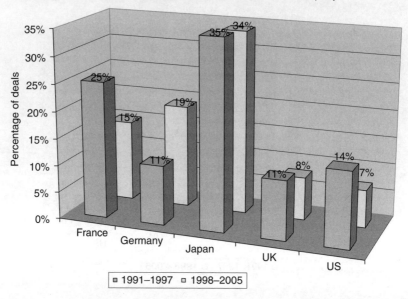

Figure 11.3:   Percentage of deals involving the acquisition of block stakes from third parties, 1991–1997 and 1998–2005

Predictably, Germany and France follow in typically having 15–25 per cent of deals that involve stake purchases. The trend is gradually falling in France, but seems to be increasing in Germany. This indicates the growing willingness of German large blockholders to sell their shares, which has led to a rapid decline in the density of ownership stakes among the 100 largest German companies over the last ten years (Höpner and Krempel, 2003). Importantly, the number of large stake purchases increased rapidly since 1999, perhaps related to the introduction of the Eichel Plan in Germany, which eliminated capital gains taxation on the sale of large blocks (Höpner, 2000). Finally, the United States and the United Kingdom have the lowest levels of large stake purchases at less than 10 per cent of all deals. These differences reflect the overall differences in ownership dispersion between these economies.

Figure 11.4 shows the proportion of deals that involved privately nego-tiated purchases of stakes. Around 11–12 per cent of deals were privately negotiated in Japan, compared to less than 5 per cent in other countries. Among listed companies, the percentage of deals with private negotiation increased from 37 per cent in 1991–9 to 50 per cent in 2000–5. This compares to around 25 per cent or less in other countries. Private negotiation is most commonly used during acquisitions of partial stakes. In Japan, the 'brokered'

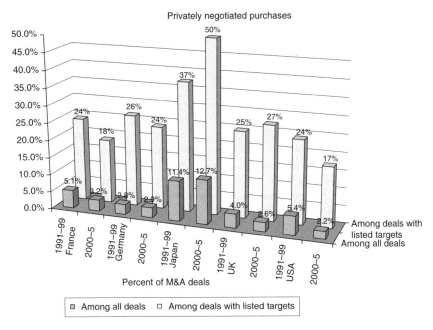

Figure 11.4:   Privately negotiated purchases, 1991–1999 and 2000–2005

Table 11.3:   Hostile takeover attempts by outcome, 1991–2005

	Hostile attempts	Sold to raider	Sold to alternative bidder	Remained independent
France	18	12	4	4
		67%	22%	22%
Germany	6	5	0	1
		83%	0%	17%
Japan	6	1	0	5
		17%	0%	83%
United Kingdom	176	74	34	68
		42%	19%	39%
United States	332	73	103	156
		22%	31%	47%

nature of transactions is also reflected in the growth of bank-related buy-out and private equity funds (Yanagawa, 2007).

Hostile bids

A final difference in M&A remains the low degree of hostile takeovers in France, Germany and Japan. Table 11.3 shows the number of attempted hostile takeovers and their outcomes for the period 1991–2005. The most hostile bids were in the United States and the United Kingdom, whereas France, Germany and Japan had relatively few bids. Notably, levels of hostile deals declined dramatically from the 1980s, when the United States had an average of 52 hostile bids per year and the United Kingdom had 31 hostile bids per year – falling to 32 and 17 bids per year respectively during the 1990s, and just 7 or 8 hostile bids per year since 2000. Of the 332 hostile bids shown for the United States, only 22 per cent of bids led to a successful takeover by the bidder. The target successfully remained independent in 47 per cent of cases and was sold to an alternative bidder in 31 per cent of cases. By contrast, hostile bids are more successful in the United Kingdom. Of the 176 hostile bids in the United Kingdom, 42 per cent were successful, 39 per cent were unsuccessful and 19 per cent led to the target being sold to an alternative bidder. Hostile bids are rare but more successful in France (12 out of 18 bids were successful) and in Germany (5 out of 6 attempts were successful). Hostile cases were the most infrequent and least successful in Japan, where only 1 out of 6 hostile attempts led to the firm being sold to the hostile bidder.[1]

The differences in the success of hostile bids may reflect some of the interesting differences in takeover defences, particularly between the United States and the United Kingdom. In the United States, the most common form of defence is the poison pill, and was found in 73 of attempted bids. White knights were involved in 23 cases and proxy fights in 15 cases. Meanwhile, poison pills are nearly impossible to implement under the UK takeover rules and proxy fights play no substantial role. Most defensive strategies in the United Kingdom therefore involve white knights. However, the overall number of defensive tactics counted in the United Kingdom was just 37 compared to 133 in the United States. The remaining countries have primarily relied on white knights in terms of defences, although Japan has implemented rules for the adoption of poison pills since 2005.

It has been widely argued that poison pills do not necessarily frustrate a deal entirely, but lead to further negotiations and may improve the price of a bid.[2] Looking at the entire sample of 538 hostile attempts in the five countries during 1991–2005, the overall success rate of hostile bids is just 30.7 per cent. However, poison pills greatly reduced the success rate of hostile bids to just 16.7 per cent (significantly different from the overall mean at $p\ 0.0018$). Likewise, the 15 cases of proxy fights led to a success rate of just 13.3 per cent (just shy of statistical significance with p value of 0.0701). In the 48 cases of white knight defences, only 10.4 per cent were successful (significantly different from the overall mean at $p\ 0.0007$). Thus, poison pills, proxy fights and white knight defences seem to lower the chance of successful hostile bids from one-half to one-third. It should be noted that this evidence is largely based on the United States, and the same might not necessarily apply to Japan or elsewhere.

Table 11.4: Proportions of firms targeted for M&A, 1991–1999 and 2000–2005

	1991–9	2000–5
Proportion of firms with low price-book ratios (less than 1) targeted in M&A		
France	4%	8%
Germany	2%	2%
Japan	1%	20%
UK	7%	8%
USA	25%	6%
Proportion of firms with negative return on assets targeted in M&A		
France	22%	13%
Germany	13%	10%
Japan	5%	21%
UK	18%	11%
USA	32%	10%

The relationship between M&A and corporate performance

The growing role of M&A across countries raises questions about the relationship of M&A and company performance. Much controversy remains in the literature as to whether M&A improves company performance. Some evidence suggests that target firm shareholders benefit, but acquiring firm shareholders may have zero or negative returns. Likewise, the impact on productivity or other operational aspects of performance post-merger is rather mixed at best (Datta et al., 1992; King et al., 2004). It is beyond the scope of this study to investigate post-merger performance using rigorous methodology. But some indirect evidence regarding the role of M&A can be gained by comparing the performance characteristics of target firms across countries. Here we use two different measures. First, we calculate the proportion of target firms with price-book ratios (PBR) lower than one. Agency theory suggests that low market valuations relative to the 'real' assets of target firms will be an incentive for acquirers to take over and restructure those poorly performing companies (Manne, 1965). Second, we calculate the proportion of target companies with negative return on assets (ROA) in a given year. Negative ROA is a sign of poor operational performance that is independent of stock market valuations, which may vary according to the business cycle or other macroeconomic factors.

Table 11.4 reports the numbers of low PBR and negative ROA firms for two time periods, 1991–9 and 2000–5. The numbers are reported as a percentage of all listed firms with low PBR and negative ROA, thus giving a standardized merger ratio that shows the proportion of low performers who became targets of M&A activity. Looking at Japan, the takeover ratio of poor performers was

Table 11.5: Average share price premiums of M&A transactions and full mergers, 1991–1999 and 2000–2005

	1991–9	*2000–5*
Average share price premium of all M&A transactions, 4 weeks prior to announcement date		
France	30.6	22.3
Germany	18.3	24.1
Japan	−2.1	1.78
UK	35.1	34.4
USA	58.1	40.8
Average share price premium of full mergers, 4 weeks prior to announcement date		
France	47	28.2
Germany	−5.1	20.3
Japan	2.5	10.9
UK	45.1	39.9
USA	46.6	52.1

very low in the 1990s, but has increased to the highest level among the five countries since 2000. For example, among firms with low PBRs, 20 per cent of Japanese firms were taken over compared to just 8 per cent of French and UK firms, 6 per cent of US firms and 2 per cent of German firms. The Japanese ratio is nearly as high as the 25 per cent of low PBR firms taken over in the US during the 1990s. These figures suggest a strong disciplinary role of the Japanese M&A market since 2000. The same pattern holds among negative ROA firms. Japanese firms with low ROA were twice as likely to be taken over as US or UK firms since 2000, demonstrating a similar level as the United States and the United Kingdom during the 1990s.

Table 11.5 shows the share price premium of target firm shareholders based on the share price four weeks prior to the announcement of the deal. These data show the importance of large share price premiums among target firms in the United States and the United Kingdom relative to France or Germany. Japan is somewhat unique in having very low or negative share price premiums during both the 1990s and thereafter. However, the low premium in Japan is typical of partial acquisitions, where firms typically are acquiring large-block stakes from other shareholders, such as when cross-shareholdings unwind and the like. Since most transactions occur on a relational basis, the players are determined first and negotiate the price without an open bid. Looking only at full-scale mergers, Japanese target firms do receive a positive premium of around 10 per cent on average. While this remains low, the premium has increased since the 1990s and reflects some growing openness in the market.

The economic interpretation of the low Japanese premiums remains somewhat puzzling. Low premiums may reflect poor market evaluation of future prospects of target firms. Likewise, low premiums are sometimes interpreted to reflect weaker legal protections of shareholders (Rossi and Volpin, 2003). In support of this interpretation, Japan does lack a mandatory bid rule and accounting rules may be less protective of investors. Against this interpretation, our summary measures of investor protection discussed in earlier sections show Japan and France with very nearly the same levels of protection as the United Kingdom or the United States. Alternatively, premiums may measure the private benefits of control for acquiring firms. Here low premiums may more positively reflect the absence of wealth transfer among stakeholders associated with 'breach of trust' and post-merger restructuring. This interpretation seems plausible in the case of Japan, since the protection of stakeholders remains strong and we further noted that many acquiring firms are particularly cautious in approaching issues such as employee restructuring.

Summary

The comparative analysis in this section suggests that the M&A market reflects a broad contrast between the arm's length markets in liberal market economies and more relationship-based markets in coordinated market economies. In the United States and the United Kingdom, the importance of markets was reflected in the fact that less M&A activity was based around inter-firm networks, either through partial acquisitions or reflecting previous ties between acquirer and target firms. Takeover bids were more common. Hostile bids also remain an important phenomenon in the United States and the United Kingdom, although their importance was less in the 1990s and 2000s than in the heyday of hostile deals in the 1980s.

By contrast, the M&A markets in France, Germany and Japan remain a more 'coordinated' type of market. A higher proportion of deals involve partial acquisitions of independent firms, and stronger prior relationships exist between acquiring and target firms. This feature is particularly true in Japan. France and Germany maintain a somewhat intermediate position, reflecting inter-firm groups with higher ownership concentration but also a somewhat greater element of change in those groups. Hostile bids remain very rare in Germany and Japan, whereas France has a growing but still low level of hostile bids. Hostile bidders have been the least successful in Japan, whereas some watershed cases have occurred in France and Germany.

These comparisons confirm the growing importance of the M&A market in France, Germany and Japan, but also important differences between these countries and the United States and the United Kingdom. The characteristics of M&A deals reflect continued institutional differences leading to different degrees of 'coordination' of M&A transactions themselves. Despite these differences, M&A has become an important tool of corporate strategy for

n new industries. Moreover, some preliminary evidence of corporate
ance also suggests an important disciplinary role of the M&A market.
e was shown to have become particularly strong in Japan during the
period after 2000, where M&A have become a major vehicle for corporate
restructuring.

The future of takeovers

Despite the general picture of coordination discussed above and the low levels of hostile bids in the United States and the United Kingdom during the
last ten years, hostile takeovers remain a crucial issue for the further development of the market for corporate control. A growing number of firms have
become exposed to potential hostile bids due to erosion on non-legal barriers
(as mentioned above). Hence, the issue of defensive measures has increased
and sparked widespread political debate. This section briefly discusses the
legal frameworks regarding takeovers with a particular emphasis on defensive
actions (see detailed discussed in Jackson, 2007).

Takeover rules can be distinguished by two broad approaches: the UK
approach and the US approach. The UK approach is probably the most restrictive of frustrating actions of the board ('board neutrality') and stresses the
shareholder rights aspects of takeovers through mandatory takeover bids.
Meanwhile, the US approach allows a much wider range of defensive actions
and has no mandatory bid rule. English case law in the 1960/70s and the
1968 City Code do not charge directors to deal with hostile bids on behalf of
the target's shareholders, but give the essential power of decision to the shareholders. Consequently, the UK rules clearly contradict the rationale of poison
pills to discriminate against the hostile bidder. It also implies that most preda-
tory bidding techniques common in the United States cannot be applied
in the UK/EU and coercive bids become ineffective because of the mandatory bid rule aimed at protecting the rights and the equality of the target's
shareholders and thus their ability to decide on the outcome of the bid.

In the United States, directors deal with the hostile bidder on behalf of
the target's shareholders. US law lacks the same emphasis on the equality of
the target's shareholders. This reflects the importance of political federalism
in the United States, where takeover rules are created by individual states.
Following the hostile takeover wave of the 1980s, large corporations lob-
bied state governments to introduce protective legislation and regulate the
use of certain takeover defences. The limits placed on such defences often
relate to court decisions, such as the Revlon and Unocal rules. The Unocal rule stipulates that defensive measures may only be taken in response to
a threat to corporate policy provided the response is proportionate to the
threat. Meanwhile, Revlon duties impose a fiduciary duty on the board to
evaluate competing proposals and refrain from implementing defensive measures that deprive shareholders of the opportunity to consider competing

proposals. Thus, under the Delaware Law, US firms can adopt a 'poison pill' whereby new shares are issued, at a heavily discounted price, to shareholders other than the hostile bidder so as to substantially dilute the hostile stake.

The EU Takeover Directive has taken the UK approach as its baseline, but still allows for substantial variation across countries in terms of defensive actions. France and Germany remain able to opt out of some elements of board neutrality. Legislation in France, for example, will allow a form of poison pill through authorized capital that does not discriminate against any shareholder (unlike poison pills under the Delaware Law). Germany has not allowed poison pills under its existing law, but does allow the shareholders to give the board a reserve authorization to undertake other sorts of defensive measures. The future deployment and impact of such measures remain highly uncertain, although their impact will likely be quite limited relative to the US-style approach.

Japan has adopted a more US approach in granting managers some degree of autonomy to develop takeover defences. The Ministry of Economy, Trade and Industry (METI) has led efforts since 1997 to liberalize the M&A market, and make it easier for companies to engage in M&A transactions. However, given the largely domestic orientation, most of the deals have been friendly and the issue of takeover defences was not acute. Likewise, deregulation of cross-border deals had been undertaken, but stalled over a key issue of share-to-share exchanges with foreign companies. Specifically, the idea of a triangular merger of Japanese and foreign companies using share swaps has met with difficulties, delays, and continued problems regarding tax treatment and so on. As a result, Japan has not seen a large-scale hostile takeover of a blue chip company along the lines of Mannesmann in Germany. Given the salience of the Livedoor bid for TBS and the use of 'poison pill' defence tactics, one central issue was under what conditions defensive actions could be taken (Jackson, 2007). The METI and Ministry of Justice 'Takeover Defense Guidelines' were issued in May 2005 and outlined conditions for introducing a 'poison pill' type of defence under certain conditions. Meanwhile Japanese courts have promoted the principle that most firms should use the AGM to assure that rights plans are considered reasonable and proportional to the takeover threat (Milhaupt, 2005). As such, the Japanese rules appear to be more restrictive of defensive actions than under most US state laws, while allowing for some degree of defences.

Conclusions

This chapter has presented some preliminary comparative evidence on the characteristics of M&A in France, Germany, Japan, the United Kingdom and the United States. All five countries have experienced a significant M&A wave starting in the 1990s driven by a number of common features, such as the emergence of new technologies and growth in information and communications technology, and the consolidation of older industries. In Europe, cross-border transactions fuelled these trends as European markets became increasingly integrated. Meanwhile, Japan and the US remain more domestically oriented.

The 'coordinated economies' of France, Germany and Japan have now gone a long way in terms of promoting an active M&A market. In addition, the 'catching up' of M&A in Japan, France and Germany reflects some important changes in the institutions governing corporate governance. All three countries have increased investor protection and transparency, facilitated new methods of financing transactions through share swaps, and faced erosion of stable shareholding among firms and banks.

In this chapter, we have argued that M&A has developed along a path-dependent trajectory characterized by more relational, brokered types of transactions and a continued absence of hostile bids (although most strongly in Japan). Thus, institutional differences still influence a number of important aspects of M&A making the takeover market much more 'coordinated' as opposed to the more 'arm's length' deals in the United States and the United Kingdom. In particular, a greater proportion of deals were among related firms, and target firms were more likely to retain legal independence after being acquired. Also, the degree of hostility in France, Germany and Japan has grown but remains lower than in the United States or the United Kingdom. The 'new' market for corporate control in France, Germany and Japan is nonetheless real and represents a fundamental shift in corporate governance in these countries and emerging sets of complementarities based on 'new' M&A-related activities and 'old' bank-based monitoring and strong relationships among stakeholders (Aoki, 2007). Thus, although M&A transactions have distinct sets of characteristics, the economic functions of the M&A market may be increasingly 'functionally equivalent' in terms of promoting corporate restructuring. In Japan, the proportion of low performing firms targeted in M&A has increased dramatically and become comparable to liberal market economies, such as the United States or the United Kingdom.

As to whether these economies would benefit from a more open market, this chapter can only provide a speculative answer. France, Germany and Japan have all made efforts to retain some protections against hostile bids, in particular. The future role played by defensive measures remains uncertain, and will emerge only slowly through political debates in Europe and the development of legal interpretation by courts over the next decade. In the meantime, the increased use of M&A transactions in this context seems like a healthy development in promoting corporate restructuring, but may also represent a distinct 'variety' of market that potentially avoids some of the high social costs of the more open US and UK takeover markets associated with 'breaches of trust'. Given that the costs of exposure to a market for corporate control may be high, the coordinated nature of M&A may help

Japanese and European firms retain their capacity for competitive advantages based on long-term business relationships and high levels of firm-specific human capital.

Acknowledgements

We would like to thank Virginia Doellgast, Yuji Hosoya, Chris Hughes, Ellis Krauss, Izumi Kubo, Ricardo Peccei, Kotaru Tsuru and Masaru Yoshitomi for helpful comments and suggestions. Valuable research assistance was provided at various stages by Stefan Horn, Marc Rufo, Mao Wada and Yukiko Yamazaki. Special thanks are extended to Bruce Hearn for extensive and energetic assistance in organizing the statistical data. All errors remain our own.

Notes

1. In 1999, Cable & Wireless PLC raised its stake to 97.69 per cent from 17.69 per cent by completing a hostile tender offer to acquire a 80 per cent interest in International Digital Communications for 84.2 billion Japanese yen (US$699 million). Previously, NTT Corporation and Cable & Wireless were bidding for the entire share capital in International Digital Communications.
2. For example, in 2000, MGM Grand Inc initially offered a choice of $17 in cash or a combination of $7 in cash and $10 in common stock per share in Mirage Resorts Inc. The Mirage Resorts board rejected the original offer, and adopted a poison pill plan giving shareholders the right to purchase stock at a deep discount in the event of an acquisition or an attempt to acquire a stake of 10 per cent or more of the company. MGM later offered a sweetened $21 in cash per share, or a total value $6.483 billion, including the assumption of approximately $2 billion in liabilities.

Bibliography

Aguilera, R. V. and Jackson, G. (2003). 'The cross-national diversity of corporate governance: dimensions and determinants'. *Academy of Management Review*, 28(3): 447–65.
Amable, B. (2003). *The diversity of modern capitalism* (Oxford: Oxford University Press).
Aoki, M. (2001). *Toward a comparative institutional analysis* (Cambridge, MA: MIT Press).
Aoki, M. (2007). 'Whither Japan's corporate governance? Toward external monitoring of internal linkage'. In M. Aoki, G. Jackson and H. Miyajima (eds), *Corporate governance in Japan: institutional change and organizational diversity* (Oxford: Oxford University Press).
Aoki, M. and Patrick, H. (eds) (1994). *The Japanese main bank system: its relevance for developing and transforming economies* (Oxford: Oxford University Press).
Armour, J., Deakin, S. and Konzelmann, S. (2003). 'Shareholder primacy and the trajectory of UK corporate governance'. *British Journal of Industrial Relations*, 41(3): 531–55.
Baums, T. (1993). 'Takeovers versus institutions in corporate governance in Germany'. In D. D. Prentice and P. R. J. Holland (eds), *Contemporary issues in corporate governance* (Oxford: Clarendon Press), pp. 151–83.
Burkhart, M. and Panunzi, F. (2006). 'Takeovers'. ECGI – Finance Working Paper no. 188.

Cieply, S. (2001). 'Bridging capital gaps to promote innovation in France'. *Industry & Innovation*, 8(2): 159–78.

Conyon, M. J., Girma, S., Thompson, S. and Wright, P. (2001). 'Do hostile mergers destroy jobs?' *Journal of Economic Behavior & Organization*, 45(4): 427–40.

Conyon, M. J., Girma, S., Thompson, S. and Wright, P. (2002). 'The impact of mergers and acquisitions on company employment in the United Kingdom'. *European Economic Review*, 46(1): 31–49.

Datta, D. K, Pinches, G. P. and Narayanan, V. K. (1992). 'Factors influencing wealth creation from mergers and acquisitions: a meta-analysis'. *Strategic Management Journal*, 13(1): 67–84.

Deakin, S., Hobbs, R., Nash, D. and Slinger, G. (2002). 'Implicit contracts, takeovers and corporate governance: in the shadow of the city code'. ESRC Centre for Business Research, Working Paper no. 254.

Deeg, R. (2005). 'Path dependency, institutional complementarity, and change in national business systems'. In G. Morgan, R. Whitley and E. Moen (eds), *Changing capitalisms? Institutional change and systems of economic organization* (Oxford: Oxford University Press).

Goergen, M., Martynova, M. and Renneboog, L. (2005). 'Corporate governance convergence: evidence from takeover regulation reforms in Europe'. Utrecht School of Economics, Discussion Paper 05-19.

Goyer, M. (2003). 'Corporate governance, employees, and the focus on core competencies in France and Germany'. In C. Milhaupt (ed.), *Global markets, domestic institutions: corporate law and governance in a new era of cross-border deals* (New York: Columbia University Press).

Hackethal, A., Schmidt, R. H. and Tyrell, M. (2005). 'Banks and German corporate governance: on the way to a capital-market based system?' *Corporate Governance: an International Review*, 13(3): 397–407.

Hall, P. A. and Soskice, D. (2001). *Varieties of capitalism: the institutional foundations of comparative advantage* (Oxford: Oxford University Press).

Hall, P. A. and Thelen, K. (2005). 'The politics of change in varieties of capitalism'. Paper presented at the APSA Conference.

Hancké, B. (2002). *Large firms and institutional change: industrial renewal and economic restructuring in France* (Oxford: Oxford University Press).

Höpner, M. (2000). 'Unternehmensverflechtung im zwielicht. Hans eichels plan zur auflösung der Deutschland AG'. *WSI-Mitteilungen*, 53(Heft 11): 655–63.

Höpner, M. and Jackson, G. (2001). 'An emerging market for corporate control? The case of Mannesmann and German corporate governance'. Köln, Max-Planck-Institut für Gesellschaftsforschung, Discussion Paper 01/4.

Höpner, M. and Jackson, G. (2006). 'Revisiting the Mannesmann takeover: how markets for corporate control emerge'. *European Management Review*, 3: 142–55.

Höpner, M. and Krempel, L. (2003). 'The politics of the German company network'. Köln, Max-Planck-Institut für Gesellschaftsforschung, Working Paper 2003/09.

Hoshi, T. and Kashyap, A. (2001). *Corporate financing and governance in Japan: the road to the future* (Cambridge, MA: MIT Press).

Howell, C. (2003). 'Varieties of capitalism: and then there was one?' *Comparative Politics*, 36(1): 103–24.

Jackson, G. (2005). 'Stakeholders under pressure: corporate governance and labour management in Germany and Japan'. *Corporate Governance: an International Review*, 13(3): 419–28.

Jackson, G. (2007). 'An emerging market for corporate control in Japan? Hostile takeover bids in comparison'. RIETI Discussion Paper, forthcoming.

Kester, W. C. (1990). *Japanese takeovers: the global contest for corporate control* (Boston, MA: Harvard Business School Press).

King, D. R., Dalton, D. D., Daily, C. M. and Covin, J. G. (2004). 'Meta-analysis of post-acquisitions performance: indications of unidentified moderators'. *Strategic Management Journal*, 25(2): 187–200.

Kuroki, F. (2003). 'The relationship of companies and banks as cross-shareholdings unwind: fiscal 2002 cross-shareholding survey'. *NLI Research*, 157.

La Porta, R., Lopez-de-Silanes, F., Schleifer, A. and Vishny, R. W. (1998). 'Law and finance'. *Journal of Political Economy*, 106(6): 1113–55.

Mahoney, J. (2000). 'Path dependence in historical sociology.' *Theory and Society*, 29(4) 507–48.

Manne, H. (1965). 'Mergers and the market for corporate control.' *Journal of Political Economy*, 73(2): 110–20.

Martynova, M. and Renneboog, L. (2005). 'Takeover waves: triggers, performance and motives'. ECGI – Finance Working Paper no. 97.

Milhaupt, C. (2005). 'In the shadow of Delaware? The rise of hostile takeovers in Japan'. Columbia Law School, Center for Law and Economic Studies, Working Paper no. 278.

Pagano, M. and Volpin, P. (2005). 'The political economy of corporate governance'. *American Economic Review*, 95(4): 1005–30.

Paunescu, M. and Schneider, M. (2004). 'Wettbewerbsfaehigkeit und dynamik institutioneller standortbedingungen: ein empirischer test des "varieties of capitalism"'. Ansatzes: University of Trier.

Podolny, J. M. (2001). 'Networks as the pipes and prisms of the market'. *American Journal of Sociology*, 107(1): 33–60.

Rossi, S. and Volpin, P. (2003). 'Cross-country determinants of mergers and acquisitions'. ECGI – Finance Working Paper no. 25.

Schnitzer, M. (1995). ' "Breach of trust" in takeovers and the optimal corporate charter'. *Journal of Industrial Economics*, 43(3): 29–259.

Vitols, S. (2001). 'The origins of bank-based and market-based financial systems: Germany, Japan, and the United States'. In W. Streeck and K. Yamamura (eds), *The origins of nonliberal capitalism: Germany and Japan in comparison* (Ithaca: Cornell University Press).

Vitols, S. (2005). 'Changes in Germany's bank-based financial system: implications for corporate governance'. *Corporate Governance: an International Review*, 13(3): 386–96.

White, H. C. (2002). *Markets from networks: socioeconomic models of production* (Princeton, NJ: Princeton University Press).

Yamamura, K. and Streeck, W. (eds) (2003). *The end of diversity? Prospects of German and Japanese capitalism* (Ithaca: Cornell University Press).

Yanagawa, N. (2007). 'The rise of bank-related corporate revival funds'. In M. Aoki, G. Jackson and H. Miyajima (eds), *Corporate governance in Japan: institutional change and organizational diversity* (Oxford: Oxford University Press).

12
The Continuing Diversity of Corporate Governance Regimes: France and Britain Compared

Mairi Maclean and Charles Harvey

Introduction

Corporate governance has been defined as 'the system by which companies are directed and controlled' (Committee on the Financial Aspects of Corporate Governance, 1992: 15), or more specifically as 'the ways in which suppliers of finance to corporations assure themselves of getting a return on their investment' (Schleifer and Vishny, 1997: 737). Such definitions, however, do not address the pluralism of corporate governance regimes, reflected, for example, in the growing number of national codes. The past decade has witnessed extraordinary global change, driven by heightened competition, and characterized by extensive corporate restructuring across national boundaries. At the same time, partly as a corollary of this, there is an increasing focus on matters of corporate responsibility, accountability and transparency. Internationalization has raised questions regarding the extent to which best practice may be transported, or transplanted, from one national business system to another (Cheffins, 2001a; Djelic, 1998; Whitley, 1999), spawning numerous studies on the likelihood of international convergence (Carati and Tourani Rad, 2000; Peck and Ruigrok, 2000; Rhodes and van Apeldoorn, 1998; Toms and Wright, 2005). Yet, as Aguilera and Jackson (2003: 447) observe, the diversity of corporate governance practices around the world is such as almost to defy a common definition.

This chapter stems from a cross-nationally comparative research project on *Business Elites and Corporate Governance in France and the UK* (Maclean et al., 2006, 2007). The project began in 1999 and consists of four related sub-projects: first, a study of the institutional histories of the top 100 companies in 1998 in France and the United Kingdom respectively; second, a prosopographical study of the education, qualifications, careers, roles and responsibilities of 2,291 directors of the top 100 French and UK companies; third, an in-depth study of the social backgrounds and accomplishments of the top 100 most powerful directors in France and the UK respectively, the 'super-elite', analysing their social origins and career trajectories; and fourth, a study of the social reality of business elites based upon a set of semi-structured interviews with past and present business leaders in France and the United Kingdom. A 'census date' of 1 January 1998 was selected to ascertain organizational and individual membership of the corporate elites of France and the United Kingdom. The study period covers the years 1998 to 2003 inclusive: a length of time felt to be long enough to reveal patterns and trends, but short enough to constitute a distinct historical period. Data were gathered from a wide range of publicly available sources on each of the directors identified as belonging to the business elites of France and the United Kingdom in 1998.

A key objective in studying the top 100 companies in both countries has been to profile their respective governance characteristics related to matters of ownership, control, board membership, board structure and use of committees, decision-making, accountability and responsibilities to shareholders. Thus, our study aims to evaluate the possible convergence of governance regimes in France and Britain to be explored in a systematic, exacting manner; and likewise, the potential resistance of national business systems to external change (Whitley, 1999). To this end, our interviewees included experts on corporate governance on both sides of the Channel.

This chapter explores the issue of continuing diversity in corporate governance regimes of Britain and France, and particularly the extent to which France may be embracing the Anglo-American model (see also Morin, 2000). We find that, although clearly great strides have been made in corporate governance reform in both countries, nevertheless pre-existing structures and practices remain, retaining much of their intrinsic systemic integrity, whilst interacting with new influences (Clift, 2007). We interpret this finding in terms of how and why corporate governance regimes may to a large extent become self-referring and self-reinforcing, possessing or possessed of what we term 'referential integrity', a coherence or cognitive similarity of organizing principles (Crouch, 2005), which restricts their capacity to adapt to new influences whilst not precluding change. Empirical continuities may be partly explained by the fact that governance regimes are 'animated' by individual directors, each of whom occupies his or her own 'habitus' or 'life world' (Bourdieu, 1986, 1990, 1994), which arguably has been neglected in the literature.

The chapter develops this argument by examining the challenges or interventions made against incumbent CEOs by company boards during the period in question, reflective of degrees of board independence, often seen as a measure of a company's accountability and responsibility to shareholders. By 'challenge' we mean a variety of actions or interventions on the part of board members which have to do with holding top executives accountable for their behaviour and performance, resulting perhaps in the removal of poorly performing managers or those who have engaged in some form of inappropriate or unethical behaviour. We see this indicator as being related to the extent to which power is distributed evenly throughout the board, or concentrated at the top. This may also be gauged to some degree by the separation (or otherwise) of chairman and CEO functions, and the extent to which board members, particularly non-executives, are independent from top management, reflected, for example, in their ability or willingness to challenge the head of the company where this is judged to be appropriate.

Competing models of capitalism

The notion that the raw forces of capitalism are bounded and directed according to different rules in different countries owes much to the work of Michel Albert (1991), who explores the notion of two vying capitalist systems: the neo-American model founded on individual achievement and short-term financial gain; and the Rhenish model, of German extraction but with strong Japanese connections, which prizes collective success and consensus. While the former is market-oriented, characterized by equity finance, relatively dispersed ownership, and dominated by 'the tyranny of the quarterly report' (Albert, 1991: 87), the latter is network-oriented, and characterized by long-term debt finance, more concentrated ownership, and a close partnership between banking and industry. Observers regularly contrast the active market for corporate control, which distinguishes the Anglo-American model, with the far weaker market for corporate control, which typifies the Rhenish model (Franks and Mayer, 1990; Goergen and Renneboog, 2001; Hall and Soskice, 2001; La Porta et al., 1998). The national business system of France is generally perceived to be positioned towards the middle of the spectrum, somewhere between the US and Japanese systems, and is often defined as a variant of the continental European model of managed capitalism (Maclean, 2002; Rhodes and van Apeldoorn, 1998; Schmidt, 2003). The UK system, needless to say, is situated towards the US end of the spectrum (Cheffins, 2001b; Goergen and Renneboog, 2001; Scott, 1990; Toms and Wright, 2002).

Building on this analysis, Whitley and his colleagues speak of 'divergent capitalisms', different models of capitalism that can be identified by comparing and contrasting the main features of national business systems, implicitly challenging the view that systems are converging on the Anglo-American model (Quack et al., 2000; Whitley, 1999). They favour taking an institutional approach to the interpretation of global economic realities. This draws on the work of North (1990), who emphasizes important lock-in effects occurring in national business systems, influenced by the timing of industrialization, and leading to path dependency (Fligstein and Freeland, 1995; Pedersen and Thomsen, 1997). To a degree, an institutional system becomes self-referential, as regulation fosters particular organizational structures and thereby reinforces existing patterns of regulation. Actors involved in rule making at international level thus remain embedded in national cultures and environments, from which they extend their behaviours and strategies into the global domain (Djelic and Quack, 2003). Meanwhile, corporate governance is traditionally studied within a framework of agency theory, focused on the potential separation of ownership and control (Berle and Means, 1932) and the consequent need to align the interests of principals and agents (Fama, 1980; Fama and Jensen, 1983; Schleifer and Vishny, 1997). This perspective fails fully to take account of the extent to which corporate governance regimes are informed and moulded by institutional embeddedness (Aguilera and Jackson, 2003; Granovetter, 1985; Prowse, 1995). According to Aguilera and Jackson (2003: 448), agency theory has contributed to an 'undersocialized view of corporate governance'. Scott points out (1990) that control is fundamentally a *relational* phenomenon. Indeed, Aguilera and Jackson (2003) suggest that the social relations and interactions among stakeholders should form the basic unit of analysis in corporate governance, since the *interplay* between firm-level actors and wider sets of institutions explains the different configurations of corporate governance regimes. The domain of managers themselves, and their ideas, ideologies and habitus, is a crucial one, but has tended to be overlooked by the literature on international convergence thus far (Aguilera and Jackson, 2003). In examining corporate governance in conjunction with the behaviour of business elites, our own study seeks to go some way towards addressing this deficit.

In recent times, however, change has been relentless at both the national and international levels. Powerful, all-pervasive agents – including technological advances, the emergence of newly industrialized countries, and the globalization of markets – have combined to create a world in which competition is heightened, global and increasingly uncertain (Cadbury, 2002). Far-reaching transformations are underway with respect to the internationalization of production and ownership, and these changes have led to the introduction of corporate governance practices more in tune with shareholder-value oriented or financialized economic systems (Froud et al., 2000; Morin, 2000; Williams, 2000). These transformations are common in Western society, arguably part-and-parcel of a general isomorphic tendency (DiMaggio and Powell, 1991).

The strength of global competition has forced French companies to provide value for their shareholders, to become more transparent, and to focus more resolutely on financial issues and return on capital. The foreign ownership of French listed companies has risen dramatically since the late 1990s (Maclean, 2002; Morin, 2000; Plihon and Ponssard, 2002), such that foreign investors, especially Anglo-American institutional investors, now own approximately 43 per cent of the share capital of CAC 40 firms (Mauduit, 2003). In addition, September 2000 saw the birth of Euronext, uniting the stock exchanges of Paris, Brussels and Amsterdam, and offering a fully integrated trading, netting, clearing and settlement solution on a pan-European basis. Companies listed on Euronext now have to conform to international accounting standards, and issue quarterly reports in English (Bloch and Kremp, 2001).

In 2002 and 2003, the volumes of equity trading on Euronext actually exceeded those of the LSE.[1]

The boards of directors of leading French firms are increasingly international, reflecting the changing composition of the shareholding body – at least at board level, if not at the very top (Maclean et al., 2006). Leading companies are taking the issue of corporate governance much more seriously than hitherto. In this they are backed by the legal muscle of the Nouvelles Régulations Economiques (NRE) of 2001 and the *loi sur la sécurité financière* on financial market regulation, which established the new Autorité des Marchés Financiers (AMF) in 2003 (Clift, 2007; Egan et al., 2003). The NRE builds on the Viénot (1995, 1999) and Bouton Reports (2002) – essentially self-regulatory and inspired by the UK Cadbury (1992), Greenbury (1995) and Hampel Reports (1998) which comprise the Combined Code – as well as the government-backed Marini Report (1996). The NRE comprises a wide-ranging set of corporate governance measures, whose primary objectives, to all intents and purposes, would seem to be informed by the shareholder value paradigm, thus bringing France closer to the Anglo-American model. In sum, it encourages the separation of chairman and CEO functions; restricts the number of board memberships which may be held concurrently to five; strengthens the board vis-à-vis top management; facilitates the participation of minority shareholders through, *inter alia*, the introduction of new technologies (electronic voting and video-conferencing); and reinforces transparency of ownership by bolstering disclosure requirements. In a similar vein, the AMF, which unites the existing prudential institutions, the COB (Commission des Opérations de Bourse) and CMF (Conseil des Marchés Financiers), is designed to improve the efficiency of the French system, and to render it more comparable to those of other countries.

Yet the philosophy that traditionally has underpinned the French business system lies firmly in the 'social interest' of the firm, as enshrined in the *arrêt Freuhauf-France* of May 1965. This may be defined as a belief in the common weal uniting the interests of workers and employers; a belief that economic and social affairs cannot be separated; and an expectation that employers should pay attention to their responsibilities as well as to their rights (Maclean, 2002; Weber, 1986). Interestingly, despite its apparent shareholder value ethos, the NRE originated in the cause of *intérêt social*. It was initiated by the former socialist prime minister, Lionel Jospin, who sought, in the wake of the 'Affaire Michelin' of 1999 (when Michelin laid off 7,500 workers, despite a 17 per cent increase in profits for the first six months of the year), to redress the balance in favour of other stakeholders. Specifically, Jospin sought to reduce the likelihood of what were termed 'abusive lay-offs' in the pursuit of higher profits. The NRE thus grants rights to all stakeholders to challenge managerial decisions (Clift, 2007; Frison-Roche, 2002). That said, such powers may prove deceptive in practice. Action by minority shareholders, for example, may collide with the fundamental principle governing French company law, which accords priority to the company interest – the survival of the firm, in effect, is paramount. A fundamental confusion obtains in the law of July 1966, moreover, whereby the person of the Président Directeur Général (PDG) and the company itself are seen as one and the same, he or she being granted 'the most extensive powers to act at all times in the name of the company' (Letreguilly, 1998). Challenges to an incumbent PDG by the board are therefore extremely rare; merely to take a vote on a decision, Alcouffe observes, would be viewed as 'bad manners' (2000: 129, cited in Clift, 2007). French business leaders remain largely autocratic, with the heads of Alcatel, AXA, Saint-Gobain and Vinci all recently reported as seeking to control the battle for their own successors (Betts, 2006; Maclean et al., 2006).

Enduring differences in governance regimes

Here, we conceptualize a governance regime as existing on three interrelated levels – at the pinnacle, the practical or regulatory level, underneath which is the systemic and organizational, with the sedimentary, ideological level, grounded in 'habitus' (Bourdieu, 1986, 1990, 1994), located at the bottom (see Figure 12.1). According to this schema, the rules, regulations and practices at the uppermost level are more visible and open to change than the organizational systems and ideologies at the two lower, less visible levels. The most visible and easily apprehended features are formal rules and regulations, shown in Figure 12.1 as close to the pinnacle. In legal or constitutional terms, we might think of the ways in which companies are set up and dissolved, the composition of boards of directors and the ground rules for financial reporting. Each of these is relatively simple to observe and document. Conversely, underlying ideologies, assumptions and deeply held values, which Bourdieu terms 'habitus', and which inform rules and practices, are located closer to the base of the pyramid, being more difficult to circumscribe. Habitus, the ingrained and socially constituted dispositions of social classes that lead actors to make choices and decisions that reproduce existing social structures and status distinctions, is defined by Bourdieu as 'structured structures predisposed to function as structuring structures, that is, as principles which generate and organize practices and representations' (1990: 53). As the means by which life chances are 'internalized and converted into a disposition' (Bourdieu, 1986: 170), habitus serves principally as a mechanism for social reproduction. Arguments for international convergence tend to stress the practical and systemic aspects, while neglecting the ideological level. However, changes at the organizational level, such as changes to corporate governance practices introduced in response to legislation, regulation or governance reports, are only ever likely to be enduring if matched by parallel changes in assumptions, values and beliefs at the deeper, ideological level.

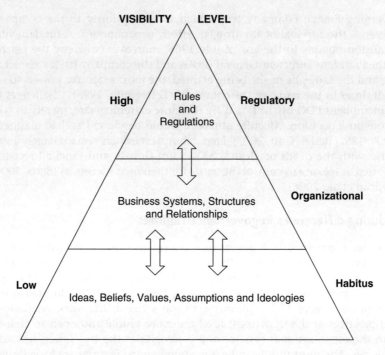

VISIBILITY   LEVEL

High   Rules
        and   Regulatory
        Regulations

        Business Systems, Structures   Organizational
        and Relationships

Low   Habitus
        Ideas, Beliefs, Values, Assumptions and Ideologies

Figure 12.1:   Elements of a governance regime
Adapted from Maclean, 2002: 7

The proposition that flows from this is that while corporate governance policies and practices may tend to converge as a result of isomorphic pressures (DiMaggio and Powell, 1991), as between France and the UK since 1995, their actual implementation and consequences for action will continue to differ because of the lesser potentiality for change that exists in business systems, and yet more so in dominant ideologies which inform the habitus of individual managers, who play a critical role in governance regimes. Key features continue to differentiate the governance regimes of France and the UK, which are fundamental to what is generally regarded as 'best practice' in corporate governance. These include the extent of separation in the roles of CEO and chairman, and the independence of non-executive directors from top management – the extent to which board members are willing, and able, to challenge the head of the company when necessary.

According to much of the latest thinking on the composition and conduct of corporate boards, the interests of shareholders are best safeguarded when the big strategic and tactical moves proposed by top executives are fully scrutinized, tested and approved by all members of the board (Aguilera, 2005; Hermalin and Weisbach, 1998; Roberts et al., 2005; Young, 2000); in direct consultation, in exceptional circumstances, with major investors. In order to avoid the destructive, sometimes catastrophic situations that have embroiled companies across the world, Vivendi, Alstom and Marconi included, governance systems are seen to be needed that might help in preventing situations from spiralling out of control, wherein risks are fully assessed and discussed before irreversible actions are taken. In this context, it is often recommended that power should be more evenly distributed throughout a board, and that all directors should be equally well informed and directly engaged in the decision-making process. This is seen to require the separation of the roles of chairman and CEO, and the appointment of non-executive directors who are genuinely independent of top management. To this end, formal but flexible decision-making processes are recommended, abandoning the comfortable informality that once characterized some boards.

Movement towards this 'ideal' has been most rapid in the UK in consequence of regular changes to the Combined Code. Following the Higgs Review (2003), the criteria for qualification as a genuinely independent director were spelled out as not having been employed by the company in a five-year period prior to appointment to the board; having no close ties with the company's advisers, directors or senior employees; not serving on the board for longer than ten years; and not serving as the representative of a single large shareholder or group of shareholders. If a non-executive director is appointed to an LSE listed company who does not satisfy these requirements, then the annual report must specify the reasons in accordance with the fundamental principle of the Combined Code, 'comply or explain'. UK companies have tended to opt for 'comply' rather than 'explain' with respect to most aspects of the Combined Code, such that by 1998 the functions of chairman and CEO had been separated in 91 of the top 100 companies, rising to include all 100 by 2003–4.

In France, the prevailing situation is very different because corporate governance regimes, in their reality and essential dynamics, are more the product of history, embraced in systems and mindsets, than conformance to a set of universally espoused principles (Roe, 1994, 2003). The option exists under French company law to separate the roles of chairman and CEO, but in many quarters the belief persists that effective decision-making requires that power be concentrated in the hands of the PDG. In 1998, 23 of the top 100 French companies had separated the roles of chairman and CEO and the figure remained at just 37 in 2003, highlighting the importance of cultural reproduction as a mechanism for moderating pressures for change (Bourdieu, 1994; Bourdieu and Passeron, 1990). Several companies that had split the roles of chairman and CEO subsequently elected to reunite them: this occurred in the cases of Alstom and Suez. There is an understandable reluctance to abandon the perceived competitive advantages of long-standing institutional arrangements: elites are naturally unwilling to promote change to a degree where it is likely to erode their own power and positions (Rhodes and van Apeldoorn, 1998). This applies, too, to interlocking directorships. Many of the most powerful PDG still hold multiple non-executive directorships. French business elites continue to value corporate networking as a mechanism for coordinated action and fruitful engagement with their peers and with the state (Burt et al., 2000; Yeo et al., 2003).

As an additional indicator of the extent of change in board structures, we compared the extent to which specialized governance committees had been adopted in both France and the United Kingdom. The introduction of audit, remuneration and nomination committees were found to have progressed significantly in both countries over the period, though France still lagged behind. By 2003, audit committee take-up on the part of the top 100 companies in each country stood at 67 per cent in France, as against 98 per cent in the UK. Nomination committees were less popular, increasing in number from 14 to 37 in France, and from 74 to 93 in the UK; while the take-up of remuneration committees progressed from 31 to 58 per cent in France, and from 95 to 97 per cent in the UK (Maclean et al., 2006).

The obvious natural affinities in outlook between the UK and other Anglo-American countries (Australia, Canada, New Zealand and the United States) have ensured that the latter have borrowed significantly from the Combined Code, whereas French companies have clearly struggled with key governance concepts such as the independence of directors. This is hardly surprising. In the UK, a manifest divide exists between the owners and managers of companies, shareholdings are dispersed, and institutional investors control just over 70 per cent of equity. A standard corporate form matches a standard governance code, whereas an enduring diversity exists in relations between owners and managers in France (Grant and Kirchmaier, 2005; Bloch and Kremp, 2001), with ownership and control not widely separated (Roe, 2003). Some companies conform to the Anglo-American norm, but many others differ in remaining family-owned or state-owned, or in having close relationships with other companies. In this situation, directors are often appointed to boards specifically to represent a family, institution or interest group, and for this reason alone cannot be classified as 'independent'. The logic of institutional arrangements thus runs counter to the ideals of the Combined Code, as highlighted by the differing perceptions of independence in Britain and France. Higgs (2003) views independence as a commodity which may be certified and audited (a view promoted by the Foundation for Independent Directors),[2] while Sir Adrian Cadbury (2002) favours training for directors, as well as a legislative statement setting out what is expected of them, enumerating their legal duties.[3] Senator Philippe Marini, author of the Marini Report (1996), however, doubts whether non-executive directors in France will ever be fully independent given the quintessential importance of their ties to one another:

> The notion of the independent director is an empirical notion. I often prefer to speak of 'professional' directors rather than 'independent' directors.

In French practice, to be a director, is a complement of activities. It is linked to the ties with capital, it is linked to the ties of friendship; it is linked to all kinds of things.[4]

Table 12.1: Corporate governance interventions faced by the boards of top 100 companies in France and the UK, 1998–2003

Type of challenge	France	UK
No major intervention	77	64
Board liquidated or merger or takeover	17	23
Performance of directors challenged	3	12
Conduct of director(s) challenged	3	1

The implications are considerable. In France, the prevalence of 'ties that bind' (Geletkanycz and Hambrick, 1999; Palmer et al., 1986) means that members of the business elite exhibit considerable 'class solidarity', marked by an 'enforceable trust' as articulated by Kadushin (1995: 219). Consequently, they are less exposed to challenge on the grounds of personal performance than their counterparts in the UK, as Table 12.1 confirms.

Boards of directors are open to challenge or intervention in their affairs in three main ways. First, a board may be liquidated or reconstituted when shareholders accept an offer of merger or takeover. Second, shareholders may require the departure of one or more directors, often the CEO or chairman, on account of perceived under-performance. Third, either shareholders or the authorities may take action with respect to conduct on the part of one or more directors that is perceived to have been inappropriate or unethical.

It can be seen that between 1998 and 2003, just three of the 100 most powerful directors of French companies suffered a career reversal as a result of alleged poor corporate performance. Jean-Marie Messier was forced to resign in 2002 when Vivendi-Universal was weighed down by onerous debts, significant operating losses and reputational damage, and Michel Bon exited France Télécom in 2002 for much the same reasons. These departures were acrimonious and atypical, requiring leading members of the elite to join forces and turn exceptionally against one of their own number. In these cases, as in that of Pierre Bilger, who left Alstom when financial crisis began to bite, corporate insiders were sacrificed, symbolically almost, to preserve the legitimacy of the majority. Such exemplary punishment of a member of the elite is not, of course, new in French history. From time to time, in a symbolic catharsis and confirmation of national identity and values, heads must roll: examples include the Revolutions of 1789 and 1848, the seizure of power by Louis Bonaparte in 1851, the 1871 Commune, and the execution of alleged collaborators after the 1944 Liberation. Such punishment arguably works to sustain the stability and cohesion of the group as a whole, 'cleansed' and absolved by the act of retribution (Turkle, 1975). It was in such terms that one former PDG explained Messier's fall from grace:

> A lot of French businessmen were thinking that the time had come to end the story.... The reputation of the country was at stake, and that of the French stock market, especially as a consequence of the involvement of Americans in the story.[5]

Both Jean-Marie Messier of Vivendi and Pierre Bilger of Alstom, stunned by the turn of events, fought brave rearguard actions to defend their business reputations, the latter handing back a golden handshake of €4 million. Bilger's resignation in March 2003 as chairman of the board of Alstom, a role he had assumed on ceasing to be PDG in December 2002, was prompted by the decision taken by the company's nomination and remunerations committee, chaired by a Briton, Sir William Purves, to decline to honour his outstanding stock options. It was not the material impact of this decision that caused him to resign, but rather its unusual and therefore shocking nature (Bilger, 2004), the very rarity of such decisions being implicit in Alcouffe's (2000) allusion to 'bad manners'. The two men accused of personal misconduct – Jean Peyrelevade and François Pinault – were caught up in the legal storm that raged for many years in the US concerning the purchase of the defunct insurance company Executive Life in 1991, led by Crédit Lyonnais, in contravention of US laws preventing the takeover of an insurance company by a bank, from which Pinault is said to have profited handsomely. He was finally cleared of fraud after a two-month trial in 2005.

The dramas surrounding the resignations of Messier, Bon and Bilger for alleged poor performance as PDG indicate the rarity of the event. In the UK, by contrast, there is a more sanguine attitude to the precariousness of life at the top, and a widespread understanding that loss of office is the price to be paid when share prices consistently fall below expectations, whether or not this can be attributed fairly to those in command. The 'bitter pill' of enforced resignation is almost invariably sweetened by a large payoff, and the prospect of taking up fresh assignments elsewhere. The system is paradoxical in that it is at once harsh and forgiving. Mounting shareholder criticism led to the resignations of Derek Wanless as CEO of National Westminster in 1999, Robert Ayling as CEO of British Airways in 2000, George Simpson as CEO of Marconi in 2001, Peter Bonfield as CEO and Iain Vallance as Chairman of BT in 2002, Philip Watts as Chairman of Shell and Peter Davis as CEO of Sainsbury's in 2004. The 'soft landing' typical of top executives' fall from grace is exemplified by Wanless, who between 2001 and 2004 was commissioned by the British government to produce a series of reports on healthcare funding and service provision. Only one member of the UK super-elite, Greg Hutchings of Tomkins, suffered serious adverse criticism on the grounds of personal conduct, an inquiry in 2000 suggesting that he had taken liberties in using the company jet for private purposes. Following his resignation in October 2000, Hutchings admitted that as a large shareholder he had run the company in a proprietorial manner, and that there had been some personal excesses for which he was apologetic, but that the financial significance of these had been much exaggerated (Bennett, 2000).

Discussion

The different economic paths pursued by Britain and France are indicative of profound differences in elite mindsets and institutional structures. Despite the enormous influence exercised by the British Combined Code internationally, and despite talk of the 'Americanization' of both Britain and France, in different ways, the systems of governance obtaining in these two countries are rooted in each case in a distinct 'habitus' (Bourdieu, 1986, 1990, 1994), the origins of which go deep. As O'Sullivan (2005) argues, both structural and cultural factors continue to impede any wide-ranging adjustment to an Anglo-American system. Clift (2007) agrees, noting that observers exhibit a tendency to over-emphasize evolutions at the international level, whilst underplaying continuities. The argument that France is gradually embracing the shareholder value paradigm, as evinced by the growing presence of Anglo-American institutional investors in the share capital of listed French firms, is not consistently borne out at this fundamental level. Share buy-backs by leading listed companies are common (O'Sullivan, 2003), casting growing stock market activity in a different light. Meanwhile, the French government remains happy to intervene to help struggling firms, such as Alstom in 2003–4, in the teeth of EU opposition, or to prevent takeovers or mergers that it sees as being against the national interest (the abortive takeover, for example, of Danone by Pepsi in 2005). As President Nicolas Sarkozy, then Finance Minister, put it at the time: 'It is not a right of the State to help its industry. It is a duty' (Sage, 2004: 23). This is reflective of a very different mindset than that which prevails in the UK, where there is typically little government interference in major corporate collapses, or international takeovers or mergers of UK-based corporations (Franks and Mayer, 1990; Scott, 1990).

Nevertheless, for every difference between the two countries it is possible to point to a similarity. French and British companies have adopted a proactive stance towards globalization. They are both major international investors and have rapidly embraced the potentialities of global restructuring in pursuit of lower costs and increased market share. The business systems of France and the UK may differ considerably in their *modus operandi*, but this should not mask their proven capacity to adapt pragmatically when gripped by the challenges of global competition. What we are witnessing, in effect, are the responses of two *competing capitalisms* to globalization, rather than the struggle between two 'divergent capitalisms', as perceived by Richard Whitley (1999). Perhaps this is nit-picking, but our essential point remains: while

French and British companies and business leaders will continue to think and do many things differently, they will simultaneously think and do many other things that are very similar. Cultural reproduction (Bourdieu, 1994; Bourdieu and Passeron, 1990) should be confused neither with a lack of change nor with the triumph of difference over similarity.

That said, the arguments of comparative advantage and economic efficiency suggest that national elites are unlikely to wish overly to alter institutions and structures from which they have long benefited; unless, of course, that change may be seen to be of benefit to themselves – as in the case of endogenous pressures for change on the part of business elites in France and the United Kingdom in favour of US-style remuneration. Despite the increasing espousal of many of the principles of sound corporate governance on both sides of the Channel, outward expressions of convergence, depicted at the uppermost level of Figure 12.1, are regularly challenged by the more deep-rooted structural continuities expressed in social, legal, institutional, political and intellectual practices (Roe, 2003). When we consider the key issue of convergence, it is often very difficult to discern precisely what is actually happening due, at times, to the blur created by the sheer number of signs and symbols of change on display, from the widespread adoption of governance committees to the increasingly sophisticated interventions of institutional investors. However, when we look deeper, we find incontrovertible evidence of inner structural continuity. In the course of the past twenty years, the French have privatized, engaged in mega-mergers, ceded the franc for the euro, and, since 1995, adopted many of the tenets of good corporate governance as recommended by a succession of French governance committees, following the British lead. This has led to new laws, the NRE and the *loi sur la sécurité financière* in particular. Yet their inner structures arguably retain their essential integrity. There is, for example, little prospect of the French abandoning the dense corporate networks, bound together by multiple director interlocks, that are deemed by the British to compromise the independence of non-executive directors; or their fundamental belief in the social interest of the firm.

Conclusions

The economic historian Douglass North emphasizes the importance of structural and institutional continuity in determining the performance of present-day economies (North, 1990, 2005). He is concerned with the underlying determinants of how economies evolve and rules change, finding that 'adaptive efficiency' depends very much on a society's ability to create and preserve institutions that are stable, broadly accepted and productive. 'Once a development path is set on a particular course', he observes, 'the network externalities, the learning process of organizations, and the historically derived subjective modeling of the issues reinforce the course' (1990: 99).

This perspective on institutional and cultural change is one that we share. The United Kingdom, since the publication of the Cadbury Report, has come a long way in matters of corporate governance. Evolutionary rather than revolutionary change has been the order of the day. Widespread acceptance of the strictures of the Combined Code elsewhere in the world has put British companies in the vanguard of a process of international governance reform. Yet, even in the UK, the impact cannot be described as transformational. It will take many years yet before regulatory and procedural reforms percolate downwards to modify permanently the behaviour of members of the business elite. Compliance with a corporate governance code, as Roberts et al. point out, should never be taken as a proxy for board effectiveness. Their research into the roles of non-executive directors suggests instead that 'the key to board effectiveness lies in the degree to which non-executives acting individually and collectively are able to create accountability within the board in relation to *both* strategy *and* performance' (Roberts et al., 2005: 56). In other words, what matters most are not the technical or legal aspects of a governance regime, but rather the quality of the performances of individual actors who 'breathe life' into them, and the interactions between them, conditioned by the framework within which they operate (Huse, 2005). A boardroom is more than a place where the agents of shareholders take decisions within a carefully specified set of rules and regulations. Boardrooms are in essence small, elite communities that function in accordance with established cultural norms and standards.

Though rules and regulations may be copied from another society (Roe, 2003), governance regimes are, to a considerable degree, self-reinforcing, with their own referential integrity, and differences in the governance of French and British companies cannot be expunged simply by insisting on compliance with a universal code of best practice. Continuing diversity is therefore a likely outcome, at least in the foreseeable future. Our research points not to international convergence, but rather to the persistence of national distinctiveness and the strength of cultural reproduction, despite globalization and more than a decade of governance reform.

Acknowledgements

The authors wish to thank the Leverhulme Trust and Reed Charity, which funded the research on which this chapter is based. They also wish to thank the business leaders and corporate governance experts who kindly agreed to be interviewed, and the reviewers for their helpful comments.

Notes

1. Statistics according to FESE, year to date, December 2003. Data provided by Euronext.

2. Interview with Chairman of Foundation for Independent Director, 26 November 2002, Bristol.
3. Interview with Sir Adrian Cadbury, 12 June 2003, Solihull.
4. Interview with Senator Philippe Marini, French Senate, 14 January 2004, Paris.
5. Interview with former PDG of leading listed French company, 3 January 2003, Paris.

Bibliography

Aguilera, R. V. (2005). 'Corporate governance and director accountability: an institutional comparative perspective'. *British Journal of Management*, 16(s1): s39–s53.

Aguilera, R. V. and Jackson, G. (2003). 'The cross-national diversity of corporate governance: dimensions and determinants'. *Academy of Management Review*, 28(3): 447–65.

Albert, M. (1991). *Capitalisme contre capitalisme* (Paris: Seuil).

Alcouffe, C. (2000). 'Judges and CEOs: French aspects of corporate governance'. *European Journal of Law and Economics*, 9(2): 127–44.

Association Française des Entreprises Privée/Conseil National du Patronat Français (1995). *Le conseil d'administration des sociétés cotées*. Viénot Report I (Paris: Institut d'Etudes Politiques).

Association Française des Entreprises Privée/Mouvement des Entreprises de France (1999). *Rapport du comité sur le gouvernement d'entreprise présidé par M. Marc Viénot*. Viénot Report II.

Bennett, N. (2000). 'Tumbril at Tomkins'. *Sunday Telegraph* (15 October).

Berle, A. A. and Means, G. C. (1932). *The modern corporation and private property* (New York: Macmillan).

Betts, P. (2006). 'The Vinci code of corporate governance'. *Financial Times* (31 May): 14.

Bilger, P. (2004). *Quatre millions d'euros: le prix de ma liberté* (Paris: Bourin).

Bloch, L. and Kremp, E. (2001). 'Ownership and voting power in France'. In F. Barca and M. Becht (eds), *The control of corporate Europe*, pp. 106–27 (Oxford: Oxford University Press).

Bourdieu, P. (1986). *Distinction: a social critique of the judgement of taste*. Translated by R. Nice (London: Routledge & Kegan Paul).

Bourdieu, P. (1990). *The logic of practice*. Translated by R. Nice (Stanford: Stanford University Press).

Bourdieu, P. (1994). *The state nobility: elite schools in the field of power*. Translated by L. C. Clough (Cambridge: Polity Press).

Bourdieu, P. and Passeron, J.-C. (1990). *Reproduction in education, society and culture*. Second edition. Translated by R. Nice (London: Sage).

Burt, R. S., Hogarth, R. M. and Michaud, C. (2000). 'The social capital of French and American managers'. *Organization Science*, 11(2): 123–47.

Cadbury, Sir A. (2002). *Corporate governance and chairmanship: a personal view* (Oxford: Oxford University Press).

Carati, G. and Tourani Rad, A. (2000). 'Convergence of corporate governance systems'. *Managerial Finance*, 26(10): 66–83.

Charkham, J. P. (1994). *Keeping good company: a study of corporate governance in five countries* (Oxford: Clarendon Press).

Cheffins, B. R. (2001a). 'Corporate governance reform: Britain as an exporter'. *Hume Papers on Public Policy*, 8(1): 10–28.

Cheffins, B. R. (2001b). 'History and the global corporate governance revolution: the UK perspective'. *Business History*, 43(4): 87–118.

Clift, B. (2007). 'French corporate governance in the new global economy: mechanisms of change within models of capitalism'. *Political Studies*, 55(3): 546–67.

Committee on the Financial Aspects of Corporate Governance (1992). *The financial aspects of corporate governance* (The Cadbury Report) (London: Gee).

Crouch, C. (2005). *Capitalist diversity and change: recombinant governance and institutional entrepreneurs* (Oxford: Oxford University Press).

DiMaggio, P. and Powell, W. W. (1991). 'The iron cage revisited: institutional isomorphism and collective rationality in organisational fields'. In W. W. Powell and P. DiMaggio (eds), *The new institutionalism in organisational analysis*, pp. 63–82 (Chicago: University of Chicago Press).

Djelic, M.-L. (1998). *Exporting the American model: the postwar transformation of European business* (Oxford: Oxford University Press).

Djelic, M.-L. and Quack, S. (2003). 'Introduction'. In M.-L. Djelic and S. Quack (eds), *Globalization and institutions: redefining the rules of the economic game* (Cheltenham: Edward Elgar).

Egan, M. L., Mauléon, F. and Wolff, D. (2003). 'France's *nouvelles régulations économiques*: using government mandates for corporate reporting to promote environmentally sustainable economic development'. Paper presented at 25th Annual Conference of the Association for Public Policy and Management, Washington, D.C., November.

Fama, E. F. (1980). 'Agency problems and the theory of the firm'. *Journal of Political Economy*, 88(2): 288–307.

Fama, E. F. and Jensen, M. (1983). 'Separation of ownership and control'. *Journal of Law and Economics*, 26: 301–25.

Financial Reporting Council (2003). *The combined code on corporate governance*.

Fligstein, N. and Freeland, R. (1995). 'Theoretical and comparative perspectives on corporate organization'. *Annual Review of Sociology*, 21: 21–43.

Franks, J. and Mayer, C. (1990). 'Capital markets and corporate control: a study of France, Germany and the UK'. *Economic Policy*, 5(10): 191–231.

Frison-Roche, M.-A. (2002). 'Le droit français des sociétés cotées entre *corporate governance* et culture de marché'. In D. Plihon and J.-P. Ponssard (eds), *Le montée en puissance des fonds d'investissement*, pp. 77–92 (Paris: La Documentation Française).

Froud, J., Haslam, C., Johal, S. and Williams, K. (2000). 'Shareholder value and financialization: consultancy promises, management moves'. *Economy and Society*, 29(1): 80–110.

Geletkanycz, M. A. and Hambrick, D. C. (1999). 'The external ties of top executives: implications for strategic choice and performance'. *Administrative Science Quarterly*, 42: 654–81.

Goergen, M. and Renneboog, L. (2001). 'United Kingdom'. In K. Gugler (ed.), *Corporate governance and economic performance*, pp. 184–200 (Oxford: Oxford University Press).

Granovetter, M. S. (1985). 'Economic action and social structure: the problem of embeddedness'. *American Journal of Sociology*, 91: 481–510.

Grant, J. and Kirchmaier, T. (2005). 'Corporate control in Europe'. *Corporate Ownership and Control*, 2(2): 65–76.

Hall, P. A. and Soskice, D. (2001). 'An introduction to varieties of capitalism'. In D. Soskice and P. A. Hall (eds), *Varieties of capitalism: the institutional foundations of comparative advantage*, pp. 1–68 (Oxford: Oxford University Press).

Hermalin, B. E. and Weisbach, M. S. (1998). 'Endogenously chosen boards of directors and their monitoring of the CEO'. *American Economic Review*, 88(1): 96–118.

Higgs, D. (2003). *Review of the role and effectiveness of non-executive directors* (The Higgs Review) (London: Department of Trade and Industry).

Huse, M. (2005). 'Accountability and creating accountability: a framework for exploring behavioural perspectives on corporate governance'. *British Journal of Management*, 16: 65–79.

Kadushin, C. (1995). 'Friendship among the French financial elite'. *American Sociological Review*, 60: 202–21.

La Porta, R., Lopez-de-Silanes, F., Schleifer, A. and Vishny, R. W. (1998). 'Corporate ownership around the world'. *Journal of Finance*, 54: 471–517.

Letreguilly, H. (1998). 'France'. *International Financial Law Review*, Supplement on Corporate Governance (April): 18–22.

Maclean, M. (1999). 'Corporate governance in France and the UK: long-term perspectives on contemporary institutional arrangements'. *Business History*, 41(1): 88–116.

Maclean, M. (2002). *Economic management and French business from de Gaulle to Chirac* (Basingstoke: Palgrave Macmillan).

Maclean, M., Harvey, C. and Press, J. (2006). *Business elites and corporate governance in France and the UK* (Basingstoke: Palgrave Macmillan).

Maclean, M., Harvey, C. and Press, J. (2007). 'Managerialism and the post-war evolution of the French national business system'. *Business History*, 49(4): 531–51.

Marini, P. (1996). *La modernisation du droit des sociétés* (The Marini Report) (Paris: La Documentation Française).

Mauduit, L. (2003). 'Du capitalisme rhénan au capitalisme américain, la mutation de l'économie s'accélère'. *Le Monde* (29 July).

Morin, F. (2000). 'A transformation in the French model of shareholding and management'. *Economy and Society*, 29(1): 36–53.

Mouvement des Entreprises de France/Association Française des Entreprises Privée (2002). *Pour un meilleur gouvernement des entreprises cotées* (The Bouton Report).

North, D. C. (1990) *Institutions, institutional change and economic performance* (Cambridge: Cambridge University Press).

North, D. C. (2005). *Understanding the process of economic change* (Princeton: Princeton University Press).

O'Sullivan, M. (2003). 'The political economy of comparative corporate governance'. *Review of International Political Economy*, 10(1): 23–72.

O'Sullivan, M. (2005). 'Analysing change in corporate governance: the example of France'. In K. Keasey, S. Thompson and M. Wright (eds), *Corporate governance: accountability, enterprise and international comparisons*, pp. 351–87 (Chichester: John Wiley).

Palmer, D., Friedland, R. and Singh, J. V. (1986). 'The ties that bind: organizational and class bases of stability in a corporate interlock network'. *American Sociological Review*, 51: 781–96.

Peck, S. and Ruigrok, W. (2000). 'Hiding behind the flag? Prospects for change in German corporate governance'. *European Management Journal*, 18(4): 420–30.

Pedersen, T. and Thomsen, S. (1997). 'European patterns of corporate ownership: a twelve-country study'. *Journal of International Business Studies*, 28(4): 759–78.

Plihon, D. and Ponssard, J.-P. (eds), (2002). *Le montée en puissance des fonds d'investissement* (Paris: La Documentation Française).

Prowse, S. (1995). 'Corporate governance in an international perspective: a survey of corporate control mechanisms among large firms in the US, UK, Japan and Germany'. *Financial Markets, Institutions and Instruments*, 4: 1–63.

Quack, S., Morgan, G. and Whitley, R. (eds) (2000). *National capitalisms, global competition and economic performance* (Amsterdam: John Benjamins).

Rhodes, M. and van Apeldoorn, B. (1998). 'Capital unbound? The transformation of European corporate governance'. *Journal of European Public Policy*, 5(3): 406–27.

Roberts, J., McNulty, T. and Stiles, P. (2005). 'Beyond agency conceptions of the work of the non-executive director: creating accountability in the boardroom'. *British Journal of Management*, 16, S6.

Roe, M. J. (1994). 'Some differences in corporate governance in Germany, Japan and America'. In T. Baums, K. J. Hopt and R. M. Buxbaum (eds), *Institutional investors and corporate governance* (Berlin: De Gruyter).

Roe, M. J. (2003). *Political determinants of corporate governance: political context, corporate impact* (Oxford: Oxford University Press).

Sage, A. (2004). 'French minister pledges state sell-offs', *The Times* (5 May): 23.

Schleifer, A. and Vishny, R. W. (1997). 'A survey of corporate governance'. *Journal of Finance*, 52(2): 737–83.

Schmidt, V. (2003). 'French capitalism transformed, yet still a third variety of capitalism'. *Economy and Society*, 32(4): 526–54.

Scott, J. (1990). 'Corporate control and corporate rule: Britain in an international perspective'. *British Journal of Sociology*, 41(3): 351–73.

Toms, S. and Wright, M. (2002). 'Corporate governance, strategy and structure in British business history, 1950–2000'. *Business History*, 44(3): 91–124.

Toms, S. and Wright, M. (2005). 'Divergence and convergence within Anglo-American corporate governance systems: evidence from the US and UK, 1950–2000'. *Business History*, 47(2): 267–91.

Turkle, S. R. (1975). 'Symbol and festival in the French student uprising (May–June 1968)'. In S. Falk Moore and B. G. Myerhoff (eds), *Symbol and politics in communal ideology*, pp. 68–100 (Ithaca: Cornell University Press).

Weber, H. (1986). *Le parti des patrons: le CNPF (1946–1986)* (Paris: Seuil).

Whitley, R. (1999). *Divergent capitalisms: the social structuring and change of business systems* (Oxford: Oxford University Press).

Williams, K. (2000). 'From shareholder value to present-day capitalism'. *Economy and Society*, 29(1): 1–12.

Yeo, H.-J., Pochet, C. and Alcouffe, A. (2003). 'CEO reciprocal interlocks in French corporations'. *Journal of Management and Governance*, 7(1): 87–108.

Young, S. (2000). 'The increasing use of non-executive directors: its impact on UK board structure and governance arrangements'. *Journal of Business, Finance & Accounting*, 27: 9–10.

13
A Financialized Account of Corporate Governance

Tord Andersson, Colin Haslam, Edward Lee and Nick Tsitsianis

Introduction

The literature on governance is generally organized within an international, national or industry framework of analysis, taking either a political economy or economic perspective. There is a need for governance because of a general reorientation of international, national and local economies away from political blocks to a neo-liberal paradigm of global free product, labour and capital markets. At a national level, withdrawal of the state further strengthens the demand for local governance which, in turn, requires new forms of regulatory institutions and policy frameworks around, for example 'participative governance'. The political economy debates on governance stress the importance of institutions and how changed relations between society and markets can, possibly, be controlled and regulated. On the other hand, an economic perspective would place more weight and emphasis on the role of markets and particularly 'non-market' controls which are employed to correct market imperfection(s).

In the last two decades the attention of both economists and political science has been drawn towards the narrower issue of 'corporate governance' and specifically the implications of the modified agency relationship between managers and institutional shareholders apparent in a shareholder-value led economy.

In the first section of this chapter we review the arguments for and against capital market control for shareholder value and implications for corporate governance, strategy and economic performance. Jensen (1993) and Lazonick and O'Sullivan (2000) share a 'productionist' framework which is employed to structure connections between capital market institutions, governance and resulting corporate/national economic performance. In contrast, the second section of this chapter constructs a complementary financialized account of corporate governance employing a framework of analysis grounded in accounting and finance. Specifically, our concern is with the use of *fair value* reporting in the US and the implication(s) of blending market value into corporate sector balance sheets. In the US fair value reporting, combined with an active market for corporate control, has forced S&P 500 balance sheet capitalization ahead of cash earnings. In section three we argue that to contain value at risk managers employ strategic arbitrage to extract additional cash from operations and shift the pattern of cash distribution towards shareholders and away from other stakeholders. A large proportion of cash remitted to shareholders arises from the need to finance share buy-backs which reduces balance sheet capital employed. Fair value reporting and active market for corporate control is reinforcing a reorientation of corporate governance towards equity stakeholders and this is evidenced in section four where we provide a stakeholder account of cash distribution in the S&P 500. In the final section of this chapter we discuss the possibility of constructing a financialized account of the reorientation of corporate governance outside the US and the conditions required for convergence.

Capital market control and corporate governance

Corporate governance may be loosely defined as the rules and arrangements structuring the exercise of control over company assets and the pattern of interaction between different stakeholders within the firm. Because it is inherently connected with the allocation of power, resources and the distribution of surplus, corporate governance structures most other relationships within firms and the wider political economy, shaping its whole logic (Lane, 2003).

Lane outlines two perspectives on corporate governance. The first draws from economics and considers the relationship between those that provide finance and the 'formal and informal rules structuring it' (Lane, 2003: 4). The second draws from outside economics and 'focuses on the entire network of formal and informal relations which determines how control is exercised within corporations and how the risks and returns are distributed between the various stakeholders' (Lane, 2003: 4). These two perspectives are employed to categorize corporate governance systems as either 'outsider' or 'insider'. The outsider perspective emphasizes the importance of the external capital market and how a combination of rules and incentives operates to discipline managers, whilst an insider perspective is concerned with how internal management boards are able to exert control over corporate governance (Vitols et al., 1997). Often these two perspectives are employed to construct good–bad typologies. On the one hand, the capital market controls operate at a distance to discipline corporate sector managers to deliver maximum return to shareholders (Lazonick and O'Sullivan, 2004; Lazonick, 2005). On the other hand, corporate control is exerted by internal management boards in the interests of all stakeholders where there is a commitment to long-term growth, innovation and sustainable return on capital employed. These typologies are often used to benchmark the extent to which national forms of corporate governance are converging, hybridizing or resisting new forms of governance.

Berle and Means (1932) observe, in an earlier period, that share ownership is dispersed, separating ownership from control to raise a concern about the principal-agent relationship between investors and managers. The motivations of managers may not coincide with those of stockholders, for example, managers may prefer to retain cash and profit for expansion and maintenance of employment at the expense of cash distribution to shareholders. Management is also able to assume strategic corporate control, employing appropriate organization structures to manage strategy where, for example, decisions on whether to outsource or internalize production acknowledges a positive role for management (Chandler, 1962, 1977).

Over the last two decades households have generally transferred active management of their equity holdings to investment banks such as JP Morgan, Chase, Goldman Sachs, Merrill Lynch and UBS. Investment banks underwrite new share issues and dominate the equity markets in terms of volume trading and are actively involved, as investors, in a market for corporate control and determining corporate market value (MV). In a highly competitive market where fee structures have eroded (McKinsey, 2003) there is additional pressure on corporate sector managers to increase return on funds invested by equity investors which, it is generally argued, will strengthen share prices and the aggregate MV of FUM. Stockhammer (2004: 720) argues that a central feature of post-war managerial capitalism has been the relative autonomy of management, but that 'through the shareholder revolution, its interests were realigned with those of shareholders, who have a stronger preference for profits, as opposed to growth.'

Jensen's (1986) concern is with the agency cost of management control, arguing that managers in mature industries tend to invest cash in low return investments rather than return cash to investors. In these industries firms are wasting investment resources because there is excess capacity arising from technological change, obsolescence or too many competitors implementing high productivity innovations (Jensen, 1993: 839). Jensen identified four 'control forces' which could resolve the discrepancy between what managers want to do and what productive conditions dictate and these include: capital markets, legal political and regulatory systems, product and factor markets and internal control systems. Of this group of 'control forces' Jensen is predisposed to capital market mechanisms and how, for example, an active market for corporate control coupled with financial and contractual incentives could motivate change, expedite corporate renewal and facilitate exit.

Debt financing, he argues, forces managers to invest only in projects that cover the cost of capital because there is a contractual obligation to service the cost of debt whereas, with dividend payments, there is no such obligation (Jensen, 1989). 'By issuing debt in exchange for stock, managers are bonding their promise to pay out future cash flows in a way that cannot be accomplished by simple dividend increases' (Jensen 1986: 324). Jensen's concern is with how capital market regulations and incentives modify corporate governance towards 'accomplishing change before losses in the product markets generate a crisis' (Jensen, 1993: 851).

Jensen's arguments are developed within a 'productionist' framework where the capital market functions to facilitate a selective and orderly exit of financial resources which are then relocated in industries and firms where new technology and innovation offers up new business opportunity, higher demand and improved financial returns. Significantly, Jensen argues, the market for corporate control is not about wealth transfer from one group of stakeholders to another but about increasing productive efficiency (Jensen, 1993: 838).

Lazonick and O'Sullivan similarly employ a 'productionist' framework to establish connections between forms of corporate governance, innovation and competitiveness. Lazonick and O'Sullivan argue that innovative business requires an appropriate form of corporate governance where: financial investment is a long-term commitment, workforce skills and employee commitment are enhanced and decision-makers are integrated into the learning and innovation process (O'Sullivan, 2003: 60).

In an era of shareholder value and increasing pressure from the capital market Lazonick and O'Sullivan (2000) employ evidence on the share of US corporate profit distributed to equity investors, in the form of dividends and share buy-backs, to construct an argument about a reorientation of corporate governance from 'retain and invest' to 'downsize and distribute'. Capital market demands on the corporate sector to service the cost of debt, fund higher dividends and increase share buy-backs undermine corporate cash resources available for innovation which is the key to sustaining commercial competitiveness. The force of Lazonick and O'Sullivan's argument is that it calls into question the assumption that liberal market economies can deliver superior economic performance (Lane, 2003: 2). For example, they cite differences in the productive and financial priorities of firms in the US and Japan employing this bifurcation to explain variation in economic performance.

Jensen's and Lazonick and O'Sullivan's 'productionist' framework is employed to link capital market control, forms of corporate governance, management of resources, and economic performance. Cutler is critical of studies which attempt to establish causal linkages between capital market control, corporate governance and firm performance and then extrapolate these findings to explain differences in national economic performance (Cutler, 2004).

In this chapter we do not attempt to establish linkages, for example, between 'appropriate' forms of corporate governance, firm and national economic performance. Rather the purpose of this study is to explore the difference that emerges between Jensen's notion of selective capital market control and Lazonick and O'Sullivan's observation that there has been a general increase in the share of US corporate profit exiting to shareholders to finance dividends and share buy-backs.

Jensen's position is that the capital market, coupled with appropriate corporate control and governance, will facilitate an orderly exit and transfer of capital resources from mature firms, with excess capacity, into alternative higher growth investments that deliver positive net present value (NPV). Managers of firms operating in mature markets with over-capacity should be encouraged to increase the share of cash remitted to 'investors' because this facilitates selective downsizing and exit of capital. Lazonick and O'Sullivan's work on corporate governance, in an era of shareholder value, raises significant doubts about whether capital market agencies promote a selective exit of capital from the corporate sector. Lazonick and O'Sullivan's findings reveal that there has been a general increase in the profit distributed to shareholders and their explanation for this rests on the financial incentives rewarding managers who increase shareholder value.

In order to move this debate forward, we construct a financialized account of the reorientation of corporate governance, strategy and cash distribution to equity stakeholders. This alternative perspective on corporate governance is located in the accounting and finance literatures and considers the significance of an active market for corporate control and use of *fair value* in the balance sheet. Our argument is that an active market for corporate control coupled with fair value reporting is forcing corporate balance sheet capitalization ahead of current cash earnings in the United States. When this takes place, value is at risk because cash earnings are not sufficient to support the market value (or wealth accumulation) absorbed onto corporate sector balance sheets. To limit the value at risk, senior executives will employ product, procurement, labour and capital market arbitrage. Arbitrage modifies existing stakeholder settlements and contracts so that additional cash can be extracted out of operations and the proportion of cash distributed to equity investors increased to contain value at risk through share buy-backs.

Financialized accounts and the reorientation of corporate governance

Since the 1990s, the Finance Accounting Standards Board (FASB) in the United States has progressively moved towards *fair value* or *mark to market* accounting for general corporate transactions (SFAS 157). This movement towards fair value reporting is of particular significance with regards to how the US corporate sector accounts for capital market transactions, for example, business purchases (SFAS 141), accounting for the expense of stock options (SFAS 123R) and derivatives and other financial instruments (SFAS 133).

Penman (2006) argues that the motivation for fair value reporting is to reconstruct the corporate sector in the image of the asset management industry where the market value of transactions in the balance sheet reflects the

Table 13.1:   The value of M&A deals in the United States, 1996–2006

Year	Deals no.	Value $ mil	Value per deal $ mil
2006	11,750	1,483	126.2
2005	11,013	1,235	112.1
2004	10,296	823	80.0
2003	8,232	530	64.4
2002	7,411	442	59.6
2001	8,545	683	79.9
2000	11,123	1,269	114.1
1999	9,628	1,387	144.1
1998	8,047	1,283	159.5
1997	7,848	675	86.0
1996	5,862	469	80.0
Total	99,755	10,279	103.0

Source: Mergerstat, http://www.mergerstat.com/new/indexnew.asp & Thomson Financial (Communication, March 2007).

bid-ask spread and cash earnings. Fair value reporting shifts the focus for corporate valuation from the income and cash statements to the balance sheet, which now records, and continually re-calibrates, the market value of the enterprise for shareholders.

Putting aside measurement issues, fair value accounting conveys information about equity value and managements' stewardship by stating all assets and liabilities on the balance sheet as their value to shareholders (Penman, 2006: 8). Fair value accounting is in accordance with the widely accepted Hicksian definition of income as a change in wealth because 'fair value accounting is a solution to the accountant's problem of income measurement' (Penman, 2006: 2). Coincident with the phasing in of fair value accounting there has also been an active market for corporate control in the US. Over the period 1996 to 2006 the US corporate sector invested $10.3 trillion financing merger and acquisition (M&A), a sum equivalent to absorbing 88 per cent of S&P 500 outstanding market value (MV) as at 1 January 2007 (see Table 13.1).

A Merrill Lynch report notes that during the 1990s, 55 per cent of all acquisitions in the US corporate sector involved 'pooling' the consolidated accounts of the acquired firm into the acquirer accounts. This left a significant 45 per cent that employed the 'purchase method' (Merrill Lynch, 1999) where the acquiring firm absorbed the fair value of the purchase into the balance sheet. Since the year 2000 all corporate acquisitions in the United States are accounted for using the purchase method (SFAS 141 Business Combinations). In the five-year period since adoption of the purchase method the US

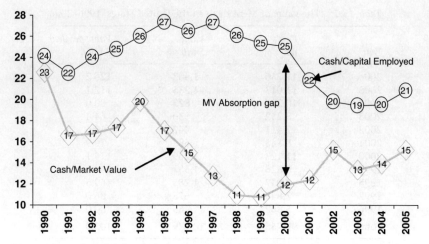

Figure 13.1:   The cash/capital employed and cash/market value ratios for S&P 500 survivors, 1990–2005
Source: Standard and Poor's Washington, 10-K annual report and accounts.
Note: S&P survivor group is all firms that survive in the S&P 500 constituent list continually throughout the period 1990 to 2005, that is, 235 out of 500 firms.

corporate sector absorbed $6.5 trillion of MV into the balance sheet and this forced corporate sector balance sheet capitalization ahead of cash earnings.

In Figure 13.1, we show the reported cash ROCE and cash to market value ratios for S&P survivors (those firms surviving in the S&P 500 over the period 1990–2005). The gap between these two ratios is the 'MV absorption gap'. When the acquiring company completes the acquisition, fair value reporting converts the acquired firm's historic balance sheet capital employed into a current market value. This has the effect of mechanically reducing the ROCE of the acquired companies. To improve consolidated company financials and close the MV absorption gap, managers in the acquiring company will need to step up product, labour and capital market arbitrage to extract additional cash from operations which, in turn, helps to finance additional share buy-backs. Both these moves impact favourably on the reported cash ROCE, bringing balance sheet capitalization back into line with cash earnings and containing value at risk.

Strategy: arbitrage, cash extraction and distribution to equity

To realign value at risk metrics managers need to stretch cash generated out of operations, and during the 1990s, and relative to the 1980s, managers in the S&P 500 group of companies have increased cash extracted out of income from a relatively steady 15 per cent of income in the 1980s to roughly 18–20 per cent in recent years (Andersson et al., 2006). Strategic arbitrage in product, procurement, labour and capital markets forms the basis upon which internal and external contracts can be renegotiated with the objective of increasing cash extracted from operations. Managers will employ a combination of outsourcing, offshoring, transfer pricing and offshore subsidiaries to stretch income and reduce procurement, labour, capital and income tax expenses so as to extract additional cash resources that can be used to limit value at risk (Sikka and Haslam, 2007). Gordon et al. (2005) reveal how strategic arbitrage by City of London based financial services firms is employed to renegotiate internal and external contracts around the objective of cash extraction and value for shareholders. Internal realignments are set in motion by the threat of contracting out, or offshoring work, with the result that internal processes are, in the first instance, simplified to reduce costs before they are eventually offshored. Total financial resource flows into developing economies have steadily increased in recent years (UNCTAD, 2006), reflecting the financial attractiveness of low cost expanding product markets such as India and China.

Although S&P 500 survivor firms have managed to extract additional cash from operations from strategic arbitrage during the 1990s this was offset by increased balance sheet capitalization coincident with an active market for acquisitions and increased use of fair value accounting (Andersson et al., 2006). In these circumstances managers need to dampen inflated balance sheet capitalization. One way to do this is to change the pattern of cash distribution by financing share repurchases for treasury stock. Shares acquired using cash are accounted for as a deduction against capital employed in the balance sheet, thereby helping to improve reported cash ROCE. In the US the value index of M&A spend and that for share buy-backs track each other (see Figure 13.2). There are also additional benefits associated with repurchasing share capital and these include:

- Banking shares so as to improve reported earnings per share (EPS), which is also a key financial metric governing managerial remuneration and bonus packages (Vermaelen, 1981; Comment and Jarrell, 1991; Deloitte, 2005).
- Issuing treasury stock options to employees and senior managers in performance-related pay packages.
- Using treasury stock as an acquisitions currency where holding gains are employed to provide financial leverage (Andersson et al., 2006).

Over the last fifteen years S&P 500 survivor companies have increased spend on share buy-backs relative to dividends. In 1990 the ratio of dividends to share buy-backs was 3:1 and in 2005 the ratio was 0.7:1 as the share of cash used to buy back shares outstripped the growth of conventional cash dividends.

To construct a more detailed account of the changed pattern of cash distribution, we have added: sales of common and preferred stock, property

Figure 13.2: The value of M&A deals and share buy-backs by S&P 500 survivors, 1990–2006
Source: Mergerstat http://www.mergerstat.com/newsite/ and S&P Washington for share buy-back data for S&P survivor group.

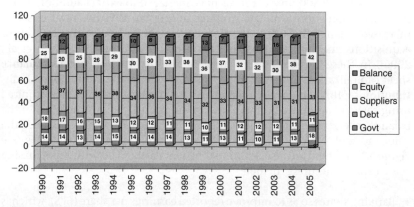

Figure 13.3: Cash distribution by S&P 500 survivors, 1990–2005
Source: S&P 500 10-K's Washington, US.

plant and equipment, and net issuances of long and short-term debt to cash from operations (after net working capital adjustments) to calculate total cash resources for the S&P 500 survivor group. Figure 13.3 reveals the changing pattern in cash distribution for the period 1990–2005. This shows the share of cash resources distributed each year to: government (as tax), debt holders (net interest payments excluding capitalized interest), tangible asset suppliers (capital expenditure) and equity holders (as cash dividends, share buy-backs and cash used to finance acquisitions).

Figure 13.3 reveals a number of changed patterns. Statutory income taxes claim a relatively steady share of S&P 500 survivor group cash resources throughout the period at 13–14 per cent, apart from 2005, when the share

Table 13.2: Cash used for acquisitions, share buy-backs and dividends by S&P 500 survivors, 1990–2005

	Cash acquisitions (%)	Purchase of common and preference stock (%)	Cash dividends (%)	Increase in cash distributed to equity (%)
1990–2005	20.4	54.5	25.1	100

Source: S&P 500 survivor group, 10-K's Washington.
Note: Total cash distributed to equity holders includes: cash acquisitions, cash dividends paid and the purchase of common and preference stock from investors.

of tax paid out of cash jumps to 18 per cent, due to an increase in tax paid by one company, Exxon Mobil. Cash employed to finance debt repayments (net interest) falls from 18 per cent of total cash into the range 11–12 per cent of cash as the cost of debt financing falls in the US during this period. After statutory income tax and contractual obligations to pay net-interest charges the residual cash can be employed to finance capital expenditure (cash payments to tangible asset suppliers), paid out to shareholders or retained as an end of year balance. Our analysis reveals that the share of cash resources employed to finance capital expenditure dropped from 38 per cent to 31 per cent by 2005, thus freeing up cash. The combination of a reduced share of net interest charges and capital expenditure released additional cash, which was then distributed to equity holders. In total the share of cash resources distributed to equity holders increased by twenty percentage points from 25 to 45 per cent over a period of fifteen years. Of the total increase in cash distributed to equity holders during period 1990–2005, half was accounted for by the increase in share buy-backs (see Table 13.2).

In the final section of this chapter we argue that global accounting standards are converging with those established in the United States for fair value reporting and this, coupled with an active market for corporate control, has the potential to financialize international business strategy and corporate governance.

Financialized accounts: international business strategy and governance

The scope for extending a financialized account of the reorientation of corporate governance and strategic priorities outside of the US corporate sector depends on the extent to which fair value reporting is adopted globally and the degree to which there is a significant market for corporate control which forces balance sheet capitalization ahead of cash earnings.

In November 2006 the International Accounting Standards Board (IASB) published its discussion document on 'fair value measurements' and announced its intention to receive comments by April 2007 on how to consolidate the accounting principles governing fair value reporting. In the United States the FASB has recently issued an accounting standard, SFAS 157 Fair Value Measurements, on which work was well advanced before the IASB launched its own project. SFAS 157 establishes a single definition of fair value together with a framework for measuring fair value for financial reports prepared in accordance with US generally accepted accounting principles (US GAAP). Consistent with its commitment to the convergence of IFRSs and US GAAP, the IASB decided to use the US standard as the starting point for its own deliberations.[1]

The IASB's starting point is the US standard on fair value, SFAS 157, and how this can be used to help consolidate a range of 'fair value' approaches that are spread across individual International Financial Reporting Standards (IFRSs). This discussion document asks respondents to address a series of twenty-seven questions about the principles and methods proposed in relation to fair value where the principle itself is non-negotiable.

Accounting practitioner responses to the FASB, and the more recent IASB's proposal documentation on fair value accounting, concentrate on the underlying accounting and value recognition logics employed to record or estimate the market value of balance sheet assets and liabilities (KPMG, 2006). And academics concerned with exploring the superiority (or not) of asset-liability over revenue recognition report that there is a difficulty in matching investments with their returns (Macve and Serafeim, 2006).

Fair value reporting is now adopted in most of the developed economies. However, not all regions have sophisticated capital markets where there is an active market for corporate control. These two conditions are, however, met in Europe. The combination of fair value reporting and an active market for corporate control have the potential to modify strategy and governance in European firms. Table 13.3 summarizes the volume of M&A deals and their value in Europe where spend on M&A deals was roughly $8.1 trillion and equivalent to churning the market value of the Europe 350 S&P index of firms two-fold during this period.

Although there is significant M&A activity in Europe it is not clear how much of the market value of M&A deals was absorbed into corporate sector balance sheets. This is because International Accounting Standard 22 (IAS 22) permitted firms a choice of 'pooling' the acquired company's financials or using the 'purchase method'. Pooling involves amalgamating the historic accounts of both companies with some minor adjustments made to reflect variations in accounting treatment. In contrast, the purchase method reports the market value of the transaction in the acquiring firm's balance sheet (Andersson et al., 2006).

This arrangement recently changed when the International Accounting Standards Board issued draft IFRS3 'Business Combinations' (2004), which recommended that all transactions are to be accounted for using the purchase

Table 13.3: The value of M&A deals in Europe, 1996–2006

Year	Europe		
	Deals no.	Value $ mil	Value per deal $ mil
2006	11,989	1,322	110.2
2005	10,726	1,005	93.7
2004	9,936	720	72.5
2003	10,037	515	51.3
2002	9,549	485	50.8
2001	12,472	535	42.9
2000	15,965	1,001	62.7
1999	12,621	1,192	94.5
1998	9,478	584	61.6
1997	8,605	449	52.2
1996	8,044	305	37.9
Totals	119,422	8,112	67.9

Source: Mergerstat, http://www.mergerstat.com/new/indexnew.asp & Thomson Financial (Communication, March 2007).

method. This IFRS is issued as part of a joint effort by the IASB and the FASB (referred to as the boards) to improve financial reporting while promoting the international convergence of accounting standards (IASB, 2005: 17). The IASB and the FASB began deliberating the second phase of their projects at about the same time. The boards decided that a significant improvement could be made to financial reporting if they had similar standards for accounting for combinations (IASB, 2005: 17–18).

As of 1 January 2005, IFRS3 superseded IAS 22 and European firms now have to report the market value of business acquisitions employing the purchase method to account for business combinations. As the market value of capital market transactions was absorbed into the balance sheet of European firms, this coincided with a substantial leap in share buy-backs:

> European companies' love affair with share buybacks grew by leaps and bounds last year: the value of new programmes in 2005 was almost equal to all those announced in the previous five years combined. This was good news for shareholders. (McCauley, 2006)

In a KPMG advisory note on IFRS3, 'Uncovering the true value of an acquisition', managers are advised to ensure that earnings improvements are sustained in order to limit market value at risk:

> you may have your work cut out convincing stakeholders that the deal is indeed good business, given that earnings improvements may be two,

three or four years down the line instead of in the next set of results. Indeed, with firms now obliged to recalculate asset values annually, the acquisition – and the price paid – is likely to continue to be under the spotlight for several years. (KPMG, 2005: 5)

Discussion and conclusion

In this chapter, we have constructed a financialized account of corporate strategy and governance, in the S&P 500. This account is located in the finance and accounting literatures and specifically considers how fair value reporting combined with an active market for corporate control has the potential to modify corporate governance priorities.

Jensen argues that capital markets operating within certain regulatory frameworks can promote an orderly exit of capital from low return to higher return economic activity. Lazonick and O'Sullivan describe the decade of the 1990s in terms of a general increase in the share of profit distributed to equity investors and argue that the driving force underlying this reorientation are shareholder value metrics and their use in executive management remuneration and incentive packages.

In a financialized account of corporate governance, we reveal how fair value reporting in the US corporate sector blends stock market value (wealth accumulation) with current cash earnings in financial accounts inflating balance sheet capitalization ahead of cash earnings to increase value at risk. Arbitrage in product, procurement, labour and capital markets sets existing contracts and settlements up against all other new possibilities as managers struggle to extract additional cash from operations and modify the pattern of cash distribution to equity. We find that there has been a significant adjustment in the share of cash distributed to equity stakeholders: a pattern which is sustained regardless of firm size and the degree to which firms are more or less cash rich.

Stakeholder settlements are malleable because financial arbitrage demands a continuous renegotiation of formal and informal stakeholder contracts. We are, however, cautious about the degree to which this financialized account can be extended beyond the US corporate sector. This depends on whether fair value reporting is adopted in a particular country or region considered and the extent of an active market for corporate control. In combination, fair value reporting and an active market for corporate control can inflate balance sheet capital employed ahead of cash earnings. In 2005 the IASB adopted fair value reporting in Europe and this was followed by a significant jump in the value of share buy-backs. This, we believe, goes someway towards confirming that fair value reporting and the follow-on need to limit value at risk is a strong force driving the reorientation of corporate governance towards equity stakeholders.

Note

1. See http://www.iasb.org/News/Press+Releases/IASB+publishes+Discussion+Paper +on+fair+value+measurements.htm

Bibliography

Andersson, T., Haslam, C. and Lee, E. (2006). 'Financialized accounts: restructuring and return on capital employed in the S&P 500'. *Accounting Forum*, 30: 21–41.

Andersson, T., Haslam, C., Lee, E. and Tsitisianis, N. (2007). 'Financialized accounts: share buy-backs, mark to market and holding the financial line in the S&P 500'. *Accounting Forum*, 31: 165–78.

Berle, A. A. and Means, G. C. (1932). *The modern corporation and private property* (New York: Macmillan).

Chandler, A. (1962). *Strategy & structure: chapters in the history of the industrial enterprise* (Cambridge, MA: MIT Press).

Chandler, A. (1977). *The visible hand: the managerial revolution in American business* (Cambridge, MA: Harvard University Press).

Ciesielski, J. (2006). 'Comment letter on FASB proposal for "fair value option"'. *The Analyst's Accounting Observer*. Available at: http://www.accountingobserver.com/ commentary/letters/2006/Fair_Val.asp

Comment, R. and Jarrell, G. A. (1991). 'The relative signalling power of Dutch-auction and fixed-price self-tender offers and open-market share repurchases', *Journal of Finance*, 46(4): 1243–71.

Copeland T., Koller, T. and Murrin, J. (2000). *Valuation: measuring and managing the value of companies*. Third edition (New York: John Wiley & Sons).

Cutler, A. (2004). 'The wages of capital: the rise and rise of corporate governance'. *Competition & Change*, 8(1): 65–83.

Deloitte (2005). 'Rise above FAS 123R's golden opportunity: performance-based equity compensation comes into its own' (London: Deloitte Development).

Erturk, I., Froud, J., Solari, S. and Williams, K. (2005). 'The reinvention of prudence: household savings, financialisation and forms of capitalism'. University of Manchester, CRESC Working Paper no. 11.

Financial Accounting Standards Board (1998). *Accounting for derivative instruments and hedging activities*. Statement of Financial Accounting Standards 133 (Norwalk, CT: FASB). Available at http://www.fasb.org/st/

Financial Accounting Standards Board (2001). *Business combinations*. Statement of Financial Accounting Standards 141 (Norwalk, CT: FASB). Available at http://www. fasb.org/st/

Financial Accounting Standards Board (2004). *Share-based payment*. Statement of Financial Accounting Standards 123R (Norwalk, CT: FASB). Available at http:// www.fasb.org/st/

Financial Accounting Standards Board (2006). *Fair-value measurements*. Statement of Financial Accounting Standards 157 (Norwalk, CT: FASB). Available at http:// www.fasb.org/st/

Fink, R. (2006). 'Will fair value fly? Fair-vale accounting could change the very basis of corporate finance'. *CFO Magazine* (1 September). Available at: http://www. cfo.com/article.cfm/7851757/c_2984361?f=singlepage

Gordon, I., Haslam, C., McCann, P. and Scott-Quinn, B. (2005). *Off-shoring and the City of London* (London: Corporation of London).

Ikenberry, D., Lakonishok, J. and Vermaelen, T. (1995). 'Market under-reaction to open share repurchases'. *Journal of Financial Economics*, 39: 2373–97.
International Accounting Standards Board (2005). *Exposure draft of proposed amendments to IFRS3 Business Combinations* (London: IASB). Available at: http://www.iasb. org/NR/rdonlyres/1C3066EC-3FEF-4966-A42E-E8AC8F341869/0/Proposedamendto-ifrs3.pdf
International Accounting Standards Board (2006). 'Fair value measurements. Part 1: invitation to comment and relevant IFRS guidance'. Discussion paper (London: IASB). Available at: http://www.iasb.org/NR/rdonlyres/6C8AF291-EB14-4034-84F1-54305F72024D/0/DDFairValue.pdf
Jensen, M. (1986). 'Agency cost of free cash flow, corporate finance, and takeovers'. *American Economic Review*, 76(2): 323–9.
Jensen, M. (1989). 'Eclipse of the public corporation'. *Harvard Business Review*, 67(5): 61–74.
Jensen M. (1993). 'The modern industrial revolution, exit, and the failure of internal control systems'. *Journal of Finance*, 48(3): 831–80.
Johnson, T. (1994). 'Relevance regained: total quality management and the role of management accounting'. *Critical Perspectives on Accounting*, 5(3): 259–67.
KPMG (2005). 'IFRS 3: uncovering the true value of an acquisition' (Dublin: KPMG Ireland). Available at: http://www.kpmg.ie/services/cfinance/publications/Valuations_ifrs3.pdf
KPMG (2006). 'IFRS Briefing Sheet – Issue 60: Fair Value Measurements' (London: KPMG). Available at: http://www.kpmgifrg.com/pubs/pub_brief.cfm#
Lane, C. (2003). 'Changes in corporate governance of German corporations: convergence to the Anglo-American model?' University of Cambridge, ESRC Centre for Business Research, Working Paper no. 259.
Lazonick, W. (2005). 'Corporate governance, innovation enterprise, and economic development'. Available at: http://www.minds.org.br/arquivos/Lazonick_CGIE&ED_%20September_2005.pdf
Lazonick, W. and O'Sullivan, M. (2000). 'Maximizing shareholder value: a new ideology for corporate governance'. *Economy and Society*, 29(1): 13–35.
Lazonick, W. and O'Sullivan, M. (2004). 'Corporate governance, innovation and economic performance in the EU-CGEP'. Available at: http://cordis.europa.eu/documents/documentlibrary/2352EN.pdf
Macve, R. and Serafeim, G. (2006). ' "Deprival value" vs "fair value" measurement for the contract liabilities in resolving the "revenue recognition" conundrum: towards a general solution'. London School of Economics, Department of Accounting and Finance. Available at http://www.lse.ac.uk/collections/accountingAndFinance/facultyAndStaff/liabrevrec300606ssrn.pdf
Manne, H. G. (1965). 'Mergers and the market for corporate control'. *Journal of Political Economy*, 73(2): 110–20.
McAuley, T. (2006). 'Crashing the buyback party'. *CFO Europe* (February). Available at: http://www.cfoeurope.com/displayStory.cfm/545985
McKinsey & Company (2003). *Will the goose keep laying golden eggs?* The fifth annual survey on the profitability of European asset management (London: McKinsey & Company).
Merrill Lynch (1999). *Valuing the new economy* (London: Merrill Lynch).
O'Sullivan, M. (2003). 'The financing role of the US stock market in the 20th century', INSEAD Working Paper.

Penman, S. (2006). 'Financial reporting quality: is fair value a plus or a minus?' Paper presented at the Conference on 'Information for Better Markets', Institute of Chartered Accountants in England and Wales, 18–19 December. Available at: http://www.icaew.co.uk/index.cfm?route=143928

Sikka, P. and Haslam, C. (2007). 'Transfer pricing and its role in tax avoidance and flight of capital: some theory and evidence'. Available at: http://www.aabaglobal.org

Stern Stewart Research (2002). 'Stern Stewart's EVA Clients Outperform the Market and Their Peers' (New York: Stern Stewart & Co.). Available at: http://www.sternstewart.com/content/evaluation/info/102002.pdf

Stockhammer, E. (2004). 'Financialization and the slowdown of accumulation'. *Cambridge Journal of Economics*, 28: 719–41.

UNCTAD (2006). *World investment report 2006. FDI from developing and transition economies: implications for development* (New York and Geneva: United Nations).

Vermaelen, T. (1981). 'Common stock repurchases and market signalling: an empirical study'. *Journal of Financial Economics*, 9: 139–83.

Vitols, S., Casper, S., Soskice, D. and Woolcock, S. (1997). 'Corporate governance in large British and German companies' (London: Anglo-German Foundation).

14
The Adoption of an American Executive Pay Practice in Germany
Trevor Buck and Amon Chizema

Introduction

This chapter focuses on one element of German corporate governance –
executive pay, specifically, executive stock options (ESOs) – as an American
pay innovation dating from around 1960 (Lewellen, 1968). ESOs have been
transplanted into many countries, even in Germany, with its distinctive cultural institutional environment. However, institutional theory has predicted
conformism, isomorphism, path dependency and resistance to this kind of
potentially illegitimate transplant (Tuschke and Sanders, 2003; Sanders and
Tuschke, 2007). Perhaps this could explain why ESOs took over thirty years
to penetrate German firms.

At the same time, neo-institutional theory does consider the circumstances
in which institutional change can occur (Greenwood and Hinings, 1996).
Indeed, Hall and Thelen (2005), Greif (2005) and Aoki (2007) have recently
begun the process of modelling a dynamic conception of how institutions
change at a micro-level (Deeg and Jackson, 2007). There is also now recognition that the perception of institutional complementarities as a positive
influence could be mistaken, since the relations between institutions may be
characterized as tensions and sources of inefficiency (Crouch, 2005): institutions may be seen as constraints as well as resources that facilitate change
(Hall and Thelen, 2005).

This chapter follows only a few others (e.g. D'Aunno et al., 2000; Sanders
and Tuschke, 2007) and extends neo-institutional theory as a theoretical
framework all the way to empirical testing. In this context, it must be recognized that institutional theory has not yet fulfilled the promise of its
early years. While early papers referred to its 'adolescence' (Scott, 1987),
this has recently shifted to notions of 'adulthood' and 'maturity' (Scott,
2007), where this might imply a gradual loss of vigour. Nevertheless, we
feel that neo-institutional theory can offer insights into the prediction of
institutional change. The analysis of the topic is important in the context of
the alleged 'Americanization' (Djelic, 1998) of corporate governance, i.e. the

means by which the behaviour of senior executives is constrained. Americanization represents convergence on the Anglo-American model of 'stock market capitalism' or shareholder system based on dispersed shareholders (often coalesced in financial institutions), laws that protect the rights of minority shareholders, open information disclosure, liquid stock markets, hostile takeovers, stock-based executive pay, and single-tier boards including independent directors (Dore, 2000). Alternatives to this Anglo-American system have collapsed in centrally planned economies and severe problems have been faced by relational governance in, for example, Japan, Korea and Germany. This has led to an element of triumphalism in some quarters in relation to convergence. For example, Hansmann and Kraakman (2001) foresee the end of comparative corporate law as the world converges on the Anglo-American model.

This triumphalism may prove to have been premature in what has been called an international 'clash of capitalisms' (Ahmadjian and Robbins, 2005). China is developing its own variety of relational or stakeholder system (Dore, 2000) and countries like Germany and Japan still manage to produce corporations that are world-leaders. However, if convergence on the American model does not occur, why not? Conversely, where some convergence does occur, *which firms may be predicted to adopt institutional change?* This chapter addresses the latter research question in the context of German executive pay.

It begins by identifying in more detail the German institutional context in comparative terms and the strength of path dependency. In section 2, neo-institutional theory is used to develop twelve hypotheses in relation to the adoption and non-adoption of ESOs in Germany. These hypotheses are then tested, using data and methodology explained in section 3. The test results are presented in section 4, followed by some discussion and conclusions in the final section 5.

The German institutional context

While the typical features of Anglo-American stock market capitalism were listed above, it must be concluded that the German version of stakeholder capitalism reverses most of them in a world where executives are mainly influenced not by share price movements, but by the voice of various stakeholders (Noteboom, 1999). In Germany, this voice is exercised by family owners, banks and other blockholders and by employees, usually supported by incumbent managers, on the upper tier of a two-board system. Stock liquidity is low as a result of 85 per cent of large firms having at least a 25 per cent (blocking minority) blockholder, plus stable cross-holdings between firms (Franks and Mayer, 2001). Banks are a significant part of such stable shareholdings in what has been called a bank-centred governance system

(Jackson, 2003) but otherwise there is a relative absence of financial institutions as investors, such as the pension funds and insurance companies that dominate US/UK governance (Vitols, 2004).

Despite some recent convergence in this context, in 2005, 56 of 120 large German listed firms still did not prepare accounts to IAS or US GAAP standards, still relying on the local HGB standard (authors' own database). Of DAX 30 firms in 2005, nine still only disclosed executive pay data for the board as a whole with no data on individual directors, and another three identified only CEO pay individually. Nevertheless, new regulations legalized and encouraged ESOs in 1998 (Cioffi, 2002; Höpner, 2001), though some firms did *de facto* manage to introduce them earlier without calling them ESOs. By 2005 all DAX 30 firms had ESOs with the single exception of BMW. However, such ESO schemes may bear little resemblance to their American counterparts (Buck and Shahrim, 2005). Minority shareholders are still only offered weak legal protection in Germany (La Porta et al., 1999), and managers have yet to face the development of an active market for hostile takeovers, despite some institutional developments in this direction (Franks and Mayer, 2001; Höpner and Jackson, 2006). Full stock market capitalism therefore remains a distant prospect for Germany. At the same time, voice-based, relational governance does 'work' in a German context in the sense that global product market leaders have emerged, and Kaplan (1994) reports similar relations between share price movements and discipline over executives, measured by CEO dismissal, in Germany, Japan and the United States.

One implication of these multifaceted elements of German governance institutions, bound together by regulative, normative and cognitive forces (Scott, 1987), is that they have helped to produce an economic system that does not resemble pure stock market capitalism, and that has changed very little in governance terms over many decades (Buck and Shahrim, 2005). From the perspective of the 'varieties-of-capitalism' literature (Hall and Gingerich, 2001), German corporate governance institutions represent a web of mutually supporting institutions and the attempted, piecemeal borrowing of 'best practices' may reduce efficiency (Deeg and Jackson, 2007). For example, takeovers could not be resisted without weak minority shareholder protection, strong employee representation and low stock liquidity, but these elements at the same time do facilitate stakeholder voice as a locally effective alternative to stock market capitalism. It follows that a single American governance innovation such as the ESO faces significant institutional resistance, dependent as it is upon liquid stock markets and upper-tier board support, and made even more unlikely given the high degree of employee control in German firms. ESOs may be expected to be rejected or at least 'translated' by German firms, to preserve their legitimacy, i.e. to suit the interests of salient stakeholders (Buck and Shahrim, 2005).

Despite such inertia, however, German firms have certainly adopted ESOs in large numbers, and a theoretical framework is needed to analyse this recent phenomenon. Traditional institutional theory, with its emphasis on path dependency, is clearly unsuitable for that purpose, and agency theory, such a frequently used paradigm in the study of executive pay (Gomez-Mejia et al., 2005), is 'under-socialized' in this context (Lubatkin et al., 2006; Aguilera and Jackson, 2002, 2003). Nevertheless, it is proposed that neo-institutional theory may be adopted for this purpose, and the next section develops hypotheses for one of the few empirical applications of this body of theory, here in the context of German ESOs. A related study by Sanders and Tuschke (2007) does analyse German ESOs using a neo-institutional theory, though in a piecemeal fashion, supplemented by an 'upper echelons' approach (Hambrick, 2007) embracing CEOs' personal characteristics. This chapter, however, is distinguished from their approach by using a longer time-horizon of twelve years (1992–2003) compared with a shorter period (1996–2000) in Sanders and Tuschke (2007), and by employing a more comprehensive neo-institutional approach.

We analyse the adoption of ESOs through intra-organizational dynamics, with an emphasis on the power dependencies, interests and commitment of organizational actors. By considering the power dependencies and value commitments implied by different forms of ownership structure, our study contributes to the understanding of how organizations adapt to environmental change (Suarez and Oliva, 2005). Specifically, why and how do organizational innovations become adopted (Nelson et al., 2004)?

Theory and hypotheses

A typical challenge in institutional theory is the identification of the particular species of institutional theory adopted. As Scott (1987: 493) observed, 'the beginning of wisdom in approaching institutional theory is to recognize at the outset that there is not one but several variants.' The main sub-species of institutional theory are new institutional sociology (NIS, e.g. DiMaggio and Powell, 1983; Meyer and Rowan, 1977), new institutional economics (NIE, e.g. Coase, 1937; Williamson, 1973; North, 1990) and old institutional economics (OIE, e.g. Commons, 1934). For this chapter, we use NIS and OIE, together with insights from political science and organization theory.

The focus of NIS is primarily on how and why firms conform to societal institutions, defined as rules exogenously pre-determined outside the domain of economic transactions carried out through a hierarchical order (Aoki, 2007). Legal rules as well as informal social norms are included in this definition. Indeed, organizations change and adapt to external pressures because of the need to gain legitimacy and have access to resources (DiMaggio and Powell, 1983). Organizations are thus forced to adopt practices (coercive isomorphism), imitate other organizations (mimetic isomorphism) or have to be

246 Corporate Governance and International Business

professionally compliant (normative isomorphism). However, the processes of institutionalization, through organizational routines (Nelson and Winter, 1982; Becker et al., 2005), over time are not well developed by NIS. Thus, on its own, NIS cannot answer our main research question, above, but its ability to accommodate dynamic external pressures (in this case changes in German corporate governance as a result of globalized financial and product markets) is useful.

On the other hand, OIE maintains that human action is constrained by institutions, but it also recognizes that institutions enable people to develop meaningful actions. For example, Sjöstrand (1995) regards institutions as infrastructures for human action, but also argues that institutions are constituted by, and reinforced through, social (inter)actions. Moreover, OIE argues that institutions are not independent of the individuals that inhabit various social settings. Rather, institutions exist through the behaviours of these individuals manifested through organizational routines. Consistent with this argument is Aoki's (2007) treatment of institutionalized rules as something spontaneously and/or endogenously shaped and sustained in the repeated operational plays of the game itself. Thus, OIE sees individual behaviour as an integral part of the institutions that govern much of social life, and 'institutions simplify action choices; they are not separate from, but are part of, the individual (inter)actions' (Sjöstrand, 1995: 21). This reasoning, alluding to the 'endogenizing' of institutions (Aoki, 2007), qualifies OIE for the analysis of micro-level (intra-organizational) dynamics and the better understanding of institutional change.

However, OIE does not tell us the source of change, nor when the time is ripe to start the process of change within the organization. This is where NIS complements OIE: *the desire to gain legitimacy by conforming to the external environment signals changes to which individual actors within an organization respond.* This actor-centred approach to institutions (Aguilera and Jackson, 2003; Crouch, 2005) may further help us to understand the diffusion, adaptation and contesting of institutional change (Fiss and Zajac, 2004; Sanders and Tuschke, 2007). Moreover, is institutional change radical, incremental or non-existent? Deeg and Jackson (2007) suggest that more dynamism may be introduced into the comparative capitalism literature by proceeding on three distinct levels of analysis: the micro, meso and macro levels. While external/exogenous pressure may point to a high possibility of radical change, the subsequent reaction by endogenous actors, through repeated operational routines, suggests that institutional change may occur through incremental adjustment or transformation and adaptation (ibid.).

To address the macro and micro dynamics of organizational change, therefore, we synthesize the new and old institutionalism in neo-institutional theory (Greenwood and Hinings, 1996) which provides the framework for the derivation of our hypotheses at two of the levels (micro, macro) suggested by Deeg and Jackson (2007).

Macro-level dynamics

The salience of institutional forces, or the strength of their influence on what constitutes social legitimacy and hence firm survival, is the basis for analysing the firm's interactions with its external market and institutional environment (Pugh and Hickson, 1997; Pfeffer and Salancik, 1978). If organizations lack any crucial resource (materials, finance, personnel, information or technology), the providers of these resources become salient, and the firms' actors must effectively act to gain legitimacy with those who possess and control these resources (Pugh and Hickson, 1997; Ulrich and Barney, 1984). Expressed in simple terms, firms faced with competitive pressures to attract investment financing are likely to seek legitimacy first in order to survive through financial markets, often foreign. Thus, these resource pressures may shape new organizational behaviour and the adoption of practices is seen as legitimate by the salient resource providers. In Germany, institutional pressure for the adoption of a standard American element of executive pay packages could be seen as partially filling the legitimacy gap (Chizema and Buck, 2006) and subsequent access to American capital (Cheffins, 2003; Fuerbringer, 2004). While long-term finance could be provided by German financial institutions, their resources are limited and they have not so far emerged as a source of finance for firms' global expansion strategies. However, American finance for German firms has been growing (Sanders and Tuschke, 2007) and many DAX 100 firms are listed on American stock exchanges. American investors are familiar with the ESO and may be suspicious of executives who receive rewards mainly in the form of merely salary and bonus, at quite low levels by American standards (Towers Perrin, 2003). Hence, we propose our first hypothesis:

> *Hypothesis 1a: ESO adoption will be positively associated with the extent of a German firm's dependence on American investors.*

Of course, ESOs are characteristic of most English-speaking countries, and foreign share ownership as a whole may indicate a firm's willingness to adopt innovations such as ESOs. In Germany, foreign ownership has increased from 8.2 per cent of total equity in 1995 to 12.5 per cent in 2000 and 16.8 per cent by 2004. Following Ahmadjian and Robbins (2005), therefore, we propose a second hypothesis as follows:

> *Hypothesis 1b: ESO adoption will be positively associated with a firm's level of foreign ownership.*

Micro-level dynamics

Intra-organizational dynamics may also contribute to organizational responses to institutional pressures. Indeed, neo-institutionalists and other transformation researchers have pointed to the need to integrate micro-level aspects into organizational change models in order to explain 'when and how' (Newman and Nollen, 1998: 49). Johnson et al. (2000) showed how actors within the organization enact and cope with change in their institutional environment. Focusing on privatization processes, they identified three micro-level mechanisms which influence an organization's transition from a public to a private sector 'template' or 'behavioural script': the involvement of actors, reciprocal behaviour by other actors confirming the adapted behavioural routines, and symbolic reinforcement of the new template in interactive processes.

The focus on organizational actors and their potential to effectively influence change draws attention to issues of power (Blazejewski and Dorow, 2003; Newman, 2000; Greenwood and Hinings, 1996), interests, value commitment and capacity for action (DiMaggio and Powell, 1991; Greenwood and Hinings, 1996). Indeed, an actor's influence in organizational change processes depends on micro-level dynamics, e.g. the availability and applicability of an actor's power base in relation to vested interests and the resources available to opponents who might build up resistance to reforms. Greenwood and Hinings (1996) refer to these micro-level dynamics as endogenous (or within-firm) and classifies them under precipitating and enabling factors. Interests and value commitments are precipitating dynamics and enabling dynamics are power dependencies and capacity for action.

Interest group dissatisfaction and value commitment

Different groups with diverse interests and value perceptions exist within firms and 'organizations are . . . arenas in which coalitions with different interests and capacities for influence vie for dominance' (Palmer et al., 1993: 103). Different groups are able to convert their interests into favourable allocations of organizational resources according to the extent to which they are dissatisfied with the accommodation of their interests. A high degree of dissatisfaction may become a precipitating pressure for change (Covaleski and Dirsmith, 1988; Walsh et al., 1981). Recently, Hall and Thelen (2005) have added weight to this argument by noting that institutional change results from a perception by actors that existing institutions no longer satisfy their self-defined interests. Thus, actors can defect from behaviours associated with previously established equilibriums and can reinterpret existing institutions in a manner that safeguards their interests by changing the content of practices or behaviours associated with that institution (Deeg and Jackson, 2007).

Taken together, these precipitating influences, of interests and value commitment, are reflected in three proposed hypotheses (explained below). First, weak firm performance is seen as a key outcome of the market context capable of generating interest group dissatisfaction and pressure for change. With weak firm performance (e.g. share price and/or employment level reductions), organizational groups (shareholders, employees, managers, etc.) may express their dissatisfaction by tilting the balance of forces in favour of institutional change. Of course the direction of causation is an issue here, because institutional change may precede firm performance, e.g. performance-related executive pay may motivate executives to make decisions that raise shareholder value or vice versa. The notion of performance may imply another host of issues (e.g. profitability, employment levels, customer satisfaction) suggesting, in this chapter's context, diverse causes and consequences of different patterns of pay. For example, as is normally the case in stakeholder systems, if managers place priority on maintaining high employment levels at the expense of shareholder returns, profits may be lower. This may suggest that change towards the use of a different remuneration pattern may not necessarily be driven by performance, nor that remuneration may cause better performance.

However, the neo-institutional view taken in this chapter is that a firm's financial performance may cause an erosion of commitment, and groups less committed to prevailing governance elements may legitimately raise and promote alternative perspectives (Child and Smith, 1987; Oliver, 1992; Tushman and Romanelli, 1985). While accepting that high profitability may increase discretionary resources available for executive pay, we propose tentatively to go along with a neo-institutional view on ESO adoption:

Hypothesis 2: ESO adoption will be associated with low profitability in firms.

Besides value commitment and profitability, Greenwood and Hinings (1996) add that organizations will also vary in patterns of value commitment because of their different locations within the institutional field. Leblebici et al. (1991) show that more peripheral, and therefore less embedded, organizations (e.g. in terms of technology or size of firm) are less committed to prevailing practices and readier to develop new ones. They lack the intensity of commitment to the status quo found in firms that are more centrally located and embedded within their organizational field. While the DAX 100 comprises Germany's top 100 firms, DAX 30 firms may additionally be identified as a 'core' group of massive firms in terms of market capitalization. Within the context of the top 100 firms, therefore, firms outside the DAX 30 may be considered as being peripheral.

In relation to institutional peripherality, we follow Leblebici et al. (1991) and an earlier study by Hinings and Greenwood (1988), who report in their analysis of municipalities that change occurs more quickly where organizations are small and undiversified, with low structural and task complexity. Organizations that are peripherally located within the institutional sector may lack the intensity of commitment to the status quo. We therefore suggest:

Hypothesis 3: ESO adoption may be positively associated with the peripherality of firms.

The third precipitating influence addresses the value commitment of firms directly, or rather declarations of value commitment. In the context of the German system of corporate governance, declared commitments to shareholder value orientation rather than to the *Gemeinschaft* (community) of the firm represent a contingency that favours the adoption of a pay innovation itself associated with the values of shareholder capitalism. Indeed, evidence of shareholder value orientation has been shown by German firms, manifesting through the number of times the words 'shareholder value' appear in the chairman's report (Bradley and Sundaram, 2004) and the establishment of investor relations' departments and share-based executive compensation (Fiss and Zajac, 2004; Tuschke and Sanders, 2007). Therefore, we propose:

Hypothesis 4: ESO adoption will depend on the declared value commitments of firms.

However, it should be emphasized that H2, H3 and H4 only constitute precipitating mechanisms and change may fail to occur without enabling dynamics. For example, the value commitment of firms may interact with employee power (see Hypothesis 5a below).

Capacity for action and power dependencies

Greenwood and Hinings (1996) propose that radical change will occur only in conjunction with enabling dynamics: an appropriate *capacity for action* and supportive *power dependencies*. Ranson et al. (1980) argue that organizational groups vary in their ability to influence organizational change because different groups have different power to effect or resist it. Positions of power can be used to enable or suppress the prevailing archetype (Covaleski and Dirsmith, 1988). The most distinctive feature of German governance institutions is a legal requirement for the presence of employee representatives on supervisory boards, contributing at least half the boards of the largest firms. Employees, undiversified compared with shareholders, may be expected to favour job security and resist labour retrenchment (Fernandez and Rodrik, 1991), and ESOs that link executive pay directly with share price may be perceived as a threat to job security. Consequently, employees may use their power on boards to block ESOs.

Hypothesis 5a: ESO adoption may be negatively associated with employee power within the firm.

The German government has largely established employees through its co-determination laws, and governance institutions hang together in a nexus of parallel interests (Hall and Gingerich, 2001). In addition, employee representation on supervisory boards may be reinforced by state ownership (at a federal and Land level) of a firm's shares, which may also be associated with board representation as employees and politicians collude. Although ownership by the government has declined by 50 per cent between 1995 and 2004 from 1.8 per cent to 0.9 per cent, this influence could be substantial where it exists. Hence:

> *Hypothesis 5b: ESO adoption may be negatively associated with state ownership of a firm's shares.*

The organizational templates of enterprise founders have been found to have a persistent influence on the institutions and strategies of firms (Baron et al., 1999). The ownership of shares in large German firms by founding families still represents an important obstacle to the high stock liquidity, and may also be expected to act as a conservative influence in relation to ESO adoption, another feature of stock market capitalism, like stock liquidity.

> *Hypothesis 5c: ESO adoption may be negatively associated with the proportion of founding family ownership.*

Besides the question of power dependencies and who owns a firm's stock (e.g. the state or founding families), the concentration of stock ownership may be an important element in relation to power dependencies. Dispersed share ownership is associated with stock market capitalism, where the exit of shareholders from a particular stock can put pressure on executives to adopt organizational changes. Höpner and Jackson (2006) note that the number of firms with dispersed ownership has not increased over the period 1995 to 2004. In 2002, for example, 22 of the 100 largest German companies had a majority of dispersed ownership, however, the average company from the top 100 listed had 52 per cent dispersed ownership. Historically, such dispersed ownership is not characteristic of the German system, but where it exists:

> *Hypothesis 5d: ESO adoption may be associated with the dispersed ownership of shares.*

In apparent contradiction of H5d, the coalescence of stock into significant blocks has been an important influence on corporate strategies in US firms (Maug, 1998). Blockholders may provide more powerful pressures for institutional change, and in Germany, blockholdings not in the hands of families or the state may press for a reform with the capacity to boost shareholder value through an incentive effect for executives. Thus:

> *Hypothesis 5e: ESO adoption may be associated with the presence of significant blockholders.*

Besides these hypotheses H5a–5e relying on power dependencies, it must be recognized that capacity for action must also buttress motivation if reform is to occur. Actual reform requires the skills, competencies and resources needed to achieve, and function with, a new template (Clarke, 1994; Nadler and Tushman, 1989). Thus, capacity for action embraces different kinds of resources: financial, human and technological etc. Sherer and Lee (2002) consider that resource endowments are linked with the prestige of an organization, important to the initiation of change in many organizational fields. Large organizations with prestige may have the legitimacy and access to resources to act as initial and early adopters (Rogers, 1995). Therefore, we propose:

Hypothesis 6: ESO adoption may be positively associated with the size and prominence of firms on capital markets.

Networks are a resource that does not appear in conventional financial statements, yet repeated exposure to reformed templates in contacts with trading partners can be an important source of information on reforms. Thus, inviting equity ownership by foreigners, participating in foreign product and capital markets, adopting International Accounting Standards (IAS) or American Generally Accepted Accounting Principles (GAAP) could all be considered as part of the process of de-institutionalizing a corporate governance system. Such activities may facilitate the process of change. Oliver (1992: 577) claims that, 'firms that diversify their operations into other sectors or markets, particularly in different countries are likely to be exposed to alternative organizational customs.'

It has been suggested that greater exposure to international product markets may encourage a firm to move towards a shareholder value orientation (Hansmann and Kraakman, 2001; Vitols, 2001). Competition in international product markets may bring German firms in direct contact with American firms, for example, and executives may make direct comparisons with their own pay packages, stimulating mimetic isomorphism (DiMaggio and Powell, 1983). This implies:

Hypothesis 7: Greater foreign links will be associated with the adoption of ESOs.

Besides these twelve hypotheses developed from neo-institutional theory, other variables are proposed as controls in empirical tests, without formal hypothesizing. As with peripherality, embeddedness may be related to the age of the firm, which is included here as a control, plus debt-to-equity ratio (leverage) as a possible influence on executive pay packages through risk mechanisms (Gray and Cannella, 1997). In addition, time may have an influence on ESO adoption through the legislative process. With these hypotheses and controls in hand, the next section explains how the data were derived and used to test them.

Data and methodology

Data

The data were collected from a sample comprising German firms listed in the DAX 100 at any time between 1992 and 2003. This yielded a sample n = 120. Information disclosure by German firms is notoriously thin (Buck and Shahrim, 2005) and so a focus on large, DAX firms is inevitable, with the smaller firms of the *Mittelstand* comprising unincorporated partnerships and sole proprietorships that account for around half German GDP, but with even weaker disclosure standards (Edwards and Fischer, 1994). Firms with less than eight years of complete data were excluded from the sample. Thus, firms established after 1995 were omitted, and firms that stopped operating as a result of bankruptcy, amalgamation or acquisition with fewer than eight years in the DAX 100 were excluded. For example, Mannesmann was acquired by Vodafone in 2000, but was included in the sample for the period 1992–2000. Firms that were DAX 100 members but were wholly owned subsidiaries of other firms in the sample were excluded, to avoid double-counting. For example, while RWE-DEA was listed, 1992–8, another firm, RWE AG, held more than 99 per cent of its shares, making RWE-DEA a subsidiary of RWE AG.

The choice of time period (1992–2003) was determined by changes in corporate governance in Germany, which began to occur in the early 1990s and are still ongoing. Specifically, the German government enacted the first of three financial market promotion laws in 1990, aimed at liberalizing financial regulation and promoting the growth of the German stock market, and declarations of shareholder value orientation first emerged among German firms around 1992 (Bradley and Sundaram, 2004; Fiss and Zajac, 2004).

The dependent variable

ESO valuation is impossible with current levels of executive pay disclosure in Germany, so the focus here is on the adoption/non-adoption of ESOs. Information was collected for each year 1992–2003 on whether a firm had adopted an ESO, including executive-only schemes, schemes for executives-plus-other managers but not all-employee stock option schemes. The unit of analysis being the firm-year, each observation was coded 1 if the firm adopted an ESO (excluding phantom ESOs, that are effectively annual cash bonuses related to share price) in that year and 0 otherwise.

Data were collected on the composite DAX 100 sample (as defined above, n = 120) for the years 1992 through 2003. Information on ESOs was compiled by hand from the executive compensation reports within companies' annual reports. Specifically, the adoption and date of adoption of ESOs were recorded. Where the date of adoption was not stated or appeared vaguely in annual reports, the investor relations departments of firms were contacted directly. Journal publications on German corporate governance in general and on executive compensation in particular (e.g. Bradley and Sundaram, 2004) were used as supplementary sources of information on ESOs.

The independent variables

Information was collected for each year 1992–2003 for each firm. Dependence on American capital markets (H1a) is represented by whether firms have American depository receipts (ADRs, at levels 2 or 3) on US exchanges (AMEX, NASDAQ and NYSE), coded 1, 0 otherwise. These data were obtained from the website www.adr.com as well as directly from these three exchanges. This information was cross-checked for reliability with companies' annual reports and Form 20-Fs supplied to the US Stock Exchange Commission.

In relation to (H1b), the foreign ownership of German firms was established from a number of sources. A database derived from *Hoppenstedt Aktienführer* was the principal source of ownership data for the majority of firms.[1] This database was checked with and complemented by data taken from Deutsches AktienInstitut (DAI) and directly from companies' annual reports. Where data were incomplete, the investor relations departments of firms were contacted directly.

Firm performance (H2) was measured for each year by an accounting-based variable, namely Return on Assets (ROA), from Datastream International, Thomson and Deutsche Börse. ROA is taken as the ratio of net income to total average assets, expressed as a percentage. In relation to peripherality (H3), firms were coded 1 if not in the DAX 30 (the thirty largest German firms) during each observation year, and 0 otherwise. For (H4), the dependence of the accounting system used by firms on American standards (i.e. IAS, US GAAP or HGB, where the latter represents the German standard) was again obtained from annual reports and the Deutsche Börse website www.deutscheboerse.de. To complete missing data, companies' annual reports were searched and the investor relations departments contacted. Firms were coded 1 for using either International Accounting Standards (IAS), now known as International Financial Reporting Standards (IFRS), or US GAAP, and 0 for German GAAP known as HGB.

Data on firms' ownership proportions and ownership concentration (subsets of H5) were taken from a number of sources, as described for H1b, above. However, the measurement of employee power (H5a) is problematic in Germany. Large German firms exhibit little variation in employee board representation since 50 per cent of the supervisory board must be employee representatives for firms with more than 2,000 employees, uniform across all firms. Employee power may be related to the number of employees in a firm. We therefore propose the number of employees as a proxy for the interests and power of employees, obtained from Datastream International, supplemented by Thomson Financial and Deutsche Börse. A dichotomous variable was used to measure state ownership (H5b), coded 1 if state (federal or Land) ownership exceeded 10 per cent and was the largest blockholder, and 0 otherwise. The same criterion and dummy variables were used for family ownership (H5c). Information on dispersed shareholdings and blockholdings was taken from the *Hoppenstedt Aktienführer*, as noted above.

The logarithm of total assets (H6) comprised a variable representing the prestige and abundance of resources available to a firm, with total assets for each year obtained from Datastream International, Thomson Financial and Deutsche Börse. Concerning the extent of foreign links (H7), the ratio for foreign to total sales was obtained for each firm from the same sources.

Control variables

The Deutsche Börse website was useful in identifying the date on which firms were established, and firm ages were obtained for each year by subtracting the observation year by the firm's founding year. These estimates were cross-checked with data taken from *Europe's 15,000 Largest Companies Handbook* (2003). Debt-to-equity ratios were obtained from Datastream International, supplemented by Thomson Financial and Deutsche Börse. Finally, year dummies were introduced for each year after 1996, the year of the first ESO adoption in Germany, with 1998 the year when they were fully legalized, to pick up any effects of regulatory change and any other time-related institutional changes.

Methodology

A dichotomous, single event-history measure was employed as dependent variable: whether or not a firm adopted an ESO scheme during the observed years, 1992–2003. Thus, from firm histories, a twelve-year window was analysed, i.e. the data were right-censored to the end-date, 2003. Left-censoring was not a problem as data were collected from 1992 onward, while the first adoption in our sample was reported in 1996. Right-censoring can be dealt with effectively by employing discrete time-event history analysis (Allison, 1984) as in the following logistic regression:

$$\text{Log} \frac{P(ESO_t)}{P(1 - ESO_t)} = \alpha_t + \Sigma \, \beta \, i \, X_{t-1} + \varepsilon \tag{1}$$

In Model 1, $P(ESO_t)$ is the probability of a firm adopting an ESO at time t. The term α_t implies that the hazard rate for adoption varies across time. To estimate α_t, a set of eight year dummies was entered in Model 2. β denotes the parameter estimates on X_{t-1} which represents the independent variables lagged by one year. Estimates of parameter β are obtained using Maximum Likelihood. This method treats the data as quasi-cross-sectional; if a firm adopts ESOs in the first year of observation, i.e. 1992, it contributes one firm-year, and at year two, two firm-years and so on. Non-adopting firms contribute as many firm-years as there are in the sample. Thus each of the censored firms contributes a maximum of n firm-years, where n is the longest time interval.

Results

To assess the extent of multicollinearity, we calculated the correlations between the independent variables. Table 14.1 reports means, standard deviations and zero-order correlation coefficients and Table 14.2 shows tolerance and variation inflation factors (VIF). The tolerance levels were all above 0.4 and the highest VIF was 2.008. These results implied a tolerable level of interdependence among the variables.

Table 14.3 provides the main results of this study. Chi-squares for each model are significant at the 0.01 level, implying an acceptable model fit. The classification accuracy is also good with 95 per cent and 95.5 per cent correctly classified for Model 1 and Model 2 respectively.

Model 1 focuses on the control and independent variables. The results support H1a: ESO adoption is significantly and positively associated with the extent of a German firm's dependence on American investors. Similarly, H1b is supported by a significant, positive coefficient on foreign share ownership. Although a similar result was produced for H2, a negative relation was hypothesized, and it seems that high profits should be regarded as a resource that enables change, rather than low profits representing a performance crisis that stimulates ESO adoption.

There is no support for the peripherality variable which is the subject of H3, and another insignificant result for firm size (H6), which suggests that ESO adoption is unaffected by firms being small or large. On the other hand, public declarations of commitment to shareholder value are significant and consistent with H4. H5a is supported by a significant, negative coefficient on employee power, suggesting potential resistance from German workers. Results for H5b and H5c show no significant relation between ESO adoption and state and family ownership as power dependencies.

The outcome of tests on dispersed ownership (H5d) and blockholder presence (H5e) appear to be contradictory at first sight, with both being positively and significantly associated with ESO adoption. Further consideration suggests that no contradiction need be involved, however, since both dispersed shareholdings (through shareholder exit and share price) and blockholder presence (through internal voice) may have a separate, positive influence on firms' decisions and ESO adoption. There is no support for H7 (foreign sales) or for the two control variables (firm age and debt-to-equity ratios), which are not significantly associated with the adoption or non-adoption of ESOs.

Model 2 focuses on the same independent and control variables as Model 1, but with the addition of the time dummies. Adding time variables contributes significantly to the amount of explained variation and improves the overall robustness of the findings. The same independent variables found to be significant in Model 1 are also significant in the time-augmented Model 2. In addition, the time dummies for 1999, 2000 and 2001 are positive and significant, drawing attention to the fact that ESO adoption was concentrated into this period. Thus, the comparison between Model 1 and Model 2 shows

Table 14.1: Means, standard deviations and correlations

Variable	Mean	SD	1	2	3	4	5	6	7	8	9	10	11	12	13	14
1. US investors	.04	.20	1													
2. Foreign ownership	9.77	18.88	.18	1												
3. Profitability	4.88	8.68	.03	.04	1											
4. Peripherality	.86	.35	-.34	-.21	.04	1										
5. Value commitment	.15	.34	.18	.20	.05	-.12	1									
6. Employee power	3565	265.57	-.09	-.13	-.05	.06	-.07	1								
7. State ownership	.17	.27	.07	-.05	-.11	-.08	-.01	-.15	1							
8. Family ownership	.37	.42	-.10	-.16	.15	.11	-.09	.18	-.26	1						
9. Dispersed ownership	42.47	27.71	.19	.10	-.02	-.34	.06	-.02	-.03	-.23	1					
10. Block ownership	.90	.29	-.14	.01	-.03	.17	-.07	-.11	.10	.16	-.55	1				
11. Firm size	6.34	.90	.25	.26	.04	-.46	.15	-.34	.34	-.32	.18	-.05	1			
12. Foreign sales	40.12	25.71	-.01	.04	.04	-.12	.11	.07	-.22	.01	.11	-.15	-.01	1		
13. Firm age	87.82	57.24	-.06	.17	-.10	-.02	.10	.08	-.08	-.11	.06	.01	.17	.17	1	
14. Leverage	243.23	237.39	.06	-.02	-.09	-.00	-.02	-.14	.09	-.10	-.02	-.00	.25	-.04	-.07	1

Table 14.2:   Collinearity diagnostic tests

Independent variable	Tolerance	VIF
US investors	0.835	1.198
Foreign ownership	0.834	1.199
Profitability	0.915	1.093
Peripherality	0.628	1.592
Value commitment	0.918	1.089
Employee power	0.658	1.790
State ownership	0.767	1.303
Family ownership	0.764	1.309
Dispersed ownership	0.580	1.725
Block ownership	0.630	1.588
Firm size	0.498	2.008
Foreign sales	0.880	1.137
Firm age	0.850	1.177
Leverage	0.896	1.116

the hazard rate (i.e. the likelihood of ESO adoption) to be time dependent. Comparing the models with and without the six-year dummies shows an improvement of Model 2 over Model 1 (a significant ($p = 0.01$) chi-square difference of the -2 Log-Likelihood at 55.58).

Discussion and conclusions

This chapter has used neo-institutional theory as a framework for the analysis of organizational change focused on one particular corporate governance innovation (the ESO) in the single country of Germany, whose governance system seems capable of divergence from, or convergence on, the American model. Many neo-institutional variables were found to be significant, and advocates of the notion of the Americanization of German corporate governance may gain strength from this study of ESO adoption. In terms of exogenous dynamics (US investors and foreign ownership), value commitment (shareholder value orientation) and power dependencies (dispersed shareholdings and blockholdings), these elements of Anglo-American governance in German firms were positively associated with the adoption of ESOs. These results complement those of Ahmadjian and Robbins (2005), who found that American-style downsizing strategies were limited to those firms not deeply embedded in the Japanese version of relational governance or stakeholder capitalism.

These significant relationships support the use of neo-institutional theory in this context and it may be extended usefully to other areas of international governance and strategy determination. However, while the study is

Table 14.3: Adoption of stock-based compensation

	Model 1			Model 2		
	β	S.E	Wald	β	S.E	Wald
Intercept	**−8.368****	2.142	15.263	**−9.545****	2.807	11.849
US investors	**1.186****	0.511	5.403	1.291	0.603	4.589
Foreign ownership	**0.023****	0.006	12.590	**0.019****	0.007	6.825
Profitability	**0.023****	0.014	2.672	**0.024****	0.015	2.637
Peripherality	−0.603	0.421	2.053	−0.439	0.508	0.749
Value commitment	**2.536****	0.330	58.592	**1.867****	0.386	26.573
Employee power	**−1.027****	0.497	3.799	**−1.028****	0.501	3.800
State ownership	−0.224	0.731	0.093	0.023	0.767	0.001
Family ownership	0.120	0.480	0.062	0.095	0.498	0.036
Dispersed ownership	**0.020****	0.008	5.657	**0.026****	0.009	8.073
Block ownership	**1.965****	0.670	8.415	**1.898****	0.770	6.040
Firm size	0.244	0.239	1.045	0.237	0.314	0.570
Foreign sales	0.006	0.007	0.767	0.006	0.007	0.636
Control variables						
Firm age	0.003	0.003	1.098	0.002	0.003	0.474
Leverage	0.000	0.000	0.133	0.000	0.000	0.164
Year dummies						
1996				0.668	1.253	0.284
1997				0.264	1.255	0.044
1998				0.931	1.165	0.639
1999				**2.845****	1.095	6.728
2000				**2.232****	1.117	3.961
2001				**2.381****	1.128	4.492
2002				1.196	1.209	0.978
Chi-Square (X^2)		148.92****			204.50****	
Nagelkerke R^2		36.70			49.60	
Hosmer and Lemeshow		0.56			0.51	
Log-Likelihood (-2LL)		318.20			264.67	
DF		14			20	

Improvement of Model 2 over Model 1 55.58 (6 DF).
Significant levels: *p < 0.10, **p < 0.05, ***p < 0.01.

presented as progressing neo-institutional theory, it has some weaknesses. Many are related to standards of disclosure on executive pay in Germany, and in this respect Germany certainly has not achieved the stock market capitalism that convergence theorists predict.

Executive pay disclosure in Germany is still quite weak. Germany's public companies were given three years (dating from the recommendation of the Cromme Commission in 2002) to comply with the voluntary Corporate Governance Code recommending the full disclosure of individual directors' pay. By mid-2005, only 70 per cent of DAX 30 firms had announced that they were intending to comply, forcing the German Federal Council in July

2005 to approve a law on the Disclosure of Management Board Remuneration (*VorStog*, see DSW, 2005). The expectation was that all annual reports for the financial year 2006 would for the first time disclose individual directors' remuneration. However, with the so called opt-out rule in the *VorStog*, shareholders may pass a resolution, with a three-quarters majority of the shares represented at the meeting, allowing the company to refrain from publishing individual board members' remuneration. For example, at the AGM of Sixt AG, 98 per cent of the shares represented at the meeting voted against the disclosure of individual pay, a decision made easier by the fact that its founder Erich Sixt holds 57 per cent of the company's shares. Thus, while ESOs may be adopted in German firms, how many are awarded to which directors often remains a mystery to outside shareholders. It is for this reason that this study must rely on dummy variables for ESO adoption, rather than sophisticated valuations of ESO awards, as in the USA and UK (Tosi et al., 2000). In addition to this weakness, the study has not addressed the question of the timing of ESO adoption among early/late adopters. This is the subject of further research by the authors.

Finally, some of the independent variables suggested by neo-institutional theory proved to be insignificant in predicting the probability of a firm having an ESO. For example, peripherality, state and family power dependencies were all insignificant, together with access to resource and information variables involving asset values and foreign sales. In the case of low profits as a possible catalyst in the adoption of ESOs, the hypothesized peripheral relation was reversed, and the level of profit was positively associated with ESO adoption, emphasizing a role for profits as a resource for the award of ESOs, rather than low profits as a push factor towards ESO adoption.

However, one important caveat should be entered: we have no way of telling, given the current state of German information disclosure, whether German ESOs are equivalent to their American template or not. It seems likely that they may have been 'translated' in transit, to suit the German institutional context (Buck and Shahrim, 2005). For example, an ESO focused on five senior executives in the US bank, JP Morgan Chase is a very different institution to one applying to 2,498 senior managers in Deutsche Bank. Finally, it seems clear from the coefficients on the year dummies in Model 2 that some changes in political and legal institutions have not been captured by the independent variables used in hypotheses so far. Evidence of legislation as an external contingency, influencing endogenous forces, can be inferred from the passing of the German stock company law (*Aktiengesetz*) in 1998. This legalized the use of ESOs as a compensation instrument. The effect of this legislation started to be felt in 1999, as the results of this study show in the significance of the 1999 year dummy. In fact, out of the 65 ESO adoptions reported in this study, 29 of them took place in 1999 alone representing 45 per cent of the total. The representation of these changes in legal institutions in regressions remains as an outstanding challenge. Meanwhile, other institutional elements measuring the embeddedness of German firms in their German environment, and conversely their willingness to change, have been demonstrated as being important in the analysis of the adoption of an American pay innovation in Germany.

While this chapter considered a number of internal and external institutional influences on the adoption of (or resistance to) ESOs, it must be understood that ESO adoption is ambiguous, and a 'power' perspective sees senior managers as the drivers of ESO adoption, seeking higher rewards for themselves. In line with this argument, executive pay may reflect agency problems rather than their resolution (Bebchuk and Fried, 2004). The recent adoption of ESOs by German firms may therefore be seen as a manager-serving or efficiency-enhancing innovation, or perhaps both. Besides efficiency and opportunism, German-style ESOs (arguably a more egalitarian, camouflaged variation on the American template; see Buck and Shahrim, 2005) may also have been legitimized in the eyes of employee stakeholders.

Note

1. Thanks to Professor Stefan Winter of Bochum University for his enormous help with these data.

Bibliography

Aguilera, R. V. and Jackson, G. (2002). 'Institutional changes in European corporate governance'. *Economic Sociology*, 3: 17–26.
Aguilera, R. and Jackson, G. (2003). 'The cross-national diversity of corporate governance: dimensions and determinants'. *Academy of Management Review*, 28: 447–65.
Ahmadjian, C. L. and Robbins, G. E. (2005). 'A clash of capitalisms: foreign shareholders and corporate restructuring in 1990s Japan'. *American Sociological Review*, 70: 451–71.
Allison, P. D. (1984). *Event history analysis* (Beverly Hills: Sage).
Aoki, M. (2007). 'Endogenizing institutions and their changes'. *Journal of Institutional Economics*, 3(1): 1–31.
Baron, J. N., Hannan, M. T. and Burton, M. D. (1999). 'Building the iron cage: determinants of managerial intensity in the early years of organizations'. *American Sociological Review*, 64: 527–47.
Bebchuk, L. and Fried, J. (2003). 'Executive compensation as an agency problem'. *Journal of Economic Perspectives*, 17: 71–92.
Bebchuk, L. and Fried, J. (2004). *Pay without performance: the unfulfilled promise of executive compensation* (Cambridge, MA: Harvard University Press).
Becker, C. M., Lazaric, N., Nelson, R. R. and Winter, S. G. (2005). 'Applying organizational routines in understanding organizational change'. *Industrial and Corporate Change*, 14: 775–91.

Blazejewski, S. and Dorow, W. (2003). 'Managing organizational politics for radical change: the case of Beiersdorf-Lechia S.A., Poznan'. *Journal of World Business*, 38: 204–23.

Bradley, M. and Sundaram, A. (2004). 'The emergence of shareholder value in the German corporation'. Thunderbird University, Working Paper.

Buck, T. and Shahrim, A. (2005). 'The translation of corporate governance changes across national cultures: the case of Germany'. *Journal of International Business Studies*, 36: 42–61.

Cheffins, B. R. (2003). 'Will executive pay globalize along American lines?' *Corporate Governance: an International Review*, 11: 8–24.

Child, J. and Smith, C. (1987). 'The context and process of organizational transformation'. *Journal of Management Studies*, 24: 565–93.

Chizema, A. and Buck, T. (2006). 'Neo-institutional theory and institutional change: towards empirical tests on the "Americanization" of German executive pay'. *International Business Review*, 15: 488–504.

Cioffi, J. W. (2002). 'Restructuring "Germany Inc": the corporate governance debate and the politics of company law reform'. *Law and Policy*, 24: 355–402.

Clarke, L. (1994). *The essence of change* (New York: Prentice Hall).

Coase, R. (1937). 'The nature of the firm'. *Economica*, 4: 386–405.

Commons, R. (1934). *Institutional economics* (New York: Macmillan).

Covaleski, M. A. and Dirsmith, M. W. (1988). 'An institutional perspective on the rise, social transformation, and fall of a university budget category'. *Administrative Science Quarterly*, 33: 562–87.

Crouch, C. (2005). *Capitalist diversity and change: recombinant governance and institutional entrepreneurs* (Oxford: Oxford University Press).

D'Aunno, T., Succi, M. and Alexander, J. A. (2000). 'Role of institutional and market forces in divergent organizational change'. *Administrative Science Quarterly*, 45: 679–703.

Deeg, R. and Jackson, G. (2007). 'The state of the art: towards a more dynamic theory of capitalist variety'. *Socio-Economic Review*, 5: 149–79.

DiMaggio, P. J. and Powell, W. W. (1983). 'The iron cage revisited: institutional isomorphism and collective rationality in organizational fields'. *American Sociological Review*, 48: 147–60.

DiMaggio, P. J. and Powell, W. W. (1991). 'Introduction'. In W. W. Powell and P. J. DiMaggio (eds), *The new institutionalism in organizational analysis*, pp. 1–38 (Chicago: University of Chicago Press).

Djelic, M.-L. (1998). *Exporting the American model* (Oxford: Oxford University Press).

Dore, R. (2000). *Stock market capitalism: welfare capitalism, Japan and Germany versus the Anglo-Saxons* (Oxford: Oxford University Press).

DSW (2005). 'Recent changes in German corporate and capital market law'. Available at: www.dsw-info.de (accessed 20 February 2006).

Edwards, J. and Fischer, K. (1994). *Banks, finance and investment in Germany* (New York: Cambridge University Press).

Europe's 15,000 Largest Companies Handbook (2003) (Oxford: William Snyder Publishing Associates).

Fernandez, R. and Rodrik, D. (1991). 'Resistance to reform: status quo bias in the presence of individual-specific uncertainty'. *American Economic Review*, 81: 1146–55.

Fiss, P. C. and Zajac, E. J. (2004). 'The diffusion of ideas over contested terrain: the (non) adoption of a shareholder value orientation among German firms'. *Administrative Science Quarterly*, 49: 60–83.

Franks, J. and Mayer, C. (2001). 'Ownership and control in Germany'. *Review of Financial Studies*, 14: 943–77.

Fuerbringer, J. (2004). 'US investors are buying more foreign stocks, bonds'. Available at: http://www.signonsandiego.com/uniontrib/20041216/net (accessed 5 December 2005).

Gomez-Mejia, L., Wiseman, R. M. and Johnson, B. D. (2005). 'Agency problems in diverse contexts: a global perspective'. *Journal of Management Studies*, 42: 1507–17.

Gray, S. R. and Cannella, A. A. Jr. (1997). 'The role of risk in executive compensation'. *Journal of Management*, 23: 517–40.

Greenwood, R. and Hinings, C. R. (1996). 'Understanding radical organizational change: bringing together the old and the new institutionalism'. *Academy of Management Review*, 21: 1022–54.

Greif, A. (2005). *Institutions: theory and history* (Cambridge: Cambridge University Press).

Hall, P. A. and Gingerich, D. W. (2001). 'Varieties of capitalism and institutional complementarities in the macroeconomy: an empirical analysis'. Paper presented at the American Political Science Association Conference, San Francisco, August.

Hall, P. A. and Thelen, K. (2005). 'The politics of change in varieties of capitalism'. Paper presented at the American Political Science Association Conference, March.

Hambrick, D. C. (2007). 'Upper echelons theory: an update'. *Academy of Management Review*, 32: 334–43.

Hansmann, H. and Kraakman, R. (2001). 'The end of history for corporate law'. *The Georgetown Law Journal*, 89: 439–68.

Hinings, C. R. and Greenwood, R. (1988). *The dynamics of strategic change* (Oxford: Basil Blackwell).

Höpner, M. (2001). 'Corporate governance in transition: ten empirical findings on shareholder value and industrial relations in Germany'. Köln: Max-Planck-Institut für Gesellschaftsforschung, Discussion Paper 01/5.

Höpner, M. and Jackson, G. (2006). 'Revisiting the Mannesmann takeover: how markets for corporate control emerge'. *European Management Review*, 3: 142–55.

Jackson, G. (2003). 'Corporate governance in Germany and Japan: liberalization pressures and responses'. In K. Yamamura and W. Streeck (eds), *The end of diversity? Prospects for German and Japanese capitalism*, pp. 261–305 (Ithaca: Cornell University Press).

Johnson, G., Smith, S. and Codling, B. (2000). 'Microprocesses of institutional change in the context of privatization'. *Academy of Management Review*, 25: 572–80.

Kaplan, S. N. (1994). 'Top executives, turnover and firm performance in Germany'. *Journal of Law, Economics and Organization*, 10: 142–59.

La Porta, R., Lopez-de-Silanes, F. and Shleifer, A. (1999). 'Corporate ownership around the world'. *Journal of Finance*, 54: 471–517.

Leblebici, H., Salancik, G. R., Copay, A. and King, T. (1991). 'Institutional change and the transformation of inter-organizational fields: an organizational history of the US radio broadcasting industry'. *Administrative Science Quarterly*, 36: 333–63.

Lewellen, W. (1968). *Executive compensation in large industrial corporations* (New York: Columbia University Press).

Lubatkin, M., Lane, P. J., Collin, S. and Very, P. (2006). 'An embeddedness framing of governance and opportunism: towards a cross-nationally accommodating theory of agency'. *Journal of Organizational Behavior*, 28: 43–58.

Maug, E. (1998). 'Large shareholders as monitors: is there a trade-off between liquidity and control?' *Journal of Finance*, 53: 65–98.

Meyer, J. W. and Rowan, B. (1977). 'Institutionalized organizations: formal structure as myth and ceremony'. *American Journal of Sociology*, 83: 340–63.
Nadler, A. D. and Tushman, M. L. (1989). 'Organizational frame bending: principles for managing reorientation'. *Academy of Management Executive*, 3: 194–203.
Nelson, R. R., Peterhansl, A. and Sampat, B. (2004). 'Why and how innovations get adopted: a tale of four models'. *Industrial and Corporate Change*, 13: 679–99.
Nelson, R. R. and Winter, S. (1982). *An evolutionary theory of economic change* (Cambridge, MA: Belknap Press of Harvard University Press).
Newman, K. L. (2000). 'Organizational transformation during institutional upheaval'. *Academy of Management Review*, 25: 602–19.
Newman, K. L. and Nollen, S. D. (1998). *Managing radical organizational change* (Thousand Oaks: Sage).
North, D. C. (1990). *Institutions, institutional change and economic performance* (Cambridge: Cambridge University Press).
Noteboom, B. (1999). 'Voice and exit forms of corporate control: Anglo-American, European, Japanese'. *Journal of Economic Issues*, 33: 845–60.
Oliver, C. (1992). 'The antecedents of deinstitutionalization'. *Organization Studies*, 13: 563–88.
Palmer, D. A., Jennings, P. D. and Zhou, X. (1993). 'Late adoption of the multidivisional form by large US corporations: institutional, political, and economic accounts'. *Administrative Science Quarterly*, 38: 100–31.
Pfeffer, J. and Salancik, G. R. (1978). *The external control of organizations: a resource dependence perspective* (New York: Harper & Row).
Pugh, D. S. and Hickson, D. J. (1997). *Writers on organizations* (Thousand Oaks: Sage).
Ranson, S., Hinings, B. and Greenwood, R. (1980). 'The structuring of organizational structure'. *Administrative Science Quarterly*, 25: 1–17.
Rogers, E. (1995). *The diffusion of innovations* (New York: Free Press).
Sanders, W. G. and Tuschke, A. C. (2007). 'The adoption of institutionally contested organizational practices: the emergence of stock option pay in Germany'. *Academy of Management Journal*, 50: 33–56.
Scott, W. R. (1987). 'The adolescence of institutional theory'. *Administrative Science Quarterly*, 32: 493–511.
Scott, W. R. (2007). 'Approaching adulthood: the maturing of institutional theory'. *Theory and Society*, forthcoming.
Sherer, P. D. and Lee, K. (2002). 'Institutional change in large law firms: a resource dependency and institutional perspective'. *Academy of Management Journal*, 45: 102–19.
Sjöstrand, S. E. (1995). 'Towards a theory of institutional change'. In J. Groenewegen and S. E. Sjöstrand (eds), *On economic institutions*, pp. 19–44 (Aldershot: Edward Elgar).
Suarez, F. F. and Oliva, R. (2005). 'Environmental change and organizational transformation'. *Industrial and Corporate Change*, 24: 1017–41.
Tosi, H., Werner, S., Katz, J. and Gomez-Mejia, L. (2000). 'How much does performance matter? A meta-analysis of CEO pay studies'. *Journal of Management*, 26: 301–39.
Towers Perrin (2003). 'Worldwide remuneration survey'. Available at: http://www.towers.com/towers_publications (accessed 5 December 2005).
Tuschke, A. and Sanders, W. G. (2003). 'Antecedents and consequences of corporate governance reform: the case of Germany'. *Strategic Management Journal*, 24: 631–49.

Tushman, M. L. and Romanelli, E. (1985). 'Organizational evolution: a metamorphosis model of convergence and reorientation'. In L. L. Cummings and B. M. Staw (eds), *Research in organizational behavior*, pp. 171–222 (Greenwich, CT: JAI Press).

Ulrich, D. and Barney, J. B. (1984). 'Perspectives in organizations: resource dependence, efficiency, and population'. *Academy of Management Review*, 9: 471–81.

Vitols, S. (2001). 'The construction of German corporate governance: reassessing the role of capital market'. Wissenschaftszentrum Berlin für Sozialforschung, Working Paper.

Vitols, S. (2004). 'Negotiated shareholder value: the German variant of Anglo-American practice'. *Competition and Change*, 8(4): 357–74.

Walsh, K., Hinings, C. R., Greenwood, R. and Ranson, S. (1981). 'Power and advantage in organizations'. *Organization Studies*, 2: 131–52.

Williamson, O. E. (1973). 'Markets and hierarchies: some elementary considerations'. *American Economic Review*, 63: 316–25.

15

A Comparison of Corporate Social Responsibility Reporting in the United States, Germany and Australia

Stephen Chen and Petra Bouvain

Introduction

Corporate social responsibility (CSR) reporting is not mandatory in most countries, but has been adopted by many large companies from around the world. The terms corporate social responsibility, global citizenship and sustainability can now be found in the corporate reports and websites of large and small corporations from around the world. However, considerable variation exists among firms worldwide. While some companies (e.g. Henkel, BHP, Johnson and Johnson) have a long-standing tradition in reporting information and have created separate internet sites to show all facets of their corporate responsibility and sustainability, other companies provide only limited information, in many cases related to corporate giving and sponsorship, or in some cases no information at all.

CSR reporting and corporate governance are obviously related since corporate reporting is both an input to and a product of the corporate governance process (Bebbington, 2004). It could also be argued, taking a social constructionist perspective, that CSR reporting is a means of influencing how others view and see the corporation and corporate governance issues (Parker, 2007). To the extent that one observes differences in corporate governance, one would, therefore, also expect to observe differences in CSR reporting. This argument does seem to be borne out by the few studies that have examined this issue. For instance, Aguilera and Cuervo-Cazurra (2004) contrast CSR reporting in the United States and the United Kingdom and argue that national differences in CSR can be related to differences in corporate governance systems. Because business organizations are embedded in different national business systems and different corporate governance systems, they will experience divergent degrees of internal and external pressures to engage in social responsibility initiatives (Logsdon and Wood, 2005; Matten and Crane, 2005).

The aim of this study is to test if similar country-specific differences can be found in a different set of countries and to examine in more detail the types of issues reported. To this end, we use a new content analysis software package that enables more objective and detailed analysis of the text in the reports. We examined the CSR reporting of leading companies from the US, Germany and Australia. First, we compared the extent of reporting across countries. Second, we used a content analysis software package called 'Leximancer' (Smith and Humphreys, 2006) that enabled us to identify key themes in the corporate social responsibility reports.

The rest of the chapter is set out as follows. First, we examine some of the motives for CSR reporting and the link between CSR reports and corporate governance systems. Second, we examine some of the differences between countries in the content of CSR reporting, in particular contrasting the Anglo-American system with that of continental Europe. Then we explain the methodology and sample of companies used in our study and the results obtained. Finally, we discuss some of the implications and areas for further research.

Corporate social responsibility and corporate governance

In spite of the extensive previous research on CSR, much debate remains as to the exact definition of the concept. However, a definition that integrates much of the previous work is that of Wood (1991: 693) who defines corporate social performance as the 'configuration of the principles of social responsibility, processes of social responsiveness, and policies, programs, and observable outcomes as they relate to the firm's societal relationships'. As Aguilera et al. (2006) note, there are many factors that motivate companies to engage in CSR initiatives, including factors at the micro (individual), meso (organizational), macro (country) and supra (transnational) levels, involving multiple actors (e.g. employees, consumers, management, institutional investors, governments, non-governmental organizations and supranational governmental entities) with multiple motives (instrumental, relational and moral). Reasons that have been advanced for firms to engage in CSR initiatives range from reaction to pressures from internal and external stakeholders, on the one hand, to a proactive strategy by companies to influence stakeholders or bring about social change, on the other hand.

Many of these reasons are the same as those that have been advanced for corporate governance initiatives (Aguilera and Jackson, 2003). Indeed Aguilera and Cuervo-Cazurra (2004) explicitly make the point that corporate social responsibility is intimately related to corporate governance systems and subject to similar pressures. It seems reasonable, therefore, to expect that differences in corporate governance systems should be reflected in corporate social responsibility reporting.

Drivers of international diversity in CSR reporting

In this chapter we focus on the country level and examine how differences in corporate governance systems at the national level may lead to differences in the extent and type of issues reported. Aguilera and Jackson (2003) show how national differences in the dimensions of corporate governance such as capital, labour and management are shaped by differences in the institutions in each nation such as ideology, property rights, financial systems, union organization, etc. We suggest that national differences in institutions also shape reporting of corporate social responsibility by companies.

A number of studies have shown that a key factor influencing both the nature and extent of disclosure is the country in which the business is headquartered (e.g. Kolk et al., 2001; Meek et al., 1995; Niskala and Pretes, 1995; Roberts, 1992). For instance, Burchell et al. (1985) demonstrate that the rise and fall of reporting on value-added in the United Kingdom was heavily influenced by the political agenda in the United Kingdom. Political factors are often intertwined with social and cultural factors. Adams and Harte (1998) linked the portrayal of women in UK banks and retail companies between 1935 and 1993 to the social, political and economic context in which the disclosures were made.

Other studies have highlighted the relationship between the cultural context (Langlois and Schlegelmilch, 1990; Adams and Kuasirikun, 2000; Salter and Niswander, 1995), ethical relativism (Lewis and Unerman, 1999) and reporting. Culture influences moral values which one would expect in turn to influence at least the issues which companies select as being worthy to report. For instance, compared with Southern Europe, the Nordic countries have traditionally been much more strongly engaged in environmental protection (Halme and Huse, 1997), as exemplified by Norway's Enterprise Act in 1989 that require corporations to include information in the directors' report about emission levels, contamination, and planned and realized measures by the corporation to clean up the environment.

As Aguilera and Jackson (2003: 449) comment in their paper on corporate governance, the unmet theoretical challenge in comparative studies is 'to conceptualize corporate governance in terms of its embeddedness in different social contexts (Dacin, Ventresca and Beal, 1999; Granovetter, 1985)'. They propose an 'actor-centred' institutional approach, which integrates agency theory, stakeholder theory and institutional theory in order to overcome some of the shortcomings of each theory in explaining differences in corporate governance. Agency theory views corporate governance systems and processes as a means of managing the differences in the interests of principals (shareholders) and agents (managers). In this perspective, CSR reporting could be similarly viewed as a means of ensuring that the CSR objectives of shareholders and managers converge.

However, as Aguilera and Jackson (2003) note, agency theory has some deficiencies. Most notably it neglects important interdependencies between other stakeholders such as employees and society at large. This shortcoming can be compensated by incorporating an institutional perspective. Institutional theory views corporations as being in a nexus of formal and informal rules (North, 1990) ranging from overt political regulation (Roe, 2003) to less formal constraints such normative pressures to establish legitimacy (DiMaggio and Powell, 1983). Where institutional environments are nationally distinct, institutional pressures may drive corporate governance systems to become more similar within countries while, at the same time, causing them to differ across countries. Two distinct models of corporate governance are often contrasted in the literature: Anglo-American and continental European (Hall and Soskice, 2001). The former is characterized by equity financing, dispersed ownership, active markets for corporate control, and flexible labour markets, while the latter is characterized by long-term debt finance, ownership by large blockholders, weak markets for corporate control, and rigid labour markets.

We expect that these national differences in the institutional environment will also be reflected in CSR reporting. For example, Aguilera et al. (2006) note that another striking difference between the UK and US markets is the greater attention being paid by both companies and institutional investors in the United Kingdom to issues of long-term social and environmental risk. To explore this question further we compared the CSR reporting of the leading companies in three countries: the United States, Germany and Australia.

The United States is typically cited as an example of a business system where private investors play a powerful role in businesses compared with government and the view that the role of business in society is to generate profit for investors has been widely accepted (Friedman, 1970). One might, therefore, expect CSR issues to figure least prominently in CSR reports of US companies in comparison to reports of companies in the other two countries.

In contrast, Germany is a country that is commonly cited as being representative of the continental European system where banks and government play a strong role in the business system (Whitley, 1999). There are also significant differences in the political sphere. Germany is also well known as a stronghold of the environmental movement in Europe. The German Green Party (die Grünen), founded in 1980, has been the most successful 'Green' party in the world, entering the Bundestag (parliament) in 1983 with 5.6 per cent of the national vote and later forming a governing coalition with the Social Democratic Party from 1998–2005, with the party's leader, Joschka Fischer, serving as the country's foreign minister. The Greens follow a coherent ideology that includes not only environmentalism, but also other concerns such as social justice, consensus decision-making and pacifism. Given the apparent importance of these concerns to the German electorate, one might, therefore, expect CSR to figure more prominently in the CSR reports of German companies.

Australia displays characteristics of both systems (Griffiths and Zammuto, 2005; ASX, 2000; Humphrey and Armstrong, 2003). On the one hand, while Australian companies and governments have copied much from the United States in terms of market-driven policies, there still remain significant differences in other areas. For instance, although there have been significant changes in recent years, in comparison with the United States, Australia is still characterized by relatively strong employee representation in the workplace. Prior to the 1990s, employment conditions in the majority of Australian workplaces were heavily dependent on highly prescriptive multi-employer awards determined by labour unions on behalf of their members, with set standard awards across enterprises for a particular industry or occupation (Wooden, 2003). Nowadays although legislative changes allow employers to negotiate directly with employees on an individual basis without union involvement, legally enforceable enterprise-based collective bargaining arrangements, in the form of certified agreements, are still commonplace.

Sample and analysis

We first identified the leading companies in each country as being those in the leading stockmarket indices of each country: the DAX 30, ASX 30 (now ASX 20) and the Dow Jones Industrial Average (comprising the 30 largest US companies). The breakdown of the sample by country and industry is shown in Table 15.1.

Table 15.1:   Sample of firms analysed for CSR reporting

Industry	Australia	Germany	US	Total
Chemical	0	4	3	7
Consumer	0	0	3	3
Financial	4	2	2	8
High tech	1	2	3	6
Gen. industrial	0	1	0	1
Manufacturing	1	3	4	8
Resources	4	2	4	10
Retail	1	1	0	2
Transport	0	1	0	1
Total	11	16	19	46

Table 15.2:   Summary of results on CSR reporting

Website checked during April 2006	Link for CSR related issues on homepage	At least 1 separate report of more than ten pages and no older than 3 years (CSR, citizen-ship, sustainability or similar)	Mean (S.D.) report page length
Australia ASX 30	15 (50%)	14 (47%)	71 (65)
Germany Dax 30	11 (36%)	17 (57%)	80 (30)
US Dow Jones industrial average (30 companies)	11 (36%)	21 (70%)	71 (30)

Extent of reporting

In the first stage, we examined the websites of each of the 90 companies and determined:

- if there was a link to CSR on the homepage;
- if companies had a separate CSR report of at least ten pages in length and no older than 3 years in a PDF format;
- the average number of pages of CSR reports.

A summary of the results is shown in Table 15.2.

Content analysis

In the second stage of our research, we used a content analysis software package called 'Leximancer' (Smith and Humphreys, 2006) to identify the major themes in each report. The Leximancer software goes beyond the searching and counting of keywords, which is most commonly used in content analysis studies. Rather, the software uses intelligent algorithms that permit both supervised and unsupervised learning to discover and extract concepts from the text data. Details of the algorithms used can be found in Smith and Hunphreys (2006), but in brief the software works by analysing the text in two phases. First, the software creates a list of relevant thesaurus words from the text data either from scratch or from 'seeds' provided by the user. The optimization algorithm, derived from a 'word disambiguation' technique (Yarowsky, 1995), finds the nearest local maximum in the lexical co-occurrence network from each concept seed. Second, the thesaurus words extracted are then used to tag the text and to create a matrix showing the concepts that co-occur in the text. The resulting asymmetric concept co-occurrence matrix is then used to generate a concept map that represents

Figure 15.1:   Concept map for the Australian companies

visually the relative importance of the concepts and how they are related to each other.

A major advantage of using the Leximancer software is that it shows the global context and significance of concepts and helps avoid fixation on particular anecdotal evidence, which may be atypical or erroneous. We identified five core concepts from the initial concept maps generated: community, employee, environment, social and sustainability. We then used these concepts to 'seed' the thesaurus of Leximancer to see how these five concepts are related to other concepts that are identified in the reports. The number of possible concepts that were related to those four was set fairly high (at 60) to enable broad concept identification.

Although Leximancer can process text in languages other than English, all of the German companies also provided reports in English. We thus used the English version in all cases to facilitate comparison with the US and Australian companies. First, we amalgamated all the reports from each country to show concepts that were present in each sub-sample of companies from the US, Australia and Germany. Figures 15.1–15.3 show the concept maps for each country.

The concept maps show the relatively high importance placed on community- and employee-related issues in Australian companies compared with an emphasis on employee, environmental and safety issues in the United States. Meanwhile, the picture in German companies is more complex with CSR being discussed in the context of other issues such as environment, employees and society.

The Leximancer software can also produce a list of the most important concepts in each report. From our initial analysis of each company, five key CSR concepts recurred consistently in the reports: community, employee,

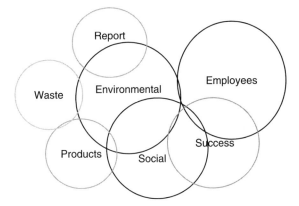

Figure 15.2:   Concept map for the German companies

Figure 15.3:   Concept map for the US companies

environment, society and sustainability. Therefore, in the second stage we focused on these concepts and compared the relative importance, as measured by relative frequency, of each concept (and related words such as social, sustainable and environmental) in the reports of each company separately. In order to determine if there were significant country or industry differences we tested the differences in relative frequencies in our sample companies using the GLM multivariate analysis procedure in SPSS (SPSS, 2001). Tables 15.3–15.5 show the results.

Table 15.3 shows that there is a highly significant difference between countries, but no significant differences between industries. The Pillai's Trace, Wilks' Lambda and Hotelling's Trace statistics are all highly significant for country but insignificant for industry. Interaction effects were also insignificant. Table 15.4 shows that the most significant differences were

Table 15.3:   Multivariate tests

Effect	Test statistic	Value	F	Hypothesis df	Error df	Sig.
Country	Pillai's Trace	0.658	2.352	10.000	48.000	.024
	Wilks' Lambda	0.408	2.599(a)	10.000	46.000	.014
	Hotelling's Trace	1.288	2.833	10.000	44.000	.008
Industry	Pillai's Trace	1.099	0.951	40.000	135.000	.559
	Wilks' Lambda	0.239	1.001	40.000	103.049	.483
	Hotelling's Trace	1.959	1.048	40.000	107.000	.413
Country* industry	Pillai's Trace	1.075	0.924	40.000	135.000	.603
	Wilks' Lambda	0.277	0.881	40.000	103.049	.669
	Hotelling's Trace	1.561	0.835	40.000	107.000	.737

in the relative importance of the community, social and sustainability concepts. In contrast, the employee and environment concepts showed little differences across countries. The Tukey and Bonferroni (SPSS, 2001: 9) test results in Table 15.5 confirm this interpretation by comparing the relative importance of each concept for each pair of countries. The tests show that there is a significant difference in the community score for Australian companies compared with the US and German companies, but less difference between the US and German companies. In contrast, there is a significant difference in the social score between German companies compared with the US and Australian companies, but little difference between the US and Australian companies along this dimension. Finally there is a significant difference in the sustainability scores for US companies compared with German companies but less difference between Australian companies compared with US companies or Australian companies compared with German companies.

Discussion

The findings do seem to show clearly that companies based in the three countries hold substantially different perspectives on: (1) the importance attached to publicity of corporate social responsibility and (2) the importance attached to particular CSR issues. This is consistent with the institutional arguments presented earlier that highlight the different views of the role of business in society found in different countries and the effects on company behaviour (Aguilera and Jackson, 2003; Griffiths and Zammuto, 2005). Not all institutional differences were reflected in significant differences in the CSR reports we examined. For instance, although we expected the importance attached to environmental issues to vary significantly between the three countries, the differences in the reporting of environmental issues were not significant. This may reflect a general increase in environmental concerns worldwide that masks any differences between countries. On the other hand,

Table 15.4: Tests of between-subjects effects

Source	Dependent variable	Type III sum of squares	df	Mean square	F	Sig.
Corrected Model	community	18,506.489(a)	18	1028.138	1.350	.235
	employee	10,791.924(b)	18	599.551	.967	.519
	environment	15,096.132(c)	18	838.674	1.231	.305
	social	7338.025(d)	18	407.668	1.054	.440
	sustainability	12,605.217(e)	18	700.290	1.274	.278
Intercept	community	18,280.253	1	18,280.253	23.996	.000
	employee	37,323.455	1	37,323.455	60.204	.000
	environment	35,315.874	1	35,315.874	51.855	.000
	social	2619.701	1	2619.701	6.775	.015
	sustainability	6374.119	1	6374.119	11.595	.002
Country	community	7885.479	2	3942.739	5.175	.013
	employee	1932.595	2	966.298	1.559	.229
	environment	822.876	2	411.438	.604	.554
	social	2949.931	2	1474.966	3.815	.035
	sustainability	3377.889	2	1688.945	3.072	.063
Industry	community	2435.137	8	304.392	.400	.911
	employee	2150.479	8	268.810	.434	.890
	environment	9672.364	8	1209.046	1.775	.126
	social	1688.988	8	211.123	.546	.811
	sustainability	6616.028	8	827.003	1.504	.202
Country * industry	community	3135.960	8	391.995	.515	.835
	employee	6347.532	8	793.441	1.280	.295
	environment	8871.233	8	1108.904	1.628	.163
	social	1825.444	8	228.180	.590	.777
	sustainability	1896.245	8	237.031	.431	.892

(a) R Squared = .474 (Adjusted R Squared = .123).
(b) R Squared = .392 (Adjusted R Squared = −.013).
(c) R Squared = .451 (Adjusted R Squared = .085).
(d) R Squared = .413 (Adjusted R Squared = .021).
(e) R Squared = .459 (Adjusted R Squared = .099).

some differences such as the greater emphasis on communities in CSR reports of Australian companies seem difficult to explain solely in terms of institutional theory and might be better explained in terms of national history and culture. This suggests that institutional theory, while useful, may not explain all differences in CSR reporting and that some differences in CSR reporting might best be explained by reference to other theories. This raises a more general question of what CSR issues are best explained by what theories or factors, and whether or not an approach that integrates various theories might work better. This is a question that could be usefully explored in future research.

However, these results should be interpreted with caution, keeping in mind some limitations of our study. First, the analysis was based on only one type of communication – websites – and did not investigate other means of

Table 15.5:   Multiple comparisons tests

Dependent variable				Mean diff.	S.E.	Sig.
Community	Tukey HSD	Australia	Germany	45.927(*)	10.8106	.001
			US	25.743	10.4571	.052
		Germany	Australia	−45.927(*)	10.8106	.001
			US	−20.184	9.3653	.098
		US	Australia	−25.743	10.4571	.052
			Germany	20.184	9.3653	.098
	Bonferroni	Australia	Germany	45.927(*)	10.8106	.001
			US	25.743	10.4571	.061
		Germany	Australia	−45.927(*)	10.8106	.001
			US	−20.184	9.3653	.121
		US	Australia	−25.743	10.4571	.061
			Germany	20.184	9.3653	.121
Employee	Tukey HSD	Australia	Germany	5.463	9.7523	.842
			US	14.598	9.4334	.285
		Germany	Australia	−5.463	9.7523	.842
			US	9.135	8.4485	.534
		US	Australia	−14.598	9.4334	.285
			Germany	−9.135	8.4485	.534
	Bonferroni	Australia	Germany	5.463	9.7523	1.000
			US	14.598	9.4334	.400
		Germany	Australia	−5.463	9.7523	1.000
			US	9.135	8.4485	.868
		US	Australia	−14.598	9.4334	.400
			Germany	−9.135	8.4485	.868
Environment	Tukey HSD	Australia	Germany	.553	10.2215	.998
			US	8.693	9.8873	.658
		Germany	Australia	−.553	10.2215	.998
			US	8.140	8.8550	.633
		US	Australia	−8.693	9.8873	.658
			Germany	−8.140	8.8550	.633
	Bonferroni	Australia	Germany	.553	10.2215	1.000
			US	8.693	9.8873	1.000
		Germany	Australia	−.553	10.2215	1.000
			US	8.140	8.8550	1.000
		US	Australia	−8.693	9.8873	1.000
			Germany	−8.140	8.8550	1.000
Social	Tukey HSD	Australia	Germany	−6.89	7.702	.648
			US	13.90	7.450	.168
		Germany	Australia	6.89	7.702	.648
			US	20.79(*)	6.672	.012
		US	Australia	−13.90	7.450	.168
			Germany	−20.79(*)	6.672	.012

(*Continued*)

Table 15.5:   (Continued)

Dependent variable				Mean diff.	S.E.	Sig.
	Bonferroni	Australia	Germany	−6.89	7.702	1.000
			US	13.90	7.450	.219
		Germany	Australia	6.89	7.702	1.000
			US	20.79(*)	6.672	.013
		US	Australia	−13.90	7.450	.219
			Germany	−20.79(*)	6.672	.013
Sustainability	Tukey HSD	Australia	Germany	−6.32	9.183	.772
			US	14.45	8.883	.252
		Germany	Australia	6.32	9.183	.772
			US	20.77(*)	7.956	.037
		US	Australia	−14.45	8.883	.252
			Germany	−20.77(*)	7.956	.037
	Bonferroni	Australia	Germany	−6.32	9.183	1.000
			US	14.45	8.883	.346
		Germany	Australia	6.32	9.183	1.000
			US	20.77(*)	7.956	.044
		US	Australia	−14.45	8.883	.346
			Germany	−20.77(*)	7.956	.044

Based on observed means.
*The mean difference is significant at the .05 level.

communication or actual social responsibility practices. Second, our measure of relative importance of CSR-related issues is based largely on word frequency in the reports, and although we would argue that this measure indicates the relative importance of the issue that the company wishes to portray to readers of the reports, this may not necessarily equate with the importance attached to the issue in actual implementation of CSR by the company. Further work would be required to establish if this is the case. Third, the conclusions were drawn from a relatively small number of companies in just three countries and the results need to be tested with a larger sample of companies. In addition, the companies included in this study were among the largest firms in their home markets and their CSR reporting might not be representative of those adopted by smaller companies. Nevertheless, we are hopeful that the methodology and initial findings presented here will serve as a sound basis for further research in this area.

Bibliography

Adams, C. A. and Harte, G. F. (1998). 'The changing portrayal of the employment of women in British banks' and retail companies' corporate annual reports'. *Accounting, Organisations and Society*, 23(8): 781–812.

Adams, C. A. and Kuasirikun, N. (2000). 'A comparative analysis of corporate reporting on ethical issues by UK and German chemical and pharmaceutical companies'. *European Accounting Review*, 9(1): 53–80.

Aguilera, R. V. and Cuervo-Cazurra, A. (2004). 'Codes of good governance worldwide: what is the trigger?' *Organization Studies*, 25(3): 415–43.

Aguilera, R. V. and Jackson, G. (2003). 'The cross-national diversity of corporate governance: dimensions and determinants'. *Academy of Management Review*, 28(3): 447–85.

Aguilera, R. V., Williams, C. A., Conley, J. M. and Rupp, D. E. (2006). 'Corporate governance and social responsibility: a comparative analysis of the UK and the US'. *Corporate Governance: an International Review*, 14(3): 147–58.

ASX (2000). *Australian shareownership study* (Sydney: Australian Stock Exchange).

Bebbington, J. (2004). 'Governance from the perspective of social/environmental accounting'. *Social and Environmental Accounting Journal*, 24(2): 15–18.

Burchell, S., Clubb, C. and Hopwood, A. G. (1985). 'Accounting in its social context: towards a history of value added in the United Kingdom'. *Accounting, Organizations and Society*, 10(4): 381–413.

Dacin, T., Ventresca, M. J. and Beal, B. D. (1999). 'The embeddedness of organizations: dialogue & directions'. *Journal of Management*, 25(3): 317–56.

DiMaggio, P. and Powell, W. W. (1983). 'The iron cage revisited: institutional isomorphism and collective rationality in organizational fields'. *American Sociological Review*, 48(2): 147–60.

Friedman, M. (1970). 'The social responsibility of business is to increase its profits'. *New York Times Magazine*, 33 (13 September): 122–6.

Granovetter, M. (1985). 'Economic action and social structure: the problem of embeddedness'. *American Journal of Sociology*, 91(3): 481–510.

Griffiths, A. and Zammuto, R. F. (2005). 'Institutional governance systems and variations in national competitive advantage: an integrative framework'. *Academy of Management Review*, 30(4): 823–42.

Hall, P. A. and Soskice, D. (2001). *Varieties of capitalism: the institutional foundations of comparative advantage* (Oxford: Oxford University Press).

Halme, M. and Huse, M. (1997). 'The influence of corporate governance, industry and country factors on environmental reporting'. *Scandinavian Journal of Management*, 13(2): 137–57.

Humphrey, R. and Armstrong, L. (2003). *2002 Australian shareownership study* (Sydney: Australian Stock Exchange).

Kolk, A., Walhain, S. and Van de Wateringen, S. (2001). 'Environmental reporting by the Fortune Global 250: exploring the influence of nationality and sector'. *Business Strategy and the Environment*, 10: 15–28.

Langlois, C. C. and Schlegelmich, B. B. (1990). 'Do corporate codes of ethics reflect national character? Evidence from Europe and the United States'. *Journal of International Business Studies*, 21(4): 519–39.

Lewis, L. and Unerman, J. (1999). 'Ethical relativism: a reason for differences in corporate social reporting?' *Critical Perspectives on Accounting*, 10: 521–47.

Logsdon, J. M. and Wood, D. J. (2005). 'Global business citizenship and voluntary codes of ethical conduct'. *Journal of Business Ethics*, 59: 55–67.

Matten, D. and Crane, A. (2005). 'Corporate citizenship: toward an extended theoretical conceptualization'. *Academy of Management Review*, 30: 166–80.

Meek, G. K., Roberts, C. B. and Gray, S. J. (1995). 'Factors influencing voluntary annual report disclosure by US, UK and continental European multinational corporations'. *Journal of International Business Studies*, 26: 555–72.

Morhardt, J. E., Baird, S. and Freeman, K. (2002). 'Scoring corporate environmental and sustainability reports using GRI2000, ISO14031 and other criteria'. *Corporate Social Responsibility and Environmental Management*, 9: 215–33.

Niskala, M. and Pretes, M. (1995). 'Environmental reporting in Finland: a note on the use of annual reports'. *Accounting, Organizations and Society*, 457–66.

North, D. C. (1990). *Institutions, institutional change and economic performance* (Cambridge: Cambridge University Press).

Parker, L. D. (2007). 'Financial and external reporting research: the broadening corporate governance challenge'. *Accounting and Business Research*, 37(1): 39–54.

Roberts, R. W. (1992). 'Determinants of corporate social responsibility disclosure: an application of stakeholder theory'. *Accounting, Organizations and Society*, 17: 595–612.

Roe, M. J. (2003). *Political determinants of corporate governance* (New York: Oxford University Press).

Salter, S. B. and Niswander, F. (1995). 'Cultural influence on the development of accounting systems internationally: a test of Gray's 1988 theory'. *Journal of International Business Studies*, 16: 379–97.

Smith, A. E. and Humphreys, M. S. (2006). 'Evaluation of unsupervised semantic mapping of natural language with Leximancer concept mapping'. *Behavior Research Methods*, 38(2): 262–79.

SPSS (2001). *SPSS Advanced Models 11.0* (Chicago: SPSS).

Whitley, R. (1999). *Divergent capitalisms: the social structuring and change of business systems* (Oxford: Oxford University Press).

Wood, D. (1991). 'Corporate social performance revisited'. *Academy of Management Review*, 16(4): 691–718.

Wooden, M. (2003). 'Industrial relations reform in Australia: causes, consequences and prospects'. *Australian Economic Review*, 34(3): 243–62.

Yarowsky, D. (1995). 'Unsupervised word-sense disambiguation rivalling supervised methods'. In *Proceedings of the 33rd Annual Meeting of the Association for Computational Linguistics (ACL-95)*, pp. 189–96 (Cambridge, MA). Available at: http://www.cs.jhu.edu/~yarowsky/pubs.html

16

Corporate Governance Challenges for Dual-Registered Companies from Emerging Markets: Focus on South Africa

Viola Makin, Ruth Clarke and Mark G. Albon

Introduction

Emerging market companies are increasingly undertaking dual registrations on local and foreign stock exchanges to access global finance, and consequently are becoming exposed to wider concerns with corporate governance. These wider concerns are fostered by globalization as emerging economies increasingly develop ties with other countries, either regionally or with more distant economies in the developed world. Aguilera and Cuervo-Cazurra (2004) postulate that this convergence of economies leads to the diffusion of organizational practices, such as corporate governance practices, and potentially creates both a greater efficiency of these processes and greater external legitimation. The challenge for corporate governance acceptance lies in the type of convergence that corporate governance measures can take, which can be either in form or in function (Palepu et al., 2002; Gilson, 2000). While formal convergence implies the coalescing of legal rules and institutions, functional convergence implies adaptations within different existing institutions to perform the functions of good governance. Although formal convergence may not be in evidence in an emerging market, *de facto* convergence may well be encouraged by the requirements that increasing numbers of dual listed companies face. Coffee (1999) also adds contractual convergence, where foreign companies submit to United States stock exchange governance rules and stock exchange regulation in order to expand their organization for potential growth opportunities. Thus this chapter explores the impact of dual registration on corporate governance and the potential for changing the nature of emerging market governance conditions.

For many emerging economies, an effective system of corporate governance is essential for several reasons. At the micro level, it encourages outside shareholders to invest in companies and attracts partner firms from developed economies, pushes up market valuations, and enhances the competitiveness of the companies in the marketplace. At the macro level it encourages inflows of both direct and portfolio foreign investment, with the corresponding expected benefits for economic growth and development. Outside investment encourages companies in emerging markets to respond to outside pressures to meet the governance standards of other countries, while still meeting the internal standards. When South African companies list in foreign markets this pressure for change becomes a mandatory regulation that they must face.

For companies in South Africa, one way to raise external finance is to seek capital on the Johannesburg Stock Exchange in which case the company will be required to abide by the guidelines set out in the South African 2002 King II Report. But some companies also seek finance overseas and a growing trend away from registering on European exchanges is towards registering on US stock exchanges. Such a strategy may bring benefits in terms of cheaper and more available finance but it also means that the company becomes subject to the requirements of the 2002 Sarbanes-Oxley (SOX) Act. On the one hand, this can impose an additional cost on dual-registered South African companies and put them at a disadvantage relative to single-registered companies, and this additional cost may be considerable for companies with smaller market capitalization. On the other hand, in addition to the potential direct benefits of cheaper finance, dual registration may lead to a strengthening of corporate governance through the impact of SOX requirements, with consequent indirect benefits for the companies concerned and the corporate governance system in South Africa, in turn.

The focus of this investigation is on the issue of voluntary versus mandated corporate governance that companies based in South Africa face as they move to become dual registered on the South African and US stock exchanges. Voluntary governance in South Africa follows the King II Report's code of conduct based on a set of principles, while mandated (legislated) governance in the US based on SOX is implemented with specific legislative measures. The study looks at whether the additional requirements of SOX, concomitant with dual listing, provide enough value to be commensurate with the costs incurred in its implementation. Some early evidence suggests that cross-listed foreign private issuers experience abnormal stock returns of −10 per cent, on average, in both the United States and their home markets in response to the implementation of SOX. Many companies also voluntarily delist and deregister in order to avoid SEC reporting obligations (Li, 2007). The rest of this chapter is organized as follows. The next section briefly reviews the literature on corporate governance, and then proceeds to discuss this in the context of South Africa and the United States. The following section presents the research methodology and the analysis of results. Finally we discuss limitations of the study and draw our conclusions for the state of corporate governance in South Africa.

Literature review

The field of corporate governance has developed over time from a theoretical approach initiated by Berle and Means in the 1930s, to the stakeholder approach (Bowen, 1953), and finally to today's emphasis on codes of conduct, both voluntary and mandatory. Advocating the separation of ownership and control and a consequent focus on the maximization of shareholder profits as the primary driver for firms led to a resultant emphasis on the market as the absolute arbiter of adequate governance (Fama and Jensen, 1983). Although Berle and Means (1967) foresaw the problems of lack of structure for control of corporate actions, the popularity of this theory led to a mostly short-term view for business and left little room for consideration of other stakeholders, both internal and external. This narrow view of the role of the corporation meant that financial and ethical excesses appear to have occurred in the name of maximizing shareholder value.

Following on from this perceived need for more appropriate corporate governance, the stakeholder approach developed in the early 1950s. Stakeholder theory seeks to take a broader view of the responsibility of the corporation and to include workers, the community and the broader society as groups who have an interest in the behaviour of corporate management and in the overall governance of companies. The theory suggests that the interests of shareholders and stakeholders need to find equilibrium in order to ensure that there is equity and balance in the system. During the 1990s, critics widely noted the reliance on market forces and subsequent lack of good corporate governance being practised by large corporations. While market-based control of corporations in the United States is supplemented by legal measures of protection of shareholders' rights, plus internal mechanisms of control (Aldrighi, 2003), this was not perceived as sufficient. Increasingly company operations around the world were becoming more transparent, due in part to the efforts of Transparency International, and to the more frequent global reporting of company actions in the media. As the obvious shortcomings of a self-regulating process became clearer, this led to the recognition of a need for the development of a set of principles or regulations that would serve as guidelines for companies in terms of their governance. This recognition led directly to the development of a variety of corporate governance codes of conduct, such as the King II guidelines in South Africa, the Cadbury Report in the United Kingdom, and the 2005 Code of Corporate Governance in Singapore. These codes use voluntary enforcement methods. After the Cadbury Report (1992), Aguilera and Cuervo-Cazurra (2004: 19) state that there was an exponential rise in the adoption of codes and that by the end of 1999, twenty-four industrialized and developing countries had issued at least one code of good governance, resulting in a total of 72 codes of good governance. Competition between governance systems has led to little formal convergence, but empirical studies highlight the possibility of functional convergence. Kaplan (1994a), comparing company rewards systems in the United States, Germany and Japan, demonstrates that, despite differences in corporate governance systems, all these countries are sensitive to poor performance (Gilson, 2000).

While US corporations as a whole have performed well and added value (Coffee, 2002), failures of large corporations have become widely publicized, such as Enron and WorldCom in the United States, and the increasing evidence of poor financial management of companies such as Tyco, Global Crossing and Xerox (Guardian, 2002). These scandals led to a renewed focus on the importance of the practice of corporate governance in the United States and worldwide (see Holmström and Kaplan, 2003). While regulatory changes by the NYSE and NASDAQ were introduced subsequent to these events and play a major role in competition for foreign listings, the major change for corporate governance is the enactment of the Sarbanes-Oxley (SOX) Act by the United States Congress in 2002 (Congress of the United States of America, 2002). SOX brings into play a legislated (outsider) requirement for corporate governance procedures with direct legal responsibility by the executive officers (Holmström and Kaplan, 2003).

The creation of enlightened self-interest, which is a cornerstone of corporate governance, has allowed modern corporations to remain competitive in a demanding and regulated environment. The creation of good governance has been costly; however, the costs should nevertheless be offset against the value of the social and legal licence to operate, and the capacity of the corporation to remain competitive in the business environment. Protection of the interests of investors, and in particular the interests of small or minority investors, from expropriation by larger investors and professional managers is a key aspect of almost all models of corporate governance. The creation of a level playing field where the influence of investors is seen to be as equal as possible is a main factor in driving up corporate valuations (La Porta et al., 2002). This in turn enhances the competitiveness of the company in the marketplace. The self-fulfilling prophecy of corporate governance extends also to the macroeconomic level where the ability of a particular country to attract foreign direct investment, which is critical for economic growth, is directly related to the state and quality of corporate governance (Rueda-Sabater, 2000). As the economy grows – and the companies within the economy grow along with it – so their competitiveness also improves.

The SOX Act has as its fundamental objective the protection of investors by ensuring the accuracy and reliability of corporate disclosures. It specifically includes the following factors: public company accounting oversight boards; the independence of auditors; corporate responsibility; enhanced financial disclosures; analysts' conflicts of interest; commission resources and authority; studies and reports; corporate and criminal fraud accountability; white-collar crime penalty enhancements; corporate tax returns; and corporate fraud and accountability.

Prior to the introduction of SOX the relationship between some firms and their auditing bodies had arguably become somewhat blurred and doubt could be cast on the independence and accuracy of audit reports published by both parties. The SOX Act sought to ensure the accuracy and independence of auditors and of the reports they prepare through the establishment of the Public Company Accounting Oversight Board (PCAOB), which is mandated by the Act to oversee the audit of public companies. The Act also requires public accounting firms to register with the PCAOB and determines conflicts of interest particularly between executives of a public company who may not be executives of a public accounting firm employed by the corporation.

The diffusion of codes of corporate governance around the world has now been exacerbated by the legal requirements faced by companies listed in the United States. The issue now becomes a question of the effects that result through the extension of the extra-territoriality of one nation's laws to another, incurred when companies are dual-listed. Companies from emerging markets that dual-list must meet the SOX requirements, or face penalties and potential threat of delisting. Does this bring additional pressure to bear on the home country to move towards legislated corporate governance? In the following sections we discuss these issues in greater detail in relation to corporate governance in emerging countries, and then proceed to discuss the case of South Africa.

Corporate governance in emerging countries

As the global political paradigm has shifted with the demise of the bipolar superpower system and developing countries are increasingly forced to compete in the global economy on their own merits, the importance of corporate governance has become apparent. There is some empirical evidence so far that supports the relationship of the implementation of voluntary codes of conduct with an increase in firm value (Kouwenberg, 2006). According to Reed (2002), two fundamental reasons exist for the intensification of interest in corporate governance in emerging countries.

First, as a result of policies implementing the import substitution industrialization (ISI) model of economic development in the period following World War Two, a downturn in economic activity has occurred in some emerging countries. Highly protectionist policies designed to stimulate domestic industrial growth have led to declining industries, especially as protections have been removed in the wake of free-trade agreements and the advent of a global economy. In an attempt to offset this decline of industries in developing economies there is now an increasing focus on corporate governance in line with international standards by domestic firms. Responsible corporate governance can help to attract investment from and partnership with companies operating in more developed economies, where expectations of governance are higher.

The second reason is the role played by international institutions (such as the International Monetary Fund, the World Bank, the World Trade Organization (WTO), the European Union, and the United Nations) engaged in the process of integrating developing economies into the global market. In South Africa, the European Commission (EC) funds the European Programme for Reconstruction and Development (EPRD) in conjunction with European Investment Bank loans, following on with strong historical ties (see the website of the Delegation of the European Commission to the Republic of South Africa). WTO initiatives are a prime mover in reducing trade barriers worldwide and enhancing a more open system for trade. The recent WTO (2002) ruling against US foreign sales corporations (FSCs) emphasizes the desired transparency that the WTO is seeking, and the extension of corporate governance practices at the governmental level (Dispute Settlement Body, 2002).

In the particular case of South Africa, WTO rulings are affecting its prior preferential relationship with the European Union. Countries that are part of the ACP (African, Caribbean and Pacific) sub-regions, including South Africa, will no longer be afforded preferential treatment under the GATT Article 1 waiver of the Cotonou Agreement, which expired on 31 December 2007. This agreement refers to countries with EU ties, which will now be on equal terms with all other developing countries under the Generalized System of Preferences scheme, consistent with international rules of trade. Previous trade ties with the European Union will be more likely to change now that this is the case and ACP countries face worldwide competition in the European Union. Given the amount of change taking place in terms of trade and investment between emerging and developed countries, inevitably corporate governance becomes a central issue.

In the next section we turn to an examination of South Africa and the growing importance of corporate governance under a voluntary code of conduct.

South Africa: the development of voluntary corporate governance

The transformed political landscape of South Africa after 1994 has led to a move from a siege economy to a liberalized economy competing globally on its own merits. The divisions of race and resultant effects on capital and labour under apartheid are being addressed by affirmative action of the government to redress these inequalities. Combining aspects of Third and First World economies, South Africa has the largest and most diversified economy in Africa and as such is quite visible in the global economy which leads to an essential requirement for sound corporate governance for South African companies. Corporate governance in South Africa has developed with a focus on voluntary (termed 'internal' in South Africa) governance beginning with the King Reports, I and II.

In the early 1990s, the Institute of Directors of Southern Africa commissioned Judge Mervyn King to investigate and make recommendations on the implementation of good financial and ethical corporate governance in South Africa. Drawing on a wide variety of resources, the report sought to look beyond the confines of the corporation itself and to define the corporation's impact on the community within which it operates. Armstrong (1995) and Ryan (1995) clarify and explain the conclusions of the report in respect to the role and function of boards of directors, and make specific recommendations on the separation of the roles of chief executive officers and chairpersons of company boards. The King Code also addressed issues of remuneration paid to directors, disclosure on auditing practices, introducing a code of ethical practice of business in South Africa, and the importance of bringing formerly disadvantaged South Africans into the business world.

The development of King II (2002) was a response to the increasing need of South African companies to comply with international best practice, as they sought foreign capital and foreign markets, as well as a reaction to the shortcomings of the first report. The King II Code aims to provide South African companies with a world-class system that can be implemented by the country's business community to foster strong corporate governance.

Whether a voluntary code is sufficient as international economic ties develop is an important consideration for companies in South Africa as we discuss in the next section.

Comparison of SOX and King II for South African companies

For South African companies registered on US stock exchanges, sections 302 and 404 dealing with corporate responsibility for financial reports and with management assessment of internal controls, respectively, are of the most relevance. These sections have imposed the greatest cost on corporations (Coustan et al., 2004).

The difference between voluntary and mandatory measures for corporate governance lies in the legislated measures that can be implemented and can lead to penalties for non-compliance. Concern has therefore been expressed that the quantifiable costs associated with SOX in particular, are higher than estimated by the Securities and Exchange Commission (SEC) prior to implementation. A concern is also expressed that the cost of the implementation of SOX may negatively impact US stock exchanges themselves as the costs of initial public offerings and the associated SOX costs become prohibitive, particularly for small market capital companies who make up the majority of registered firms. This could also be an inhibiting factor for companies from emerging economies.

Much of the cost associated with the implementation of SOX may arise out of an inadequate evaluation and documentation of system controls required under the Act. Once these requirements have been adequately systemized, the prognosis is that costs will decrease as a learning curve effect takes hold (The Institute of Internal Auditors Research Foundation, 2005). Costs also relate to the need for qualified individuals to prepare reports and for management time spent on implementation. These costs are especially high in emerging economies where qualified labour may be limited in supply and where management in general is dealing with issues pertinent to an emerging economy and its concomitant institutional voids (Khanna and Palepu, 2006). In South Africa, the development of qualified labour continues to be a paramount concern; although in terms of infrastructure the country is fairly well developed, this development is still sporadically applied nationwide. The attention of companies might tend to be on these issues rather than on the legislated requirements of corporate governance.

While corporate governance generally develops independently within a given country context, firms are increasingly pressured to adhere to both the norms and laws of their home country and to the norms and laws of other countries. There is a great deal of commonality between the various country-based approaches, as they seek to address the same fundamental problems and challenges. This phenomenon would seem to hold true for a comparison between King II and SOX. While the approach and philosophy is different in some cases, a high degree of alignment, commonality and convergence exists between the two, as each of these systems seeks to address the same or similar issues. As an example, Table 16.1 outlines some of the similarities and differences between South Africa (King II), the United States (SOX), the United Kingdom and Singapore. Other systems that have been revised recently are the OECD Principles (2004), which were originally adopted by the 30 member countries of the OECD and used extensively by governments, regulators, investors, corporations and stakeholders (Jesover and Kirkpatrick, 2005).

We now proceed to a discussion of the research methodology and present five research questions to guide the qualitative research undertaken in South Africa.

Research methodology

The review of the literature shows that corporate governance is growing in prevalence in the emerging economies of the world. In South Africa the system of corporate governance is well entrenched and highly codified through the widely accepted mechanism of the King II Code on corporate governance. A comparison of SOX with the King II Code indicates that in general terms the requirements of each are very similar. The fundamental difference therefore is that SOX has the status of law, which must be adhered to. While it is generally accepted that good corporate governance enhances competitiveness because it provides investors with a sense of security regarding the restrictions on executives to expropriate funds (among other dubious actions), the

Table 16.1: Comparison of corporate governance measures between South Africa (King II), the United States (SOX), the United Kingdom and Singapore

---

Board of Directors and Audit Committee
Composition:

King II	Must be of sufficient size and comprise both executive and non-executive directors some of whom at least must be independent. The chairperson should also be independent.
SOX	Does not separately address the issue.
United Kingdom	At least half the members should be independent non-executive directors. Chairman should also be independent.
Singapore	At least a third of the members should be independent.

Responsibility:

King II	The board is ultimately accountable for the affairs of the company. It should adopt a charter and make provision to deal with the issues of whistleblowing.
SOX	No specific reference is made, although whistleblowing is made the responsibility of the Audit Committee.
United Kingdom	Provides entrepreneurial leadership within a framework of effective control. It sets company values and ensures obligations to shareholders are understood and met.
Singapore	Must set out internal guidelines setting out matters that require board approval and the material transaction requiring board approval.

Audit Committee to Board:

King II	Majority of members must be independent and financially literate. Outlines various responsibilities.
SOX	All members must be independent and at least one must be a financial expert. Various responsibilities outlined.
United Kingdom	Must consist of at least three members all of whom should be independent directors. At least one member must have financial/accounting expertise.
Singapore	Must consist of at least three members the majority of whom, including the chair, should be independent. At least two members are expected to have accounting or financial expertise.

Financial Reporting and Internal Control

Financial reporting responsibility:

King II	Board must report certain items annually and regarding preparation of financial statements and implementation of internal controls.
SOX	Quarterly certifications by the CEO and CFO regarding compliance with the exchange act.
United Kingdom	No current requirements.
Singapore	No current requirements.

Financial Disclosures:

King II	No specific requirements.
SOX	Required disclosure of all material off balance sheet transactions and other defined relationships in the quarterly reports.

(Continued)

Table 16.1:   (Continued)

	All correcting adjustments to the financial statements must be made. Prohibition of certain non-GAAP info.
United Kingdom	No specific requirements.
Singapore	No specific requirements.

Internal Controls:

King II	Part of the risk management process. Board must maintain recognized systems and make disclosures about risk management process.
SOX	CEO and CFO must certify quarterly regarding their responsibility over disclosure and control procedures. Annual internal control report must be prepared and included with annual SEC filings.
United Kingdom	Board responsible for maintaining a system of internal control and for reporting to shareholders at least annually. Controls must cover: material, finance, operational, compliance and risk controls.
Singapore	Management required to maintain a control system under board supervision. Financial, operational and compliance controls are specifically cited. The Audit Committee is charged with reviewing materials and risk controls on an annual basis. The board is required to comment on the adequacy of the controls.

Accounting and Auditing

Independence:

King II	External auditors should uphold the highest personal and professional ethics and maintain an awareness of their responsibility to shareholders.
SOX	Prohibits defined activities by the external auditor. Limits employment of former external auditors, and prohibits fees begin earned for non-audit functions. Stricter rotation rules.
United Kingdom	No specific reference.
Singapore	No specific reference.

Interaction with companies:

King II	Requires an effective internal audit function with formal audit charter.
SOX	Requires mandatory communications between external auditor and the Audit Committee.
United Kingdom	No specific internal audit function required; however, the Audit Committee should consider the need on an annual basis.
Singapore	Internal auditor must report to the Audit Committee chair. The internal auditor must maintain the highest possible standards.

New Attestation Report:

King II	Not separately addressed.
SOX	External auditor must issue an attestation on management's internal controls.
United Kingdom	Not separately addressed.
Singapore	Not separately addressed.

(Continued)

Table 16.1:   (Continued)

Disclosure:

King II	Requires separate disclosure of fees paid to the external auditor for non-audit services and a detailed description of the services.
SOX	Requires disclosure paid to the external auditor for the two most recent years and a description of the services.
United Kingdom	Not separately addressed.
Singapore	Not separately addressed.

Organizational Ethics and Remuneration

Code of Ethics:

King II	Standards of ethical behaviour should be codified in a code of ethics and adherence disclosed.
SOX	Disclose whether code of ethics applicable to senior management has been adopted. Must make code publicly available and disclose changes or waivers.
United Kingdom	Requires that the highest ethical standards be maintained at all times and that the requirements be contained in a defined document.
Singapore	Not yet specifically addressed.

Compensation:

King II	Performance-related elements of compensation should form a substantial portion of the package. Vesting periods, re-pricing of options must be approved by shareholders.
SOX	Illegal to extend loans to directors or executive officers. Requires reimbursement of some compensation by CEO and CFO if financial statements are restated.
United Kingdom	Requires remuneration to be performance-related, and performance criteria should be challenging. Recommends vesting periods of up to three years and longer.
Singapore	Remuneration should take into account industry norms, the relative performance of the company and the performance of individuals. Long-term, share-based, incentive-based schemes are encouraged so as to align the interests of shareholders and directors.

Source: Price-Waterhouse-Coopers (2003).

involuntary nature of the SOX compliance requirements means that companies cannot tailor their governance actions to their needs and size of their company.

In addition, the costs associated with compliance may begin to outweigh their value and ultimately begin to affect competitiveness, not only of the companies themselves but of the capital markets upon which they rely for funding. In particular, the costs of compliance in emerging economies are high due to limits to the availability of qualified individuals, and a greater focus on country-specific development issues. As the sample of companies used in this study have high market value, and as such attract many qualified employees, we would not expect this to be perceived as a highly relevant issue. However, in any extension of the study this would be more relevant. The following research questions were used to guide the research in seeking the views of interviewees:

- How applicable are the principles set out in the King II Code, and how do the principles of King II and the SOX Act relate?
- How does the King II Code provide potential investors with confidence?
- Is the King II Code preferable to an outsider governance code such as the SOX Act?
- What elements of the SOX Act should be introduced in South Africa?
- Do the costs of complying with the SOX Act outweigh the potential benefits?

The South African respondents

Nine South African companies were dual-registered on the American and South African stock exchanges at the time of this research. This small target population comprises: AngloGold Ashanti Limited, DRDGold Limited, Gold Fields Limited, Harmony Gold Mining Company Limited, Highveld Steel and Vanadium Corporation Limited, Randgold & Exploration Company Limited, Sappi Limited, Sasol Limited and Telkom SA Limited. It is notable that these nine companies represent a collective market capitalization on the Johannesburg Stock Exchange in excess of R470 billion, making them a significant part of the economic landscape of South Africa. Therefore in this exploratory research we are looking at large companies only, leaving potential for further research on small market-capitalized companies whose issues may be greater in relation to cost concerns and competitive issues.

The research is conducted using a qualitative approach, which effectively means 'any kind of research that produces findings not arrived at by means of statistical procedures or other means of quantification' (Strauss and Corbin, 1990: 17). Qualitative research takes an involving and interpretive, naturalistic approach to its subject matter (Denzin and Lincoln, 1998: 3). The rationale for this approach rests on two factors, the first being the size of the target population. Only nine companies (out of a total of fifty-seven dual-listed) are listed in the United States, and this in turn is a fraction of the 387 companies registered on the Johannesburg Stock Exchange. The population is sufficiently small that a quantitative approach would not be appropriate to fully describe the phenomenon being studied.

The second and possibly more important reason is that the questions being asked are inherently qualitative in nature and require a qualitative and insightful assessment which can be based on the experience and opinions of corporate officers charged with corporate governance implementation within each of the companies that make up the target population. While there is obviously a 'natural bias' of respondents to support the corporate governance processes of the corporation, the research questions aim to elicit considered responses by comparing the two systems. The validity of the research rests on the accuracy of the findings obtained from the respondents and the faithful representation of these findings by the researchers (Creswell, 2003).

All nine companies were targeted, and contact was made with corporate officers in each company to explain the background to the study, as well as the nature of the research being conducted. The primary data-gathering technique used in this study was a standardized, semi-structured interview which according to Henning et al. (2004: 53) 'is still the dominant conception of an interview as a mechanism or a technology, if used methodically according to strict principles of objectivity and neutrality, that will yield information that represents reality more or less "as it is" through the response (and filters) of an interviewee.' However, only five of the nine companies approached finally consented to be interviewed: these were AngloGold Ashanti Limited, Goldfields Limited, Harmony Gold Limited, Sappi Limited and Sasol Limited. The Appendix outlines some details on these companies. The remaining four companies did not respond to requests for interviews in this time period.

Analysis of results

All of the interviewees in the study were corporate officers charged with the responsibility of implementation of corporate governance measures within their particular organization, specifically including measures mandated under the King II Codes as well as the implementation of the requirements of the Sarbanes-Oxley Act. The analysis of results follows using categorized responses to the research questions.

How applicable are the principles set out in the King II Code, and how do the principles of King II and the SOX Act relate?

All of the respondents communicated that they have a very clear understanding of the differences in fundamental approach to the requirements of corporate governance, and drew a clear distinction between the legislative approach of SOX and the principle-based approach of the King II Code of Corporate Governance. The respondents noted, with regard to internal audit and accounting functions, that King II does not make specific recommendations in the same mould as SOX and that as a result of this less specific language there is in fact a high degree of complementarity between SOX and King II, as applied in South Africa. There is also a strong common opinion among the respondents that notwithstanding the virtues of SOX and the rules-based approach, there is a great deal to be said for the principled approach of the King II Code. The overall conclusion that can be drawn therefore is that there is indeed a strong sense of comfort about the validity and applicability of King

II, but that there are aspects of SOX that serve to enhance the overall process of corporate governance in South Africa.

How does the King II Code provide potential investors with confidence?

The balance of opinion among the respondents interviewed is that King II provides a more than sufficient basis for confidence among investors. The strong performance of South African equity markets in recent years was offered as an example of the confidence of investors that South African companies are well governed and managed within a strong governance framework. Respondents believe that King II provides confidence in key investor markets such as the United States and thus enables South African companies to compete for capital funding with confidence. From the analysis of the data it can be concluded that King II is indeed a confidence-building measure for investors and managers in South African companies. This position is prevalent among the interviewees, notwithstanding the revelations in recent years regarding corporate scandals and mismanagement by professional managers. This cohesive body of positive opinion can be considered a strong endorsement of the King II Code among South African corporate governance managers.

Is the King II Code preferable to a legal (outsider) governance code such as the SOX Act?

Opinion among the interviewees appears evenly divided on the issue of legal, outsider governance. Although there is a consensus of understanding on the differences between a voluntary system such as King II and a legal, outsider system such as SOX, there are comparatively differing views as to which is a preferable approach overall. If a common theme can be detected among the responses it is rather that each approach has its particular value and merit and given the specific requirements of implementation of SOX, in particular for foreign private issuers (as all South African companies listed in the United States are), there is a high degree of complementarity between the two approaches. While the flexibility of the voluntary system remains attractive, there is room for the implementation of some legal aspects in the domestic South African context which may carry legal sanctions in the mould of SOX. The promulgation of suitably tempered and adapted 'SOX-like' regulations in South Africa will be a welcome adjunct to the current insider regime under King II.

What elements of the SOX Act should be introduced in South Africa?

The data clearly indicate that corporate governance professionals in South African multinational companies recognize the need for the implementation of stricter and more enforceable rules governing the roles of internal auditors and the application of accounting standards. Some interviewees go so far as to suggest that the South African government may even be well advised to consider the implementation of legal requirements, possibly under a revised Companies Act. Here South African companies would report regularly on their audit and accounting practices. A universal theme among those interviewed is that King II provides many useful and valuable guidelines for companies in terms of their corporate governance, but it does fall short of providing the kind of scrutiny of internal audit and accounting practices that SOX does.

While interviewees agreed that there is a high degree of commonality between King II and SOX, in the critical area of reporting on accounting and audit practice, SOX is seen as having a distinct benefit over the King II Code. Equally, other aspects of SOX, outside those mentioned above, are seen as exceeding the needs of the business community (because they are already adequately covered under King). A strong sense exists that as time passes and both businesses and regulators become more comfortable with SOX and its implementation, a tendency will emerge towards moderation and practicality.

Do the costs of complying with the SOX Act outweigh the potential benefits?

The fundamental issue of cost garners unanimity of response that strong and sound corporate governance is seen as a value adding exercise for companies operating in South Africa. All of the respondents indicate that the implementation of universally accepted and credible corporate governance measures provides all stakeholders, and in particular investors and shareholders, with the necessary confidence that administration of the enterprise is being undertaken in an open, honest and transparent manner.

On the issue of the cost of SOX measures specifically, the overwhelming body of opinion is that costs associated with the implementation of SOX are indeed significant. It is worth noting that on average costs for the implementation of SOX are estimated at R20 million, with staff time costs being estimated as significantly higher. It is also noted that these costs are incurred in addition to costs already incurred in terms of the implementation of existing (and largely adequate) governance measures. When compared with the cost of implementation with King II, respondents believe that the difference in costs is indeed significant. As to whether these costs are ultimately excessive and whether or not the costs ultimately detract from the value added by the compliance measures, opinion is more divided. Respondents indicate that while costs are high they have to be measured against the value accrued by the company due to having access to US capital markets, which after all is the reason for having to comply with SOX in the first place. The final analysis therefore appears to be that the cost is high, in fact very high, and the value added in terms of better governance is not that high, but the benefit in terms of access to crucial investment outweighs both the cost and the low added value.

Limitations of the study

This exploratory study draws on a small number of respondents, as initial research propositions are investigated. The comparative newness of the requirement to implement SOX in the companies of the target population (a period of only one year in most cases) means that there is little experience and learning for respondents to draw upon in their consideration of the questions asked of them. Therefore we are not drawing any generalizable conclusions from the data, but intend to use this as a starting point for further research.

A key consideration to bear in mind during the analysis of the data is the social context within which the research is conducted and the likelihood of an occurrence of so-called 'natural bias' arises. The responsibilities of the interviewees are the very reason for their continued tenure within the organization and therefore it is to be expected that there would be a natural bias towards favouring corporate governance measures in general. It seems highly unlikely that any of the respondents would characterize corporate governance as a waste of corporate time, effort and resources, and this 'natural bias' must be borne in mind when evaluating the outcome of the research.

Conclusions

From the data analysis, it is possible to draw a series of conclusions with regard to each of the propositions presented. We conclude that the King II Code of Corporate Governance compares very favourably as a whole with Sarbanes-Oxley in the minds of the respondents. The strong acceptance of King, both in South Africa and internationally, where it has been used as a benchmark and guideline for systems of governance, would seem to underscore this view. There is indeed confidence among South African based multinational corporations that the South African system of corporate governance provides adequate protection for investors and accountability for managers and companies. There is strong evidence to show that prior to the requirement to implement SOX, South African companies trading on international, and specifically US, stock markets were considered to be stable and well-governed and therefore a worthwhile and safe investment destination. Strong capital inflow over the past five years has underscored this point.

It is clear that companies appreciate the flexible nature of the voluntary based system under the King II Code and the ability to tailor the requirements of good corporate governance to meet their specific needs. Equally, however, companies have recognized that there is merit to the mandatory (outsider) approach, and the specifically legal sanctions based approach, of SOX.

The commonalities between King II and SOX are widely recognized. However, the one area where SOX does seem to have a greater appeal to governance professionals is in the area of reporting on internal accounting and audit practices. In this area, King II does not have the same capacity for enforcement and discipline that seems to be highly favoured among companies. There is a strong view that by drawing on the strengths of both approaches (SOX and King II) it is possible to achieve better corporate governance that covers all the critical aspects of the business.

And finally, the issue of costs must be seen in two distinct contexts. First, in the context of the value-added to companies in terms of their ability to effectively manage and implement internationally sound and accept-able corporate governance. Here the answer is strongly in the negative, the value-added by the measures required by SOX is negligible, with the notable exceptions of the requirements related to internal accounting and audit standards. Second, from the perspective of the ability of South African multinational companies to access lucrative US capital markets, it is clear that the costs of SOX, while still seen as significant, are considered to be an acceptable cost to bear in return for the access to capital at this time. Costs related to the need for qualified individuals are not a major issue for these companies; however, this would be a major concern for smaller companies from emerging markets. However, if the cost to valuation of dual-registered companies is in fact high, as early evidence shows (Li, 2007), then companies must reconsider dual listing in the United States.

In the final analysis there seems to be a strong sense of commitment and support for the indigenous King II regulations, but it appears that the system can be improved and strengthened by the addition of elements of the SOX regulations, provided that this can be done at a much more moderate cost.

Recommendations

From the research and the conclusions, it would seem that there is merit in a detailed review of the requirements of the King II Code with regard to the standards for the implementation and regulation of internal auditing and accounting controls, with a view to aligning them with the requirements under SOX. Additionally, it would be best if a review of this specific aspect of the King Code is based on further detailed research. This research should specifically focus on the issue of the development of appropriate accounting standards that serve the best interests of sound corporate governance.

While the implementation of improved reporting on internal accounting and auditing standards is desirable, it must be achieved at a lower cost than is the case under SOX. The achievement of such a cost-effective regime for South Africa would serve as an ideal arena for further research, which should seek to draw on the experiences of South African companies that have already found innovative ways of mitigating the costs by incorporating many of the measures of SOX into their internal reporting systems.

As stated, one of the key weaknesses in this research is that the compara-tive newness of the requirement to implement SOX among the companies of the target population (a period of only one year in most cases) means that there is little experience and learning for respondents to draw upon in their consideration of these questions. A comparative study over the next three or four years, targeting the same companies and individuals within those companies, may well reveal significantly different experiences and views, as practitioners and organizations learn to do SOX better, faster and – most significantly – cheaper, or if company stock value is seen to decline significantly after dual listing on the US exchanges a reconsideration of the practice will take place.

In the course of the research process a number of interviewees made reference to rumours and discussions circulating in the market regarding SOX-style changes to the Companies Act of South Africa in the wake of recent corporate financial scandals in the country (Saambou, Leisurenet and most recently the so-called Kebble scandal at JCI). If a SOX-style regime of corporate governance is implemented in South Africa, with similar associated costs, it can be expected that there will be the effect of driving smaller-capitalized companies out of the capital markets.

The question, however, arises whether the South African stock market can absorb such impacts. If such a course of action is contemplated in South Africa (or any emerging economy) a recommendation of caution to policy-makers is advised. There is further merit in recommending that any such action should be carefully researched before implementation.

Appendix: Brief background information on the South African companies in the sample

AngloGold Ashanti

AngloGold Ashanti Limited is a global gold producer with 21 operations on four continents, a substantial project pipeline and an extensive, worldwide exploration programme. The company is listed on the New York, Johannesburg, Ghanaian, London and Australian stock exchanges, as well as the Paris and Brussels bourses.

Market Capitalization at 2 October 2006: R81, 723,957,094.

Gold Fields

Gold Fields is one of the world's largest unhedged pure gold producers, providing investors with maximum leverage to the gold price. The company has an annual gold production of approximately 4.1 million ounces from mines in South Africa, Ghana, Australia and Venezuela, as well as a developing mine at Cerro Corona in Peru and has ore reserves of 65 million ounces and mineral resources of 179 million ounces. The company employs 48,467 people globally and is listed on the NYSE, LSE, JSE, DIFX, Euro next and Swiss Exchanges. All of Gold Fields' operations are ISO 14001 certified.

Market Capitalization at 2 October 2006: R70, 972,259,171.

Harmony Gold

Harmony Gold is the fifth largest gold producer in the world with operations and projects in South Africa, Australasia and Papua New Guinea (PNG). Founded in 1950 as a Rand Mines-managed company, Harmony was independently listed on the JSE Limited in 1997. Today Harmony is listed on seven bourses worldwide: London, Paris, Brussels and a dual listing in New York, on the NASDAQ and the NYSE.

Market Capitalization at 2 October 2006: R41, 735,956,463.

Sappi

Sappi is the leading worldwide producer of coated fine paper in a variety of applications, from books to wine labels, from magazines and brochures to catalogues and calendars. Sappi is a company with global brands, global assets, global shareholding and a global structure focused on meeting the needs of customers in more than 100 countries around the world. Sappi is also the world's largest producer of chemical cellulose (dissolving pulp), used primarily in the manufacture of viscose fibre and consumer and pharmaceutical products. In addition, it produces uncoated graphic and business papers, premium quality packaging papers and a range of specialty papers.

Market Capitalization at 2 October 2006: R23, 715,931,686.

Sasol Group

The Sasol Group of companies comprises diversified fuel, chemical and related manufacturing and marketing operations, complemented by interests in technology development and oil and gas exploration and production. Its principal feedstocks are obtained from coal, which the company converts into value-added hydrocarbons through Fischer-Tropsch process technologies. Sasol also uses various petrochemical feedstocks in its chemical plants outside of South Africa. It also has interests in crude oil refining and chemical production and marketing through a number of global strategic partners or joint ventures. More recently, Sasol has embarked on developing international gas-to-liquids ventures, based on its unique Slurry Phase Distillate process. Sasol is listed on the Johannesburg Securities Exchange (JSE), symbol SOL and on the New York Securities Exchange (NYSE), symbol SSL.

Market Capitalization at 2 October 2006: R173, 557,952,350.

Bibliography

Aguilera, R. V. and Cuervo-Cazurra, A. (2004). 'Codes of good governance worldwide: what is the trigger?' *Organization Studies*, 25(3): 415–43.

Aldrighi, D. M. (2003). 'The mechanisms of corporate governance in the United States: an assessment'. *Revista Brasiliera de Epidemologia*, 57(3): 469–513.

Armstrong, P. (1995). 'The King report on corporate governance'. *Boardroom*, 1: 16–25.

Berle, A. A. and Means, G. C. (1967). *The modern corporation and private property.* Revised edition (New York: Harcourt, Brace & World Inc).

Bowen, H. R. (1953). *Social responsibilities of the businessman* (New York: Harper and Brothers).

Coffee, J. C. (1999). 'The future as history: the prospects for global convergence in corporate governance and its implications'. Columbia Law School, Center for Law and Economic Studies, Working Paper no. 144. Available at SSRN: http://ssrn.com/abstract=142833

Coffee, J. C. (2002). 'Racing towards the top: the impact of cross-listings and stock market competition on international corporate governance'. *Columbia Law Review*, 102(7): 1757–1831.

Congress of the United States of America (2002). *The Sarbanes-Oxley Act of 2002.* H.R. 3763-3. Available from: http://www.soxlaw.com

Coustan, H., Leinicke, L. M., Rexroad, W. M., Ostrosky, J. A. and Thomas, A. (2004). 'Sarbanes-Oxley (SOX): what it means to the marketplace'. *Journal of Accountancy* [online] (New York: American Institute of Certified Public Accountants). Available at: http://www.aicpa.org/pubs/jofa/feb2004/coustan.htm

Creswell, J. W. (2003). *Research Design.* Second edition (Sage Publications).

Delegation of the European Commission to the Republic of South Africa (2007). Website at: http://www.eusa.org.za

Denzin, N. K. and Lincoln, Y. S. (1998). *The landscape of qualitative research* (Thousand Oaks: Sage Publications).

Dispute Settlement Body (2002). 'Tax treatment for foreign sales corporation'. Available at: http://www.wto.org

Fama, E. and Jensen, M. (1983). 'Separation of ownership and control'. *Journal of Law and Economics*, 26: 301–25.

Gilson, R. J. (2000). 'Globalizing corporate governance: convergence of form or function'. Columbia Law School, Center for Law and Economic Studies, Working Paper no. 174; Stanford Law School, John M. Olin Program in Law and Economics, Working Paper no. 192. Available at: http://www.law.columbia.edu/lawec/

Guardian (2002). 'Uncle Sam's scandals at a glance'. *The Guardian* (29 July): 1–2.

Henning, E., van Rensburg, W. and Smit, B. (2004). *Finding your way in qualitative research* (Pretoria: Van Schaik).

Holmström, B. R. and Kaplan, S. N. (2003). 'The state of US corporate governance: what's right and what's wrong'. ECGI – Finance Working Paper no. 23/2003. Available at SSRN: http://ssrn.com/abstract=441100

Jesover, F. and Kirkpatrick, G. (2005). 'The revised OECD principles of corporate governance and their relevance to non-OECD countries'. Available at: http://www.oecd.org/dataoecd/41/38/33977036.pdf

Kaplan, S. N. (1994a). 'Top executive rewards and firm performance: a comparison of Japan and the US'. *Journal of Political Economy*, 102(3): 510–46.

Kaplan, S. N. (1994b). 'Top executives, turnover, and firm performance in Germany'. *Journal of Law, Economics & Organization*, 10(1): 142–59.

Khanna, T. and Palepu, K. (2006). 'Emerging giants: building world-class companies in developing countries'. *Harvard Business Review*, 84(10): 60–9.

Kouwenberg, R. R. P. (2006). 'Does voluntary corporate governance code adoption increase firm value in emerging markets? Evidence from Thailand'. Erasmus University Rotterdam, Erasmus School of Economics, Working Paper. Available at SSRN: http://ssrn.com/abstract=958580

La Porta, R., Lopez-de-Silanes, F., Schleifer, A. and Vishny, R.W. (2002). 'Investor protection and corporate valuation'. *Journal of Finance*, 57(3): 1147–70.

Li, X. (2007). 'The Sarbanes-Oxley Act and cross-listed foreign private issuers'. University of Miami, School of Business Administration, Working Paper. Available at SSRN: http://ssrn.com/abstract=952433

Palepu, K., Khanna, T. and Kogan, J. (2002). 'Globalization and similarities in corporate governance: a cross-country analysis'. Harvard Business School, Working Paper no. 02-041. Available at SSRN: http://ssrn.com/abstract=323621

Price-Waterhouse-Coopers (2003). *A comparison of the King Report 2002 and the Sarbanes-Oxley Act of 2002* (Johannesburg: Institute of Directors).

Reed, D. (2002). 'Corporate governance reforms in developing countries'. *Journal of Business Ethics*, 37(3): 223–47.

Rueda-Sabater, E. J. (2000). 'Corporate governance and the bargaining power of developing countries to attract foreign investment'. *Corporate Governance*, 8(2): 117–24.

Ryan, C. (1995). 'The King Report: an outline'. *People Dynamics*, 13(7): 15–18.

Strauss, A. L. and Corbin, J. M. (1990). *Basics of qualitative research: grounded theory procedures and techniques* (Newbury Park, CA: Sage Publications).

The Institute of Directors in Southern Africa (1994). *The King Report on corporate governance* (Johannesburg: The Institute of Directors of Southern Africa).

The Institute of Directors in Southern Africa (2002). *The King Report on corporate governance for South Africa – 2002 (King II Report)* (Johannesburg: The Institute of Directors of Southern Africa).

The Institute of Internal Auditors Research Foundation (2005). *Sarbanes-Oxley Section 404: looking at the benefits* (Altamonte Springs, FL: The Institute of Internal Auditors Research Foundation).

Index